Transition and Justice

Development and Change Book Series

As a journal, *Development and Change* distinguishes itself by its multidisciplinary approach and its breadth of coverage, publishing articles on a wide spectrum of development issues. Accommodating a deeper analysis and a more concentrated focus, it also publishes regular special issues on selected themes. *Development and Change* and Wiley Blackwell collaborate to produce these theme issues as a series of books, with the aim of bringing these pertinent resources to a wider audience.

Titles in the series include:

Transition and Justice: Negotiating the Terms of New Beginnings in Africa
Edited by Gerhard Anders and Olaf Zenker

Governing Global Land Deals: The Role of the State in the Rush for Land
Edited by Wendy Wolford, Saturnino M. Borras, Jr., Ruth Hall, Ian Scoones and Ben White

Seen, Heard and Counted: Rethinking Care in a Development Context
Edited by Shahra Razavi

Negotiating Statehood: Dynamics of Power and Domination in Africa
Edited by Tobias Hagmann and Didier Péclard

The Politics of Possession: Property, Authority, and Access to Natural Resources
Edited by Thomas Sikor and Christian Lund

Gender Myths and Feminist Fables: The Struggle for Interpretive Power in Gender and Development
Edited by Andrea Cornwall, Elizabeth Harrison and Ann Whitehead

Twilight Institutions: Public Authority and Local Politics in Africa
Edited by Christian Lund

China's Limits to Growth: Greening State and Society
Edited by Peter Ho and Eduard B. Vermeer

Catalysing Development? A Debate on Aid
Jan Pronk et al.

State Failure, Collapse and Reconstruction
Edited by Jennifer Milliken

Forests: Nature, People, Power
Edited by Martin Doornbos, Ashwani Saith and Ben White

Gendered Poverty and Well-being
Edited by Shahra Razavi

Globalization and Identity
Edited by Birgit Meyer and Peter Geschiere

Social Futures, Global Visions
Edited by Cynthia Hewitt de Alcantara

Transition and Justice
Negotiating the Terms of New Beginnings in Africa

Edited by

Gerhard Anders and Olaf Zenker

WILEY Blackwell

This edition first published 2015
Originally published as Volume 45, Issue 3 of *Development and Change*
Chapters © 2015 by The Institute of Social Studies
Book Compilation © Blackwell Publishing Ltd.

Blackwell Publishing was acquired by John Wiley & Sons in February 2007. Blackwell's publishing program
has been merged with Wiley's global Scientific, Technical, and Medical business to form Wiley-Blackwell.

Registered Office
John Wiley & Sons Ltd, The Atrium, Southern Gate, Chichester, West Sussex, PO19 8SQ, United Kingdom

Editorial Offices
350 Main Street, Malden, MA 02148-5020, USA
9600 Garsington Road, Oxford, OX4 2DQ, UK
The Atrium, Southern Gate, Chichester, West Sussex, PO19 8SQ, UK

For details of our global editorial offices, for customer services, and for information about how to apply for
permission to reuse the copyright material in this book please see our website at
www.wiley.com/wiley-blackwell.

The rights of Gerhard Anders and Olaf Zenker to be identified as the authors of the editorial material in this
work has been asserted in accordance with the UK Copyright, Designs and Patents Act 1988.

Wiley also publishes its books in a variety of electronic formats. Some content that appears in print may not
be available in electronic books.

Designations used by companies to distinguish their products are often claimed as trademarks. All brand
names and product names used in this book are trade names, service marks, trademarks or registered
trademarks of their respective owners. The publisher is not associated with any product or vendor mentioned
in this book. This publication is designed to provide accurate and authoritative information in regard to the
subject matter covered. It is sold on the understanding that the publisher is not engaged in rendering
professional services. If professional advice or other expert assistance is required, the services of a competent
professional should be sought.

Library of Congress Cataloging-in-Publication data is available for this book.

ISBN 9781118944776 (paperback)

LCCN 2014027078

A catalogue record for this book is available from the British Library.

Front cover image © Géraldine Bollmann

Set in 10.75/12pt Times New Roman PS by Aptara Inc., New Delhi, India

Printed in Singapore by C.O.S. Printers Pte Ltd

1   2015

Contents

Contents

Notes on Contributors

Gerhard Anders is lecturer at the Centre of African Studies, University of Edinburgh. He has conducted research on the implementation of the good governance agenda, international criminal justice and transitional justice in Africa. He is co-editor of *Corruption and the Secret of Law: A Legal Anthropological Perspective* (Ashgate, 2007) and author of *In the Shadow of Good Governance: An Ethnography of Civil Service Reform in Africa* (Brill, 2010).

Kimberley Armstrong is based in Arusha, Tanzania. She graduated from McGill University in Canada and is currently working as a Social Research Consultant in the region. Her research interests include transitional justice, post-conflict transition, development, East Africa and research methodology.

Adam Branch is Senior Research Fellow at the Makerere Institute of Social Research in Kampala, Uganda, and Associate Professor of political science at Department of Political Science, San Diego State. His work has focused on political violence and international intervention, leading to the book, *Displacing Human Rights: War and Intervention in Northern Uganda* (Oxford University Press, 2011), as well as numerous articles and chapters on the ICC, humanitarianism and regional security.

Nigel Eltringham is senior lecturer in Social Anthropology at the University of Sussex, Brighton. He is the author of *Accounting for Horror: Post-Genocide Debates in Rwanda* (Pluto Press, 2004), editor of *Framing Africa: Portrayals of a Continent in Contemporary Mainstream Cinema* (Berghahn Books, 2013) and co-editor of *Remembering Genocide* (Routledge, 2014).

Marion Fresia is Assistant Professor at the Institute of Anthropology, Neuchâtel, Switzerland. Her research interests include humanitarianism, forced migration and the institutional fabric of the refugee regime. She has published *Les Mauritaniens réfugiés au Sénégal. Une anthropologie de l'asile et de l'aide humanitaire* [*Mauritanian Refugees in Senegal: A Critical Anthropology of Asylum and Humanitarian Aid*] (L'Harmattan, 2009), and a number of articles on the everyday work of refugee workers.

Sabine Höhn received her PhD in African Studies from the University of Edinburgh in 2010. She is currently a British Academy post-doctoral fellow in the Department of Politics, University of Glasgow.

Steffen Jensen is a senior researcher at DIGNITY-Danish Institute Against Torture in Copenhagen and an associate of the University of the Philippines. He has published on issues of violence, gangs, vigilante groups, human rights, urban and rural politics, as well as on the relationship between security and development in rural and urban South Africa and in the Philippines. He has published *Gangs, Politics and Dignity in Cape Town* (University of Chicago Press, 2008) along with edited volumes on victimhood, policing, human rights and security.

Steven Robins is a Professor in the Department of Sociology and Social Anthropology at the University of Stellenbosch. He has published on a wide range of topics including the politics of land, 'development' and identity in Zimbabwe and South Africa; the Truth and Reconciliation Commission; urban studies; and citizenship and governance. His recent authored and edited books include: *From Revolution to Rights in South Africa: Social Movements and Popular Politics* (2008); *Limits to Liberation After Apartheid: Citizenship, Governance and Culture* (2005) and *New South African Keywords* (2008, with Nick Shepherd).

Simon Turner is associate professor at Global Refugee Studies, Aalborg University, Copenhagen. His research has focused on refugees, humanitarianism, diaspora and conflict in Burundi and Rwanda. He is presently exploring the relationship between the Rwandan state and its diaspora.

Olaf Zenker is Junior Professor at the Institute of Social and Cultural Anthropology, Freie Universität Berlin, Germany. He has done research on Irish language revivalism and ethnicity in Northern Ireland and currently studies the moral modernity of the new South African state in the context of its land restitution process. He is the author of *Irish/ness Is All Around Us: Language Revivalism and the Culture of Ethnic Identity in Northern Ireland* (Berghahn, 2013) and co-editor of *The State and the Paradox of Customary Law in Africa* (Ashgate, to be published in 2015).

Transition and Justice: An Introduction

Gerhard Anders and Olaf Zenker

INTRODUCTION

Since the end of the Cold War, political new beginnings have increasingly been linked to questions of transitional justice. This can also be observed in Africa. Since the establishment of the South African Truth and Reconciliation Commission (TRC) and the International Criminal Tribunal for Rwanda (ICTR) during the mid-1990s, the African continent has loomed large in academic and political debates about how to deal with past injustices and realize political transition. The contributions to this collection examine a series of cases where peaceful 'new beginnings' have been declared after periods of violence and where transitional justice institutions played a role in defining justice and the new socio-political order.

In spite of the dramatic growth of transitional justice, there are other sites in countries and regions affected by violence and armed conflicts where ideas about justice, reconciliation, retribution and political participation are being instantiated and contested. Among the sites explored in this edited volume are re-education camps for demobilized combatants, refugee camps and prisons, as well as domestic courts, parliaments and village meetings. In these sites, former combatants and their leaders, politicians, civil society activists, village elders and ordinary people advance their views on how to realize justice or seek to secure a place in the new political system. Such negotiations of the terms of new beginnings in Africa, in which transitional justice measures are only one aspect of — and often challenged by — a multitude of much broader societal attempts at realizing more 'justice', constitute the subject matter of this collection. It is aimed at furthering our knowledge about transition and justice, including and transcending the usual transitional justice mechanisms, by presenting fine-grained case studies of sites where claims to justice are advanced and contested.

The focus on Africa in this edited volume is not accidental. Since the establishment of the TRC in South Africa and the ICTR in Arusha, Tanzania,

This edited volume is based on a special issue of the Journal *Development and Change*, 45(3), entitled *Transition and Justice: Negotiating the Terms of New Beginnings in Africa*, which developed out of a panel with the same title at the AEGIS 4th European Conference on African Studies (ECAS 4) in Uppsala, Sweden, in 2011. We are greatly indebted to all participants and contributors as well as the editorial board and the anonymous reviewers of *Development and Change* for their insightful and constructive comments.

the African continent has turned into a veritable laboratory of transitional justice. The International Criminal Court (ICC), the first permanent international criminal tribunal in history, has focused almost exclusively on Africa. At the time of writing, in March 2014, investigations or trials against accused from eight African countries have been opened at the ICC. This has attracted considerable criticism from various quarters, especially in Africa, where some see the ICC as a thinly veiled instrument of neo-colonialism. The advent of this critique is directly linked to the expansion of transitional justice mechanisms in post-conflict situations in African countries characterized by fragile state institutions, widespread poverty and considerable internal fragmentation due to ethnicity and regionalism. In Sierra Leone, for instance, no less than four transitional justice mechanisms (amnesty, truth commission, international tribunal and domestic criminal trials) co-existed in often uneasy relationships, as Gerhard Anders describes in his chapter. In Uganda, a similar pluralism of transitional justice institutions can be observed, as Adam Branch and Kimberley Armstrong show in their contributions. Uganda and Rwanda are of particular interest as these countries have experienced the most sustained efforts to create alternative transitional justice mechanisms more attuned to local culture and conceptions of justice.

In contradistinction to Latin America, where transitional justice was one of the means to address human rights violations by authoritarian military regimes, transitional justice in Africa with the exception of South Africa has focused on efforts to end violent conflicts and civil wars in societies characterized by the absence of a strong state apparatus and a plurality of de facto sovereign political and military groups. The growing importance of transitional justice in international efforts to pacify volatile regions affected by civil war has resulted in a growing convergence of international peace-building, development and transitional justice mechanisms (de Greiff and Duthie, 2009; Mani, 2008; UN, 2004). The interventions of foreign actors such as the United Nations or donor countries promoting transitional justice institutions as part of much larger military-humanitarian interventions have resulted in complex relationships with state institutions and locally operating groups. This variety and complexity is not matched by other regions and allows the comparison of different debates about transition and justice both across Africa and within specific countries. Due to this complexity and variety, the African experiences can shed light on debates about transitional justice and new beginnings elsewhere. Put differently, given that 'Africa' is often treated as a prime location for putting transitional justice into practice, African case studies seem particularly suited to decentre such approaches and to refocus on broader attempts at bringing about transition and justice.

The chapters in this edited volume cover a wide range of situations, putting an emphasis on either explicit 'transitional justice' mechanisms in the context of broader negotiations of justice and transition, or on the multifarious ways in which debates about new beginnings speak to lessons to be learnt for 'transitional justice'. In this sense, the first set of chapters aims at destabilizing the emphasis on transitional justice institutions in the analysis of new beginnings in Africa by studying other sites where past injustices are addressed. The second set contextualizes transitional justice mechanisms, situating them in relation to conflicts and negotiations about the past and the future. Widening the scope and including other sites of contestation will benefit the social-scientific study of political change and attempts to come to terms with past injustices in Africa and elsewhere. By transcending the narrow focus on institutions this edited volume seeks to address fundamental questions about transitions and justice in societies characterized by a high degree of external involvement and internal fragmentation.

We contend that the new beginnings examined in this collection are shaped by two inter-related dialectics. The first is the discrepancy between lofty promises of justice issued by lawyers, commissioners, diplomats and politicians, and the messy realities on the ground and within the institutions themselves, where the official narrative is constantly invoked and challenged by people's everyday actions. The second is the dialectic between the logics of exception, on the one hand, and the ordinary or normal, on the other hand. Re-education camps, repatriation of refugees, land restitution claims, truth commissions and war crimes trials are by no means ordinary measures; they are justified by an emergency or other exceptional circumstances. Yet there is no evidence for consensus on this, as the case studies in this collection show. In fact, there are groups and individuals who make a case for continuity by denying the extraordinary character of a situation and insisting on doing business as usual.

These dialectics, and how they play out during political new beginnings, have not been addressed by the current debate on localizing transitional justice, as the literature review in part one of this Introduction shows. The second part of the Introduction discusses the problem of new beginnings, the paradox of legitimizing a new social-political order that seeks a break with the laws and mores of the past. The third part outlines the importance of the discrepancies between lofty promises of justice and messy realities in the context of new beginnings, while the fourth examines the significance of the dialectics between logics of the exceptional and the ordinary or normal for a more comprehensive understanding of justice that transcends transitional justice as a field of study.

APPROACHING TRANSITIONAL JUSTICE: STATE OF THE ART

Transitional justice became an interdisciplinary field in its own right at the turn of the twenty-first century and has given rise to a burgeoning body of literature. Scholars from a range of disciplines including social and cultural anthropology, political science, theology and legal studies, as well as practitioners and activists, have focused on the analysis and development of institutions and processes including truth commissions, criminal prosecution, amnesty and reparations (Arthur, 2009; Bell, 2009). According to a widely quoted definition by former UN Secretary-General Kofi Annan, transitional justice comprises:

> the full range of processes and mechanisms associated with a society's attempts to come to terms with a legacy of large-scale past abuses, in order to ensure accountability, serve justice and achieve reconciliation. These may include both judicial and non-judicial mechanisms, with differing levels of international involvement (or none at all) and individual prosecutions, reparations, truth-seeking, institutional reform, vetting and dismissals, or a combination thereof. (UN, 2004: 4)

During the 1980s and the 1990s, democratically elected governments replaced military regimes across Latin America. This resulted in heated debates about how to address the human rights violations committed under military rule. In Argentina, Chile and El Salvador, truth commissions were established to signify a new, democratic beginning. These institutions had the task to throw light on the fate of tens of thousands of suspected dissidents who had 'disappeared' under military rule and to produce an authoritative historical record. Truth commissions were advanced as an alternative to amnesty provisions passed by the military rulers before relinquishing power, on the one hand, and criminal prosecutions, seen as threatening the stability of the new democracies, on the other. The first transitional justice studies were a direct response to these discussions about the merits and disadvantages of the various institutions set up to deal with the human rights violations of the military regimes in Latin America. During the 1990s, the first systematic studies under the newly coined term 'transitional justice' were published, discussing possible solutions to the problem of how to come to terms with a violent past (Cohen, 1995; Kritz, 1995; Orentlicher, 1991).

In its formative years, transitional justice was mainly seen as a tool that could be employed to effect a transition to democracy and adequately deal with past injustices regardless of the specific socio-cultural context. The field was dominated by legal scholars and political scientists who adopted a model of legal and political reform to be employed during a transitional period from autocratic rule to democracy. This reflected a broader shift during the 1980s and 1990s, away from the emphasis placed by modernization theory and Marxism on socio-economic structures (Arthur, 2009: 337–8). Instead, the quickly expanding transnational human rights movement advanced individual rights and political liberalism as the main drivers of progress. Authors like Bass (2000), Minow (1998) and Teitel (2000, 2003) legitimized the new concept of transitional justice by tracing it to the Nuremberg Trials and other trials against perpetrators of war crimes and the holocaust after World War II, although the term itself was not coined until the 1990s, as Arthur (2009) points out.

This shift is particularly striking with regard to Africa where, during the 1960s and 1970s, socio-economic structural transformation was seen as key in overcoming the legacy of colonialism. After the wave of democratization of the 1990s, when many countries across Africa introduced multi-party democracy, political liberalism and the belief in the potential of the free market became the principal paradigms in sub-Saharan Africa. The international financial institutions and the Western donor community welcomed the vision of individual rights and agency underlying both liberalism and capitalism, and vigorously promoted democracy, human rights and good governance. Transitional justice, also informed by a liberal belief in the transformative power of individual rights, became a key part of international humanitarian and development interventions and of national projects with the goal of realizing democracy, human rights and the rule of law.

On how to achieve these objectives, opinions have been divided. At one end of the spectrum are those who deem compromises necessary to maintain peace. At the other end are those who maintain that the punishment of perpetrators is the only credible means of achieving justice. This debate, known as peace versus justice, has shaped transitional justice for a long time. In this context, truth commissions were advanced as a compromise between amnesty and criminal prosecutions, creating a form of accountability but refraining from the punishment of perpetrators (Rotberg and Thompson, 2000; van Zyl, 1999). Recent studies have attempted to transcend the stark opposition between peace and justice by advocating a mix of several institutions including truth commissions and various forms of community justice, as well as criminal trials at national and international courts (Roht-Arriaza and Mariezcurrena, 2006; Sriram and Pillay, 2009).

The question of whether truth commissions or criminal trials are better suited to deal with past injustices has been partly eclipsed by the recent debate about localizing transitional justice. The idea that transitional justice institutions need to be adapted to socio-cultural specificities reflects growing doubts about the universalism of transitional justice, the ability to aid the establishment of liberal democracy in any socio-cultural setting. This universalistic outlook is mainly due to the influence of political science and law, the principal academic disciplines defining the field (Arthur, 2009; Bell, 2009).

The universality of the institutions and the objectives of transitional justice have come under critical scrutiny by a growing body of scholarship. Especially anthropologists, with their keen eye for the specificities of place and cultural difference, have been at the forefront of this critique. Wilson's (2001) anthropology of the South African TRC is one of the first examples of this approach. His book questions two basic assumptions informing the establishment of the TRC in South Africa. The first concerns the vision of a truly multicultural, non-nationalist constitutionalism after the end of apartheid based on universal human rights — a new culture not refracted by ethnicity, communalism or nationalism. The second was the idea of the existence of a unified concept of African restorative justice aimed at national reconciliation shared by all South Africans. By contrast, Wilson's ethnographic evidence shows how 'human rights talk is enmeshed in culturalist discourses on community and becomes an integral part of nation-building' (Wilson, 2001: 17). According to him, the ultimate objectives of the TRC process were the strengthening of the state's bureaucracy and legal system (ibid.) rather than realizing restorative justice and national reconciliation. He further shows that perceptions of restorative justice and reconciliation as cornerstones of the new constitutionalist national identity were by no means shared by all South Africans, some of whom favoured retributive justice (ibid.: 14–16).

This focus on the people in whose name justice is said to be done and the places where official narratives are challenged both in word and action gained in importance as more research on transitional justice in action was conducted in a number of different countries and institutions. It also became clear that the concept of transitional justice was by no means universal. A number of social-scientific studies have argued that ideas about achieving justice through truth-telling and punishment are rooted in Occidental religious and legal traditions. Research on Rwanda (Barnet, 2008; Buckley-Zistel, 2006; Eltringham, 2004; Thomson, 2011), Uganda (Allen, 2006; Finnström, 2008), South Africa (Ross, 2003) and Sierra Leone (Shaw, 2005, 2007) reveals a wide variety of voices and experiences in the regions affected by large-scale violence. For instance, Buckley-Zistel (2006) and Shaw (2005, 2007) argue that people in these regions did not share Western conceptions of truth-telling and reconciliation but preferred silence or social forgetting as a way to come to terms with the violent past.

Other studies highlight the diversity of views held by people in the regions affected by violence. Allen's research on northern Uganda (2006) traces the divisions between those preferring amnesty, those who support neo-traditional reconciliation ceremonies and those who demand retributive justice from the ICC. Finnström's (2008) ethnography of the everyday survival of the Acholi people in northern Uganda suggests an even more complex picture defying simplistic accounts of clear divisions between victims and perpetrators as people struggle to come to terms with 'bad surroundings'.

With regard to international criminal justice, several authors adopt a cultural relativist stance similar to Shaw's perspective. For instance, Clarke (2009) and Kelsall (2009) focus on the cultural differences between international criminal justice and African conceptions of justice, truth and fact-finding. Clarke argues that local conceptions of justice and law tend to be at odds with the language of human rights and international criminal law. In his study of the Special Court for Sierra Leone, Kelsall blames the problems encountered by the court on cultural differences between Western law and African culture, arguing that the Special Court failed to appreciate 'different ideas of social space and time, of causation, agency, responsibility, evidence, truth and truth-telling' (Kelsall, 2009: 17) prevalent in Sierra Leone.

Other studies situate international criminal tribunals in relation to international influences and the national political landscape, and trace how the tribunals produce historical narratives. Anders (2009) situates the Special Court for Sierra Leone in relation to the debate about international criminal justice and the national political arena in Sierra Leone. Hagan et al. (2006) show how US politics affected the prosecutorial strategy at the International Criminal Tribunal for the former Yugoslavia (ICTY). Wilson's (2011) study analyses how various features and dynamics of international criminal justice have shaped the historical accounts produced by the international tribunals. By tracing the various influences, these studies have contributed to a better, empirically more grounded understanding of the development of international criminal justice.

This revisionist scholarship has started to make some impact in the wider field of transitional justice. This is mainly due to the growing body of empirical knowledge about the manifold problems encountered when transitional justice mechanisms have been adapted to different situations and places. Even proponents of transitional justice admit that place matters, as abstract ideals such as reconciliation or justice are constantly contested and questioned by people who seek to engage, or try to avoid, the mechanisms of transitional justice at work (Orentlicher, 2007). In response to these problems, attempts have been made to localize transitional justice by advancing alternative mechanisms. Africa has been spearheading this trend with the *gacaca* courts in Rwanda and supposedly traditional reconciliation ceremonies in northern Uganda. These institutions are presented as drawing on African cultural values and concepts of justice by emphasizing community involvement and reconciliation between perpetrators and victims. Several authors such as Kelsall (2009) support the establishment of these alternative transitional justice mechanisms due to their hybrid and localized character.

Generally, the donor community has hailed these neo-traditional institutions as being more responsive to African values and expectations but a growing number of scholars have advanced a scathing critique. They argue that in fact they do not constitute manifestations of authentic African culture. In Rwanda, international humanitarian activists (Oomen, 2005) and the government (Waldorf, 2010) have promoted the *gacaca* courts as a cheap and quick way of dealing with the large number of *génocidaires*. Clark's (2010) study draws an ambivalent and complex picture of community involvement in the *gacaca* courts, which does not correspond with simplistic ideas about African culture. With regard to Uganda, Branch (2011) criticizes the essentializing culturalism driving supposedly African transitional justice mechanisms, a critique he further develops in his contribution to this collection. The edited volume *Localizing Transitional Justice* (Shaw et al., 2010) exemplifies the critique of the aloofness of transitional justice and the problems surrounding the introduction of supposedly African alternative institutions such as the *gacaca*. In the book's introduction, Shaw and Waldorf suggest adopting a 'place-based' approach to explore the multifaceted encounters between universal transitional justice discourse and 'local practices and priorities' (ibid.: 5). Their empirical evidence on local practices shows how clearly differentiated categories of victim and perpetrator fail to account for complex realities on the ground where people often prefer silence to public displays of truth-telling.

By now, the emphasis on sound empirical knowledge of the local and increasing scepticism towards the efficacy of transitional justice mechanisms are shared by a growing group of scholars in the field of transitional justice (Bell, 2009; Orentlicher, 2007; Teitel, 2003; Theidon, 2009). We agree with Shaw and others that local, place-based empirical evidence is important. Clearly, the emphasis on empirical evidence is sensible from a methodological perspective. However, it runs the risk of reproducing the scalar logic of global, national and local that tends to obscure the multifarious ways in which these scales are being made and re-made in processes of negotiation and contestation. Transcending the mainly methodological concern with scalarity, we deem three issues to be crucial to the understanding of transitional justice in the context of much wider social debates on justice and political change: the problem of 'new beginnings' — the paradox of legitimizing a novelty, of finding a foundation for that which explicitly breaks with the past; the discrepancies between lofty promises and the messy realities of transitional justice in action; and the dialectic between logics of the exception and the ordinary employed to legitimize or resist transitional justice mechanisms.

THE PROBLEM OF NEW BEGINNINGS

New beginnings have often been associated with violence. According to Arendt:

> The relevance of the problem of beginning to the phenomenon of revolution is obvious. That such a beginning must be intimately connected with violence seems to be vouched for by the legendary beginnings of our history as both biblical and classical antiquity report it: Cain slew Abel, and Romulus slew Remus; violence was the beginning and, by the same token, no beginning could be made without using violence, without violating. (Arendt,1990/1963: 20)

In Arendt's seminal analysis, the problem of beginning is key to the understanding of modern revolutions and the violence with which revolutionary change tends to be brought about. According to Arendt, the modern idea of revolution differs from pre-modern ideas of political change as it envisages the beginning of a new era, a complete break with the past to realize freedom, social equality and justice.

When Arendt was writing *On Revolution* in the early 1960s, many African countries were achieving independence. Prominent African leaders such as Kwame Nkrumah, Sekou Touré and Julius Nyerere framed the strife for national independence in the language of revolution, socialism and Pan-Africanism and did not eschew the use of violence to achieve independence. Theorists such as Fanon (2004/1961) explicitly condoned violence to end colonialism and emancipate the colonized populations from deeply entrenched racism and economic exploitation. During the 1990s, this appeared to change, and since the turn of the twenty-first century, violence is no longer seen as a legitimate means to bring about social change. Representative democracy has spread throughout the continent, but many parts of Africa have also experienced widespread violence and civil war in bitter conflicts over the control of state institutions and natural resources, with Sierra Leone, Rwanda, Uganda, Liberia and Somalia becoming the most prominent examples of state failure and armed conflict.

It was these conflicts that triggered the establishment of international tribunals, truth commissions and other transitional justice mechanisms, which are now seen as key in strengthening representative democracy and the rule of law. Following the Latin American template, South Africa was the first country in sub-Saharan Africa to establish a transitional justice mechanism in the form of the Truth and Reconciliation Commission during its transition from the apartheid regime. This was followed by the International Criminal Tribunal for Rwanda, established to hold accountable the main perpetrators of the genocide in 1994. In 2002, another ad hoc criminal tribunal, the Special Court for Sierra Leone, was set up in Freetown to hold accountable perpetrators of war crimes committed during the civil war. In the same year, the ICC, the first permanent international criminal tribunal, was established in The Hague. The ICC has mainly focused on African situations including the case against the leaders of the Lord's Resistance Army in northern Uganda, and its first concluded trial against Thomas Lubanga, who was found guilty in March 2012 of conscripting and enlisting children in the DRC.

All of these situations face the problem of new beginnings. In contradistinction to Arendt's analysis of revolutionary new beginnings and the revolutionary spirit of decolonization during the 1960s, current debates about new beginnings in Africa often revolve around transitional justice and explicitly reject revolutionary violence. Transitional justice also seeks a break with the past but by addressing past injustices rather than by violent means. The two principal techniques employed are the production of an authoritative historical record contributing to national reconciliation, and criminal trials to hold accountable the perpetrators of war crimes and human rights violations.

As mentioned earlier, liberal constitutionalism, rule of law and human rights are the ultimate objectives of fact-finding by truth commissions and criminal tribunals. For instance, the preamble of the South African Promotion of National Unity and Reconciliation Act of 1995 establishing the truth commission invokes 'a future founded on the recognition of human rights, democracy and peaceful co-existence for all South Africans, irrespective of colour, race, class, belief or sex'. Similarly, representatives of international criminal courts have highlighted the importance of criminal trials beyond the mere punishment of individuals who have committed crimes. In 2000, for instance, the UN Secretary General stated in his report to the UN Security Council that the Special Court for Sierra Leone 'would contribute to the process of national reconciliation and to the restoration and maintenance of peace in that country' (UN, 2000: 13).

Truth commissions and courts are manifestations of a reformist and legalistic approach to effecting new beginnings; they have their foundation in legal documents including national legislation, international law or peace agreements between warring factions. The South African truth commission is based on the South African interim constitution of 1993 and the Promotion of National Unity and Reconciliation Act (1995); the Special Court for Sierra Leone on an agreement between the UN and the Government of Sierra Leone authorized by the UN Security Council; the ICTR on several Security Council resolutions; and the ICC on an international treaty.

These founding documents differ from the American Declaration of Independence of 1776 or the French Declaration of the Rights of Man and of the Citizen of 1789 as they do not represent a complete break with the past. Whereas the French Declaration of 1789 rejected the sovereignty of the monarch and introduced popular sovereignty, the South African constitution was the outcome of a long process of negotiation between the apartheid regime and the African National Congress (ANC) resulting in the gradual transfer of power and a compromise between the old regime and the new political order. According to Lollini (2011: 28), the 'language of constitutional law became the syntax and shared language' of the National Party (NP) and the ANC.

Generally, the condemnation of violence is one of the hallmarks of transitional justice with its focus on legal reform and peaceful dialogue. However, violence often shapes the new beginnings. In spite of the promise of peace and inclusion even the new social and political order envisaged by transitional justice might rely on founding violence, as Branch shows in his chapter on northern Uganda. His account reveals the contradiction between the rhetoric of reconciliation and justice espoused by the advocates of transitional justice mechanisms such as *mato oput* and continued violence and injustices in the supposedly pacified districts of northern Uganda. The discrepancy between the liberal narrative informing truth commissions, courts and localized, neo-traditional initiatives, on the one hand, and the messy realities in the regions affected by violence and injustice, on the other hand, is one of the key themes addressed by this collection.

LOFTY PROMISES AND MESSY REALITIES

Tensions and contradictions between the often lofty and abstract ideals of (transitional) justice and their actual enactments and realizations in practice have a profound impact on the ways in which new beginnings in Africa evolve. The ethnographic case studies in this volume on Sierra Leone, Kenya, Uganda, Rwanda, Mauritania and South Africa explore the relationship between abstract ideas and ideals of justice, on the one hand, and often bitter political power struggles and mundane bureaucratic practices, on the other hand. Justice is always refracted in individuals' everyday experiences, challenged or instantiated in specific situations, as Riano-Alcalà and Baines (2012) argue in a recent publication on transitional justice and the everyday. It is striking how absolute ideas about justice are constantly invoked by international organizations, social activists and politicians as well as ordinary people who are engaged in complex negotiations, while ostensibly upholding justice as a non-negotiable principle. For instance, in Steffen Jensen's discussion on South African police reform in this volume, justice as such does indeed seem non-negotiable; however, quite different and conflicting versions of justice emerge in practice, depending on whether freedom is sought from a repressive state apparatus, i.e. the police itself, or from crime. Similarly, the justice of actual outcomes in South African land restitution, in the course of which the state compensates victims of former race-based dispossessions, is evaluated quite differently on the basis of divergent property regimes that are hardly ever made explicit (see Olaf Zenker, this volume). What is more, it might take a conscious effort to raise public awareness in the first place for the fact that normalized poverty actually constitutes an unacceptable state of injustice, as the recent 'toilet wars' in South Africa show (Steven Robins, this volume) — whether such goals are pursued through spectacular or ordinary activism.

The international criminal tribunals have promoted an ambitious vision of justice and peace based on retributive justice, the punishment of political and military leaders who are held responsible for war crimes, crimes against humanity and genocide. Anders' analysis focuses on the discrepancy between the lofty promises of justice made by the Special Court for Sierra Leone and the violent conflicts between the political leaders and former commanders of the warring factions who sought to secure a place in the political order after the end of the civil war. Similarly, Nigel Eltringham's ethnography of the experiences of lawyers and judges at the ICTR raises fundamental doubts about the promise of new beginnings heralded by the tribunal. The contributions by Kimberley Armstrong, Adam Branch and Sabine Höhn on the interventions by the ICC in Uganda and Kenya also highlight the conflicts and contestations about new beginnings and justice in the affected regions where the international project of global justice is often challenged by individuals and groups.

BETWEEN EXCEPTIONS AND BUSINESS AS USUAL

Transitional justice institutions are exceptional instruments established to address extraordinary situations. None of these institutions is meant to be permanent. Even investigations of the ICC, a permanent international organization, are conceived as temporary interventions in the internal affairs of a country in response to extraordinary circumstances sanctioned by international law. And yet special tribunals or truth commissions follow a well-established set of templates with criminal trials at one end of the continuum and blanket amnesty at the other end. Arendt's (2006/1963) account of Eichmann's trial reminds us that ordinary measures such as criminal trials often seem barely adequate to deal with the most extraordinary crime of genocide (see also Drumbl, 2007: 1–10).

In her history of transitional justice, Teitel (2003: 71–2) points out that in 'this contemporary phase, transitional jurisprudence normalizes an expanded discourse of humanitarian justice'. In her view, 'there is no clear boundary between ordinary and transitional periods' (ibid.: 93). We would like to interrogate this boundary between the extraordinary and the ordinary, which we think is key to understanding new beginnings in Africa and elsewhere. The contributions to this edited volume question the clear boundary between the transition phase and normality. For instance, the chapters on South Africa illustrate that, more than a decade after the TRC published its report, the transition phase is not over. At the ANC National Policy Conference in June 2012, President Zuma called for a 'second transition' to highlight the ongoing need to come to terms with apartheid's legacy. As a consequence, debates about justice, compensation and recognition have expanded in various arenas, as Jensen, Zenker and Robins show in their case studies.

Logics of the exception are invoked and employed by a wide range of actors. This includes the classical 'state of exception', as declared in a foundational act of state sovereignty (Agamben, 2005; Benjamin, 1996; Schmitt, 1985). In a reconfiguration of such sovereign power, a similar logic of exception is also utilized within foreign interventions and by various transitional justice institutions, drawing on a pan-human ethic of compassion, international humanitarian law and universalized human rights standards in order to justify local engagements (Fassin and Pandolfi, 2010). But logics of exception are by no means the prerogative of modern states, international organizations or humanitarian activists alone, as a multitude of voices advances similar or divergent claims to sovereignty (Hansen and Stepputat, 2005). Negotiations of new beginnings in Africa are thus shaped by competing logics — logics that vary not only between different actors, but also possibly within a unitary agent such as 'the state'.

The multitude of voices and claims to exceptionality are mirrored by logics of the ordinary instantiated by states, international agencies and Africans from all walks of life. For instance, international organizations and transitional justice mechanisms often emphasize a normal sequence from chaos to order based on a tried and tested model or tool to aid transition and reconciliation. However, it is important to note that these claims — even though backed up by an overwhelming military-humanitarian apparatus — do not go unchallenged. Often the envisioned beneficiaries of these good intentions refuse to adopt the proclaimed reading of exceptionality. Instead, they invoke an alternative logic of the ordinary in seeing a neo-colonial agenda or other perfectly mundane political and economic interests at work behind the rhetoric of exception. We hence propose to pay particular attention to the dialectics of various logics of the exception, which justify extraordinary measures in exceptional times, as well as different logics of the ordinary that envision the transition towards a just(er) future as a difficult, yet perfectly mundane affair. We argue that these entanglements of logics of the exception and the ordinary have a crucial bearing on the peculiar trajectories that the discursive and practical negotiations of 'justice' can take in particular settings. This is so because a certain incident or 'move' within such negotiations acquires variable connectivity, depending on the concrete logics of the exception and/or the ordinary, in which it becomes embedded. A focus on these two analytical dimensions in their interrelation is thus crucial for a deeper understanding of transitions to justice in specific African settings.

THE CHAPTERS

Simon Turner's chapter on the repatriation from camp life to post-genocide Rwanda succinctly illustrates the dialectics between the two logics. Here subtle similarities and differences are at work between Hutu refugee camps under the UNHCR and Hutu re-education camps called *ingando* that are run by the Tutsi-dominated new Rwandan state as a specific transitional justice measure. While the refugee camps conform closely to the logic of exception, in which Hutu refugees (i.e. potential *génocidaires*) are reduced to the 'bare life' of an a-historical humanity, the *ingando* camps make use of a profoundly historical logic of exceptionality, conceiving ex-combatants as 'bad life' in need of purification. Both camps aim for reintegration and new beginnings; yet whereas the UN invokes a logic of the ordinary that wants to turn Hutu refugees into universal citizens with no specified history, the Tutsi-dominated state seeks the production of 'good citizens' in terms of an ethnically cleansed Rwandan history. Given that *ingando* is only compulsory for Hutu ex-combatants, while Tutsi join separate solidarity camps (*itorero*) that merely enhance their elite careers, quite different ideals and practices of 'justice' emerge from these three spaces of exception and from the divergent transitional trajectories inscribed in them.

Marion Fresia's study of the official repatriation of Mauritanian refugees as both an act of transitional justice and as a prerequisite for further transitional justice measures equally focuses on the camp as an exceptional site where the terms of new beginnings are intensely debated. Her ethnography of refugee camps in Senegal shows how a dominant politico-humanitarian narrative about past human rights violations was co-constructed by both the refugee elite and human rights organizations. Based on humanitarian law, they portrayed the refugees as being in a state of exception in relation to the ordinary logic of the international law of sovereign states. However, these refugees were by no means a homogeneous group. They comprised different subsets with divergent interests and Fresia further shows how the dominant narrative was also contested by counter-narratives, putting forward quite different understandings of new beginnings and desirable transitions to other forms of justice. Moreover, her analysis reveals substantial discrepancies between locals' discourses and their practices: on the one hand, many highlight the importance of the order of nation states, underlying their predicament as 'refugees', while, on the other hand, deviantly disregarding precisely this order and thus the 'refugee'/'citizen' dichotomy in their everyday practices.

Police violence in post-apartheid South Africa also seems to be under the spell of two alternating logics of exceptionality, each one forming the background of the other. The first of these, as Jensen points out, refers to the need, immediately recognized and addressed with the end of apartheid, to profoundly transform the old apartheid police within the transitional justice measure of a security sector reform, in order to prevent further human rights violations (such as torture). However, in the mid-1990s, a second emergency moved to centre stage, namely the threat to national liberation posed by high levels of crime, apparently necessitating hefty police violence as a means to protect the citizens. While on the level of abstract ideals these two exceptional logics seem complementary, Jensen shows how, on the level of messy everyday practices, they actually clash. They end up giving preference to different notions of 'justice' — freedom from police violence *versus* freedom from crime — with each logic of exceptionality dismissing the concern of the other as 'ordinary'. In this sense, the first logic conceives police violence as requiring exceptional measures (and frames crime as ordinary), whereas the second logic sees excessive crime as justifying exceptional police violence (and treats security sector reform as ordinary). The transitional justice of institutional reform is thus left in a state of ambiguity, since — depending on which exceptional logic is activated — excessive police violence constitutes either an obstacle or a means to create a new beginning for South Africa.

Robins' discussion of the recent 'toilet wars' in South Africa provides another example of the relevance of different logics of the exception and the ordinary. In the run-up to the 2011 local government elections, the existence of open (i.e. unenclosed) porcelain toilets in Western Cape townships run by the Democratic Alliance provincial government was suddenly elevated to a public scandal by activists from the African National Congress Youth League (ANCYL). This was achieved by what Robins calls a 'politics of the spectacle', which — drawing on a logic of exceptionality — represented the 'anti-dignity toilets' as a high-profile incident of gross injustice. The spectacle involving the mass media, High Courts and the South African Human Rights Commission soon deteriorated into opportunistic politicking. By contrast, social movements such as the Social Justice Coalition have engaged the sanitation problem for a much longer time through a 'politics of the ordinary'. Rather than using spectacular acts of resistance, such social movements have patiently deployed personal testimonies, protests, petitions, scientific reports, statistics and litigation to render politically legible everyday forms of structural injustice, thereby projecting a quite different avenue towards a more just society. Robins argues that the logic of exceptionality, underpinning both the short-lived politics of the spectacle and the narrowly conceived transitional justice mechanism of the Truth and Reconciliation Commission, is ultimately ill-equipped to deal with the structural inequalities still haunting post-apartheid South Africa. By contrast, in fighting structural violence, the ordinary logic of 'slow activism' stands a better chance of contributing towards a much broader 'transitional social justice'.

The justice of South African land restitution is also evaluated differently, and hence contested, depending on whether restitution is read in terms of a logic of the exception or of the ordinary. As a transitional justice measure of the state, aimed at restoring justice in the light of the exceptional condition of massive, racially motivated land dispossessions in the past, post-apartheid restitution law retrospectively transforms the conception of landed property on which past dispossessions had built. However, as Zenker shows, many former (white) landowners expect restitution to still operate as an ordinary process within an unchanged property system, whereas, in fact, it is driven by an exceptional process of a new transformative property regime. Rather than making restitution's instituted logic of exceptionality their own, such former owners end up reading the events in terms of an ordinary logic of 'victor's justice', in which the allegedly politically motivated transfer of land to Africans is interpreted as being merely dressed up as 'restitution'. In this way, the proclaimed ideal of bringing about justice and reconciliation through the restitution process is seen as being undermined, in practice, through an unjust and politically motivated implementation process. Zenker argues that if all parties in a claim had to interact face-to-face with each other and share their histories of (dis)possessions, there would be a better chance for the development of more 'common sense'. Given the current institutional format, however, deeply entrenched differences regarding the justice of restituted lands remain. Under such conditions, agreements on the terms of a new beginning seem difficult to reach.

International criminal tribunals are based on the idea that exceptional circumstances justify interventions in countries where the national authorities are unable or unwilling to hold accountable the perpetrators of crimes against humanity and war crimes. This is what happened in Sierra Leone where the government requested the United Nations to set up a special tribunal to hold accountable those 'bearing the greatest responsibility' for war crimes and crimes against humanity committed during the civil war. This UN-backed tribunal was supposed to deliver justice and contribute to a peaceful new beginning of Sierra Leone but, as Anders' analysis shows, this promise was never realized. Instead, the volatile transition period at the turn of the twenty-first century was characterized by a violent struggle over positions of power and influence that suggest the continuity of patterns of Sierra Leonean politics rather than a new beginning. Sierra Leone provides an illuminating case, as an international criminal tribunal operated in

parallel to a truth commission. Moreover, the government had already declared a state of emergency in 1998 and used these powers to arrest and
detain hundreds of former combatants in an attempt to remove the former
rebels from the political arena.

Eltringham makes a similar point in his ethnography of lawyers and judges
at the International Criminal Tribunal for Rwanda. The ICTR was meant to
mark a new beginning both for Rwanda and internationally, by contributing
to a global legal order. Over time, emphasis shifted from its contribution
to Rwandan reconciliation to the idea of a new beginning for international
criminal justice. At the court, however, lawyers and judges held different
opinions regarding the tribunal's national and international impact. These
differences and contradictions are particularly stark with regard to discussions at the tribunal about the failure to indict members of the Rwandan
Patriotic Army for alleged war crimes in 1994 and accusations of 'victor's
justice'.

The three chapters dealing with the interventions of the ICC in Kenya and
Uganda highlight the growing importance of this permanent international
criminal tribunal for debates about the terms of new beginnings in Africa.
Höhn's analysis of the impact the ICC investigations have had on the political
arena in Kenya illustrates the growing salience of the ICC. The violence
surrounding the 2007 elections were widely perceived as exceptional. Due
to the failure of the Kenyan authorities to hold accountable those responsible
for organizing the violence, the ICC stepped in as an extraordinary response
to an exceptional situation. The ICC's intervention signalled the expansion
of the scope of the tribunal's activities, which had been limited to civil
wars, into a new domain. This development highlights the role the ICC is
likely to play in expanding and consolidating a specific model of multi-party
democracy promoted by the UN and other actors. According to Höhn, it
is less clear whether the ICC's intervention represents a new beginning for
Kenya. It seems unlikely that the political elite will embark on the social and
political reforms that would be needed to address the root causes of electoral
violence.

Armstrong and Branch both address the debates about transitional justice
and the intervention of the ICC in northern Uganda. In many ways this
case symbolizes the contradictions and tensions underlying the project of
advancing global justice. The arrest warrants against five leaders of the Lord's
Resistance Army issued in 2005 were the first to be issued by the ICC. Since
then the investigation has entered a limbo as the Ugandan government, which
originally had referred the case to the ICC, has removed its support for the
ICC, considering various domestic options instead. As elsewhere, the debate
in Uganda has been framed in terms of justice and peace, with justice serving
as shorthand for a retributive justice mechanism and peace denoting amnesty
and other non-retributive forms of restorative justice. Armstrong unpacks this
debate and shows how supporters and opponents of the ICC have sought to
relate to and adapt ideas about justice and peace in the negotiations about a
new beginning in northern Uganda.

Branch examines a localized model of transitional justice in northern Uganda that has been promoted as an alternative to the retributive vision of transitional justice promoted by the ICC. This form of supposedly traditional justice, or what Branch refers to as 'ethnojustice', is said to represent African, or more specifically Acholi, concepts of justice and to be much better adapted to the local socio-cultural context in northern Uganda than Western criminal justice. Branch's analysis reveals to what extent ethnojustice is shaped by essentialist ideas about African cultural authenticity that strengthen the claims to political authority advanced by traditional leaders who lost much legitimacy during the violent conflict. His evidence challenges the dominant official narrative of a new beginning in northern Uganda. Branch argues that transitional justice in northern Uganda did not bring liberal peace but instead has legitimized new and old forms of everyday violence and injustice.

The proposed perspective on 'justice' between the exceptional and the ordinary thus enables the contributing authors to explore issues and themes commonly deemed to fall outside the scope of analysis of transitional justice. They situate courts and other transitional justice mechanisms within wider debates about justice, human rights discourses and humanitarian interventions. They combine analyses of the interventions of international criminal tribunals in Kenya, Uganda, Rwanda and Sierra Leone with studies of restitution and human rights in South Africa and debates about justice among refugees in Mauritania and Rwanda. These debates about the terms of new beginnings are key to the study of contemporary Africa and its place in a wider world. The various case studies show the considerable differences between divergent situations, fleshing out the wide spectrum of debates about justice and transition across Africa. All situations share, however, the prominent role played by foreign influences, either in the form of institutions such as courts, or globally circulating ideas about justice. In addition, foreign interventions have generally had profound economic, social and political consequences influencing African debates about a just order, whilst being shaped in often unforeseen ways by the local settings they are operating in. The case studies address these dynamics within settings shaped by transnationally circulating ideas, state-driven processes and variable place-based aspirations. In focusing on the discursive and practical negotiations of justice, situated within entanglements of logics of the exception and the ordinary, they thus ultimately aim for a better understanding of current debates about transition, justice and 'transitional justice' in Africa.

REFERENCES

Agamben, G. (2005) *State of Exception*. Chicago, IL: University of Chicago Press.
Allen, T. (2006) *Trial Justice: The International Criminal Court and the Lord's Resistance Army*. London: Zed Books.
Anders, G. (2009) 'The New Global Legal Order as Local Phenomenon: The Special Court for Sierra Leone', in F. von Benda-Beckmann, K. von Benda-Beckmann and A. Griffiths (eds)

Spatializing Law: An Anthropological Geography of Law in Society, pp. 137–56. Farnham: Ashgate.

Arendt, H. (1990/1963) *On Revolution*. London: Penguin.

Arendt, H. (2006/1963) *Eichmann in Jerusalem: A Report on the Banality of Evil*. New York: Viking Press.

Arthur, P. (2009) 'How "Transitions" Reshaped Human Rights: A Conceptual History of Transitional Justice', *Human Rights Quarterly* 31(2): 321–67.

Barnet, J.E. (2008) 'The Injustice of Local Justice: Truth, Reconciliation and Revenge in Rwanda', *Genocide Studies and Prevention* 3(2): 173–93.

Bass, G. (2000) *Stay the Hand of Vengeance: The Politics of War Crimes Tribunals*. Princeton, NJ: Princeton University Press.

Bell, C. (2009) 'Transitional Justice, Interdisciplinarity and the State of the "Field" or "Non-Field"', *International Journal of Transitional Justice* 3(1): 5–27.

Benjamin, W. (1996) 'Critique of Violence', in M. Bullock and M.W. Jennings (eds) *Walter Benjamin: Selected Writings. Volume 1: 1913–1926*, pp. 236–52. Cambridge, MA: Belknap Press.

Branch, A. (2011) *Displacing Human Rights: War and Intervention in Northern Uganda*. Oxford: Oxford University Press.

Buckley-Zistel, S. (2006) 'Remembering to Forget: Chosen Amnesia as a Strategy for Local Coexistence in Post-Genocide Rwanda', *Africa* 76(2): 131–50.

Clark, P. (2010) *The Gacaca Courts, Post-Genocide Justice and Reconciliation in Rwanda: Justice without Lawyers*. Cambridge: Cambridge University Press.

Clarke, K.M. (2009) *Fictions of Justice: The International Criminal Court and the Challenge of Legal Pluralism*. Cambridge: Cambridge University Press.

Cohen, S. (1995) 'State Crimes of Previous Regimes: Knowledge, Accountability, and the Policing of the Past', *Law and Social Inquiry* 20: 7–50.

Drumbl, M. (2007) *Atrocity, Punishment, and International Law*. Cambridge: Cambridge University Press.

Eltringham, N. (2004) *Accounting for Horror: Post-Genocide Debates in Rwanda*. London: Pluto Press.

Fanon, F. (2004/1961) *The Wretched of the Earth*. London: Penguin Books.

Fassin, D. and M. Pandolfi (eds) (2010) *Contemporary States of Emergency: The Politics of Military and Humanitarian Interventions*. New York: Zone Books.

Finnström, S. (2008) *Living with Bad Surroundings: War, History, and Everyday Moments in Northern Uganda*. Durham, NC: Duke University Press.

de Greiff, P. and R. Duthie (eds) (2009) *Transitional Justice and Development: Making Connections*. New York: Social Science Research Council.

Hagan, J., R. Levi and G. Ferrales (2006) 'Swaying the Hand of Justice: The Internal and External Dynamics of Regime Change at the International Criminal Tribunal for the Former Yugoslavia', *Law and Social Inquiry* 31(3): 585–616.

Hansen, T.B. and F. Stepputat (eds) (2005) *Sovereign Bodies: Citizens, Migrants, and States in the Postcolonial World*. Princeton, NJ: Princeton University Press.

Kelsall, T. (2009) *Culture under Cross-Examination: International Justice and the Special Court for Sierra Leone*. Cambridge: Cambridge University Press.

Kritz, N. (ed.) (1995) *Transitional Justice: How Emerging Democracies Reckon with Former Regimes* (3 vols). Washington, DC: United States Institute of Peace Press.

Lollini, A. (2011) *Constitutionalism and Transitional Justice in South Africa*. Oxford: Berghahn.

Mani, R. (ed.) (2008) 'Special Issue: Transitional Justice and Development', *International Journal of Transitional Justice* 2(3).

Minow, M. (1998) *Between Vengeance and Forgiveness: Facing History after Genocide and Mass Violence*. Boston, MA: Beacon Press.

Oomen, B. (2005) 'Donor-driven Justice and its Discontents: The Case of Rwanda', *Development and Change* 36(5): 887–910.

Orentlicher, D. (1991) 'Settling Accounts: The Duty to Prosecute Human Rights Violations of a Prior Regime', *Yale Law Journal* 100: 2537–2615.

Orentlicher, D. (2007) '"Settling Accounts" Revisited: Reconciling Global Norms and Local Agency', *International Journal of Transitional Justice* 1(1): 10–22.

Riano-Alcalà, P. and E. Baines (eds) (2012) 'Special Issue: Transitional Justice and the Everyday', *International Journal of Transitional Justice* 6(3).

Roht-Arriaza, N. and J. Mariezcurrena (eds) (2006) *Transitional Justice in the Twenty-First Century: Beyond Truth versus Justice.* Cambridge: Cambridge University Press.

Ross, F. (2003) 'On Having Voice and Being Heard: Some After-Effects of Testifying before the South African Truth and Reconciliation Commission', *Anthropological Theory* 3(3): 325–41.

Rotberg, R. and D. Thompson (eds) (2000) *Truth v. Justice: The Morality of Truth Commissions.* Princeton, NJ: Princeton University Press.

Schmitt, C. (1985) *Political Theology: Four Chapters on the Concept of Sovereignty.* Cambridge, MA: MIT Press.

Shaw, R. (2005) 'Rethinking Truth and Reconciliation Commissions: Lessons from Sierra Leone'. Special Report No. 130. Washington, DC: United States Institute of Peace.

Shaw, R. (2007) 'Memory Frictions: Localizing the Truth and Reconciliation Commission in Sierra Leone', *International Journal of Transitional Justice* 1(2): 183–207.

Shaw, R., L. Waldorf and P. Hazan (eds) (2010) *Localizing Transitional Justice: Interventions and Priorities after Mass Violence.* Stanford, CA: Stanford University Press.

Sriram, C.L. and S. Pillay (eds) (2009) *Peace versus Justice? The Dilemma of Transitional Justice in Africa.* Scottsville: University of KwaZulu-Natal Press.

Teitel, R. (2000) *Transitional Justice.* Oxford: Oxford University Press.

Teitel, R. (2003) 'Transitional Justice Genealogy', *Harvard Human Rights Journal* 16: 69–94.

Theidon, K. (ed.) (2009) 'Special Issue: Whose Justice? Global and Local Approaches to Transitional Justice', *International Journal of Transitional Justice* 3(3).

Thomson, S. (2011) 'The Darker Side of Transitional Justice: The Power Dynamics behind Rwanda's Gacaca Courts', *Africa* 81(3): 373–90.

UN (2000) 'Report of the Secretary-General on the Establishment of a Special Court for Sierra Leone'. UN Doc. S/2000/915, 4 October. New York: United Nations.

UN (2004) 'Report of the Secretary-General on the Rule of Law and Transitional Justice in Conflict and Post-Conflict Societies'. UN Doc. S/2004/616, 23 August. New York: United Nations.

Waldorf, L. (2010) '"Like Jews Waiting for Jesus": Posthumous Justice in Post-Genocide Rwanda', in R. Shaw, L. Waldorf and P. Hazan (eds) *Localizing Transitional Justice: Interventions and Priorities after Mass Violence*, pp. 183–202. Stanford, CA: Stanford University Press.

Wilson, R.A. (2001) *The Politics of Truth and Reconciliation in South Africa: Legitimizing the Post-Apartheid State.* Cambridge: Cambridge University Press.

Wilson, R.A. (2011) *Writing History in International Criminal Trials.* Cambridge: Cambridge University Press.

van Zyl, P. (1999) 'Dilemmas of Transitional Justice: The Case of South Africa's Truth and Reconciliation Commission', *Journal of International Affairs* 52(2): 647–67.

2

Making Good Citizens from Bad Life in Post-Genocide Rwanda

Simon Turner

INTRODUCTION

Rwanda is mostly known to the outside world for the exceptionally brutal violence that hit the country for three months in 1994. This chapter explores not the genocide but the attempts by international humanitarian agencies and the post-genocide Rwandan state respectively to deal with exceptionality created by the genocide and return to normality. I do so by exploring two particularly disturbing, and to a great degree overlapping, groups in relation to the genocide. The first group is the Hutu who fled *en masse* to neighbouring Zaire[1] and Tanzania after the genocide and ended up in vast refugee camps that became states of exception beyond the national order of things, organized by the United Nations High Commissioner for Refugees (UNHCR). Once these camps were closed by force by the Rwandan government, a second unsettling group emerged, namely the members of various Hutu armed groups returning to the new Rwanda.

   This chapter examines the process whereby the Rwandan state is attempting to transform these returning ex-combatants into new citizens of the new Rwanda, a Rwanda devoid of ethnicity or hatred. An important instrument in transforming them from *génocidaires* to good citizens is the *ingando* education camps which are organized by the Rwandan government. I argue that the *ingando* camps act as points of transition where returning refugees are transformed from 'bad life' into good citizens. There are resemblances between the exceptional space of refugee camps, where international agencies are concerned with empowering the refugees to become 'normal' citizens upon return, and the *ingando* camps where the Rwandan government is trying to remove what it calls 'genocidal mentalities' and create a sense of 'national unity' among the ex-combatants. There are, however, also subtle differences. The international community seems to be interested in (re-)creating a universal citizen, drawing on universal tenets of human rights and democratic empowerment whilst negating the concrete historical context of politics and

I am grateful to Olaf Zenker and Gerhard Anders for their thorough critique and constructive comments, and to the anonymous referees for their feedback on an earlier version.

1. I use this name because it was the official name of present-day DRC at the time.

violence. In contrast, the Rwandan state seems intent on creating a new citizen of its own whilst being firmly situated in a concrete historical moment
of violence which it is vociferously trying to exorcize. In other words, the
Hutu in the refugee camps are reproduced as 'bare life', while the Hutu
who enter the *ingando* are reproduced as what I term 'bad life'. Finally, this
exploration of the similarities and the subtle differences between the two
exceptional spaces of the refugee camp and the re-education camp aims to
further our understanding of the specific kind of 'normality' that the Rwandan state is invoking in its process of transitional justice and creating a new
beginning.

TRANSITION AND JUSTICE IN RWANDA

In the aftermath of the genocide, Rwanda pursued transitional justice through
a number of international, national and local mechanisms such as the International Criminal Tribunal for Rwanda (ICTR) in Arusha (Peskin, 2011;
Webster, 2011; Wilson, 2010), the national courts and, most notably, the
local *gacaca* courts (Brouneus, 2008; Kanyangara et al., 2007; Tiemessen,
2004; Waldorf, 2011). The *gacaca* courts have been criticized for not being
authentically Rwandan, as claimed (Oomen, 2005), for not living up to standards of the rule of law (Webster, 2011), and for conflicting with ordinary
Rwandans' perceptions of justice (Ingelaere, 2009). Whatever the criticism,
they may also be seen as a pragmatic means to deal with the enormous
challenge of prosecuting more than 120,000 genocide suspects (Zorbas,
2004).

As mentioned in the Introduction to this volume (see also Anders and
Zenker, 2014), transitional justice concerns more than simply punishing the
guilty. Truth telling is another option that has become popular since the
end of the Latin American dictatorships and, in particular, since the well-
known South African Truth and Reconciliation Commission (TRC). It has
been argued that *gacaca* may have been more successful in facilitating truth
telling than in punishing the guilty (Zorbas, 2004). Others have argued that
truth in Rwanda is relative and relational, and that locally the *gacaca* courts
were perceived as mere state spectacles (Ingelaere, 2009).

The Rwandan state has, however, taken a number of other initiatives
that go beyond the legalistic limits of tribunals and truth commissions in
order to create a new Rwanda devoid of ethnic animosity. Central to the
project of creating a new Rwanda is the National Unity and Reconciliation
Commission (NURC), which was established in 1999 with the vision to
strive for 'a peaceful, united and prosperous nation'.[2] It mainly tries to

---

2. See the website: www.nurc.gov.rw

achieve its goals through various forms of civic education and monitoring what are perceived as 'genocidal mentalities'. Under its auspices a number of events, studies, institutions and policies have emerged — all in the name of moving beyond the genocide and preventing it from happening again. For instance, the genocide is memorialized in numerous ways, from the month of mourning every April to the establishment of an increasing number of memorial sites all over the country (Buckley-Zistel, 2006b; Ibreck, 2010). The *ingando* re-education camps are also examples of dealing with the past in order to create a specific new beginning. Here, a state-sanctioned version of history is taught in order to be able to rectify the mistakes of the past and create a present that is shared by all Rwandans (Buckley-Zistel, 2006a). The Rwandan state is, in other words, managing transition by meting out justice and controlling the past in order to create a new beginning that is radically different to pre-genocide Rwanda.

At first glance, the process of transitional justice in Rwanda fits into the general mould of present-day notions of transitional justice, following a liberal ideology of human rights and good governance. As mentioned in the Introduction to this volume, the international hegemonic discourse on rights no longer accepts violence as a legitimate means to bring about social change. This chapter argues that despite the apparent resemblances with the dominant international liberal rights discourse on transition, the Rwandan state also relies on a revolutionary idea of violence as a precondition for a new beginning. Although it was the enemy, and not the revolutionary movement itself, that was responsible for the genocide, genocidal violence as an act of cleansing, enabled the Rwandan Patriotic Front (RPF) to create something radically new. The genocide can thus be said to be a founding moment of the new nation, albeit in a negative sense. The aim of the new state is to prevent this moment ever occurring again — as popularized in the 'never again' campaigns. As with other nation states founded on a violent rupture, there is an ever-present threat which calls for constant vigilance in order to avoid any kind of relapse. The new nation that RPF is creating is, in other words, not simply a question of re-establishing universal liberal rights through transitional justice. It is a revolutionary political project of creating a specific nation in a specific political image. Therefore, the objectives of transitional justice mechanisms that are being deployed are different from the objectives of the international community. This also goes for the reintegration of refugees and ex-combatants into the new nation.

REFUGEE CAMPS AS SPACES OF EXCEPTION

It has often been pointed out in the literature that refugees are perceived as 'matter out of place' (Douglas, 1966: 48) in the 'national order of things' (Malkki, 1995: 495). Nevzat Soguk refers to refugees as a Derridean supplement, both destabilizing and reinforcing the nation–state–citizen trinity (Soguk, 1999). In this manner, refugee camps become the containers within which to put and maintain this anomalous humanity, these fragments of 'bare life' (Turner, 2005, 2010).

Following Agamben, we may argue that the camp is an exceptional space and that it is here that we reach the limit of bio-politics; *zoë* or 'naked life' is produced and political life stops.[3] '(T)he camp is the structure in which the state of exception is permanently realised' (Agamben, 2000: 40), which means that 'all notions of political agency are, in a word, emptied from refugee subjectivity' (Nyers, 1998: 18) — they are in effect naked life. The main point here is that the refugee camp is a space where the normal law is suspended and where exceptionality results in sovereign power over the lives of the refugees.

Agamben argues that the camp is symptomatic of our times where the old trinity of nation (from the Latin *natio*: birth), state and territory has been broken up. 'The increasingly widening gap between birth (naked life) and nation-state is the new fact of the politics of our time and what we are calling "camp" is this disparity' (Agamben, 2000: 43–44). In other words, as citizens — the political life of the state — are no longer inscribed in the nation state through birth, the state needs the camp to separate political life from naked life (life that is not part of the *polis*). The camp becomes the hidden matrix and *nomos* of modern political space (Agamben, 1998: 166; Agamben, 2000: 37).

Such a production of biological life was obvious in the camps for Rwandan refugees which were set up across the borders in Zaire and Tanzania after the 1994 genocide. The international community responded to the 'humanitarian crisis' in the Great Lakes within weeks of its eruption, providing drinking water, hospitals, food and thousands of humanitarian experts to assist the millions of refugees. The refugees were perceived as bare humanity, victims of a humanitarian tragedy that needed the international community's attention and care. That the real (political) tragedy was in fact taking place across the border inside Rwanda was ignored. Indeed, these humanitarian victims were the same people who had been committing the crimes inside Rwanda, and who had made a collective military retreat into Tanzania and in particular into Zaire. Notwithstanding their dubious past, the Hutu who crossed the borders to Tanzania and Zaire instantly became refugees, incarnations of a universal voiceless 'humanity' and therefore helpless victims of history (Agier, 2011; Feldman and Ticktin, 2010; Nyers, 2006).

However, camps never were simply empty containers that produced time pockets to sustain a population. The international agencies in charge of the

---

3. In Agamben's books, the terms 'naked life' and 'bare life' are used interchangeably, depending on the English translations.

camps did not simply keep the biological bodies of the refugees alive and healthy but also did their best to create empowered citizen-subjects of the refugees (Turner, 2005, 2010). Although UNHCR and other agencies were primarily charged with 'care and maintenance' as it is called, they also prepared the refugees for the day they would return to 'normality'. Through various community development programmes they tried to create a responsible and reasonable 'community' out of what they perceived as a traumatized, apathetic mass of refugees (Turner, 2005, 2010). Dean (1999) and Hindess (2001), among others, have described programmes like these as attempts to create democratic citizens out of populations that are deemed unfit for political freedom in a society with a liberal government. The refugee camp, in other words, is perceived as an exceptional space, but it is a space that through its exceptionality is meant to prepare its inhabitants to return to 'normality'. In this optic, violence and displacement had created exceptional conditions, and it was the task of the camp leadership to prepare the refugees for normality.

Meanwhile, refugees themselves are not merely passive victims of history, put temporarily outside history while in the camp. Rather, they are active creators of history. Scholars have argued that refugee camps are like cities (Agier, 2002; Jansen, 2011) and that refugee agency actively negotiates the camp, creating new identities. I would take the argument further, namely that the very abnormality of the camp — a non-place outside the *polis* of men — actually creates a space for hyper-politicized subjectivities. This is the paradoxical nature of the camp, in that it is simultaneously depoliticized and hyper-politicized. It is through its very non-political nature, its attempts to become a non-place outside of history, that a vacuum is created that gives room for 'pure politics' to a much greater degree than 'normal cities'. In the camp, what used to be taken for granted is no longer valid, thus creating a space to make one's own history.

As much as they want to empower refugees, the international agencies cannot accept the political nature of the refugees. Particularly in the case of the Rwandan Hutu in 1994, the agencies could not cope with the fact that the refugees came with a bundle of history, politics and violence. These camps were, after all, occupied by the Hutu who had committed the genocide and who had retreated across the borders to Tanzania and Zaire — not as refugees fleeing state persecution but as an army that had been (temporarily) defeated on the battlefield. The camps were organized along the administrative lines of the old state, and controlled by the same *bourgmestres*, *préféts* and other civil servants who planned the genocide (Eriksson, 1996; Prunier, 1995). The solution to this dilemma was for UNHCR to maintain that the vast majority of refugees were innocent victims held in the grip of a few manipulating *génocidaires*. In this manner, the UNHCR and other agencies could continue to treat the refugees as victims without agency and without political subjectivities, as people in need of empowerment in order to return to normality in the future.

REPATRIATION AS RETURN TO NORMALITY

While transitional justice mechanisms may be perceived as steps towards new beginnings, they are often implicit attempts to 'return' to
normality — assuming that normality is defined by peace and social harmony
and that violence is the exception (Duffield, 1996). Thus, truth commissions
are concerned with removing the legacy of exceptional violence in order that
society may return to an assumed 'normal' state of peace, just as tribunals are
concerned with punishing the culprits in order to 're-establish' an assumed
social harmony. Similarly, repatriation is an exercise in moving from the
exceptional to the normal.

In the hegemonic discourse on refugees as helpless-victims-without-
political-subjectivity, repatriation is equivalent to 'normalization', where the
anomalous refugees return to their original place in the order of things. Such
a simplified understanding of repatriation has long been criticized by refugee
scholars.[4] It ignores the fact that both refugee and 'home' have changed in
the meantime and that moving to what once was home is in fact moving
to somewhere completely new. 'In this case, paradoxically, "repatriation"
might be considered the *beginning* of a refugee cycle' (Black and Koser,
1999: 9).

Although relief agencies might perceive of repatriation as a return to
normality, I would argue that they do not assume that the process is unprob-
lematic. They make significant resources available in the effort to prepare the
refugees for return from bare life to full citizenship. In the case of Rwanda,
there were two discourses on refugee repatriation that came into play. First,
there was the international community that was concerned with the 'rights'
of the refugees (land rights, right to fair trial, etc.). These rights were decon-
textualized in the sense that they were not concerned with the radical shifts in
Rwandan identity politics from pre- to post-1994. In human rights discourse,
rights hinge on a universal humanity beyond a political context, rendering
it unable to accommodate political contexts (see Anders and Zenker, 2014).
So when UNHCR prepared Hutu refugees to become democratic citizens in
a new post-conflict state, it was creating an apolitical citizenry that merely
could claim universal 'rights'.

The Rwandan state, on the other hand, was concerned with creating a
radically new Rwandan nation and therefore also with erasing any traces of
the old Rwanda. There was, however, a twist to this since the new Rwanda
was supposedly also a return to an original, authentic Rwanda untouched by
colonialism which introduced the kind of 'divisionist' thinking that led to the
genocide. The state was therefore explicit about not wanting the refugees to
return 'home' as it was before the genocide and exile. Instead, the returnees
should be created anew; hence, the camps for ex-combatants. As in the

---

4. See Black and Koser (1999), Jansen and Löfving (2009). For Rwanda, see Newbury (2005).

case of the international community, the Rwandan state wanted to imprint a new beginning on the returning refugees. However, in contradistinction to the international community, it did not perceive the refugees as bare humanity — as blank slate that is ready to be written on — but as Hutu who fled the country after the genocide against the Tutsi.[5] According to the Rwandan state, these Hutu refugees had been subject to intimidation and indoctrination by the ringleaders of the genocide, both before and after 1994 when they set up base in camps in Zaire and Tanzania, and thus needed 'de-doctrinating' before they could become citizens of the new Rwanda. Upon return, most Hutu simply returned to the villages they came from, because there were too many to realistically send through a re-education programme. Ex-combatants, however, were put through a three-month re-education camp in order to create new citizens for the new Rwanda. But first, the Rwandan state needed to persuade the refugees to return to the new, non-ethnic Rwanda.

CAPTURING THE STATE AND THE PEOPLE

While the new RPF-dominated government attempted to create national unity and reconciliation by abandoning ideas of ethnicity and race, the Hutu refugees across the borders were preparing for the day that they could return and reclaim the Rwandan state by force. Particularly in Mobutu's Zaire, arms were smuggled into camps in large quantities, and the camps became training grounds for militias and ex-soldiers. The camps thus became a security issue for the new Rwandan state as Hutu militia made raids into the northwestern parts of the country, killing civilian Tutsi.

The assumption, held by the Rwandan state and by the international community alike, was that the majority of refugees were innocent civilians who simply wanted to return to their fields but who were being held hostage by an elite of *génocidaires* who needed them as a human shield and as cannon fodder. For a long while the relief agencies and the Rwandan authorities therefore ran information campaigns in order to convince the refugees that the country was indeed safe to return to. Disappointed with the results and impatient in particular with Mobutu's lack of political will to put a stop to the armed elements in the camp, the Rwandan government decided to force the refugees home. This led the Rwandan government in late 1996 to attack the camps in Zaire, with the intention to force the refugees to repatriate. The rationale behind the attacks was essentially the same as the information campaigns run by the UNHCR, namely that the civilian refugees were being held hostage by a handful of *génocidaires*. Therefore, it was argued, by

---

5. This is now the official term for the genocide, although it is well known that many moderate Hutu were among the first to be deliberately targeted.

attacking the camp leadership, the population would be liberated from its grip and gladly return to Rwanda. Space does not permit a detailed account of the events that took place in Zaire in December 1996 and 1997, as the conflict escalated and became interwoven with local and national conflicts in Zaire, leading to the downfall of Mobutu and the creation of the Democratic Republic of Congo. Suffice it to say that by early 1997 virtually all Rwandan refugees staying in camps in Tanzania had returned while the majority from Congo had done the same.[6]

According to Dorsey, the repatriation of the Hutu from the camps in Tanzania and Zaire was the final stage of Rwandan 'normalization' (Dorsey, 2000: 321), and it followed a well-established pattern of public awareness campaigns followed by military force. In order to understand this pattern, and the kind of state that is being established in Rwanda, it is helpful to briefly explore the kind of regime that took power after 1994 and, in particular, how it took power. RPF was created in 1987 in Uganda by Tutsi refugees who had fled the pogroms against the Tutsi following the Hutu revolution in 1959. Many RPF cadres had fought alongside Museveni in his liberation war and had initially been rewarded with high posts in Museveni's government and military (Mamdani, 1996, 2000; Ottunu, 1999; Reed, 1996). The movement, which was inspired by Maoism, was characterized by a harsh discipline, hard work and an ethic of not trusting anyone, not even in the movement. There was a strong sense of purpose and mission, and the fact that the RPF managed to stop the genocide in July 1994 only added to this sense of mission. In the words of one old man, who had worked as a planner in the Tanzanian state for twenty-seven years: 'I had expected to return slowly when things had settled, but the genocide changed the premise. I had to come back straight away — although it was costing me. Oh those days! There was nothing; no planning, no infrastructure! We worked all day every day and received nothing' (interview with Mzee Justice, November 2011). In other words, the state that was taking shape after the genocide had the moral upper hand because it had stopped the genocide while the international community did nothing; it had achieved this through a strategic military leadership and a strong ethic of sacrifice and discipline. Furthermore, winning the war gave the leadership a strong sense of having been given a responsibility which it had the duty to accept.

The strategy for this movement was twofold and has remained so since. On the one hand, it believed that the ordinary population — whether Hutu or Tutsi — lacked education which made them susceptible to manipulation and oppression, whether by colonialism in the past or greedy politicians in the present. It was therefore concerned with liberating the population

---

6. When Rwanda attacked the camps in Zaire, the Tanzanian government gave the refugees one month's notice to leave the country, tacitly supported by the international community who could no longer see the reason to feed a population that was a security threat for the fledgling new Rwandan state. See Whitaker (2002).

through education and enlightenment. On the other hand, it was also poised to strike down, swiftly and severely, anything and anyone that could obstruct its mission. This double strategy could be observed in the campaigns that were launched to remove 'genocidal mentalities'.

The mission statement of the NURC emphasizes, amongst other things, the importance of: '*Educating and mobilizing* the population on matters relating to national unity and reconciliation; *Denouncing and fighting* against acts, writings and utterances which are intended to promote any kind of discrimination, intolerance or xenophobia' (www.nurc.gov.rw, emphasis added). This illustrates the twofold approach of RPF: on the one hand disseminating information about unity and reconciliation, while on the other hand monitoring and 'combating' ideologies and activities that go against unity (Beswick, 2010; Waldorf, 2011). In the concluding chapter of a report by the NURC on 'The Causes of Violence after the 1994 Genocide', it comments on what it refers to as 'wickedness' as a cause of violence, whether it is violence against genocide survivors, or domestic or sexual violence. According to the report, this kind of wickedness is caused by ignorance, and continues: 'It has become a mentality, a sub culture peculiar to some of Rwandans. It cannot be uprooted at once, as by a stroke of magic wand. It requires for the long-term efforts that must be led to (*sic*) several fights by very wide-ranging actors' (NURC, 2008: 119–20).

This mentality or subculture, characterized by 'wickedness', is what I term 'bad life'. Some elements of the Rwandan population are perceived as not simply outside the polis or the commonwealth of citizens; they are infected by wickedness, and the objective of NURC then is to 'uproot' this wickedness from their minds bit by bit. The means to achieve this objective is primarily through re-educating the masses and combating the divisive ideologies of the old regimes. In concrete terms, NURC has several so-called 'reconciliation tools' at its disposal to achieve these goals; prominent among them are the education camps *itorero* and *ingando*. At the same time, the government has taken several steps to monitor and punish what has officially been termed divisionism, negationism and most lately 'genocide ideology' (Waldorf, 2011). The 2003 Law Punishing Genocide has defined divisionism and inciting ethnic hatred so broadly that it can cover almost any criticism of the present regime's version of the truth and has indeed been used in a number of cases to silence critics (Waldorf, 2011; Zorbas, 2004). The Commission Nationale pour la Lutte contre la Génocide (CNLG) was established in 2008 with the objective of monitoring and combating genocide mentalities wherever they may be hidden in society (interview, Director of CNLG, January 2009). The *ingando* camps are key government instruments for educating the population and creating new citizens of the new Rwanda who are unblemished by the stains of the old genocidal regime. However, the RPF also relies on vigilance and the elimination of enemies in much more direct ways through the CNLG and the 2003 Genocide law. Theoretically, this is interesting because it reveals how bio-power and sovereignty are not mutually exclusive. On the contrary, bio-power relies on a security discourse that sets the limits of where bio-power applies and where sovereign power begins.

By July 1994, the RPF had won the territory through military force. The next step was not only to conquer the territory but also win the minds — and preferably the hearts — of the population that the RPF had 'liberated'. This consisted in teaching the peasants the true nature of Rwandan history and society. However, as long as the refugee camps in Tanzania and Zaire continued to exist, the mission of liberating the Rwandan people from their genocidal ideologies and colonial mentalities could not be completed. Using force to empty the camps and bring the Hutu refugees back 'home' was a necessary step in this mission. After liberating these Hutu from their leaders in the camps, the next step was to liberate them from their mentalities. This is where *ingando* and *itorero* enter the picture.

INGANDO AND ITORERO: TWO WAYS TO INCLUSION

'"Ingando" is taken from the Rwandese verb "Kugandika" that refers to halt-ing normal activities to reflect on, and find solutions to national challenges. In ancient Rwanda, Ingandos were first developed by the military. Whenever Rwanda faced disasters (wars, natural calamities, etc.), the Mwami (King) mobilized and prepared the population through Ingandos' (homepage of NURC website). *Ingandos* are called a number of different things: solidarity camps, education camps, civic education camps, reorientation camps, etc. The government claims that it is inspired by a traditional institution, although the precise meaning of the term *ingando* is under debate, as is the connec-tion between the modern *ingandos* and their presumed traditional roots (see Mgbako, 2005: 208; Purdeková, 2008: 20).

The first official *ingandos* were established in 1996 under the Ministry of Youth, Culture and Sports. They were intended for the Tutsi who had returned from Burundi, Zaire, Tanzania, Uganda and Europe after 1994 and were meant to instil a sense of nationalism in these returnees who were enthusiastic about rebuilding their homeland but who mostly had never been to Rwanda before. They were particularly meant to stave off potential divisions between the Anglophone Tutsi returning from Uganda who made up the top echelons of the new regime and the Francophone Tutsi returning from Burundi. While the former perceived of themselves as Rwandans and had been interpellated as such while in exile in Uganda, the latter had lived in a country that was deeply split along ethnic lines and had been treated as distinctly Tutsi while in Burundi. The *ingandos* were meant to impart a common identity in accordance with RPF ideology. It is believed that *ingandos* were inspired by RPF cadre schools that had been established in 1990–93 as a means of grassroots mobilization of the population in exile in Uganda and Tanzania, and in the conquered territories of northeastern Rwanda, and also by similar camps in Uganda (Mgbako, 2005: 208).

Pasteur Bizimungu, then President of the Republic, officially launched the programme for 'national political awareness' of the returning Hutu refugees in May 1997. He talked about a youth camp: 'This camp, like many others which will take place countrywide, are (*sic*) aimed at integrating the youth that have just returned from exile into the current social and political life' (Radio Rwanda, 24 May 1997, quoted in Purdeková, 2008: 21). Later, *ingando* camps were used for a number of different groups and it was the aim of NURC that all Rwandans should attend an *ingando* at some point in their lives. There are two types of *ingandos*. 'The government makes an important distinction between *ingando* solidarity camps and i*ngando* re-education camps. Solidarity camps are for politicians, civil society and church leaders, *gacaca* judges and incoming university students, whereas re-education camps are for ex-combatants, ex-soldiers, confessed *génocidaires*, released prisoners, prostitutes, and street children' (Thomson, 2011: 333–34). The solidarity camps were later renamed *itorero*.

On the one hand, there are those who have a special responsibility to stand out as role models in society due to their privileged positions in society. This means that university students, diaspora youth, schoolteachers and various civil servants are expected to attend *itorero*, and they are expected to spread the word afterwards. As this news clipping from the government-friendly *New Times* shows:

> The Executive Secretary of National Unity and Reconciliation Commission Dr Jean Baptist Habyarimana, has challenged students completing Ingando to transfer the knowledge acquired during their course to other youths in the country. . . . 'We have come from a situation marked by a very difficult past. Teachers and students need to first understand the source of this sad past in order to build a meaningful vision for the future generations', he said. (Mukombosi, 2010)

Those who have completed *itorero* are called *intore*, which is the name of the young men who served at the royal palace and the palaces of big chiefs in pre-colonial times where they learned the skills of debate as well as sports and dance. Such *intore* are thus promoted as an elite group of society. In 2011, I interviewed a representative of NURC's '*Itorero* Task Force'. He handed me a power point presentation that they had made in relation to launching *itorero*. It claims that in the past:

- Rwandans believed that Intore (people) who passed through *Itorero* were different from those that didn't pass through *Itorero* in terms of portraying ethical values, being eloquent, examplary (*sic*) in leadership, etc.
- In brief, Intore were advanced in their consciousness in the society.

In January 2012, I attended an event where a group of *intore*, mostly Rwandans studying abroad, visited a settlement in a poor region to support the local community build houses. They were shuttled from the capital to the settlement in buses, funded by the Ministry of Education, while important people from government offices arrived later in cars. They rolled up their sleeves and sang and shouted *intore* slogans while we passed the mud for the bricks from hand to hand. After a few hours the work stopped — leaving it to the villagers to clean up and finish the bricks — and everyone was ordered to sit and listen to speeches and watch an educational play on the cause of the genocide.[7] Every speaker started with shouting '*intore!*' and raising his arm, whereupon the youth from Kigali — most wearing *itorero* T-shirts and some wearing combat trousers — yelled 'Aho!' and various slogans back at him. Everyone seemed to be ecstatic and at one point they broke out in dance. The local villagers looked on in quiet disbelief, a chosen strategy of the poor in Rwanda (cf. Thomson, 2009).

This meeting illustrates the way in which the state is at once attempting to create national unity while also creating classes of citizenship. The *intore* are meant to be role models and they are meant to help the poor and the powerless. However, in doing so they are also constructing themselves as powerful and invaluable. The *intore* incarnate the new Rwanda — not as simple citizens but as a vanguard. They come from the city in buses and assist the peasants in building their houses and then teach them history and the cause of the genocide. The villagers, on the other hand, are cast as potentially misguided victims of genocide ideologies in need of assistance. The play, which explains the true nature of ethnicity and the root causes of the genocide, has the purpose of removing any wrong interpretations of ethnicity and colonialism from the minds of the villagers. This attitude towards the rural poor was confirmed in most conversations I had with representatives of NGOs, state institutions and diaspora organizations during six months' fieldwork in Kigali and the Eastern Province in 2011–12. Higher-level civil servants in particular expressed a desire to assist and save the poor and uneducated segments of the population.

While the majority of villagers are assumed to be ignorant and in need of assistance and enlightenment, other groups are positioned as a direct threat to the new Rwanda and in need of special education programmes. These are genocide suspects released from prison, ex-combatants returning from DRC and Tanzania and street children. They are, in Hindess's (2001) words, the kind of life that is perceived not yet fit for liberal freedom and

---

7. After almost eighteen years, the government (helped along by willing national and international NGOs and church groups) still uses every possible occasion to teach 'the people' that Rwandans lived in harmony before the Belgians arrived and that it was the colonialists — in this particular play in the shape of a Catholic Father — who created the 'divisionism' that led to the genocide.

self-governance. Certain groups lack the required capacities for autonomous conduct. These capacities, Hindess argues, can be developed either 'through compulsion, through the imposition of more or less extended periods of discipline [or] by establishing a benign and supportive social environment' (ibid.: 101). Hindess mentions a number of different categories of people who are more or less beyond repair, and I would argue that individuals and groups may slip from one category to another. Thus an ignorant peasant, who is a victim of indoctrination, may well become 'bad life' harbouring 'genocidal ideologies', if not taken care of in time. Therefore, all Hutu are potentially 'bad life'.

The camps for street children on Iwawa Island caught the eye of international media in April 2010, when the *New York Times* published an article titled, 'Rwanda Pursues Dissenters and the Homeless'. The author writes:

> Nearly 900 beggars, homeless people and suspected petty thieves, including dozens of children, have recently been rounded up from the nation's neatly swept streets and sent — without trial or a court appearance — to this little-known outpost. They will spend up to three years here being 'rehabilitated', learning skills like bricklaying, hairdressing and motorcycle maintenance. ... But on the mainland, people describe it as an Alcatraz. (*New York Times*, 2010)

In May 2011 the first group 'graduated' from Iwawa Island under much pomp and circumstance, including the attendance of the Prime Minister and diplomats. The Rwandan government made use of this occasion to counter international criticism. The *New Times* reported from the event: '(Prime Minister) Makuza observed that the centre achieved its initial objective which "was to transform street children into responsible and skilled" citizens' (Kagire, 2011). And in an editorial, 'Iwawa Graduation Puts Falsehood Peddlers to Shame', the *New Times* (2011) explained: 'The future, indeed, looks bright for these youths who, only yesterday, as street children, were a threat to security particularly in the urban areas where they roamed aimlessly'. In other words, the camp is about creating new citizens out of the delinquents — for their own sake and for the sake of safety and security of society at large.

The *ingando* camps for ex-combatants from Zaire last for two and a half months. They include an aid package at the end of the training and 47 per cent of their cost is financed by the World Bank. The activities include sports, singing, daily chores and lectures. The programme consists mostly of lectures on unity and reconciliation, history, democracy, development and HIV/AIDS. In other words, it is a mixture of teaching about Rwanda's pre-colonial past in order to make students proud of their heritage, teaching about the historical reasons for the genocide in order to prevent it from happening again, and teaching about present development goals in order that they can 'toe the government line', as I often heard it phrased by supporters of the *ingandos*.

Whereas the *itorero* for the elite and the first *ingandos* for returning Tutsi
had the objective to create a shared identity by being together twenty-four
hours a day and sharing the same food (Mgbako, 2005: 208), the later
camps for returning Hutu were designed to remove certain mentalities.
As Purdeková (2008: 19) argues, the '*Ingando* camps are microcosms of
the attempted linkage between repatriation and reconciliation through de-
ethnicization'. She holds that the government of Rwanda realized that full
repatriation would not be possible without some kind of reconciliation. At
the same time, it believed that in order to bring about reconciliation and create social cohesion, it was necessary to de-ethnicize the population. I would
argue that this is the crux of the matter: in order to repatriate, reconcile and
re-integrate the former combatants from Zaire, the present state is trying
to erase ethnicity by taking the Hutu out of the Hutu. De-ethnicization is
therefore not about removing ethnicity per se, but about removing the problematic ethnicity of the Hutu since it may lead to genocidal mentalities. In
other words, the state is not simply educating subjects to become citizens.
Neither is it converting 'bare life' into 'political life'. It is removing 'bad
life' in order to create 'good life'.

In November 2011, I had the opportunity to speak to a number of ex-
combatants who had been through Motobu camp, the camp for demobilized
combatants returning mostly from DRC. They responded to my questions
about the camp in a positive and superficial manner: 'we were taught about
unity', 'we were taught about history', etc. Mgbako's study of *ingandos* for
ex-combatants similarly found that participants were often optimistic about
their own future, seeing the *ingandos* as a means to a better future by starting
a new life. 'They're trying to upgrade us to the level of the local people. If you
come back from the bush and go straight to the people you don't know their
mentality. *Ingando* teaches you this' (Mgbako, 2005: 214). The participants
themselves viewed *ingando* as a transition, a means to becoming something
else or something new. They saw a need to become like other people — to
have the same mentality — in order to understand each other and cohabit.
Furthermore, there was a sense, not only of becoming different but also of
becoming 'someone'; moving from the bush to civilization.

It should be kept in mind that these participants were mainly in the *ingando*
camps because they were mandatory. They also perceived it as part of a deal
where the state promised them a future in harmony and, at a more tangible
level, a starting package if they followed the programme for two and a half
months. I also found that ex-combatants were pleased to be in possession
of a 'Demob' ID paper. It was official proof that they had been properly
demobilized and therefore no longer posed a threat to their neighbours who
otherwise would be suspicious of them. In other words, *ingando* was their
ticket back into society.

The statements of the participants were consistent with the discourse on
ingandos as transition centres that were meant to change the mentalities and
personalities of those who had been outside the new Rwandan nation one

way or another, and participants were aware that this was the intended purpose of the camps. However, participants navigated several layers of truth, as Ingelaere has demonstrated in relation to the *gacaca* courts (Ingelaere, 2009). After explaining the advantages of the demobilization process at Motobu camp, one man who had been active in the pre-genocide army, and later in DRC, changed his discourse[8] and explained how the RPF soldiers had scolded them and shouted at them that they were wrong. Another demobilized soldier who used to belong to one of the rebel movements based in DRC, at first praised the system and told me that the President was chosen by God and hence infallible. Later, under four eyes and in hushed voices he confided that 'we are being subjected to a slow genocide'. By this he meant that he had no possibilities of upward mobility and that his children would never get a good education however hard they studied. 'In twenty years we will be like dead'. The 'we' implicitly means the Hutu. He constantly talked of 'my people' versus 'them' — the government, the army and their entourage.

In these cases, it was clear that the rural Hutu population only bought into the official discourse on national unity at a superficial level. This also applied to those who had been through *ingando*. They believed that they were no longer part of the nation because 'they' lost the war and the 'others' won and that they simply had to accept their fate and play along with the rhetoric of unity and reconciliation in order to survive. Apart from this being a tragic fact, it is analytically interesting because it shows that the process of removing 'bad life' from the Hutu returning from exile has not resulted in the production of new citizens. The Hutu who returned from the camps do not feel included in the citizenry and their opinions are just as 'bad' as they were before. This is not, however, just a question of a failed programme, something that would call for more of the same. On the contrary, the *ingando* and the *itorero* programmes have been successful in creating two kinds of life in Rwanda. On the one hand, the *intore* have been moulded in the *itorero* to feel a sense of common identity and identification with the new Rwanda. They are made to feel that they can play an important role; in fact, that it is their duty to play a role, as the chairman of the Itorero Task Force emphasized. They are, in other words, full political citizens with rights and duties. On the other hand, the demobilized Hutu have been taught that their opinions are wrong. They are welcome to return to Rwanda as long as they leave their ethnicity behind them.

---

8. Due to a finely masked system of surveillance in the countryside, it was almost impossible for me to get anyone — in particular Hutu — to speak freely to me. My interviews had to be reported to the local security agent, and it was only through patience and thanks to some excellent manoeuvering by my assistant, that I was able on a few occasions to hear the other side of the story.

CONCLUSION

The horror of the genocide has called for a radical break with the past in Rwanda. Anything associated with the pre-genocide regime carries the stigma of the genocide and has been completely delegitimized. The Rwandan state has therefore taken a number of steps in order to deal with this past and to create a new beginning where the citizens are united and reconciled. The transitional justice mechanisms cover the span from retributive justice at local, national and international courts, over truth telling, to various information campaigns and programmes to uncover and eliminate 'genocidal mentalities'. In this chapter I have focused on a particular group — namely the Hutu who fled the country during and immediately after the genocide and who have subsequently repatriated. These Hutu had lived in the exceptional space of the refugee camps — neither in the past nor in the present — and needed to be reintegrated into the present post-genocide Rwanda.

I have argued that both the refugee camps, run by international humanitarian agencies, and the re-education camps, run by the new Rwandan state, were exceptional spaces that had the function of 'holding' these 'beings' that did not belong — either in the pre-genocide Rwandan state that no longer existed, or properly in the new Rwandan state in the making. Both spaces treated the Hutu as outside the normal order of things — as biological life. And both spaces were preparing this biological life for a future life; a life as citizens, as political subjects. There are, however, also important differences. The UNHCR and other agencies running the camps conceive of the refugees as pure victims. Due to their humanitarian approach, they must cast the refugees as pure victims, individuals without a history and beyond politics. They draw on universalist ideas of humanity and of citizenship. The task is thus to prepare this 'bare humanity' to become good, empowered citizens upon their return. The Rwandan state, on the other hand, conceives of the same population in overtly political and historical terms. For the new Rwandan state these refugees represent the *ancient regime*, which is projected as the antithesis of the 'New Rwanda'. Therefore the re-education camps are far more political and historical than the refugee camps where refugees are assumed to be apolitical 'bare life'. The re-education camps have been put in place to remove the 'bad life' of the Hutu refugees.

The consequence of this shift in meaning from 'bare life' to 'bad life' is that the returning Hutu are not integrated into the nation in the same way that for instance the *intore* are. While the *intore* are presumed to be a prize for the new state and therefore have a duty to contribute, the returning Hutu are perceived as a necessary evil. They are integrated because the alternative for them would be to remain within a 'genocidal mind frame', which is constantly invoked by the Rwandan media and policy as the greatest security threat to the new Rwanda. The returning Hutu should thus be grateful to the new state that they are allowed to be re-educated. By conceiving of them as 'bad life' that needs cleansing before being reintegrated, the state is also producing them as second-rate citizens who will not contribute but who are integrated in order to eradicate the 'bad life' that they used to represent.

In other words, the universalistic norms of UNHCR posit the issue of a new beginning as ahistorical, non-violent and non-political, whereas the Rwandan state treats the issue of creating a new beginning and a new just society concretely and historically. It thus does not shy away from politics and violence in its quest to create a new Rwanda that is radically different to the Rwanda that created the genocide.

REFERENCES

Agamben, G. (1998) *Homo Sacer: Sovereign Power and Bare Life*. Stanford, CA: Stanford University Press.
Agamben, G. (2000) *Means without End: Notes on Politics (Theory out of Bounds)*. Minneapolis, MI: University of Minnesota Press.
Agier, M. (2002) 'Between War and City: Towards an Urban Anthropology of Refugee Camps', *Ethnography* 3(3): 317–41.
Agier, M. (2011) *Managing the Undesirables: Refugee Camps and Humanitarian Government*. Cambridge: Polity.
Anders, G. and O. Zenker (2014) 'Transition and Justice: An Introduction', *Development and Change* 45(3): 395–414.
Beswick, D. (2010) 'Managing Dissent in a Post-genocide Environment: The Challenge of Political Space in Rwanda', *Development and Change* 41(2): 225–51.
Black R. and K. Koser (1999) *The End of the Refugee Cycle? Refugee Repatriation and Reconstruction*. New York: Berghahn Books.
Brouneus, K. (2008) 'Truth-telling as Talking Cure? Insecurity and Retraumatization in the Rwandan Gacaca Courts', *Security Dialogue* 39(1): 55–76.
Buckley-Zistel, S. (2006a) 'Dividing and Uniting: The Use of Citizenship Discourses in Conflict and Reconciliation in Rwanda', *Global Society* 20(1): 101–13.
Buckley-Zistel, S. (2006b) 'Remembering to Forget: Chosen Amnesia as a Strategy for Local Coexistence in Post-genocide Rwanda', *Africa* 76(2): 131–50.
Dean, M. (1999) *Governmentality. Power and Rule in Modern Society*. London: Sage Publications.
Dorsey, M. (2000) 'Violence and Power-building in Post-genocide Rwanda', in R. Doom and J. Gorus (eds) *Politics of Identity and Economics of Conflict in the Great Lakes Region*, pp. 311–48. Brussels: VUB University Press.
Douglas, M. (1966) *Purity and Danger: An Analysis of Concepts of Pollution and Taboo*. London: Routledge and Kegan Paul.
Duffield, M. (1996) 'The Symphony of the Damned: Racial Discourse, Complex Political Emergencies and Humanitarian Aid', *Disasters* 20(3): 173–93.
Eriksson, J. (ed.) (1996) 'The International Response to Conflict and Genocide: Lessons from the Rwanda Experience. Synthesis Report'. Copenhagen: Steering Committee of the Joint Evaluation of Emergency Assistance to Rwanda.
Feldman, I. and M. Ticktin (eds) (2010) *In the Name of Humanity: The Government of Threat and Care*. Durham, NC: Duke University Press.
Hindess, B. (2001) 'The Liberal Government of Unfreedom', *Alternatives* 26(2): 93–111.
Ibreck, R. (2010) 'The Politics of Mourning: Survivor Contributions to Memorials in Post-genocide Rwanda', *Memory Studies* 3(4): 330–43.

Ingelaere, B. (2009) 'Does the Truth Pass across the Fire without Burning? Locating the Short Circuit in Rwanda's Gacaca Courts', *Journal of Modern African Studies* 47(4): 507–28.

Jansen, B. (2011) 'The Accidental City: Violence, Economy and Humanitarianism in Kakuma Refugee Camp, Kenya'. PhD thesis, Wageningen University, The Netherlands.

Jansen S. and S. Löfving (eds) (2009) *Struggles for Home: Violence, Hope and the Movement of People*. New York: Berghahn Books.

Kagire, E. (2011) 'Excitement as 752 ex-street Kids Graduate from Iwawa Centre', *New Times* 18 May.

Kanyangara, P., B. Rime, P. Philippot and V. Yzerbyt (2007) 'Collective Rituals, Emotional Climate and Intergroup Perception: Participation in "Gacaca" Tribunals and Assimilation of the Rwandan Genocide', *Journal of Social Issues* 63(2): 387–403.

Malkki, L. (1995) 'Refugees and Exile: From "Refugee Studies" to the National Order of Things', *Annual Review of Anthropology* 24: 495–523.

Mamdani, M. (1996) 'From Conquest to Consent as the Basis of State Formation: Reflections on Rwanda', *New Left Review* 216: 3–37.

Mamdani, M. (2000) 'The Political Diaspora in Uganda and Background to the RPF', in D. Goyvaerts (ed.) *Conflict and Ethnicity in Central Africa*. Tokyo: Institute for the Study of Languages and Cultures of Asia and Africa.

Mgbako, C. (2005) 'Ingando Solidarity Camps: Reconciliation and Political Indoctrination in Post-Genocide Rwanda', *Harvard Human Rights Journal* 18: 201–24.

Mukombosi, B. (2010) 'Varsity Students Urged to Transfer Values Attained from *Ingando*', *New Times* 4 March.

Newbury, D. (2005) 'Returning Refugees: Four Historical Patterns of "Coming Home" to Rwanda', *Comparative Studies in Society and History* 47(2): 252–85.

New Times (2011) 'Iwawa Graduation puts Falsehood Peddlers to Shame', 20 May.

New York Times (2010) 'Rwanda Pursues Dissenters and Homeless', 20 April.

NURC (2008) 'The Causes of Violence after the 1994 Genocide'. Kigali: Republic of Rwanda.

Nyers, P. (1998) 'Refugees, Humanitarian Emergencies, and the Politicization of Life', *Refuge* 17(6): 16–22.

Nyers, P. (2006) *Rethinking Refugees: Beyond States of Emergency*. New York: Routledge.

Oomen, B. (2005) 'Donor-driven Justice and its Discontents: The Case of Rwanda', *Development and Change* 36(5): 887–910.

Otunnu, O. (1999) 'An Historical Analysis of the Invasion by the Rwandan Patriotic Army (RPA)', in H. Adelman and A. Suhrke (eds) *The Path of a Genocide: The Rwanda Crisis from Uganda to Zaire*, pp. 31–51. New Brunswick, NJ and London: Transaction Publishers.

Peskin, V. (2011) 'Victor's Justice Revisited: Rwandan Patriotic Front Crimes and the Prosecutorial Endgame', in S. Straus and L. Waldorf (eds) *Remaking Rwanda: State Building and Human Rights after Mass Violence*, pp. 173–84. Madison, WI: University of Wisconsin Press.

Prunier, G. (1995) *The Rwanda Crisis, 1959–1994: History of a Genocide*. London: Hurst & Company.

Purdeková, A. (2008) 'Repatriation and Reconciliation in Divided Societies: The Case of Rwanda's "Ingando"'. RCS Working Paper. Oxford: University of Oxford Refugee Studies Programme.

Reed, C. (1996) 'Exile, Reform and the Rise of the Rwandan Patriotic Front', *Journal of Modern African Studies* 34: 479–501.

Soguk, N. (1999) *States and Strangers: Refugees and Displacements of Statecraft*. Minneapolis, MI: University of Minnesota Press.

Thomson, S. (2009) 'Resisting Reconciliation: State Power and Everyday Life in Post-Genocide Rwanda'. PhD Thesis, Dalhousie University, Halifax, Nova Scotia.

Thomson, S. (2011) 'Re-education and Reconciliation: Participant Observations on *Ingando*', in S. Straus and L. Waldorf (eds) *Remaking Rwanda: State Building and Human Rights after Mass Violence*, pp. 331–43. Wisconsin, WI: University of Wisconsin Press.

Tiemessen, A.E. (2004) 'After Arusha: Gacaca Justice in Post-Genocide Rwanda', *African Studies Quarterly* 8(1): 57–76.

Turner, S. (2005) 'Suspended Spaces: Contesting Sovereignties in a Refugee Camp', in T.B. Hansen and F. Stepputat (eds) *Sovereign Bodies: Citizens, Migrants, and States in the Postcolonial World*, pp. 312–32. Princeton, NJ: Princeton University Press.

Turner, S. (2010) *Politics of Innocence: Hutu Identity, Conflict and Camp Life*. New York: Berghahn Books.

Waldorf, L. (2011) 'Instrumentalizing the Genocide: The RPF's Campaigning against "Genocide Ideology"', in S. Straus and L. Waldorf (eds) *Remaking Rwanda: State Building and Human Rights after Mass Violence*, pp. 48–67. Madison, WI: University of Wisconsin Press.

Webster, D. (2011) 'The Uneasy Relationship between the ICTR and *Gacaca*', in S. Straus and L. Waldorf (eds) *Remaking Rwanda: State Building and Human Rights after Mass Violence*, pp. 184–94. Madison, WI: University of Wisconsin Press.

Whitaker, B. (2002) 'Changing Priorities in Refugee Protection: The Rwandan Repatriation from Tanzania'. New Issues in Refugee Research Working Paper No. 53. Geneva: UNHCR.

Wilson, R.A. (2010) 'When Humanity Sits in Judgement: Crimes against Humanity and the Conundrum of Race and Ethnicity at the International Criminal Tribunal for Rwanda', in I. Feldman and M. Ticktin (eds) *In the Name of Humanity: The Government of Threat and Care*, pp. 27–58. Durham, NC: Duke University Press.

Zorbas, E. (2004) 'Reconciliation in Post-Genocide Rwanda', *African Journal of Legal Studies* 1(1): 29–52.

3

Performing Repatriation? The Role of Refugee Aid in Shaping New Beginnings in Mauritania

Marion Fresia

INTRODUCTION

In 2005, the Mauritanian President Ould Sid' Ahmed Taya, who had been in power since 1984, was overthrown by a military coup, ushering in a new era of what was presented as a 'democratic' transition. This political transition was characterized by the official recognition, for the first time in twenty years, of the massive human rights violations perpetrated against 'Black' Mauritanians in 1989–1991, including the expulsion of 120,000 to Senegal and Mali and the execution of more than 500 others. This recognition was followed, in 2008, by the official repatriation of Mauritanian refugees from Senegal under the supervision of the United Nations High Commissioner for Refugees (UNHCR). This major event was presented by many stakeholders as symbolizing the end of a period of dictatorship in Mauritania and the beginning of a new era. It was constructed as both an act of transitional justice in its own right, undoing the human rights violation of displacement, and as a prerequisite for further transitional justice measures aiming at the reconciliation of the 'Moorish' and the 'Black' components of the Mauritanian population.

Mauritania is not unique in this regard. Since the 1990s, the repatriation of displaced populations has been increasingly framed by the UN, Western donor institutions and African states as an essential component of new beginnings in post-conflict countries (Allen and Morsink, 1994). It is intended to symbolize the end of a 'refugee cycle' (Black and Koser, 1999), the return of peace, the end of discrimination and persecution, and the re-establishment of a certain 'national order of things' (Malkki, 1995) whereby all citizens of a country can live in and be protected by a nation state. The return of refugees, which is defined by international refugee law as one of the three 'durable solutions' to the refugee plight (UNHCR, 1951: Art 1.C), has thus been highlighted as a return to normalcy and ordinary life; but it has also increasingly been framed as a first step towards restoring a 'just order of things' which may, paradoxically, call for new exceptional measures such as the establishment of specific transitional justice mechanisms. In Mauritania,

The author would like to thank Olaf Zenker and Gerhard Anders, and the journal's anonymous referees, for their comments on earlier versions of this paper.

as refugees returned, intense debates over restitution of land and property and the resolution of past human rights violations have indeed appeared on the public scene for the first time since the 1989 crisis, along with the notion of 'transitional justice'. Debates over past human rights violations were therefore closely related to and provoked by the return of refugees.

'Transitional justice' refers to the institutionalized attempt to deal with past human rights violations in order to facilitate a transition towards greater justice in the future. It includes 'both judicial and non-judicial mechanisms, with differing levels of international involvement (or none at all) and individual prosecutions, reparations, truth-seeking, institutional reform, vetting and dismissals or a combination thereof'(UN, 2004: 4). Such mechanisms have gained importance everywhere in the world, but in Africa they are often part of larger military–humanitarian interventions which include the repatriation of refugees and peace-building interventions. As shown in the Introduction to this volume (see also Anders and Zenker, 2014), academic work on transitional justice has tended to focus on the most obvious and institutionalized sites in which ideas about justice are discussed or contested, such as truth commissions or international tribunals, or neo-traditional institutions such as the *gacaca* in Rwanda. Yet, there are many other sites where ideas about justice and transition circulate or are negotiated, including reparations programmes (which may include land restitutions, financial compensation, etc.), security system reform, or memorialization efforts.[1] Ideas about a 'just order' and 'new beginnings' may also be intensively discussed and framed outside transitional countries, for instance within refugee camps, through refugee assistance programmes or within diaspora associations.

Transitional justice institutions such as truth commissions or criminal prosecutions may therefore be only one part of a much broader context in which new beginnings are framed, negotiated or contested. Mauritania is a clear example of this: since the transition of 2005, various transitional justice initiatives have been suggested or demanded as part of an effort to deal with past human rights violations. Even though — as of 2013 — most of them have not been implemented, these initiatives were largely framed by transnational ideas about human rights violations, justice and transition, which had previously circulated in refugee camps outside the country.

Based on the Mauritanian case, this contribution explores the specific roles played by refugee camps, refugee aid and repatriation in shaping the terms of new beginnings in transitional countries and in building a dominant narrative about past human rights violations and ways to overcome them. It argues that taking account of the broader context in which ideas about justice and transition take shape, including developments outside transitional countries, may

1. The International Center for Transitional Justice defines transitional justice as including criminal prosecutions, truth commissions, reparations programmes, gender justice, security system reform and memorialization efforts; see http://ictj.org/sites/default/files/ICTJ-Global-Transitional-Justice-2009-English.pdf

contribute to a better understanding of when and how specific transitional justice logics based on claims for exceptional measures — as opposed to or in articulation with other, more ordinary, logics — are mobilized by social actors. It shows that discourses and ideas about justice and new beginnings in Mauritania have to be understood in the light of the political dynamics enhanced by humanitarian assistance and past experiences of refugee life in camps. Refugee camps are privileged spaces where narratives on past injustices, representations of normality and exceptionality, claims for compensation and the need for humanitarian aid are constructed through the lens of international humanitarian and refugee laws. They are places of intense politicization of memory and appropriation of the refugee label, which enhance the construction of new imagined communities based on a feeling of victimhood and abnormality, which in turn influences representations of justice, transition and normality.

The analysis which follows will examine how certain transnational discourses on human rights violations and transitional justice were introduced by humanitarian actors and appropriated and reworked by the Mauritanian refugee elite, until they became a hegemonic narrative drawing on the logic of the exception. It will also highlight how this dominant narrative over past injustices, and what should be a 'just order' in Mauritania, was at the same time contested or transcended by subaltern groups through the production of alternative accounts of past injustices and through mundane, daily practices which activated sometimes very different imaginings of the appropriate forms of 'justice' and 'transition' to be aspired to in the future.

To explore the linkages and continuities between refugee aid and new beginnings in Mauritania, I have revisited some ethnographic materials which I collected in Mauritanian refugee camps in Senegal between 2001 and 2005 for my doctoral research (see Fresia, 2009a), as well as more recent materials collected within returnee sites in Mauritania just after the repatriation of refugees in 2008. This chapter is organized in three parts: the first section looks back at the historical events that led to the expulsion of thousands of Mauritanians in 1989. The second section then explores the roles played by humanitarian interventions, refugee political leaders and human rights organizations in the social construction and circulation of a dominant narrative over past injustices and a 'just' order for Mauritania. The last substantive section will analyse the consequences of this dominant narrative for the negotiation of the terms of the 2005 political transition in Mauritania.

NAMING PAST INJUSTICES: THE *PASSIF HUMANITAIRE* OF MAURITANIA

Naming past injustices in Mauritania has been a very sensitive issue. The 1989–91 period remained taboo, given that the Ould Taya regime, in place since 1984, was directly involved in the violence perpetrated against its own citizens. Since the fall of the Ould Taya regime in 2005 and the subsequent transitional and electoral period, the 1989–91 clashes have started to be named, in the Mauritanian public and political debates, under the French notion of *passif humanitaire*,[2] which translates as 'humanitarian liability' in the accounting sense. This term, which was first mobilized by political opponents in exile and human rights organizations in the early 2000s,[3] had the advantage of implying that Mauritania still had a burden to alleviate before it could truly enter a new era of peace and democratization, while not explicitly designating past injustices as 'human rights violations', as the topic was still sensitive. Taking distance from the official terminology, I will mainly refer to this period as the 1989–91 acts of violence. Before exploring how refugees made sense of them in exile, I will provide a brief overview of what happened in Mauritania at that time.

In spring 1989, within the context of an interstate conflict with Senegal that led to the expulsion of hundreds of Senegalese living in Mauritania, the Mauritanian authorities of the Ould Taya regime also expelled 120,000 of its own citizens, belonging to Wolof, Bambara, Soninké and Haalpulaaren[4] ethnic groups. On the false pretext that they were Senegalese, they were sent to Senegal and Mali. Many of them were Haalpulaaren agro-pastoralists (FulBe) and (to a lesser extent) Haalpulaaren landlords (TorooBe) who occupied the only fertile lands of the southern part of Mauritania (Santoir, 1993). There was also a minority group consisting of government employees (civil servants and soldiers), mainly Haalpulaaren and some Wolof, who belonged to major landlord families of the middle Senegal River Valley. They were either leaders, or sympathetic to the political ideas, of a clandestine political party — the Forces de Libération Africaines de Mauritanie (FLAM) — which had repeatedly denounced the political, economic and cultural discrimination endured by an oppressed imagined community named the

---

2. On the Mauritanian main press information website (www.cridem.org), one can find 811 press articles using this notion between 2005 and 2010.
3. The notion first appeared in the Memorandum of the FLAM (Forces de Libération Africaine de Mauritanie) political party in 2000. It was then mobilized by the RADDHO, the main umbrella of human rights based NGOs in Senegal, and then by the International Federation of Human Rights in its paper on Mauritania (FIDH, 2006). Previously, most of the refugees I had interviewed during my fieldwork in Senegal had referred to the 1989–91 acts of violence as the 1989–91 'events', a depoliticized expression which was also used in the Senegalese media.
4. Haalpulaaren literally means 'people who speak pulaar' in Fulani. This term has different connotations depending on the context. For Haalpulaaren living in the middle Senegal River Valley (Fuuta Tooro), it includes all groups speaking Fulani in the region, including (but not only) FulBe populations, who were historically semi-nomadic groups who held power in the region until the end of the eighteenth century, and TorooBe, a muslim sedentary elite which took power from them and became important landlords in the region. FulBe groups from southeast Mauritania, who called themselves FulaaBe, differentiate themselves from the 'Haalpulaaren group', whom they call FutankooBe, literally 'people living in the Fuuta Tooro region' (Ciavolella, 2010: 14).

'Négro-Mauritanians' ('Black Mauritanians').[5] Herders, peasants and government employees were all dispossessed of their identity cards, herds and
ancestral lands; many women were raped; some people lost their lives in the
forced displacement; and 500 soldiers among them were arbitrarily arrested
and executed without trial in 1990–91. With the forced displacement of thousands of Mauritanians, the Ould Taya regime got rid of some of its major
political opponents belonging to the FLAM movement, while redistributing
the land of refugees to political clients and private investors belonging to the
president's own tribe or allied tribes.

Various interpretations have been suggested by Mauritanian political leaders, NGOs and the media to explain the root causes of the 1989–91 acts
of violence, but a racial understanding of the tensions between opposing
'Moorish' and 'Black' components of the Mauritanian population has often
dominated. Academic work (e.g. Leservoisier, 1999; Magistro, 1993) has
repeatedly stressed that races and ethnicities were socially constructed and
manipulated to respond to other issues at stake, such as the rivalry, rooted
in Mauritania's colonial heritage, between francophone and Arab-speaking
elites over control of the nation state and the definition of the national
identity; the competition for scarce fertile land and resources in a country
comprising 90 per cent desert, which was deeply affected by severe droughts
in the 1970s, and the forced sedentarization of thousands of Moorish and
FulBe nomads; and the land reform and large-scale irrigation projects in the
Senegal River Valley which exacerbated conflicts over land tenure and land
entitlements in the south of the country.

It is beyond the scope of this chapter to further discuss these interpretations; rather the rest of this contribution will analyse how the dominant narrative over past injustices involving racial categories has been co-constructed
by humanitarian organizations and the refugee elite in exile, and how this
narrative has influenced the terms of new beginnings in Mauritania.

MAKING SENSE OF PAST INJUSTICES IN REFUGEE CAMPS

In Senegal, the Mauritanian victims of the 1989–91 forced displacements
were recognized by the Senegalese government as refugees, and were established in small refugee camps and settlements of between 50 and 2,000
inhabitants along the 500 km Senegal–Mauritania border. They received significant assistance from the UNHCR between 1989 and 1998. In Mali, the

---

5. Although the notion of 'Black Mauritanians' has been socially constructed over the years
by a specific political group and was a contested term before the 1989–91 clashes, it is
now increasingly mobilized by a majority of stakeholders within the public political arena
in Mauritania, and used by ordinary people. In this chapter, I will refer to this term in both
its political and its emic dimensions, and take it as a social construction, which has real-life
consequences as it contributes to the racialization of social relations.

destination of mainly FulBe, the refugees received far less attention and humanitarian aid. There were a number of reasons for this, including their long-standing marginalization in Mauritanian political processes, the absence of well-connected political leaders among them, and the ambiguous position of the Malian authorities, who did not want their presence to create tensions with host communities (Ciavolella, 2010). My analysis focuses on the situation of refugees in Senegal where my research was conducted and where humanitarian aid and the categorization of Mauritanians as 'refugees' played a major role in the social construction of a dominant interpretation of past injustices.

Humanitarian Ideas over a 'Just Order': The Exceptionality of Refugee-hood

The refugee programme in Senegal has produced a specific way of understanding the situation of displaced Mauritanians by framing their situation according to international human rights law and international refugee law. According to the latter, displaced persons are perceived in terms of 'victimhood' and 'abnormality' because they have faced persecution, lost the protection of their nation state, and crossed a national border to seek protection (Coulter, 2001). The 1951 Convention relating to the Status of Refugees defines a refugee as a person who:

> owing to well-founded fear of being persecuted for reasons of race, religion, nationality, membership of a particular social group or political opinion, is outside the country of his nationality and is unable or, owing to such fear, is unwilling to avail himself of the protection of that country; or who ... is unable or, owing to such fear, is unwilling to return to it. (UNHCR, 1951: Art 1.A.2).

The Convention defines only three ways or 'durable solutions' to restore normality and find a solution to the refugee 'problem': repatriation (as the most preferable), local integration, or resettlement (ibid.: Art 1.C). All three solutions aim at reintegrating refugees in a nation state that can protect them. International refugee law therefore conveys a perception of a just order as being a 'national order of things' (Malkki, 1995), in the sense that everyone should belong to and be protected by a nation state. It is thus embedded in a sovereign and territorial vision of belonging, conveying an essentialist notion of home and identities (Black and Koser, 1999). But this just order should also be a 'human rights order of things' as nation states are also supposed to ensure the security and basic rights of their citizens.

This way of understanding the situation of forcibly displaced populations has greatly influenced the manner in which many stakeholders, including refugees themselves, have made sense of past injustices in Mauritania. In Senegal, one of the direct consequences of the implicit assumptions that refugees were in an abnormal situation was to legitimize the establishment of refugee camps that were responsible for them until their situation could be normalized (i.e. until they could go home). For humanitarian actors, camps are indeed always presented and perceived as 'exceptional' and temporary spaces, where refugees can be fed, taken care of and protected until they can be reintegrated into a 'national and human rights order of things'. The logic of the exception is therefore constantly evoked by humanitarian actors to justify their interventions. Yet many researchers have outlined how camps tend, in reality, to become long-term solutions for managing undesirable populations, thus legitimizing the permanence of the exceptional state (Agier, 2008; Turner, 2002). They have shown in particular that everyday practices of camp management and humanitarian assistance in all sectors (health, food aid, shelter, etc.) transform camps into places of governance and control over bodies, describing them through Agambian metaphors as spaces of biopolitics and power over 'bare life' (Agamben, 1995) where refugees have only the right to survive.

In Senegal, refugee camps progressively turned into small towns similar to those surrounding Senegalese villages. They became a long-term rather than a temporary solution for Mauritanian refugees, as for nearly twenty years neither the Mauritanian nor the Senegalese governments really wanted to clarify their legal position (Fresia, 2009b). Yet, far from being only places of control over bare life, they also became places of contestation, resistance and mobilization, where new forms of political expressions and claims, and new identities, took shape at the interface of international, national and local dynamics (Fresia, 2009a). As with other camps in Africa (Horst, 2007; Malkki, 1995; Turner, 2002), they have turned out to be extremely politicized arenas, in which making sense of past injustices and claiming greater justice have been a constant preoccupation for their inhabitants. One of the unintended effects and indirect consequences of humanitarian aid was to turn the camps into a physical symbol of past injustices, and spaces of production and circulation of a dominant narrative over those injustices, which drew on the same logic of the exception as that evoked by humanitarian actors.

The Power of Labelling: The Construction of a Shared Sense of Victimhood

In Senegal, the labelling of Mauritanians as 'refugees' according to international law and the subsequent intervention of the UNHCR contributed to new political and identity dynamics in the Senegal River Valley. Before 1989, all ethnic groups in the region had moved freely back and forth across the border: groups from both sides of the river were tied by close kin relationships, they had lands and herds on both sides of the river, and they were cultivating, transhuming and marrying across borders (Seck, 1991). Historically, this area formed a united political entity, that was divided by borders traced under French colonization. In 1989, Mauritanians expelled into northern Senegal therefore became 'refugees on their own ancestral territory' (Fresia, 2009a). Some Mauritanians were hosted by close kin in

Senegalese towns and villages; others decided to join UNHCR camps, either because they wanted to remain independent from their Senegalese kin (as a result of old antagonisms), or because they had no kin close to their place of arrival, had lost everything and needed immediate humanitarian assistance. A minority group composed of government employees sympathetic to the FLAM movement also decided to join the camps, mainly in order to remain visible and to assert that they were not Senegalese, as the Ould Taya government claimed, but genuine Mauritanians. For them, joining humanitarian spaces therefore had a political meaning: camps and their inhabitants were to become a physical symbol of past injustices and a proof of their nationality.

French-speakers with good rhetorical and organizational skills, these former government employees soon became the refugee representatives in Senegal and the principal intermediaries between refugees and external actors. Although not always occupying leadership positions in Mauritania before the explusions, the majority of them were part of the Haalpulaaren sedentary elite (TorooBe), and their extended families had owned some of the most fertile land across the Senegal River Valley. In all the camps, they created refugee associations which were officially presented as non-political but were actually extremely politicized. The majority of these associations were affiliated to the FLAM movement, and a minority to FRUIDEM, another political party which was also opposed to the Ould Taya regime but was part of the mainstream political opposition.[6] Through these associations, refugee leaders sought to sensitize other Mauritanians, mainly FulBe agro-pastoralists, about the need for the refugees to remain united and visible in camps in order to claim justice for what they had suffered: dispossession of their lands, goods and citizenship, and what they called 'massive deportations'. The refugee associations thus contributed to turning the label of 'refugee' from a source of stigma into a positive political identity endorsed with rights (to obtain justice and compensation) and duties (to remain visible in camps). They were also able to transcend the divisions among various refugee groups by putting them all into the same racial category: the 'oppressed Black Mauritanians'. Before 1989, this category was seldom used in Mauritania by anyone apart from FLAM activists; many FulBe in particular — who were for a large part clients of the Ould Taya regime and historically opposed to the sedentary elite — were more inclined to perceive themselves as Arabs than Black (Sall, 1999).

The refugee labelling process and the humanitarian intervention thus had important consequences in terms of politicizing camps and enhancing new categories of self-identification among Mauritanians based on race, victimhood and a desire to restore specific rights. Although they were refugees on

---

6. FRUIDEM was affiliated to the authorized mainstream political opposition in Mauritania, the Mouvement National pour la Démocratie. In the camps, the majority of FRUIDEM members were FulBe.

the territory of their ancestors and had close kin among Senegalese, many Mauritanians appropriated the refugee label as a new element of complex identities. It was invested by a strong idea that an entire community — now called the Black Mauritanians — had suffered from past injustices, discrimination and oppression and should obtain justice and compensation.

The Dominant Narrative on Past Injustices: Evoking the Logic of the Exception

While fostering the construction of a new imagined community around the refugee label, the politicization of refugee camps also enhanced the construction, legitimization and circulation of a dominant narrative over past injustices and on what should constitute a just order. I call this the 'politico-humanitarian' narrative as it took shape through the daily interactions between the refugee political elite, NGOs and human rights organizations but also because it was directly inspired by international refugee law, human rights and transitional justice discourses and drew on the same logic of the exception as humanitarian actors.

The narrative was constructed by the refugee representatives from the FLAM political party established in Senegal. They had the legitimacy, the rhetorical competence and the channels (through their associations) to disseminate among the rest of the refugees as well as among external actors (UNHCR, NGOs, journalists, etc.) a certain interpretation of past injustices. Extremely politicized and inscribed in the continuity of former FLAM discourses from the 1980s (FLAM, 1986), their narrative was embedded in a racial interpretation of the 1989–91 period, presented as an attempt by the 'Moorish State', sometimes called the 'fascist and *ethno-genocidaire* system' or the 'racist State', to proceed to an 'ethnic cleaning' of the 'Black' population in Mauritania through massive 'deportations' and 'killings', in addition to long-term discrimination (see also Fresia, 2009a: 248–81).[7] In this account, ethnic and racial categories were reified without any space to mention solidarities and alliances among the Moorish and other ethnic groups, including within the state, during and before the 1989–91 period. The politico-humanitarian narrative was also formulated to emphasize scenes of violence, humiliation and dispossession: all losses were systematically enumerated. The violence against the sedentary elite, be they government employees or landlords, was also emphasized, to the detriment of the specific acts of violence endured by other groups such as the FulBe, who were actually the major target of the forced displacement.

---

7. These quotes are based on the words spoken by FLAM leaders at the World Refugee Days in Dakar between 2001 and 2004, official statements of FLAM delegates in the refugee camp where I was staying (N'Dioum) and the party's first online forum (www.membres.tripod.fr/flamnet) which was then replaced by the official website of the party (www.flamnet.net). Since the official repatriation of the refugees and the transition period, the party's discourse has evolved and become less radical.

The politico-humanitarian discourse conveyed strong claims over justice and compensation built on an asserted intention to return home, to resist absorption in the host society, and to restore a 'lost dignity'. In various official declarations between 2001 and 2004, these claims were listed as follows: (1) the recognition of the Mauritanian citizenship of refugees; (2) the repatriation of all refugees in dignity under the supervision of the UNHCR; (3) the restitution of land; (4) the reinsertion of all government employees in the Mauritanian administration; (5) a compensation proportionate to the value of all goods lost; and (6) the identification and trial of those responsible for the 1989 crimes (see also FLAM, 2007). These claims were based on a concept of a just order, which was clearly embedded in international refugee and human rights laws (the right to return home and the right to regain citizenship) and transnational ideas of transitional justice (the right to reparation and justice). The claims thus drew on the same logic of the exception as that invoked by humanitarian actors: they too were framing the forced exile in terms of an abnormal situation as compared to the 'national order of things' — a situation which had to be addressed through exceptional measures such as repatriation, reparation and compensation under the supervision of UN organizations. Invoking this logic of the exception was both the result of the influence humanitarian aid had on the refugee elite's understanding of their situation, and a prerequisite to making their claims intelligible and heard by the international community.

Yet, this politico-humanitarian narrative also drew on the local concept of 'dignity' (*dimaagu* in Fulani), which the refugee elite mobilized to give their narrative resonance for the majority of the refugee population, including FulBe. The following official FLAM declaration, made in the context of World Refugee Day in 2002 in Senegal, demonstrates this use of the notion of dignity:

> The Mauritanian government continues to deny the very existence of deportees. Remaining attached to their nation, despite 13 years of exile, the Mauritanian refugees still claim for: the recognition of their citizenship, the organization of their return under the supervision of UNHCR as a guarantee, the restitution of their land and assets or an appropriate financial compensation for them, the rehabilitation of political refugees, the identification and judgment of the perpetuators of the 1989 deportations and all *genocidaires* and the application of international and national law to them . . . . For the dignity (*dimaagu*) and respect of refugees! Mauritanians we were, Mauritanians we will remain! 13 years of suffering, 12 years of being forgotten, it is enough! For a return with our dignity (*dimaagu*)![8]

The Fulani word *dimaagu* stems from a term for a free man, of noble status, as opposed to a slave (Mohamadou, 1991: 87). Mobilizing the notion of dignity was a way to stress that the social status and the social origin of refugees, as noble and free men, had to be acknowledged and respected by the Mauritanian government who had treated them like slaves by dispossessing them of their lands and goods and by denying their origins. Overcoming

---

8. FLAM, official declaration for the World Refugee Day, Dakar, 2002.

such humiliation thus required an official, formal and ritualized process: it called for exceptional measures that could be fulfilled, for instance, through a 'formal' recognition of their citizenship and an official repatriation to be guaranteed by a UN organization.

This politico-humanitarian narrative became dominant not only because it was constructed by refugees belonging to the sedentary elite within the camps and inspired by both transnational and local ideas about justice, but also because it was progressively institutionalized, legitimized and disseminated by external actors such as human rights organizations and the media. In the early 1990s, these actors tended to make regular visits to the same camps — the most visible, accessible and politicized ones — and to keep interviewing the same refugee leaders, those belonging to the FLAM movement. Through that process, the refugee leaders' narratives, which were based on a specific grid of interpretations of the 1989–91 acts of violence and mainly reflected the human rights abuses that were perpetrated against them and their relatives, were gradually transformed into a 'historical' collective memory of the past. Basing their written reports on these testimonies alone, NGOs have thus contributed to institutionalizing and widely circulating the politico-humanitarian narrative constructed by a specific politicized sedentary elite. For instance, the Human Rights Watch report entitled *Mauritania's Campaign of Terror: State-sponsored Repression of Black Africans* (Fleischman, 1994), which constitutes a major institutional reference for the 1989–91 acts of violence, mainly focuses on human rights abuses perpetrated against government employees and cultivators, and interprets these through the same racial categories as those mobilized by the refugee elite in Senegal.

Besides NGO reports, the politico-humanitarian narrative was also widely disseminated through the lobbying, commemorative and sensitization activities undertaken by the refugee elite, which were unexpectedly facilitated by UNHCR's humanitarian interventions. The narrative was transmitted to younger generations through refugee schools which were financed by UNHCR to ensure the 'right to education' for all refugee children. Most teachers were recruited among refugees themselves and many of them belonged to the FLAM leadership: they saw refugee schools as a vehicle to pass on to younger generations a certain memory of past injustices. During my research, when asking the youth born after 1989 to account for the causes of their exile, they frequently answered that it was because a 'genocide' had been attempted against 'Black people' by the 'Moorish people', or that 'the Moorish have massacred and deported the Blacks and done everything that can humiliate a man in his life'.[9] For these young people, it was not just the state that was held responsible for past injustices, but the Moorish in general.

The politico-humanitarian narrative over past injustices also circulated widely in Europe and the United States, not only through NGO reports but

9. I asked several teenagers to write an essay on the 1989 period; all of them used such expressions.

also because many refugee political leaders were resettled to Western countries in 2001 through UNHCR resettlement schemes. If their resettlement was first considered a way of moving them out of Senegal, where their political activities were perceived as a threat to the stability of the region, its unintended effect was actually to reinforce their capacity to lobby for their rights directly in Europe and the US. In their resettlement countries, refugee leaders created a number of associations and organized regular demonstrations, commemorative events and conferences, websites and fora, not only to keep alive the memory of the past among the Mauritanian diaspora, but also to claim their rights and to claim a just order in Mauritania. The legitimacy of this narrative for the 1989–91 period was therefore to a great extent reinforced with the resettlement of refugee leaders.

The humanitarian aid programme in Senegal, and the recognition of Mauritanians as refugees, therefore had significant, although often unintended, consequences in terms of producing, legitimizing and facilitating the circulation of a certain discourse over past injustices, which soon became hegemonic. This narrative was based on a specific racial grid of interpretation, on the social experiences of violence of one part of the refugee population only and on a strong sense that a deep humiliation had to be repaired. In this discourse, the repatriation of refugees under the supervision of UNHCR, the recognition of their Mauritanian citizenship, the restitution of lost assets and the criminal prosecution of the perpetrators of violence appeared to be the only way to atone for this humiliation, to regain dignity and re-establish a just order.

Counter-narratives and Pragmatic Attitudes among Subaltern Groups

The dominant narrative over past injustices and claims for compensation conveyed by the elite was appropriated by many refugees who were not as politicized as the former government employees, but who regularly participated in commemorative events and political meetings in the camps. Although this narrative did not represent the diversity and complexity of individual experiences of past injustices, it provided ordinary people with a rather simple frame to make sense of the 1989–91 acts of violence. During my research, I collected many similar politico-humanitarian accounts of the past among ordinary people, as well as similar claims with regard to repatriation. Claims for compensation were also expressed in ways similar to the political formulations of leaders, although with greater insistence on the local conception of *dimaagu* and with more references to the situation of herders. This quotation, collected in 2004, is illustrative:

> We want to return with our dignity. Because there, it is as if we are not important. If we go back home, the government will not respect us. Or the one who does not respect you and who does not recognize you for who you are can bring you some problems. This is what stops us from returning home. We want that the government knows who we are, we want to have our

place and our rank in Mauritania. If your land was taken, it should be given back to you. If your herds were taken, the value of what you lost should be given back to you. But the one who thinks you do not have any importance and is not ready to welcome you back home in a proper way, will never give you back what you have lost.[10]

Yet, these discourses, mainly collected in a formal context of interviews, sharply contrasted with alternative narratives produced in other, more informal settings, which were based on different frames of understanding, different norms of what can and cannot be said, and different modes of expressing one's emotions.

Among the alternative accounts of the past that I have identified, I will mention two here. The first, which I call the 'Marxist narrative', was conveyed by FRUIDEM, the minority political party in the camps. According to their representatives, the 1989–91 acts of violence are to be explained in Marxist terms, as the result of the domination of a politico-commercial class willing to exploit the majority, be it Black or Moorish. Members of FRUIDEM rejected the racial interpretations proposed by the FLAM movement, and denounced the tendency of FLAM leaders to 'exploit' the suffering of the FulBe majority for their own ends. FRUIDEM was in favour of claiming rights for compensation and justice from the 'inside' rather than the 'outside', and without calling for specific external interventions. It was also in favour of returning home at the first opportunity rather than waiting for the government to organize an official repatriation under UNHCR supervision. In that sense, they were not drawing on the logic of the exception, as in the politico-humanitarian narrative, but rather on a logic of the ordinary, as class exploitation is not a deviation from a normal order of things but rather the staple of ordinary injustice. The influence of this narrative was, however, less far-reaching than that of the FLAM movement, especially with regard to external actors; FRUIDEM members decided to return to Mauritania soon after the Senegal–Mauritania border was reopened in 1992, leaving the FLAM movement occupying the main political space in exile.

The other alternative account was the one adopted by many ordinary people outside formal interview contexts, especially herders who constituted the majority of the refugees. I call this the 'epic narrative' in the sense that it accounted for past injustices not in terms of humiliation and dispossession or of class exploitation, but rather in terms of courage, bravery and acts of resistance of herders in face of the 1989 acts of violence. The epic narrative did not set racial groups in systematic opposition, but offered a more nuanced interpretation of the conflict, mentioning allies among the enemies, traitors among the Black population (such as certain TorooBe), solidarities with certain Moorish, as well as the acts of (cross-border) vengeance organized by FulBe to preserve their honour against those who had stolen their herds and chased them off their land. This narrative did not directly invoke scenes

10. Interview with Ousseyni, Ndioum, Senegal (2004).

of violence and was, in that respect, closer to the oral historical tradition of FulBe, which is more inclined to celebrate heroic acts of the past rather than focus on humiliation and dispossession.

In contrast to the Marxist narrative, the epic narrative can therefore be interpreted as another type of exceptional discourse, in which the extra-ordinary deeds of specific individuals or groups under extreme circumstances are emphasized as a way to celebrate the honour of the group and restore its dignity. This narrative thus did not include specific claims for justice or calls for external actors to restore justice: justice had already or at least partly been restored through acts of vengeance during or immediately after the 1989 events. The will to return 'home' was also not as clear as in other narratives. Without denying their Mauritanian nationality, the authors of the epic narrative often indicated, although not always, that they would rather become Senegalese. The 1989 events had brought them back to where their ancestors came from; furthermore, the pastoral lands belonging to their clan spanned both Mauritania and Senegal, and nationality was not such an important issue for them. Other groups such as the youth insisted that they actually considered themselves Senegalese, Mauritanian *and* Haalpulaaren and that they would stay where their interests and social relations are. Many women (apart from those married to the political leaders) insisted that although past injustices have been hard to overcome, they were satisfied with life in Senegal where they had found peace, but also better access to basic infrastructure such as water, schools and hospitals.

The hegemonic politico-humanitarian discourse on past injustices conveyed in formal interview contexts not only contrasted with other alternative accounts collected in informal settings. It also sharply contrasted with pragmatic attitudes and ordinary practices I had observed in refugee settlements between 2001 and 2005. After fifteen years of exile, although many refugees were still living in camps in order to remain visible and to strengthen their claim for an official repatriation to be organized, most families were dispersed across several locations: elders, women and children remained in refugee sites for visibility, while men and youth either worked as small entrepreneurs in Senegalese cities or elsewhere in West Africa, went back to Mauritania to work in major cities, or stayed in Senegalese pastoral zones with their herds. As soon as the Mauritania–Senegal border reopened in 1992, some refugees started to move back and forth across the border again, as they had done before, making use of multiple identities according to the context. In 1995, when UNHCR initiated a reinsertion programme in Mauritania to informally encourage refugees to return outside of any official recognition from the government, many families divided themselves, one part staying in camps and the other returning to try to get their assets back. Apart from the political leaders, who mainly lived in camps where they were hired by UNHCR to manage refugee infrastructures, the coping strategies of the majority were thus organized, as before their forced excile, according to cross-border and transnational logics — an observation already made in many other refugee contexts (e.g. Horst, 2007; Van Hear, 2003). Furthermore, to regain the legal protection of a nation state and be able to move around and work more freely, most of them had also bought Senegalese or Mauritanian identity papers, while officially keeping their refugee status.

Overall, therefore, there were important discrepancies between, on the one hand, the dominant political discourse over past injustices and claims for reparation for lost dignity (employed by almost all refugees in formal interviewing contexts) as well as counter-narratives of subaltern groups such as herders in informal conversations; and, on the other hand, the pragmatic attitudes of the majority of refugees, who had already rebuilt their lives or attempted to recover their rights through the mobilization of transnational strategies and multiple identities. An important disjuncture was thus revealed between the lofty ideals and the messy practical realities of seeking justice in transition. On the discursive level, each of the identified narratives activated different imaginings of past injustices, people's responses to them, as well as the appropriate forms of transition or 'just order' to be aspired to for the future. Yet, the dominant politico-humanitarian narrative, inspired by transnational ideas about a just order and embedded in a nation state ideology, still had the strongest performative effects, because it was institutionalized and disseminated at the international level by actors such as the UNHCR, the refugee elite, and NGOs who had the legitimacy to speak on behalf of the refugees. This narrative thus became hegemonic and contributed to sustaining the idea that the only way to overcome past injustices, and make good what was presented as a loss of dignity, was to restore a national and human rights order of things through a formal and ritualized process based on the logic of the exception.

RETURNING HOME AND CLAIMING JUSTICE: CONTINUITIES WITH THE PAST

The consequences of the humanitarian intervention in Senegal are crucial to understanding how new beginnings have been shaped in Mauritania since the fall of the Ould Taya regime. This section therefore describes how the labelling of Mauritanians as 'refugees', and the social construction of a hegemonic narrative on past injustices, have contributed to giving the return of refugees a political and symbolic meaning in the Mauritanian transitional context, while deeply influencing the dominant models of justice that have been mobilized by victim associations since 2005. It also outlines how the dominant meaning given to the repatriation process has erased alternative and ordinary ways of making sense of new beginnings in Mauritania.

Going 'Home' as an Act of Transitional Justice

With the fall of the Ould Taya regime in 2005, and the opening of a new transitional period, the repatriation of refugees was to become the symbol of new beginnings in Mauritania. Although state officials and UNHCR knew very well about the pragmatic attitudes of a majority of refugees and the fact that many of them had de facto repatriated or regained Senegalese or Mauritanian identity papers through informal channels, the 'performance' of an official return movement under the supervision of UNHCR within a legally bounded framework was perceived as essential to re-establish a just order in Mauritania. It was constructed as both an act of transitional justice in its own right (undoing the human rights violation of displacement) and a prerequisite for further transitional justice measures such as the restoration of citizenship, the restitution of land, compensations and reparations.

At the level of the new Mauritanian authorities, the need to perform an official repatriation had been directly influenced by the lobbying activities of the refugee political elite in exile: their claim for an official repatriation to be organized under the supervision of UNHCR had made its way up to the European Union and its fulfilment became one of the conditions imposed by the EU Council to support the new transitional authority (Council of the European Union, 2006). In search of legitimacy, the newly elected government (in 2007) had therefore to respond to that condition to gain political support from donor countries. The logic of the exception, on which the refugee elite based its narrative of past injustices, thus eventually succeeded, in that the international community pressurized the new transitional regime into repatriation.

At UNHCR level, too, the organization of an official return of refugees was crucial: first, to restore credibility after the failure of its first attempt to encourage refugees to return home in 1995, when the Mauritanian authorities were not willing to recognize their citizenship; second, because it is part of the core mandate of UNHCR to find a 'durable solution' to the refugee 'problem' and to ensure that displaced persons can be re-embedded in a nation state able to protect their rights. Repatriating Mauritanian refugees through a formal and official ritual therefore became an urgent matter for both the Mauritanian authorities and UNHCR's legitimacy. As a result, only three months after his investiture, the newly elected President Sidi Abdellahi officially and solemnly invited all Mauritanian refugees to come back to their country, asked the UNHCR to assist him in organizing their return, and announced his intention to organize 'national days of consultations' on the resolution of the *passif humanitaire*. The return of refugees was presented as an act of transitional justice in itself as it implied the official recognition, by the authorities, that hundreds of thousands of Mauritanians had been forcibly displaced in 1989. This acknowledgement symbolized the end of the Ould Taya regime, associated with state violence, and the beginning of a new era, but it was also constructed as a first and necessary step towards a wider reconciliation of all Mauritanians.

On the side of refugees, the social meaning given to repatriation was strongly embedded in the dominant interpretation of past injustices framed by the refugee elite. The call by the newly elected President for refugees to come back to their country was indeed perceived by many of them as a unique opportunity to 'show to the world that we are Mauritanians and not Senegalese'.[11] This attitude was clearly influenced by the politicization of memory in camps, which led to the construction of a new imagined community (the oppressed Black Mauritanians) and hence reinforced the link to the nation state. When I asked why they had finally decided to go back to Mauritania, the majority of returnees I interviewed in 2008 answered by insisting on their origins: 'It is love towards our country that made us came back; we are all born in Mauritania, it is from here that we come from, here that we had grown up and where we were used to, here that we had found our parents and grand-parents; it is also here that we have a large part of our kin'.[12] These words from a returnee representative were repeated in almost the same formulation by most of my respondents in formal interview context.

The dominant and legitimate discourse therefore presented repatriation as a way to reassert their autochthony in Mauritania. Despite extremely harsh conditions in returnee areas, which were deprived of basic infrastructure and access to water, and despite encouragement from state officials to establish themselves close to major cities, returnees were firm in wanting to rebuild their own villages in the same place as before. There was a clear political and identity statement in this repatriation process. If it was 'performed' — in the sense that many families had actually already gone back (or back and forth) to Mauritania — it still had real-life consequences with the rebuilding of more than 150 villages in the South of Mauritania. In parallel to this strong political statement, returning home was also presented by certain returnees as a way of fulfilling their consistent position — to assert their will to go home if certain conditions were satisfied, among which the official recognition of the 1989–91 acts of violence by the government and the official involvement of UNHCR in the repatriation. Refusing to repatriate when those conditions had been met would have exposed them to the ridicule of their Senegalese kin,[13] who had often suspected them of staying in camps only to take advantage of humanitarian assistance and not because of a genuine attachment to their country of origin. Repatriation was therefore also associated with the will to maintain their reputation *vis-à-vis* their Senegalese kin and avoid shame.

Lastly, but just as importantly, returnee representatives have also apprehended repatriation as a way to obtain restitution of their lands and compensation for what was lost in 1989. They perceived the official involvement of UNHCR in that process as an important opportunity to claim their rights with the support of the international community. As a women's representative stated: 'we came back because this time, we had UNHCR and big donor countries behind us: we were not trusting the new governments, but we were

---

11. Interview with the returnee representative of Houdallaye returnee village, July 2008.
12. Interview with the chief of the Bounguel Thille returnee village, June 2008.
13. Interview with Mayri, Bounguel Thille, June 2008.

trusting the countries which were behind our country; if we don't get our rights, at least, the entire world will know it'.[14] For all stakeholders, the performance of an official repatriation thus had a strong symbolic dimension to which various meanings were attached: it could simultaneously reinforce the legitimacy of the new authorities, save the credibility of UNHCR, and assert the refugees' political and identity claims for citizenship recognition, land restitution and compensation.

Dominant Discourses on Justice among Victim Associations

Although it needed to be 'performed', the repatriation of refugees and the high expectations associated with it were far from being only symbolic; they have had major real-life consequences in Mauritania. With the recognition of their citizenship, the reconstruction of hundreds of villages in the south and the revival of discourses over autochthony, Mauritanians are now legally rooted again in Mauritania in terms of official residence, civil rights and property rights, but also in terms of rights for compensation and justice. This explains why the official return of refugees has also enhanced a pro-liferation of victim associations. According to my research there are around ten such associations in Mauritania, in addition to the dozens of refugee and victim associations already established by the refugee political elite in Senegal, Europe and the US. The model of justice they have adopted since 2005 is based on transnational ideas over transitional justice such as claims for justice, truth and material compensations. This draws directly on the politico-humanitarian narrative framed in exile and is based on the same logic of the exception, calling for exceptional transitional measures to be taken. The associations emphasize the right for all victims of the 1989–91 acts of violence to know the truth, to have the perpetrators of violence — and particularly the 1991 killings of military personnel — identified and prosecuted. They also demand the right for civil servants and the military to recover their place in the Mauritanian administration, for families (widows) to be financially compensated for the loss of their husbands, and for peasants to be given back their land.

While this proliferation of associations was positively perceived by the international community as a sign that civil society was flourishing, most of them were either not known at the local level, or were criticized as being not representative. Most of them conveyed the views and interests of the sedentary elite: former government employees, widows of the soldiers killed in 1991, and landlords. Just as in the politico-humanitarian narrative over past injustices, claims for justice during the transitional period seldom seemed to take into account the interests of the majority (agro-pastoralists

---

14. Interview with Djennaba, head of the women's committee, Houdallaye, July 2008.

FulBe), who had endured other types of violence and destitution (such as the loss of their herds, pastoral lands, etc.) and who needed other types of compensation than those listed by victim associations.

As of 2013, the claims for justice conveyed by these associations, although dominant within public debates, were not fulfilled. In August 2008, the new transitional authorities, which had promised to establish a truth commission, were overthrown by a new military coup, as a part of the army which had been involved in the former Taya regime was not willing to let that happen. The main author of the military coup, General Mohamed Ould Abdel Aziz, defended another model of justice drawing on the ordinary logic of the Islamic notion of forgiveness. On 25 March 2009, while visiting one of the main cities of the south of the country (Kaédi), he supervised a collective prayer, called the 'prayer of the absent' and dedicated to the memory of the victims of the Taya regime, in order to gain support from the returnee population. In a speech before the prayer, he called upon the Muslim culture to overcome the pain of the past: 'Today, I am both sad and fulfilled. Sad because there was human loss without any reason. But fulfilled because Allah has given to the victims the courage to overcome their pain ..., without any resentment' (Radio France Internationale, 2009). He also agreed to establish a financial compensation scheme for 244 people in exchange for their renouncing any claim for exceptional measures of truth telling or special trials. Far from being satisfied with these measures, victim associations have continued to demand the establishment of 'genuine' transitional justice institutions and to undertake a variety of lobbying activities inside and outside the country.

Alternative Discourses and Pragmatic Attitudes of the Majority

The dominant social meaning given to repatriation among returnees tended to erase alternative views on new beginnings. Indeed, the ethnographic materials I have collected among returnees in 2008 show that it was not always perceived, by ordinary people, as an act of transitional justice in its own right. In returnee areas, some of my respondents mentioned in informal discussions that they had been 'pressurized' to go home by their leaders, but also by Mauritanian authorities, UNHCR or foreign diplomatic missions who promised them that once at home, they would receive their land back as well as significant assistance to facilitate their reintegration. At the household level, the decision was generally made by men, leaving women with no other choice than to follow them. Yet, apart from politicized women occupying leadership positions within returnee villages, or spouses of political activists, many of the women did not want to go back to Mauritania, as returnee areas were lacking basic infrastructure, including access to water points. They said they would rather 'forget' about the 1989–91 period and enjoy their lives in Senegal, than return to Mauritania where painful memories may come back and where life conditions were so harsh. Many children and youth were also not keen to go back, as they identified more with Senegal than Mauritania, had the perception that they would suffer discrimination back in their own country, and did not want to integrate into the Mauritanian school system which in-cluded Arabic, which they did not speak. Some refugees actually asserted that they wanted to be naturalized as Senegalese: Senegal was for them a place where they had restored their 'dignity', built new social relationships and found 'peace', or had developed fruitful commercial activities.

Furthermore, while the majority of refugees who were officially registered for repatriation did return to Mauritania and asserted their will to reaffirm their autochthony, in practice many of them resumed their former practice of going back and forth across the Senegal–Mauritania border. After the official repatriation was performed, children at secondary school, for instance, were sent back to Senegal to finish their studies; those who had commercial activities in Senegalese or Mauritanian cities went back to live there; herders went back to pastoral zones in Senegal, where they had left their herds. It is therefore mainly women, small children and elders that have been left in returnee villages (often in harsh conditions) to assert political claims over autochthony and justice, just as it was the women, children and elders who had previously been left in refugee camps to maintain the visibility of refugees and past injustices. In that sense, these subaltern groups have played a central but also instrumental role in the symbolic meaning that was given to repatriation by the elite — often to the detriment of their own interests and will. In addition, as in the past, there were still major discrepancies between the dominant narratives of returnees reaffirming their strong attachment to the nation state in transition and their will to obtain justice, and the everyday practices which remained embedded in cross-border logics and multiple identities.

NEW BEGINNINGS OR NEW CHALLENGES?

Since the end of the Taya regime in 2005, discourses on and claims for transitional justice in Mauritania have been at the centre of national political debates and are increasingly relayed by the flourishing civil society within the country as well as by the media. Although, as of 2013, no transitional justice institutions have been established, ideas about a just order have made progress in a country where the subject of past and current human rights violations had, for a very long time, remained taboo. To understand how such ideas, which draw on the logic of the exception, have emerged on the Mauritanian political scene we need to take into account the wider context of negotiations of new beginnings in Mauritania and the ways in which this was influenced by a dominant narrative on justice and transition circulating outside the country, among refugees and human rights organizations.

The dominant and legitimate interpretation of past injustices has, to a large extent, been co-constructed by the political elite among refugees in exile and by humanitarian and human rights organizations, through the lens of refugee and humanitarian law, itself derived from the ordinary logic of the international law of sovereign states. By framing the situation of refugees in terms of abnormality, exceptionality and victimhood, but also in terms of humiliation and loss of dignity, both refugee leaders and humanitarian actors have contributed to constructing the need to perform an official repatriation of refugees as an essential part of new beginnings in Mauritania and as an act of transitional justice in itself. Interestingly, in Mali — to which many Mauritanians had also been forcibly displaced in 1989 — the lack of significant involvement of UNHCR and the lack of well-connected political leaders able to speak in the name of the refugees led to very different dynamics. Less politicized, the situation of refugees there has been largely ignored by the international community and followed with less attention by the transitional authorities in Mauritania. This lack of visibility and international recognition of their refugee status also means that their situation has not been systematically and clearly framed as abnormal or as a problem to be resolved through exceptional measures. There has therefore been less interest in reintegrating these refugees into a 'national order of things' and, as a result, no initiative has been taken by the Mauritanian government to date to officially organize their repatriation.

Exploring the discrepancies between the ideals of transitional justice conveyed by the dominant politico-humanitarian narrative about past injustices and alternative narratives produced by subaltern groups in informal settings has also enabled us to better understand how ideas about justice and transition may be more messy and diverse than we expect. In that respect, it is interesting to observe that alternative ways of making sense of past injustices may trigger very different images of what has been endured in the past, but also different forms of transition to be aspired to for the future; these may draw on other exceptional logics (such as in the epic narrative) or be embedded in the logic of the ordinary (such as in the Marxist narrative). The discrepancies between the dominant narrative and the everyday, mundane practices of refugees and returnees have, at the same time, stressed that ordinary people do not wait for exceptional measures to be taken to try to re-establish a sense of order, normalcy and justice in their daily lives. This study clearly shows that Mauritanian refugees have constantly transcended the 'national order of things' on which their identification as victims of forced displacement was founded, as they mobilized transnational logics and multiple identities on a daily basis. For the majority, it seemed clear that the just order they aspired to was an order which allowed them to remain mobile, rather than an order forcing them again into one single place.

This observation, which has also been made in other refugee and returnee contexts, has led some researchers to conclude that defining repatriation as a 'durable solution', undoing the human rights violation of displacement, is to a large extent illusory: it remains embedded in a sedentary view of a just order, which does not reflect the complex patterns of movements of ordinary people (Bakewell, 2000; Van Hear, 2003: 14). Yet, this study also shows that this sedentarist view was conveyed not only by humanitarian organizations, but also by certain refugee leaders who remained attached to localities and territorialities at the level of social representations, identity and political claims. Through their political activism in camps, these leaders have led many refugees to embrace the national categorization of 'Black Mauritanians' and the external label of 'refugees', creating the need to perform an official repatriation to regain dignity, including for those who had already returned in Mauritania or whose families were spread out on both sides of the border. Far from being solely symbolic, the performance of this repatriation had a number of concrete consequences on the ground, such as the reconstitution of more than 100 villages in the south of the country, the revival of discourses of autochthony, the strengthening and affirmation of the Black Mauritanians racial category on the public scene and the strong claims for transitional justice mechanisms conveyed by victim associations. These elements have deeply influenced the terms of the country's new beginnings, not least by precipitating a new military coup in 2008, and they will continue to weigh heavily in its future.

REFERENCES

Agamben, G. (1995) *Homo Sacer: Le pouvoir souverain et la vie nue* [*Homo Sacer: Sovereign Power and Bare Life*]. Paris: Seuil.

Agier, M. (2008) *Gérer les indésirables: Des camps de réfugiés au gouvernement humanitaire* [*Managing the Undesirables: Refugee Camps and Humanitarian Government*]. Paris: Flammarion.

Allen, T. and H. Morsink (1994) *When Refugees Go Home*. London: James Currey, in assoc. with UNRISD and Africa World Press.

Anders, G. and O. Zenker (2014) 'Transition and Justice: An Introduction', *Development and Change* 45(3): 395–414.

Bakewell, O. (2000) 'Repatriation and Self-settled Refugees in Zambia: Bringing Solutions to the Wrong Problems', *Journal of Refugee Studies* 13(4): 356–73.

Black, R. and K. Koser (1999) *The End of the Refugee Cycle: Refugee Repatriation and Reconstruction*. Oxford and New York: Berghahn Books.

Ciavolella, R. (2010) *Les Peuls et l'Etat en Mauritanie. Une anthropologie des marges* [*The Fulani and the State in Mauritania. An Anthropology of the Margins*]. Paris: Karthala.

Coulter, C. (2001) 'Organizing Places and People: Humanitarian Discourse and Sierra Leonean Refugees'. Working Paper in Cultural Anthropology 10. Uppsala: Department of Cultural Anthropology and Ethnology.

Council of the European Union (2006) 'Council Decision of 29 May 2006 Concerning the Conclusion of Consultations with the Islamic Republic of Mauritania under Article 96 of the Revised Cotonou Agreement (2006/470/EC)'. Brussels: Official Journal of the European Union.

FIDH (2006) 'Mauritanie. L'établissement de la démocratie peut-il s'affranchir du règlement du passif humanitaire?' ['Can the Establishment of Democracy Avoid the Resolution of Past Injustices?']. Report No. 447 (April). Paris: International Federation of Human Rights.

FLAM (1986) 'Le Manifeste du Négro-Mauritanien Opprimé' ['The Manifesto of the Oppressed Black Mauritanians']. http://flamnet.info/index.php?option=com_content& view=article&id=90%3Ale-manifeste-du-negro-mauritanien-opprime-fevrier-1966-avril-1986-&catid=37%3Apublications&Itemid=1 (accessed 6 February 2014).

FLAM (2007) 'Plateforme pour une Mauritanie réconciliée des FLAM, phase 1 (Mars 2007)' ['Platform for a Reconciled Mauritania, Phase 1, March 2007']. http://flamnet .info/index.php?option=com_content&view=article&id=89%3Aretro-plate-forme-pour-une-mauritanie-reconciliee-des-flam-mars-2007&catid=37%3Apublications&Itemid=1 (assessed 6 February 2014).

Fleischman, J. (1994) *Mauritania's Campaign of Terror: State-sponsored Repression of Black Africans*. New York: Human Rights Watch.

Fresia, M. (2009a) *Les Mauritaniens réfugiés au Sénégal. Une anthropologie de l'asile et de l'aide humanitaire.* [*Mauritanian Refugees in Senegal: A Critical Anthropology of Asylum and Humanitarian Aid*]. Paris: L'Harmattan.

Fresia, M (2009b) 'Humanitarian Governance: Managing Mauritanian Refugees in Senegal', in P.Y. Lemeur and G. Blundo (eds) *The Daily Life of Governance in Africa. Public and Collective Services and Their Users*, pp. 279–300. Leiden: Brill.

Horst, C. (2007) *Transnational Nomads: How Somalis Cope with Refugee Life in the Dadaab Camps of Kenya*. Oxford and New York: Berghahn Books.

Leservoisier, O. (1999) 'Les réfugiés "négro-mauritaniens" de la vallée du Sénégal', ['"Black-Mauritanian" Refugees in the Senegal River Valley'], in V. Lassailly-Jacob, J.-Y. Marchal and A. Quesnel (eds) *Déplacés et réfugiés, la mobilité sous contrainte* [*Displaced Persons and Refugees: Mobility under Constraint*], pp. 283–302. Paris: IRD éditions.

Magestro, J. (1993) 'Crossing River. Ethnicity and Transboundary Conflict in the Senegal River Valley', *Cahier d'études africaines* 130: 201–32.

Malkki, L. (1995) *Purity and Exile: Violence, Memory, and National Cosmology among Hutu Refugees in Tanzania*. Chicago, IL, and London: University of Chicago Press.

Mohamadou, A. (1991) *Lexique peul-français. Parlers du Fuuta Tooro* [*Fulani–French Lexicon. Dialects of Futa Toro*]. Paris: INALCO.

Radio France Internationale (2009) 'Mauritanie: des réparations pour les familles des victimes du régime Taya' ['Mauritania: Reparation for the Families of Victims of the Taya Regime']. http://www.rfi.fr/actufr/articles/111/article_79533.asp (accessed 6 February 2014).

Sall, I. (1999) 'Crise identitaire ou stratégie de positionnement politique en Mauritanie: Le cas des Fulbe Aynaabe' ['Identity Crisis or Strategy of Political Positioning in Mauritania: The Case of Fulbe Anynaabe'], in A. Bourgeot (ed.) *Horizons nomades en Afrique sahélienne. Sociétés, développement et démocratie* [*Nomadic Horizons in the Sahel: Societies, Development and Democracy*], pp. 79–99. Paris: Karthala.

Santoir, C. (1993) 'D'une rive à l'autre. Les Peul mauritaniens réfugiés au Sénégal (département de Dagana et Podor)' ['From One Bank to Another. Mauritanian Fulani Refugees in Senegal (Dagana and Podor)]', *Cahiers des sciences humaines* 29(1): 195–229.

Seck, S.M. (1991) 'Les cultivateurs transfrontaliers "de décrue face à la question foncière"' ['Floodplains, Cross-border Peasants and Struggles over Land'], in B. Crousse, P. Mathieu and S.D. Seck (eds) *La vallée du fleuve Sénégal: évaluations et perspectives d'une décennie d'aménagements, 1980–1990* [*The Senegal River Valley: An Overview of One Decade of Technical Planning*], pp. 297–313. Paris: Karthala.

Turner, S. (2002) 'The Barriers of Innocence: Humanitarian Intervention and Political Imagination in a Refugee Camp for Burundians in Tanzania'. Doctoral dissertation, Roskilde University.

UN (2004) 'Report of the Secretary-General on the Rule of Law and Transitional Justice in Conflict and Post-Conflict Societies'. UN Doc. S/2004/616, 23 August. New York: United Nations.

UNHCR (1951) 'Convention Relating to the Status of Refugees'. Geneva: United Nations High Commissioner for Refugees.

Van Hear, N. (2003) 'From Durable Solution to Transnational Relations: Home and Exile among Refugee Diasporas'. New Issues in Refugee Research Working Paper No. 83. Geneva: UNHCR.

4

Conflicting Logics of Exceptionality: New Beginnings and the Problem of Police Violence in Post-Apartheid South Africa

Steffen Jensen

INTRODUCTION

On 16 August 2012, thirty-four miners were killed and eighty others were wounded in one of the worst ever police shootings in South Africa. Controversy shrouded the incident as police officers claimed self-defence and heightened tension in the preceding days, and ultimately apologized for the incident. The subsequent enquiry into what is now termed the Marikana massacre has unearthed a string of disastrous police actions and alludes to unsavoury relations between the mining company, powerful politicians and the police (Marinovich and Nicolson, 2013). Whatever the final outcome of the investigation, the Marikana massacre brought into sharp focus the use of force by the South African police, the seeming sense of righteousness with which they use that force, how central the police is as an institution for the future of South Africa, and how dangerous it can be if left unchecked. In this way, the Marikana massacre became part of a discussion that has been going on at least since the fall of apartheid about the role of the police and how it should be dealt with politically.

When apartheid finally ended and the African National Congress (ANC) assumed power, it was a matter of urgency to transform the state from a repressive apparatus of racial segregation into an institution that would realize ANC's National Democratic Revolution. It was in this process that the notion of transitional justice was adopted, stressing for example security sector reform. Based on the idea that a human rights focus and international law operationalized as institutional reform could provide a radical break with the past towards a new beginning, transitional justice appeared perfect to address the far-reaching reforms needed in these exceptional circumstances.[1]

The author would like to thank Amanda Dissel and the Centre for the Study of Violence and Reconciliation in Johannesburg who participated in and hosted the media study on which part of this chapter is based. I would also like to thank the editors of the special issue (on which this volume is based), and the anonymous referees of the journal *Development and Change*, for their insightful comments on earlier versions of this paper.

1. There are several reasons why human rights and transitional justice became central to the transformation of the state. In pragmatic terms, human rights provided a language that made

Transition and Justice: Negotiating the Terms of New Beginnings in Africa, First Edition.
Edited by Gerhard Anders and Olaf Zenker.
Chapters © 2015 by The Institute of Social Studies. Book compilation © 2015 John Wiley & Sons, Ltd.

Thus the democratic transformation of South Africa inaugurated a period during which unique human rights measures were adopted as mechanisms of transitional justice.[2] However, not long after the fall of apartheid, another crisis erupted and began to impact on politics. This was the crime wave that seemed to spiral out of control, endangering the prospect of a new South Africa. Most South Africans would agree with the need to both transform the state and deal decisively with the crime wave: few wanted a return to the past and no one wanted to become a victim of crime. In this way, dealing with the two urgencies was complementary rather than conflicting. It was in the everyday and mundane practices related to acting decisively that conflicts arose, for instance, when police officers used violence in the course of carrying out what they saw as their duty. From the perspective of the first urgency, police violence constitutes gross human rights violations, maybe even torture or cruel, inhuman and degrading treatment; from the perspective of the need to deal with crime, the same police violence is often necessary, legitimate and moral.

In this way, and in line with the Introduction (see also Anders and Zenker, 2014), what constitutes urgent and pressing need is not universally agreed upon and claims to exceptionality followed by calls for extraordinary measures are varied, multiple and indeed sometimes conflicting. It is within this complex field that I wish to understand police violence and reform in post-apartheid South Africa. Echoing the Introduction, it is useful to explore this as conflicting and contemporaneous logics of exceptionality. In this concept lies a notion that while reform or taking action is pressing, it is temporary. The impermanent nature of actions, and the crises that have called them forth, often legitimize quite extraordinary types of interventions that the editors refer to as logics of exceptionality (see also Anders and Zenker, 2014). In this chapter, I examine the question of how we might understand police violence in a field defined by two seemingly conflicting but simultaneously related logics of exceptionality. While the two logics of exceptionality constitute ideal, opposing totalities, in the realm of the mundane they often mesh and entangle to the extent that they shimmer (Jensen and Ronsbo, 2014: 13) in and out of focus, with one temporarily dominating the other. Rather than one proclaiming victory over the other, the two logics are constantly shifting, informing and animating each other to the extent that they are hard to perceive individually. It is this relationship that I attempt to capture through the notion of conflicting logics of exceptionality.

Exploring the contemporaneity of the two logics with reference to police violence makes sense because policing and the police are central to both

---

sense to many important actors, also within the apartheid state preoccupied with minority and property rights (personal communication, Saul Dubow, 13 October 2011). In more ideological terms, the fact that the international community spoke of South Africa as iconic of a human rights struggle simultaneously made South African politicians proud to be part of a morally superior political project.

2. Julia Hornberger (2011: 6) has aptly described this as a hyper-reality of human rights.

logics of exceptionality. As crime was perceived to spiral out of control, the South African police was given a central role in combating the crime wave. Concurrently, as the police had also been one of the repressive institutions of the apartheid regime, it was a matter of urgency to transform the institution. It was in this transformation of the police that transitional justice became central. Traditionally, transitional justice in South Africa has been identified with the Truth and Reconciliation Commission (TRC). However, the concept is broader than the TRC,[3] also including economic compensation, prosecution, memorialization and, central to my argument, security sector reforms. Within the transitional justice literature, each of these mechanisms contributes to social transformation and a new beginning where the human rights of all citizens are respected (Anders and Zenker, 2014; Teitel, 2000: 11–26).[4]

It might be useful to distinguish between transitional justice mechanisms as implemented by governments, international organizations and NGOs, and transitional justice as an analytical framework. The former clearly constitutes the empirical basis of the analysis of the first logic of exceptionality. The analytical framework is broader, and through it, we are able to explore logics of exceptionality. However, the concept of transitional justice seems to be somewhat narrow if we want to understand the conflicting and contemporaneous nature of different logics of exceptionality. Therefore, and heeding other critical voices (including the editors of this volume), we need to pay attention to the different logics at work. Despite the alleged universality of the meaning of transitional justice, there is seldom consensus on its meaning in the places undergoing transformation (Kelsall, 2005). Even if 'partners' in the South agree to interventions in principle, human rights and the mechanisms employed are appropriated and negotiated locally (Shaw, 2010). Hence, we need to pay attention to what Richard Wilson (2006) has termed 'the social life of rights', not least those that populate the institutions of transitional justice and the institutions under reform (Jefferson and Jensen, 2009). Taking into account the situated and conflicted nature of different logics of exceptionality allows us to address the three themes that the editors have identified in the Introduction: the discrepancy between ideals and practice, the problem of new beginnings, and the logics of exception and the ordinary. While in their lofty formulations the two logics of exceptionality seem to be reconcilable and non-conflicting in pointing to a new beginning, the everyday politics of both are rather mundane and constantly at odds. It is clear that the two logics of exceptionality envisage radically different new beginnings. In fact, the two logics assume particular forms of justice and injustice in ways that locate injustice with the practices of the proponents of

---

3. For a critique of this reduction of transitional justice to truth commissions, see Zenker (2011).
4. The International Centre for Transitional Justice provides useful illustrations of this kind of thinking. See, for example, 'What is Transitional Justice?' on their website: http://ictj.org/about/transitional-justice

the other logic. Put differently, while the advocates of transitional justice and the first logic regard the crime situation as worrying, they deem it ordinary in a way that does not call for exceptional measures. Reform of the police, on the other hand, is imperative. In contrast, the proponents of the second logic view police reform as a necessary endeavour but one that has been ongoing since before the fall of apartheid — and hence rather ordinary. Crime, on the other hand, does call for exceptional measures.

I present my argument in three sections. In the first section I trace the different roles attributed to the police by supporters of the respective logics from the end of apartheid to the present, showing how ambiguous and entangled the relationship between the two logics is. In the process, the different post-apartheid beginnings envisioned are revealed. In the second part of the chapter, I explore the mundane practices of police violence against the public, and police consent to public violence, utilizing three different archives: ethnographic data collected during twenty months' fieldwork on policing and gangs in Cape Town between 1997 and 1999; ten months' fieldwork on state and non-state policing between 2002 and 2004 in rural Mpumalanga; and a national media study of torture and cruel, inhuman and degrading treatment by the South African police in 2006. In the final section, on the basis of these analyses, I explore the contemporaneity and relationality of the two logics.

TWO LOGICS, DIFFERENT BEGINNINGS

When the ANC assumed power after the 1994 elections, the government faced the enormous task of having to restore the legitimacy of the South African police force among the public. Given the pivotal role it played in carrying out the oppressive policies of the apartheid government, there was a pressing need to transform the police. An avalanche of policies, laws and institutional change descended on the police, all informed by transitional justice imperatives. The name was changed from the South African Police (SAP) to become a 'service' (SAPS); a new Police Act was introduced; the principle of community policing was enshrined in the constitution; and a human rights culture, including a code of conduct, was adopted together with diversity training and policies against police brutality. The SAPS had to adhere to new labour relations practices and affirmative action with stipulated levels of representation enshrined in the legal statutes. The professionalism of the police with regard to investigation, sensitivity towards victims and methods of policing also had to be improved. New police stations had to be built to cater for the safety needs of all South Africans — not only whites in whose areas most of the police stations had hitherto been located — requiring some police officers to relocate to other stations. New units were set up and others, like the Security Branch, were either closed down or given new assignments; an Independent Complains Directorate (ICD) was introduced together with civilian oversight in the form of a Ministry for Safety and Security (Hornberger, 2011; Jensen, 2008; Marks, 2005). All or most of these new provisions were introduced to rein in and bring the police under ANC or democratic control. Human rights operationalized as transitional justice were therefore not the only rationale behind these new provisions. However, as Hornberger argues (2011: 4), a human rights discourse provided a globally accepted language for police transformation (e.g. Bailey, 2001). Thus transitional justice mechanisms and international law in many ways came to mould the understanding of the first urgency.

The human rights training policy of 1999 was a case in point. During a presentation to a group of international human rights representatives (myself included), its author, Peter Cronjé, who was the head of the human rights directorate in the SAPS, explained that it had been formulated over a four-year period as a joint project between the SAPS, local and international NGOs, academics and other state institutions. Several needs assessments during the 1990s had shown a shockingly low level of human rights knowledge among police officers on the ground. NGOs and the police leadership thus identified a fundamental need for (human rights) training. The training programme materialized in a training package including a presenter's guide with a detailed manual of how to conduct the training sessions. It consisted of a workbook/photo story/information booklet on human rights and policing; a package containing a training video, posters, and a copy of the constitution; a book on human rights standards for law enforcement officials; a booklet called 'You and the Constitution'; the SAPS code of conduct; and the United Nations High Commissioner for Refugees guidelines for the policing of refugees. The programme was implemented from 1999 through the creation of a 'train the trainer programme' as a first step in training a daunting number of 90,000 police officers nation-wide. The aim was to train 1,000 trainers by July 2001, who would subsequently be responsible for three-day workshops. Cronjé estimated that by the end of 2002 all police officers would have attended a human rights workshop.

This account amounts to what, paraphrasing Stanley Cavell (1988), we might term the 'standing language' of police reform informed by transitional justice. The police are construed as unknowing, in need of enlightenment and change; the international human rights community and its local partners are able to provide just that, through standardized training manuals, train the trainer programmes, workshops and policies. However, the reality of the human rights training programme was less rosy than Cronjé would have us believe. In an evaluation from 2002, the Swedish Aid agency published a damning report of the internationally backed programme. According to the report, there was no institutional commitment; prejudices against human rights were rife; logistical constraints and shortcomings dominated the programme itself; there was no willingness to see the benefits; and the programme had no institutional status, no trainers and sometimes even no trainees. One element, however, did emerge unscathed from the evaluation:

the evaluators regarded the internationally sponsored manual as particularly useful, also outside South Africa (Hornberger, 2011: 71–4). Thus the transitional justice ideal was vindicated; only its implementation was flawed. Accordingly, the report ends 'with an ideal type of human rights policing that is beyond scrutiny' (Hornberger, 2010: 267). Not satisfied with the failed or passed evaluation, Hornberger continued her research into the implementation of the manual. She found that, as in the case of most other issues in South Africa, police officers, including trainers, approached human rights from a racial rather than transitional justice perspective. In one of the sessions that Hornberger managed to attend, the trainer dismissed the class once it was established that there were no white police officers present, and hence no reason for the training to take place. Furthermore, human rights were basically translated into a moral or religious discourse where transformation became conversion and failure to live up to its ideals an endorsement of suffering (Hornberger, 2011: 15). Finally, Hornberger convincingly argues that human rights policing is infused with class and institutional culture, as it privileges the written and intellectual above the physical and action oriented. In this way, human rights-based policing becomes thoroughly racialized, gendered and classed (ibid.: 81). None of these issues are reflected in the evaluation of the human rights programme for transforming the South African police, despite the fact that a growing body of literature within the broad field of transitional justice suggests the need for contextualization instead of focusing on universal standards, best practices and one-size-fits-all interventions (Goodale and Merry, 2007; Jefferson and Jensen, 2009; Merry, 2006; Shaw and Waldorf, 2010; Teitel, 2003).

Parallel to the everyday and mundane problems of transitional justice implementation, the centrality of this exceptional logic demanding police reform was challenged almost from the outset by a second logic. The crime wave which gripped the country was depicted as another exceptional urgency requiring extraordinary means, but it was a crisis that posited police violence as a solution rather than as part of the problem. When the ANC assumed power in 1994, the analysis was that the tenuous hold of the state on the townships had to be addressed through a radical transformation of the institutions of the state. It was assumed that once the state had changed its relationship to the townships, and a new social contract had been negotiated and accepted by township residents, crime and violence would decrease. However, as of 1996 crime became one of the overarching political issues capable of making or breaking political aspirations. The gradual shift in focus of ANC policies from development to security is discussed in detail elsewhere (Jensen, 2005, 2010). Suffice it to say that township residents increasingly came to be seen as a threat to the democratic revolution rather than as victims of apartheid. State resources were utilized for safeguarding the state in the townships and the surrounding society instead of delivering services to township residents. State officials and municipal workers increasingly viewed residents as being caught up in a culture of dependency, poverty and violence. National and local government initiated programmes like Safer Schools and Community Policing Forums which called upon township residents to act against their own (young men) in the service of the state and its drive to fight crime.

The renewed focus on security also positioned the police differently and in 1999 President Mbeki appointed securocrat Steve Tshwete as Minister for Safety and Security. He succeeded Sydney Mufamadi who was known to be quite suspicious of the police. Tshwete fuelled hopes in the police station where I did fieldwork in 1999 regarding the relationship between gangs and police when he rehabilitated the police and made them the bulwark against crime, rather than a problem of transformation. In fact, Tshwete famously noted in 1999 that 'Criminals must know that the South African Police possesses the authority, moral and political, to ensure by all means, *constitutional or unconstitutional*, that the people of this country are not deprived of their human rights' (*Mail & Guardian*, 2000, emphasis added).

In this way, the second logic seemed to gain the upper hand. As gang wars ravaged Cape Town in particular, a war on gangs was declared with the introduction of CCTV in the inner city, gang courts, mandatory sentences and legal codes outlawing association to gangs — all measures to help the police protect society against a crime wave that was perceived to be destroying South Africa (Samara, 2003; Standing, 2006). This process seemed to gain momentum as there was now the political will to rename the South African Police Service as the South African Police Force and to finally settle the issue of police use of lethal force in favour of the police in relation to section 49 of the Criminal Procedure Act, which had been under constitutional court scrutiny for years. These initiatives made some commentators talk of a return to a pre-1994 authoritarian police state (Gumede-Johnson, 2011). However, Hornberger (2013: 599) argues that rather than being a return to the authoritarianism of the apartheid era, this state of affairs is more accurately described as a rapprochement between people and police. In keeping with the second logic, people want the police to employ violence — a reading that is supported by my own data from rural Mpumalanga (Jensen, 2009). In this way, the second logic seems to have gained the upper hand, as the South African population in general supported the reading and rationality of those arguing that the police be given the necessary means to stop the criminals. In the process, the urgent need to break with the past, fuelling the first logic of exceptionality, was severely undermined.

However, this has not remained unchallenged. In 2011, the weekly news-paper *Mail & Guardian* ran a series of articles that seemed to question the general acceptance of the dominance of the second logic. Human rights activists criticized the brutalization of trainee police officers (Gumede-Johnson, 2011); the ANC condemned police brutality during service delivery protests in the wake of an ICD report on an increase in police brutality (Ferreira, 2011); and in 2010 the ICD investigated police brutality and possible torture at a Cape Town police station (*Mail & Guardian*, 2010). In 2012 and 2013, following the brutal killing of thirty-four mine workers in the Marikana massacre and the torture and killing of a taxi driver, abhorrence of police brutality reached new heights, leading to the rehabilitation of the logic that stressed the urgent need to reform the police (*Business Report*, 2012; *The Guardian*, 2013). What is significant about these reports is not so much that they cite police violence — which is a regular occurrence — but that it is deemed problematic by the media and politicians alike. In this way, the first logic of exceptionality has retained its power as explanatory framework and as a template for action.

VICTIMHOOD AND EVERYDAY POLICE VIOLENCE

What emerges from the analysis above is that the two conflicting logics of exceptionality exist simultaneously and that the dominance of the one over the other shimmers in and out of focus throughout the post-apartheid period. The two logics imply different categories of victims. Whereas the first logic invokes victims of untransformed policing structures, the second alludes to 'citizens as crime victims' (Simon, 2007). In order to understand how the two logics co-exist, we need to pay close attention to the everyday practices of police violence against and/or in alleged protection of these victims. In this section, I explore practices of police violence; the invisibilization of illegitimate violence; the banality of violence; and the everyday policing of townships. This analysis reveals the discrepancies between lofty ideals and everyday practices, acts of bravery and idealism on the part of individual police officers and the commonplace and almost banal violence against certain groups.

Police Violence in South Africa

Police violence comes in many forms, from legitimate to illegitimate, to downright criminal. To examine the nature of police violence, I carried out a media study in 2006 of torture and cruel, inhuman and degrading treatment (CIDT) and punishment by the South African police (Dissel et al., 2009). Torture and CIDT are useful lenses through which to explore the conflicting logics as they are legal categories that exclude police crime and legitimate police violence, while focusing on practices most abhorred by proponents of the first logic of exceptionality. The UN Convention Against Torture (UNCAT), which includes CIDT, was one of the first conventions signed by South Africa to usher in a new beginning as envisaged by the first logic. In order to fall under the purview of the Convention, practices must fulfil four requirements: purpose (of extracting information, confessions or to intimidate); intention; severe suffering; and state involvement, consent or acquiescence. The criteria for CIDT are generally less rigid than for torture.[5]

---

5. For elaboration on definitions and history of torture, CIDT and conventions, see Cole (2009); Dissel et al. (2009); Nowak and McArthur (2008); Rejali (2003).

Although media reports are partial and sometimes problematic to use as data, the data obtained constitute an archive of violent, illegitimate state practices spanning a full year and covering most of South Africa.[6] This archive covered violent practices perpetrated by a number of different institutions (for example police, prisons, homes of safety, military, mental institutions and schools). In line with other reports about torture and CIDT (Nowak and McArthur, 2008), the police were responsible for the bulk of the incidents. We identified cases related to police interrogation, crowd control, police shooting, police assault, police detention and police crime. By far the most media attention was given to a few high-profile cases, where the police were under considerable pressure to produce results. It was also in these cases that some of the more blatant forms of torture were perpetrated. Most of these cases were the result of police interrogation. One such case was the 'Airport Heist'.

The airport heist case began as a crime story about a daring robbery of a plane at Oliver Tambo International Airport in Johannesburg, followed by an equally daring robbery where the recovered money was stolen from a police safe at Benoni Police Station, east of Johannesburg. Quickly, however, the case pointed to the involvement of police officers as perpetrators and colluders in the robberies. During the investigation two civilian witnesses, Frank Mampane and Solly Hangwane, died under mysterious circumstances after relatives alleged they had been tortured. Mampane had allegedly been doused with boiling water by police officers in his home immediately prior to his fatal arrest. Three police officers, Khomani Mashele, Paul Kgoedi and Serious Mthembi, were also interrogated during the investigation in ways that qualify as torture, including electric shocks. In a rather remarkable statement to investigating police officers during bail application, Judge Schutte warned the police not to harm the prisoners and not to interrogate them without the presence of their legal defence: '*Dit moet end kry*' (This must cease) (*Beeld*, 2006; *Saturday Star*, 2006a).[7]

---

6. The media review covered reports of practices that could be classified as torture and CIDT in thirty Afrikaans and English newspapers in 2006. For a number of reasons, it is problematic to use media reports to access information about torture and CIDT. Torture and CIDT are shrouded in secrecy and indifference. Journalists prioritize news they can identify with, of conflict, or news that is sensationalist, actual, newsworthy and exclusive (Schultz, 2007). Although torture and CIDT meet these news criteria, evidence of these practices is often difficult to obtain. Moreover in most cases of this study, the articles had been written soon after the alleged event, or during a trial, featuring mostly accusations. Only rarely did the news report a final verdict or finding on allegations of torture or ill-treatment. Despite these shortcomings, news reports provide one of the few avenues into understanding the nature of torture and CIDT in South Africa. Through the reports we access a variety of testimonies and stories. Unlike governing institutions like the ICD and the Judicial Inspectorate of Correctional Services (JICS), media reports cover a broader spectrum of cases and allow more voices, including those of victims, to be heard.

7. For additional reporting, see: *The Star* (2006); *Saturday Star* (2006b, 2006c).

The allegations, which attracted much attention during 2006, clearly qualify as torture, as they include boiling water thrown on suspects, threats to life, electrocution, beatings and finally murder. Media reports also covered illegitimate police violence exercised in crowd control, where the excessive use of force arguably constitutes CIDT (but not torture). We also identified cases involving unlawful police shooting as falling under the purview of the Convention, as well as several cases of police assault. Several cases dealt with crimes allegedly committed by the police, including domestic violence. Not all acts of police criminality fell within the purview of the Convention in terms of purpose, as they were often committed for personal enrichment or other criminal motives. However, cases where the police used their state authority to rob, steal or rape might still fall under the Convention.

Invisibility of Illegitimate Violence

Most of the cases in the media archive from 2006 qualify as CIDT rather than torture, but the line between these categories is notoriously difficult to draw, in many instances de facto rendering the violence invisible. Take the case of Portia Adams from Ruyterwacht in Cape Town. Portia went to the police station to report an assault but she herself ended up in police custody, as the police officer suspected that she had information about the whereabouts of her boyfriend. The police officer put Portia Adams into a male detention cell, and she was made to share the cell with her alleged attacker. She said afterwards, 'I was thinking, "Oh God, I'm going to die in here"'. According to Adams, she was released only when a female police officer found her in the cell.[8] Afterwards, she was left handcuffed in the charge office for hours while the police officer dealt with other complaints (*Saturday Cape Argus*, 2006; *Saturday Star*, 2006). After her release she went to the media with her story and the commanding officer at the police station promised to investigate. Regardless of the consequences, this kind of practice is clearly in contravention of the Convention that prohibits maltreating people to gain information about third parties. The apparently unlawful arrest and subsequent imprisonment with males, among them her attacker, would, given the frequent rapes in custody, be an extreme form of sexual harassment and threat to body and life, and could cause significant mental or psychological suffering. It is also in violation of international principles regarding the separation of female from male prisoners and of police rules regarding detention of suspects (see, for example, SAPS, 1999). Finally, Adams was made to stand handcuffed for hours in full view in the charge office. In terms of the Convention, all criteria are met: there was the intention and purpose

---

8. Personal blog, http://sooner67.blogspot.com/2006/01/woman-assaulted-then-put-in-jail-with-man-who-assaulted-her.html (accessed 12 October 2011).

of eliciting information of a third party; the impact was (potentially) very severe; and there was a state agent acting in an official capacity. Whether the incident qualified as torture or CIDT is difficult to evaluate but it clearly falls within the ambit of UNCAT.

While the officer may not have been aware that he was committing acts that fall under the purview of the UNCAT, he must have known that his actions deviated from standard procedure, at least when his female colleague released Portia. The discussions illustrate the difficulty of determining whether a case constitutes torture, CIDT or whether it is just part of what the South African police do on any given day. In any case, the ordeal of Portia Adams is a far cry from how we intuitively perceive torture and CIDT, which is often associated with white police officers in dark places torturing black activists. Portia did not qualify in that respect, not least because she lives in a neighbourhood where gang violence is a frequent occurrence and where she in all likelihood was identified as complicit in the activities of one of the gangs or other criminal elements. Under the second logic informed by the crime wave, she was a perpetrator (by proxy) rather than a victim in need of protection. The maltreatment that she suffered, to the point of qualifying as torture, was somehow invisibilized and even rendered legitimate.

The Banality of Police Violence

The forms of torture and ill-treatment included in our archive range from sustained and systematic torture of suspects in high-profile cases, callous treatment of the homeless or the vulnerable, use of excessive force in arresting suspects or volatile crowd situations, to dehumanizing and degrading treatment in detention. What also emerges from this study is how the use and abuse of force seems to have permeated the culture and conduct of the police to the point of being banal and ordinary (see also Vigneswaran and Hornberger, 2009).

What is striking is the frequent and total disregard of the police for those they are meant to serve and the almost absolute certainty of being in the right, to the extent of being above the law. In one case, a Bolebedu (Limpopo province) Captain Crime Stop police officer (appointed to do public outreach and crime prevention work with children) was asked to drive two young girls home after they participated in a radio interview. Along the way, the policeman, accompanied by a police reservist, dragged the older thirteen-year old girl from the police van, raped her, and then proceeded to drive the two girls home, after which he returned to the station (*Citizen*, 2006). This case suggests either absolute impunity or a belief on the part of the police officers that their actions were somehow legitimate.

The case of Jonas, a Congolese national, illustrates a similar disregard for life and limb by the police (*Cape Argus*, 2006). Jonas was on his way home from his job in Salt River, Cape Town when he was stopped by a car and ordered to get in by one of the female occupants. When he refused and pushed the woman away, she drew a gun and identified herself as a police officer. The officers took Jonas to the Woodstock police station where the two female police officers beat him while male officers watched. After a while, they demanded that he strip and proceeded to spray his entire body with pepper spray, notably the genitals. He was subsequently thrown into jail, where he spent another fifteen hours, most of the time naked. The officers did not ask his name, charge him or to take down an affidavit. He was simply released.

In both the rape case and the maltreatment of Jonas, the victims were vulnerable. In South Africa, which is a virulently sexist society, women are often considered as mere objects of sexual gratification (Sideris, 2007). Migrants, who are often referred to as 'ATMs' because money might be extorted from them, are habitual victims of street violence by police officers and citizens alike (Hassim et al., 2008; Madsen, 2004). Incidents like these were commonplace in 2006. However, there were also incidents of bravery. The police officer who imprisoned Portia Adams was challenged by a colleague and the case was investigated. In the case of the thirteen-year old girl, the policeman was later dismissed and charged with rape (*Sowetan*, 2006). In Jonas's case, as he was released, another police officer from the same station noticed his bruising and helped him lay charges against the officers who assaulted him. This suggests that in spite of the culture of impunity and violence within the police that is animated by the second logic, parts of the police system do function in accordance with the rules and conventions central to the first logic.

Everyday Police Practice and the War on the Criminal

The ambivalent relationship between the first and the second logic of exceptionality could also be found in the everyday police practice that I recorded during fieldwork in Cape Town and in rural Mpumalanga. Throughout my engagements with the police, they expressed considerable ambiguity towards transitional justice and the Bill of Rights. In a conversation I had with an officer in 1999, he remarked:

> The constitution that we have is a beautiful document. Everyone says that it is the best constitution in the world. But maybe South Africa is not ready for it yet. Because it allows the criminals to walk free and we can do nothing about it. So yes, I would say that it is too early for South Africa for all these rights.

The argument is that the constitution makes policing impossible. However, on closer examination, it is clear that police officers are not only expressing the impotence they feel in combating crime; they also actively bend or break the rules. As I have discussed elsewhere (Jensen, 2008), this might take the form of classifying cases according to perceptions of relevance, dodging cases and, most importantly, manifest itself through the use of violence.

Most police officers were adamant that violence was a necessary aspect in policing the townships. On one occasion, in an attempt to explain this need for violence to me, a police officer asked if I could hear muffled cries from the cells. I listened, and said that I could. 'It's a boy who stole some money from the neighbour. They found the money in his school bag. [The mother] has had problems with him before. He won't listen. So she brought him here, so that we could give him a beating'. I asked, somewhat taken aback, whether this was normal practice. He affirmed that it was.

Later I asked a sergeant, who remarked: 'I don't like doing it, and I will never do it in front of the father. If the father is there he must do it; so I don't take the authority away from him. But if they want me to, I will do it'. What was striking about the incident was that nobody seemed to take much notice of the beating; they were simply attending to their normal routines. This suggests that the co-existence of human rights norms and the 'need' for violence is made possible by silencing and ignoring the violence. As long as everybody pretended that it wasn't happening, there was no conflict between the two logics. The mother herself had wanted it; indeed many South Africans subscribe to the view that violence is a normal and necessary part of dealing with misbehaving children and youth (Morrell, 2001). Hence, the violent actions of the officers were deemed acceptable. It is only when these practices are rendered publicly visible that the contradictions emerge. This happened in a similar case, reported by the local media, where a school principal took seven boys to the same police station where the mother had taken her boy to be 'set straight'. According to the news story, the police officers told the principal to leave and let them handle the boys. In the following hours, the seven boys were severely beaten and ridiculed. After this incident, the parents of the children went to the police to complain about the maltreatment of their children. The station commander 'confirmed the incident', and assured the parents that 'we will look into internal disciplinary action once the investigation has been completed' (*Sunday Independent*, 2000).

Both logics are at play in these cases, suggesting that this practice was indeed common: there's an acknowledgement of human rights but also a sense that violence is necessary and legitimate, as evidenced by the approval and participation of the mother in the disciplining of her son, as well as the disciplinary actions visited upon the erring police officers. A case from our media archive serves to illustrate this. A young boy from northern KwaZulu-Natal was reportedly severely beaten and strangled by a school principal, a senior police officer and a member of the community policing forum, which led to his hospitalization. This happened after he was accused of stealing other pupils' lunch boxes. His mother later complained about the treatment of her son (*Sunday Tribune*, 2006). In this case, all the requirements and criteria for the case to constitute torture apply. State agents (the police officer, principal and community policing forum member) severely maltreated the child with the purpose and intent to punish him. It is reasonable to believe that while the three men of the rural elite knew their actions were wrong legally, nothing suggests that they saw themselves as being morally in the wrong. The beating of the child arguably was seen by them as necessary.

All these cases of police violence against the youth are suggestive of an inter-generational war between the state (and its allies) and the youth of the city and countryside. This war is to a large extent absent from media scrutiny except for cases like the above that involve children. In our sample of articles from 2006, only one article relates to the often dramatic confrontations between the police and township youth, especially street gangs. The article described a shoot-out between the police and a gang in the Cape Flats in which an innocent woman was caught in the crossfire (*Die Burger*, 2006). This one incident is not in any way indicative of the number of violent confrontations between the young men of the townships in major urban centres and a police force charged with the responsibility to wage war on crime and to exhibit zero tolerance (Altbeker, 2005). According to Malose Langa from the Centre for the Study of Violence and Reconciliation, a prominent human rights NGO, young men are habitually beaten up and even electrocuted by the police in Kagiso in the West Rand of Johannesburg (Langa, 2011). Elsewhere in the Johannesburg area, police are reported to have used plastic bags filled with pepper spray on suspects in order to punish and elicit information from them (Matshedisho, 2009: 52). In my own work, I describe the violent and humiliating encounters between police, young men and residents during raids in Cape Town (Jensen, 2008: 120–23). To my knowledge, none of these incidents was reported or made news in any way, apart from being published in obscure academic texts. This form of violence was generally legitimated by the second logic of exceptionality, and only rarely were such incidents brought to public light.

While the second logic does seem to prevail, the first logic of exceptionality is still alive and police need to negotiate between the two. Elsewhere (Jensen, 2009), I draw a distinction between an enchanted (transitional justice) vision of the police versus a practical (everyday) vision of the police. In order to uphold the vision of a transformed police force in accordance with the first logic, the police refrain from acknowledging the transgressions of the legal codes in the process of fighting the second crisis. This is also illustrated in the following case from the rural hinterlands of Mpumalanga involving police reactions to acts of mob violence against suspected criminals. A band of robbers had been intercepting and robbing motorists over the course of several weekends. In the end, residents of the village caught the gang and brought them to their own form of justice. Parallel to dealing with the alleged criminals, residents had also organized a huge demonstration demanding that the police take action. I asked a police officer to comment on the demonstration: 'What demonstration?', he asked. 'The one 5,000 people took part in the other day', I helped him. 'Oh that one – no, I wasn't working that day so I didn't know about it'. Somewhat surprised by his reluctance to acknowledge the event, I asked why they hadn't arrested someone. He deliberated, almost with himself, back and forth on the issue of police intervention in relation to the demonstration and the vigilante actions taken by residents:

> We don't fold our hands. We attend to complaints and open dockets. We arrest people from the community if we have to. To me, crime is crime and nobody is above the law. If there is a crime, there are procedures to be followed. These people took the law into their own hands and we investigated it. If it ever transpires that one, two, three were involved, we have no choice but to open a case. But we must understand that people are fed up with crime and violence. For me, it was the right thing they did. It was a good thing. But law is law.

He did not know about the demonstration because he was not present in his capacity as police officer. The point here is that there are different ways of seeing. Only when one wears a uniform or is on duty does one, to paraphrase James Scott (1998), have to see like a state. At the same time, the officer invokes the first logic which he is able to maintain because the vigilante practices and police knowledge of it were made invisible. The latter serves to legitimize him as a police officer within his own community concerned with the second crisis, while the former satisfies the (national and global) transitional justice proponents.

CONFLICTING LOGICS OF EXCEPTIONALITY AND THEIR DIVERGENT BEGINNINGS

In this chapter, I have examined how we might understand police violence across two conflicting but intertwined logics of exceptionality referring to two different sets of extraordinary circumstances: the urgency to transform the South African police and the urgency to combat the crime wave. On an abstract, general level, the two logics seem to complement each other. However, on the level of everyday and ordinary implementation, they are diametrically opposed to each other. Although both the untransformed police and the crime wave were said to endanger the transition to democracy, the imagined new beginnings emerging from the different logics of exceptionality were radically different. In one version of a new beginning, the police would be accountable and service minded, as opposed to before. In the other version, a dedicated police force would fight crime at every turn. While the antagonistic relationship between the different logics certainly exists, especially on the discursive level, I argue that both logics failed to fundamentally restructure the discourses and practices around policing. In this way, the logics of exceptionality as explanatory frameworks shimmer in and out of focus in ways that are interdependent as well as contemporaneous. In line with Anders' and Zenker's Introduction, the contemporaneity of the conflicting logics implies the co-existence of several extraordinary measures rather than the absolute supremacy of one state of exception over another, as much of the literature that draws on the work of Giorgio Agamben suggests.[9] Likewise, the contemporaneity of conflicting logics also implies the co-existence of very different versions of justice. Justice under the first logic is freedom from state violence, whereas under the second logic it is about freedom from crime perpetrated against the 'citizen as crime victim' by the poor as proxy for the criminal. In line with how Anders and Zenker invoke the conceptual pair of the ordinary and the exceptional, we might say that crime is worrisome under the first logic, but not out of the ordinary, whereas police violence must be addressed through exceptional means. Under the second logic, policing needs to be transformed, but it is crime, rather than 'ordinary' police violence, that demands an exceptional response.

In the first part of this chapter, I traced the simultaneous existence of the conflicting logics from the democratic transition in 1994 until the present on the discursive and political level. From a dominant beginning, where human rights were operationalized through transitional justice mechanisms, the first logic lost ground to the imperative of combating crime. While the general trend has been towards privileging the second logic, there are also clear traces and remnants of the first, for instance in the government critiques of the brutal policing of service delivery and labour protests and the Marikana massacre — practices that have been likened to apartheid policing. In the second part of the chapter, I discussed police violence with reference to media and ethnographic archives. I showed the persistent, often invisible, occurrence of police violence. On the one hand, I focused on how the violence was interpreted and rendered meaningful through the two logics while on the other hand, I illustrated the extent to which the violent acts are also banal and ordinary.

Through this analysis it became apparent that certain groups of people are more likely to be victimized than others. These include women, migrants and poor young men, where the latter two are perceived to pose a significant threat to the safety and security of South African society. Their victimization is legitimized under the second logic of exceptionality in order to protect the generalized 'citizen as crime victim'. As evidenced by our media archive, police violence against service delivery protesters has been widely condemned, as have the victimization of migrants and the brutalization of children. The targeting of and violence against rural and township youth by police and vigilante structures, on the other hand, have received very little attention and were mostly visible in obscure ethnographic archives.

Throughout my analysis, the two conflicting logics coexist but they also advance and recede. A police officer helped Jonas, the Congolese migrant, to lay a complaint against his colleagues. The policeman who raped the girl was discharged. The police promised to investigate the maltreatment of the seven school children who had been 'disciplined' by the police. Portia's

---

9. For a critique of Agamben's influence on the study of human rights and international law, see Heins (2005).

imprisonment was investigated. In all these cases, the violence legitimized by the second logic was reconfigured within the first. The subjectivity of Jonas, read through the second logic as a problematic foreigner, was recast by human rights discourses into a hapless victim of impunity. The seven thieving and misbehaving township youth were reconfigured as children in need of protection. Portia's subjectivity changed from one consorting with criminal elements (her boyfriend) into a 'slightly built' mother attacked by a 'huge guy' and left to be raped in a 'tiny, filthy, windowless cell'.[10] In this way, the same incident travels from one logic to the next and testifies to the fundamental permeability and instability of logics.

This analysis has, or should have, ramifications for the ways in which human rights and transitional justice organizations work to transform the violent practices of the police. Transitional justice mechanisms were associated with the first logic of exceptionality as it provided a (human rights) language and a framework through which to transform the state towards a new beginning. In this way, transitional justice mechanisms dominated the political field for a while until they were seen as obstacles to addressing the crisis of crime. Along with a call for institutional change, the transitional justice discourse pertaining to security reform often posited the police as ignorant subjects in need of serious personal and attitudinal change (Marks, 2005). While transitional justice organizations lamented the crime wave, they arguably failed to understand and take into account the deep-seated belief in the necessity of the use of violence shared by police and public alike (Hornberger, 2013). It was not that the police were ignorant of human rights; they just did not agree with the basic assumptions of transitional justice mechanisms. They also did not believe that they themselves, rather than the township youngsters they dealt with in everyday encounters, were the problem. Again this view was shared by most of the public. This should of course not distract transitional justice organizations from criticizing the government and police while making constructive inputs. However, it does suggest a need for transitional justice organizations to engage in a dialogue with those who hold these assumptions and are guided in their actions by the second logic of exceptionality.

Secondly, the analysis illustrates the importance of deconstructing labels and taken-for-granted categories, including the ones associated with transitional justice mechanisms. As long as the police are successful in categorizing people in terms of the second logic of exceptionality, police violence will remain legitimate. However, when the subjectivities of people are reconfigured, the moral claims of the police that they are protecting 'citizens as crime victims' are subverted. Petite women, girls, children, hard-working people, miners and political protesters are not acceptable targets of police

---

10. Personal blog, http://sooner67.blogspot.com/2006/01/woman-assaulted-then-put-in-jail-with-man-who-assaulted-her.html (accessed 12 October 2011).

violence. For the public and politicians, they share an uncanny resemblance to ordinary citizens which suggests that anybody could be a victim of police violence. However, each of them can so easily be cast as problematic, especially if they are associated with troublesome rural and township youth who can be abused seemingly at will, and who will seldom complain. Rather than only focusing on institutions, codes and difficult legal arguments, transitional justice and human rights organizations need to be of assistance also to people classified as threats to polite society. Only then can we imagine a new beginning that does not marginalize the weak once again.

REFERENCES

Altbeker, A. (2005) *The Dirty Work of Democracy: A Year on the Streets with the SAPS*. Cape Town: Jonathan Ball Publishers.

Anders, G. and O. Zenker (2014) 'Transition and Justice: An Introduction', *Development and Change* 45(3): 395–414.

Bailey, D. (2001) *Democratizing the Police Abroad: What to Do and How to Do It*. Washington, DC: US Department of Justice.

Beeld (2006) 'Polisiekluis: Landdros Looi Gesloer' ['Police Safe: Judge Criticizes Delays'], 9 June.

Die Burger (2006) 'Vrou Kry R16,600 by Polisie ná Skietery' ['Woman Receives R16,600 from Police after Shooting'], 27 May.

Business Report (2012) 'Lonmin an Example of Exploitation', 17 August. http://www.iol.co.za/business/companies/lonmin-an-example-of-exploitation-1.1365221

Cape Argus (2006) 'Refugee Says Police Beat Him Up', 10 November.

Cavell, S. (1988) *In Quest of the Ordinary: Lines of Skepticism and Romanticism*. Chicago, IL: Chicago University Press.

Citizen (2006) 'Captain Crime Stop Rape Cry', 16 March.

Cole, D. (2009) *Torture Memos: Rationalizing the Unthinkable*. New York: New Press.

Dissel, A., S. Jensen and S. Roberts (2009) 'Torture in South Africa: Exploring Torture, Cruel, Inhuman and Degrading Treatment through the Media'. Johannesburg: Centre for the Study of Violence and Reconciliation.

Ferreira, E. (2011) 'ICD: Rise in Police Abuse at Service Delivery Protests', *Mail & Guardian* 14 June. http://mg.co.za/article/2011--06--14-icd-rise-in-police-abuse-at-service-delivery-protests (accessed 14 October 2011).

Goodale, M. and S.E. Merry (2007) *The Practice of Human Rights: Tracking Law Between the Global and the Local*. Cambridge: Cambridge University Press.

The Guardian (2013) 'South African Police Suspended over Death of Man "Dragged Behind Van"', 28 February. www.guardian.co.uk/world/2013/feb/28/man-dies-south-africa-police-van

Gumede-Johnson, K. (2011) 'Police Training: Brutality Exposed', *Mail & Guardian* 3 June. http://mg.co.za/article/2011--06--03-saps-the-strong-arm-of-force (accessed 7 October 2011).

Hassim, S., T. Kupe and E. Worby (2008) *Go Home or Die Here: Violence, Xenophobia and the Reinvention of Difference in South Africa*. Johannesburg: University of the Witwatersrand Press.

Heins, V. (2005) 'Giorgio Agamben and the Current State of Affairs in Humanitarian Law and Human Rights Policy', *German Law Journal* 6: 845–60.

Hornberger, J. (2010) 'Human Rights and Policing: Exigency or Incongruence', *Annual Review of Law and Social Science* 6: 259–83.

Hornberger, J. (2011) *Policing and Human Rights: The Meaning of Violence and Justice in the Everyday Policing of Johannesburg*. London: Routledge.
Hornberger, J. (2013) 'From Colonel to Commissioner to Colonel: On the Popular State of Policing in South Africa', *Law and Social Inquiry* 38(3): 598–614.
Jefferson, A. and S. Jensen (eds) (2009) *State Violence and Human Rights: State Officials in the South*. London: Routledge.
Jensen, S. (2005) 'From Development to Security: Political Subjectivity and the South African Transition', *Development and Change* 36(3): 551–70.
Jensen, S. (2008) *Gangs, Politics and Dignity in Cape Town*. Oxford: James Currey.
Jensen, S. (2009) 'The Vision of the State: Audiences, Enchantments and Policing in South Africa', in A. Jefferson and S. Jensen (eds) *State Violence and Human Rights: State Officials in the South*, pp. 60–78 London: Routledge.
Jensen, S. (2010) 'The Security and Development Nexus in Cape Town: War on Gangs, Counterinsurgency and Citizenship', *Security Dialogue* 41(1): 77–98.
Jensen, S. and H. Ronsbo (2014) *Histories of Victimhood*. Philadelphia, PA: Penn University Press.
Kelsall, T. (2005) 'Truth, Lies, Ritual: Preliminary Reflections on the Truth and Reconciliation Commission in Sierra Leone', *Human Rights Quarterly* 27(2): 361–91.
Langa, M. (2011) *Profiling Torture and CIDT in the Hands of the Police: A Case Study of Kagiso Township, Gauteng*. Johannesburg: Centre for the Study of Violence and Reconciliation.
Madsen, M. (2004) 'Living for Home: Policing Immorality among Undocumented Migrants in Johannesburg', *African Studies* 63(2): 173–92.
Mail & Guardian (2000) 'Tshwete Gets Tough on Crime', 10 November.
Mail & Guardian (2010) 'ICD Probes Torture Complaints against Bellville Cops', 16 August. mg.co.za/article/2010--08--16-icd-probes-torture-complaints-against-bellville-cops
Marinovich, G. and G. Nicolson (2013) 'Marikana Massacre: SAPS, Lonmin, Ramaphosa and Time for Blood. Miners' Blood', *Daily Maverick* 24 October. http://www.dailymaverick.co.za/article/2013-10-24-marikana-massacre-saps-lonmin-ramaphosa-time-for-blood-miners-blood/ (accessed 18 November 2013).
Marks, M. (2005) *Transforming the Robocops: Changing Police in South Africa*. Durban: University of Kwazulu-Natal Press.
Matshedisho, R. (2009) '"We Must Fight Them!" Police Violence, Torture and Brutality', in D. Vigneswaran and J. Hornberger (eds) 'Beyond Good Cop/Bad Cop: Understanding Informality and Police Corruption in South Africa', pp. 52–55. Johannesburg: FMSP, Wits University.
Merry, S. (2006) 'Transnational Human Rights and Local Activism: Mapping the Middle', *American Anthropologist* 108(1): 52–65.
Morrell, R. (2001) 'Corporal Punishment and Masculinity in South African Schools', *Men and Masculinities* 4(2): 140–57.
Nowak, M. and E. McArthur (2008) *The United Nations Convention Against Torture: A Commentary*. Oxford: Oxford University Press.
Rejali, D. (2008) *Torture and Democracy*. Princeton, NJ: Princeton University Press.
Samara, T.R. (2003) 'State Security in Transition: The War on Crime in Post-Apartheid South Africa', *Social Identities* 9(2): 277–312.
SAPS (1999) 'Policy on the Prevention of Torture and the Treatment of Persons in Custody of the South African Police Service'. Pretoria: South Africa Police Service.
Saturday Cape Argus (2006) 'Woman Held in Men's Cell "to Sue"', 28 January.
Saturday Star (2006a) 'Witness's Death Mystery Deepens', 24 June.
Saturday Star (2006b) 'Death after Police-safe Robbery still Baffles', 1 July.
Saturday Star (2006c) 'Must it Take a Thief to Catch a Thief?', 17 June.
Saturday Star (2006d) 'Woman Locked in Cell with Four Men', 28 January.
Schultz, I. (2007) 'The Journalistic Gut Feeling', *Journalism Practice* 1(2): 190–207.
Scott, J. (1998) *Seeing Like a State: How Certain Schemes to Improve the Human Condition Have Failed*. New Haven, CT: Yale University Press.

Shaw, R. (2010) 'Linking Justice with Transitional Justice: Ex-combatants and the Sierra Leone Experiment', in R. Shaw and L. Waldorf (eds) *Localizing Transitional Justice: Interventions and Priorities after Mass Violence*, pp. 3–27. Stanford, CA: Stanford University Press.

Shaw, R. and L. Waldorf (2010) *Localizing Transitional Justice: Interventions and Priorities after Mass Violence*. Stanford, CA: Stanford University Press.

Sideris, T. (2007) 'Post-Apartheid South Africa: Gender, Rights and the Politics of Recognition', in L. Buur, S. Jensen and F. Stepputat (eds) *The Security Development Nexus, Expressions of Sovereignty and Securitization in Southern Africa*, pp. 233–50. Cape Town: HSRC Press.

Simon, J. (2007) *Governing through Crime: How the War on Crime Transformed American Democracy and Created a Culture of Fear*. Oxford: Oxford University Press.

Sowetan (2006) 'Cop Charged with Rape Fired', 19 October.

Standing, A. (2006) 'Organised Crime: A Study from Cape Flats'. Pretoria: Institute for Security Studies.

The Star (2006) 'Fear as Another Airport Heist Suspect is Slain', 22 June.

Sunday Independent (2000) 'Pupils Lay Charges after "Lesson" from Police', 27 October.

Sunday Tribune (2006) 'Beaten Pupil Fights for Life', 5 February.

Teitel, R. (2000) *Transitional Justice*. Oxford: Oxford University Press.

Teitel, R. (2003) 'Transitional Justice Genealogy', *Harvard Human Rights Journal* 16: 69–94.

Vigneswaran, D. and J. Hornberger (2009) 'Beyond Good Cop/Bad Cop: Understanding Informality and Police Corruption in South Africa'. FMSP Research Report. Johannesburg: FMSP, Wits University.

Wilson, R. (2006) 'The Social Life of Rights', *American Anthropologist* 108(1): 77–83.

Zenker, O. (2011) 'Land Restitution and Transitional Justice in Post-Apartheid South Africa'. Working Paper No. 134. Halle: Max Planck Institute for Social Anthropology.

5

The 2011 Toilet Wars in South Africa: Justice and Transition between the Exceptional and the Everyday after Apartheid

Steven Robins

INTRODUCTION

In the run-up to South Africa's 2011 local government elections, protests against unenclosed toilets in an informal settlement in Khayelitsha in Cape Town were widely reported in the media as the 'Toilet Elections' and the 'Toilet Wars'. The widely circulated media images of unenclosed modern, porcelain toilets struck a raw nerve as the nation was preparing to vote: for a few weeks running up to the elections, the images of these open toilets produced responses of shock from politicians and ordinary citizens. Both the Democratic Alliance (DA), the political party in control of the Western Cape Province, and the ruling African National Congress (ANC) government were politically compromised by scandals about the construction of such toilets in townships in the provinces that they controlled. The spectacular image of the open toilet created the conditions for the framing of sanitation as a matter of concern for politicians, activists, journalists, citizens and, most significantly, judges. As will be discussed later, in the domain of the courts, this spectacle of the open toilet came to stand in for the indignities and injustices of daily life under apartheid as well as the limits of transformation after apartheid.

The Toilet Wars in the Western Cape and recent forms of social movement activism around sanitation seem to have contributed towards a post-apartheid 'politics of shit' that has been visible in 'service delivery protests'. These protests recently involved not only burning barricades, but also the destruction of toilets and the tossing of bags of human faeces onto township streets, highways and the steps of the provincial legislature building, as well as — in June 2013 — at the vehicle convoy of Western Cape Premier Helen Zille (*Cape Argus*, 2013; *Cape Times*, 2013). A few weeks later, the 'poo protestors' dumped containers of human waste in the departure section of Cape Town International Airport. They were arrested and charged under the Civil Aviation Act for delaying flights while cleaners worked around the

The paper has benefited from the helpful insights and comments of Andrew Spiegel, Olaf Zenker and Gerhard Anders. I would also like to thank *Development and Change*'s anonymous reviewers for their constructive suggestions and comments.

Transition and Justice: Negotiating the Terms of New Beginnings in Africa, First Edition.
Edited by Gerhard Anders and Olaf Zenker.

clock to get rid of the waste and its lingering smell. These activists had literally dragged the stench from the urban periphery and its informal settlements
to the seat of political and economic power in the city centre (see Robins,
2013a, 2013b).

Figure 1. Protest action in July 2013 in which containers from portable flush
toilets are flung upon cars driving along Cape Town's N2 highway with the aim
of drawing attention to disparities in sanitation resources in Cape Town.

Source: Independent Newspapers.

Prior to the Toilet Wars, the shocking sanitation conditions in informal
settlements seldom made it into the mainstream media or national political
discourse. This observation raises a number of questions that this chapter
seeks to address. Firstly, what do these protest actions about poor sanitation,
and the increased visibility of everyday realities of structural poverty, reveal
about broader questions relating to 'transitional justice' in South Africa?
Secondly, in what ways has this ongoing politicization of issues such as sanitation challenged the dominant transitional justice narrative — that the 1994
elections which brought the ANC and Nelson Mandela to power constituted
a 'new beginning' characterized by the miraculous birth of a democratic
nation state? (See Anders and Zenker, 2014—the Introduction to this book.)
    The politicization of sanitation — for instance, in the form of the Toilet
Wars, the emptying of bags of excrement in public spaces in protest, and
social movement activism around these issues — suggests that transitional
justice is going to continue to be a protracted and messy process involving,
amongst other things, the systemic reform of the mundane conditions of
structural poverty. Unlike the human rights-based framework of transitional
justice that underpinned the Truth and Reconciliation Commission (TRC),
issues such as sanitation, housing and public education can only be addressed
by long-term state interventions at a systemic level. Conventional transitional
justice mechanisms such as commissions, courts and tribunals are seldom
able to adequately address these structural problems and inequalities (see
Anders and Zenker, 2014). For instance, the TRC focused on narrowly
framed gross human rights violations, defined in terms of political violence,
torture, abduction, murder and assault, to the exclusion of everyday violence

and more systemic violations such as daily racial discrimination in housing, land, health, education and numerous other domains. It is precisely the gaps in these transitional justice approaches that have necessitated the emergence of new forms of social activism. This contribution will show how sanitation activists have recognized this reality and responded by critically engaging with the state in order to lobby and pressure it to meet its constitutionally enshrined obligations to its citizens in terms of housing, education, sanitation and land restitution. This is a very different understanding of social justice than either the revolutionary rhetoric and practices of the anti-apartheid struggle era, or more conventional transitional justice approaches, which tend to focus on commissions and courts to establish peace building and new political beginnings in post-conflict settings in Africa (Anders and Zenker, 2014).

The chapter will use the Toilet Wars controversy to draw attention to what at first glance appear to be two distinct and contradictory political logics: first, the 'politics of the spectacle' with its association with styles of popular resistance and the exceptionality of state violence and injustice during apartheid; and second, a 'politics of the ordinary' that I describe here as 'slow activism'.[1] Whereas the former has to contend with the difficulties of sustaining media and public interest in the drama of the spectacle — and in the process often obscures the more ordinary and systemic forms of injustice — the latter has to make 'ordinary suffering' and systemic injustices politically legible to the state, the media and the wider public. The chapter will also draw attention to the ways in which proponents of slow activism may also tactically deploy the politics of the spectacle such as toilet queue protests (see below) in order to make legible these mundane realities of structural violence and poverty. In other words, although these two logics may at times appear to be distinct and contradictory, NGOs, social movements, trade unions and community-based organizations often selectively draw on both of them. It will become apparent that social justice activism that is concerned with long-term conditions of structural poverty is unlikely to find conventional transitional justice concepts and mechanisms appropriate to the task. It will be argued here that the political logic of the exception, which underpins both the concepts and mechanisms of transitional justice *and* the politics of the spectacle can, under particular circumstances, come to stand in stark contrast to the logic of the ordinary that underlies the structural violence of the everyday that social movements such as the Social Justice Coalition have tackled through their practices of slow activism and what I refer to as 'transitional social justice'.

---

1. I use this term to refer to contemporary NGO and social movement tactics that seek to render as politically legible the normalized and taken-for-granted daily realities of structural violence and racialized poverty.

MAKING HUMAN WASTE POLITICALLY LEGIBLE

In February 2011, I joined a group of American exchange students who visited the social movement for the urban poor, Abahlali baseMjondolo, in 'QQ Section', an informal settlement in Khayelitsha on the outskirts of Cape Town. Abahlali-Western Cape had been in the news in September and October 2010 as a result of its almost daily erection of barricades in Khayelitsha, and its calls for popular protests to render Cape Town ungovernable until the City management responded to service delivery needs in informal settlements. One of the leaders of the movement, Mzonke Poni, accompanied the exchange students on a walk through QQ Section. He stopped in front of a large mound of garbage and began to speak about daily conditions in the informal settlement. He told the students that residents had to relieve themselves using buckets and plastic bags, and how they would throw these bags, 'flying toilets', in the direction of a wetlands area next to the settlement where it was not possible to build houses.[2] Poni also told the students that residents walked long distances to request to use the toilets of shebeen owners and residents who lived at the adjacent formal housing scheme called Q Section. Sometimes they were charged to use these toilets, and many residents could not afford to pay these toilet fees. The students were overwhelmed both by Poni's accounts of daily conditions and by the pungent stench coming from the nearby piles of waste. Poni commented on the students' discomfort and pointed out to them that QQ residents have to endure this on a daily basis.

Having recently visited an informal settlement in Khayelitsha called RR Section, where the Social Justice Coalition (SJC) had managed to get the City of Cape Town to improve sanitation infrastructure, I too was shocked by the sight and smell of huge heaps of uncollected garbage. What neither the students nor I could have anticipated during our visit in February 2011 was that a national controversy about unenclosed toilets was about to explode in the run-up to the May 2011 elections. We could also not have anticipated the faeces-flinging protests that ANC Youth League (ANCYL) and community activists in Khayelitsha would resort to in June 2013, in the run-up to the 2014 national elections. These dramatic protests were staged against the DA-controlled city and provincial government's rollout of portable toilets rather than the permanent flush toilets demanded by residents of Cape Town's informal settlements. The ANC activists, including the former ANC Councillor Andile Lili who had been at the centre of the 2011 Toilet Wars,

---

2. Despite the target of completely eradicating the bucket system by 2007, there were still an estimated 200,000 bucket toilets in municipalities throughout the country in that year. In addition, there were over 1 million households, or 2 per cent of households in South Africa, without any toilet facilities in 2009 (The Municipal Outreach Project, 2009).

mobilized Khayelitsha residents against the provision of portable toilets. This was part of an emerging 'politics of shit' that shocked the political establishment and was even deemed unacceptable by the ANC leadership, which threatened these activists with disciplinary action.

Notwithstanding concerted efforts by social movement activists from organizations such as the SJC and Abahlali to draw attention to ongoing sanitation disasters in many informal settlements, prior to 2011, toilets and sanitation were not considered to be proper party political concerns. Instead, they were submerged and subsumed under the vague and technicist concept of 'service delivery'. Although activists and the media periodically reported on practices of open defecation, the bucket system, or the fact that large numbers of poor people have to use plastic bags to relieve themselves, these kinds of sanitation concerns did not enter into party political campaigns or mainstream political discourse. There was something quite extraordinary and shocking about the mass media image of the unenclosed modern porcelain toilet that captured the attention of politicians, activists and citizens in 2011. What the spectacle of the open toilet obscured, however, was the very ordinary, if not banal, slow activism of SJC activists who had, over a number of years, patiently lobbied and pressured the City government to respond to the absence of any budget for the maintenance, cleaning and monitoring of communal toilets in informal settlements in Cape Town. On 3 October 2011 the SJC announced that they had finally managed to persuade the Office of Cape Town Mayor Patricia de Lille to make available R 138 million for janitorial services for sanitation facilities in informal settlements. In May 2013 these janitors, who were employed by a company contracted by the City of Cape Town municipality to clean and maintain the toilets in informal settlements in Khayelitsha, were dumping bags of faeces and garbage on the highway in protest against labour conditions.

This chapter is concerned with understanding the complex relationship between this spectacular politics of shit and the slow, patient sanitation activism of the SJC. It is also concerned with why, until quite recently, toilets and 'shit matters' remained so tightly confined to the private domain of the home and seemed to resist becoming matters of public concern. These questions are addressed in relation to the moment in 2011 when it seemed as if the toilet had indeed become imbued with political and juridical meanings about race, dignity and privacy, meanings that far exceeded the functional utility of this mundane object. The public scandal of the open toilets was of such a magnitude that it prompted Tokyo Sexwale, the Minister for Human Settlements, to announce in September 2011 that he was appointing Winnie Mandela to head an eleven-member national task team which he had commissioned to investigate open toilets in poor communities throughout the country. Announcing the composition and scope of the task team to the media, the Minister stated: 'The sordid chapter [of the open toilets] must be brought to an end' (*Business Day*, 2011).

Figure 2. Open toilet in Makhaza township in Khayelitsha.

Source: Independent Newspapers.

Figure 3. Mandisa Feni of Site C, Khayelitsha, sits on a portable toilet on the steps of the provincial legislature. She is one of the many poo protesters who, in June 2013, dragged portable toilet containers of human waste from the informal settlements on the urban margins to the provincial legislature in Cape Town's city centre.

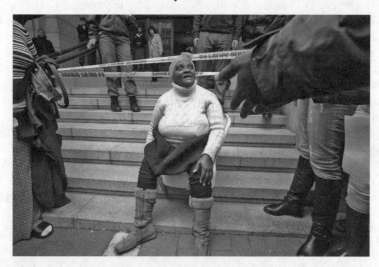

Source: Independent Newspapers.

As will become clear, the Toilet Wars catalysed public disputes that found expression in protests as well as letters to the press, court judgements, media reportage, Internet blogs and other outlets. The controversy entered a variety of legal and political settings and discursive fields: the Western Cape High Court, the Human Rights Commission, party politics, social movement activism, popular protests against poor 'service delivery', and the mass media. The controversy became a particularly productive site for mass mediated processes of contestation, definition and boundary-making by a variety of actors and networks, including bloggers, journalists, newspaper columnists and letter writers, politicians, NGOs, social movements, community residents, activists, state officials, judges, academics and many others. So what did this spectacle of the open toilet reveal, and obscure, about the politics of transitional justice in South Africa? How come 'toilet matters' managed to move out of the sequestered, private space of the home into the public sphere of the streets, the media and national party politics? In other words, how did toilets and shit matters escape the confines of the private sphere to become such a highly politicized matter of public debate? Finally, what role, if any, did this spectacle play in facilitating or inhibiting SJC's tactics of slow activism?

In trying to address these questions, the chapter will focus on two key problematics: first, the ways in which the media images and public commentary on the spectacle of the open toilets constituted various contested public and juridical discourses on 'race', dignity and privacy in the run-up to the 2011 local government elections; and second, how this media spectacle intersected with the slow and patient efforts of the SJC to render legible to the public and the state the conditions of 'ordinary suffering' in informal settlements in Cape Town. The aim of the chapter is to examine to what degree, if at all, this mass-mediated controversy about open toilets contributed towards rendering legible the mundane, and often invisible and normalized, indignities and injustices of 'slow violence' (Nixon, 2011)[3] and chronic poverty in South African cities. The chapter focuses specifically on what I refer to as the 'politics of legibility' and how various actors attempted to frame these issues as matters of public concern, thereby significantly expanding dominant

---

3. Nixon uses the term 'slow violence' to refer to slow-acting forms of violence such as climate change and desertification that pose 'formidable imaginative difficulties for writers and activists alike' because they seem to lack the symbols of dramatic urgency (Nixon, 2006: 14). For Nixon, slow violence accounts for processes of 'long dyings' and 'attritional lethality' that result from the long-term consequences of environmental catastrophes such as the Bhopal and Chernobyl disasters. Here casualties are deferred, sometimes for generations, and this makes it difficult to convince political leaders to act to avert further catastrophe or to hold accountable actors who contributed towards these disasters in the first place. While tens of thousands of people have, over many decades, suffered socially, economically and physiologically as a result of such disasters, it remains difficult to hold states and corporations accountable. So how can activists, writers and journalists represent and narrate these kinds of environmental catastrophes which are 'low in instant spectacle but high in long-term effects'? (ibid.: 15).

conceptions of transitional social justice. It also asks how this framing emerged in relation to the ordinary, daily realities of structural poverty and 'slow violence' that do not generally conform to conventional understandings of transitional justice *or* media-friendly spectacles and instantaneously disseminated images of distant suffering (Boltanski, 1999; Nixon, 2011).

SANITATION, SHIT AND THE PUBLIC SPHERE

Writing about 'excremental politics' and infrastructure (public toilets and sewage systems) in the Ghanaian city of Tema, Brenda Chalfin (2014: 93) suggests that it would seem from most scholarly and technoscientific interventions that 'the natural order of human waste is expected to give way to the political administration of excreta and the eventual sequestering of shit and shitting as base substance and private act (Morgan 2002)'. Chalfin draws on Dominique Laporte's *History of Shit* (2000) to highlight the relationship between this privatization of human waste management and the naturalization of the 'paired emergence of self-regulating private citizens and the overarching apparatus of the modern state' (Chalfin, 2014: 93). These historical developments have, in Chalfin's words, contributed towards 'the interiorization of sanitation and bodily waste as fundamental to individual well-being and to the broader project of societal improvement' (ibid.). Chalfin's ethnographic study investigates the engagement of actors in contemporary urban Ghana with waste and hygiene in ways that contribute towards creating public spaces and animating political life. This sanitation politics includes popular or subaltern political practices of claiming 'the right to the city' and 'the right to shit'.

For political theorists of democracy such as Hannah Arendt (1958), the private domain of the household (the *oikos*) and everything that took place within its walls were not considered to be 'properly political' matters of concern. Arendt would probably have struggled to envisage an 'authentic politics' located in the technical, governmental and social reproductive domains, let alone 'private matters' relating to defecation, toilets and sanitation infrastructure. For Arendt, the embodied dimensions of human existence, including the most basic bodily needs and functions, had to first be taken care of within the confines of the private domain before 'proper' public life could emerge. Yet, it would seem that in cities in Ghana and South Africa even the most basic activities of everyday life, including defecation, periodically surface in public spaces and politics. Given Arendt's association of these matters with the 'private' space of the household, it is unlikely that she would have recognized these concerns with toilets, sanitation and human waste as properly political matters.

Of course the privatization and domestication of human waste was part of a long historical process that Laporte (2000: 29) identifies as beginning in Europe with France's 1539 Degree 'requiring that every individual or individual family hold on to personal waste before carrying it out of the city'. However, Arendt is not alone in sequestering the *oikos* and its human waste from being considered as properly political matters. Jurgen Habermas (1989), the pre-eminent theorist of the bourgeois public sphere, would probably also not have envisaged that private, household-related and bodily matters such as toilets and shitting had the potential to animate public debate on political and juridical questions relating to dignity, privacy and democracy. For Habermas, the early bourgeois public sphere that emerged from the seventeenth century until its decline in the mid-twentieth was conceived of as an 'elevated' political space of rational-critical debate that transcended narrow, mundane, private interests and concerns, as well as the individual statuses of the arguers. A 'politics of shitting' (Appadurai, 2002) would no doubt have seemed beyond the pale from the perspective of the more high-minded, philosophically inflected conceptions of 'the political' shared by Arendt and Habermas.

When it comes to African scholarship, Achille Mbembe (2001) and Jean-Paul Bayart (1993) have been far less restrictive in their assessments of what counts as political. For example, they both write eloquently about the porous borders between the private and the public in their accounts of a 'politics of the belly' in terms of which the private parts and orifices of 'Big Men' are more than game for public commentary, scrutiny, parody and ridicule by citizen-subjects. Similarly, unlike European political theorists of democracy such as Arendt and Habermas, Irish Republican prisoners appear to have been fully cognizant of the potency of a 'politics of shit' when, from 1978 to 1981, they embarked upon the 'blanket protests'[4] that involved smearing their cell walls with excrement in protest at not being allowed to leave their cells because they refused to wear prison uniforms as part of their struggle to be recognized as prisoners of war (Coogan, 2002; Feldman, 1991).[5]

The open toilet controversy in South Africa in 2011, as well as the more recent faeces protests in Cape Town in 2013, suggest that a basic bodily function such as defecation, perhaps *the* most private and intimate domain of household life, can, under certain conditions, enter the circuits of public debate and political life. There are nonetheless historically constituted obstacles that may prevent such private matters from entering the public domain of debate and deliberative democracy (Laporte, 2000). For instance, deep histories of stigma and shame associated with shit and open defecation have ensured that these issues are only gradually becoming part of an emergent

---

4. Refusing to wear prison uniforms, which they referred to as 'monkey suits', these IRA prisoners wrapped blankets around their bodies. See Feldman (1991: 153–5, 166–85) for first-hand accounts and analysis of the 'blanket protests'.
5. Olaf Zenker drew my attention to the 'blanket protest' as an extraordinary measure or political logic that was used to communicate to the outside world that what appeared to be an 'ordinary situation' (i.e. criminals in prison), was in fact an exceptional situation of criminalizing 'prisoners of war' under inhuman conditions (Zenker, personal communication).

'politics of shit' (Appadurai, 2002) in India. Similarly, in a book entitled *Shit Matters*, Lyla Mehta and Synne Movik (2011) analyse how the Community-Led Total Sanitation (CLTS) Programmes that began in Bangladesh opened up such debates in villages, thereby challenging the silence and normalization of abysmal sanitation conditions in many parts of the developing world. The Bill and Melinda Gates Foundation and the Swedish environmental agency Ecosan have recently become key global actors in sanitation programmes that seek to break the silence about 'shit matters' and develop new eco-friendly 'toilets for Africa' (see Penner, 2010).

The Social Justice Coalition in Cape Town has approached the problem from a very different angle to the Gates Foundation and Ecosan. Instead of trying to come up with new-fangled toilet designs, the SJC has sought to ensure that the state provides, monitors and maintains toilets and existing sanitation technologies in poor communities. The SJC has also taken up the challenge of making more visible the appalling sanitation conditions in informal settlements in South Africa. The SJC's approach differs from ANCYL's politics of the spectacle. Instead it deploys slow, patient methods to mobilize communities around activism and to legitimize 'scientific facts' about sanitation conditions in poor neighbourhoods. It does this by producing studies that show, for example, that 500,000 people in the city of Cape Town have no access to basic sanitation facilities. These sanitation facts are then disseminated to the public through the mass media. A typical SJC press statement frames the sanitation problem in Cape Town as follows:

> In some of these [poor] communities more than 100 dwellings (or 500 people) share one toilet stall . . . Many toilets and standpipes have consequently fallen in disrepair, due largely to high use and a lack of routine maintenance, repairs and monitoring. The resulting poor hygiene conditions contribute directly to an array of illnesses including diarrhea, gastroenteritis and skin rash. Lack of access also places resident at great risk of criminal attacks. (SJC, 2011)

This framing of the problem, which is backed up by scientific studies commissioned by the SJC, seeks to transform 'private matters' of defecation into public concerns and matters of public health.

So apart from the many criticisms of Habermas's early conception of the classical bourgeois public sphere for overlooking exclusions based on race, gender, sexuality, class and education,[6] it would seem that his Europe-centred model is also guilty of privileging 'elevated' topics of deliberation and debate to the exclusion of those, such as toilets and shit, that could be considered to be too ordinary, base and banal. It is therefore not very surprising that Habermas's innovative analyses of the European bourgeois

---

6. Craig Calhoun also notes that in the 1960s 'young leftists attacked it for focusing on the bourgeois public sphere to the exclusion of the proletarian one, for an inadequate grasp of everyday life (including mass media) in advanced capitalism, and for exaggerating the emancipatory potential in the idealized bourgeois public sphere' (Calhoun, 1993: 5).

public sphere may have limited value when it comes to trying to understand how toilets and shit became 'political' in South Africa in 2011. So how can we begin to understand how the open toilet emerged as such a powerful legal, political and symbolic spectacle?

HUMAN RIGHTS, HUMAN WASTE AND THE SPECTACLE OF THE 'ANTI-DIGNITY TOILET'

During 2010, in response to public protests and statements from ANC community activists that people had to use open toilets and cover themselves with blankets in full view of the public, the City of Cape Town Municipality (hereafter 'the City') made a number of attempts to enclose the toilets with corrugated iron and timber. However, each of these attempts encountered severe resistance from Khayelitsha residents and ANCYL activists who demanded that the City build pillbox concrete structures to enclose the toilets. When the City did not comply with these demands, a group of ANCYL activists and residents set about destroying the open toilets and the corrugated iron and timber enclosures.[7] This resulted in the City laying criminal charges for the structures destroyed. Meanwhile the ANCYL approached the South African Human Rights Commission (SAHRC) which, after investigating the case, concluded that these open toilets constituted a violation of human dignity. In September 2010, Mrs Beja, a seventy-six year-old woman who had been attacked and stabbed while going to an unenclosed toilet in Makhaza informal settlement in Khayelitsha, filed an application against the City,[8] and on 29 April 2011, Judge Erasmus of the Western Cape High Court handed down judgement against the City and the Province. This series of events, from the ANCYL protests to the SAHRC and High Court applications, came to be known as the 'Makhaza toilet wars'.

Judge Erasmus's judgement in the Beja case ordered the DA-controlled City of Cape Town and the DA Premier of the Western Cape Province to enclose 1,316 toilets in the Silvertown Project, an area that included Makhaza informal settlement in Khayelitsha, a predominantly Xhosa-speaking township on the outskirts of Cape Town. The judgement, which focused on

---

7. Andrew Spiegel alerted me to the graffiti in Khayelitsha in the early 1990s that stated 'Give us houses not toilets'. The meaning behind this graffiti was that, at a time when apartheid was coming to an end, people rejected the state's pillbox structures that enclosed toilets on serviced sites, and instead demanded dwellings that included toilets inside the houses (Spiegel, personal communication).

8. Beja was the first applicant, and Western Cape ANCYL leader, Andile Lili, was the second applicant in a case that was widely seen to be spearheaded by the ANCYL. The Premier of the Western Cape, the Mayor of the City of Cape Town, the MEC for Human Settlements, Western Cape, and the South African Human Rights Commission were the respondents in the case.

Figure 4. The 2011 toilet election and toilet wars. Reproduced by kind permission. Copyright 2010-2011 Zapiro / www.zapiro.com (all rights reserved).

housing legislation and rights to dignity and privacy, declared that by erecting 225 unenclosed toilets in Makhaza in 2009, the City had violated the constitutional rights of citizens of this settlement. This landmark judgement had followed local mobilization in Makhaza, led by the ANCYL's Andile Lili, against these open toilets. The City had responded by claiming that it had entered into a prior agreement with residents that they would enclose the toilets themselves in order to stretch the available budget, and thereby enable each household to have its own toilet rather than having to rely on existing communal toilets. In fact, the City claimed that Andile Lili, the ANCYL's applicant in the Beja High Court case, had been employed by the City of Cape Town to facilitate the agreement with the residents. However, Lili had then turned against the City's scheme and began to play the leading role in the challenge to the City's open toilets in Makhaza.

The ruling given by Judge Erasmus revealed the centrality of questions of dignity and privacy in constitutional law and the democratic culture of the post-apartheid state. The ruling also revealed the pervasive ways in which historical remembrance of the violations of the apartheid past continued to animate both public political discourses and the legalistic language and jurisprudence on dignity and privacy. For the Judge, in his public performance as custodian of the rights of the citizen — and in particular the rights and

Figure 5. Both the ANC-run Free State and the DA-run Western Cape provincial governments were embarrassed by media coverage of open toilets in the run-up to the 2011 local government elections. Reproduced by kind permission. Copyright 2010–2011 Zapiro / www.zapiro.com (all rights reserved).

dignity of the poor and historically marginalized — these matters of indignity and sanitation were related to, and resonated with, the historical memory of the struggle against apartheid: 'The Constitution asserts dignity to contradict our past in which human dignity for black South Africans was routinely and cruelly denied'.[9] The language of the Beja judgement was easily assimilated into an official public script that re-enacted the commitment of the caring, post-revolutionary state, a state that claimed to protect the dignity of all South Africans and affirm their equal worth. The open toilet was intolerable given these constitutionally mandated commitments and imperatives of social justice. Here transitional justice was no longer confined to dealing with apartheid's political violence and gross human rights violations, but also included a wide range of human rights to dignity and 'a better life'.

In his description of the *in loco* inspection of the open toilets at Makhaza, Judge Erasmus reinforced these concerns with questions of human dignity and privacy. Here the Judge expressed disquiet at the poor sanitation conditions throughout the informal settlement, and wrote that

9. 'Beja vs. Premier of the Western Cape and Others', Western Cape High Court Records, p. 21.

Figure 6. In June 2010, the South African Human Rights Commission (SAHRC) released a report finding that the open toilets constructed by the DA-run local government in Makhaza informal settlement in Khayelitsha were an affront to the dignity of residents living there. Zapiro's cartoon has Mayor Zille being issued with the HRC finding. Reproduced by kind permission. Copyright 2010–2011 Zapiro / www.zapiro.com (all rights reserved). This ruling was followed by another SAHRC Report, released in July 2014, focusing on the controversial rolling out of portable chemical flush toilets ("porta potties") in Cape Town's informal settlements. The 2014 SAHRC report found that portable toilets violated the residents' rights to equality, human dignity and privacy, and that the sanitation conditions, services and infrastructure were racially discriminatory against black Africans. The report was the outcome of a SJC social audit and complaint made to the HRC by the SJC about the conditions of portable chemical toilets in Khayelitsha.

even the existing communal toilets, the lack of adequate ablution facilities for disabled people, and the self-enclosed toilets that were part of the agreement between residents and the City of Cape Town, 'were unsatisfactory to satisfy dignity and privacy':

> At the inspection *in loco* the court was accompanied by the legal representatives of all the parties. We observed [that] *most of the self enclosed toilets were unsatisfactory to satisfy dignity and privacy*. E.g. I observed a toilet, pointed out by a woman occupier that had no door. The opening faced a public thoroughfare. She indicated she could not afford a door... The communal toilets that were visited were in a bad state and it can hardly be said that it satisfied *the minimum requirement to promote dignity*.[10]

---

10. 'Beja vs. Premier of the Western Cape and Others', Western Cape High Court Records, p. 14 (emphasis added).

While the Western Cape ANCYL's involvement in the toilet wars and its High Court application were interpreted by many journalists, political commentators and DA politicians and supporters as opportunistic politicking in the run-up to the highly contested Western Cape local government elections of May 2011, few could have anticipated the degree to which toilets and sanitation would come to dominate election campaigns in South Africa. Only a couple of weeks after the April 2011 High Court judgement in the Beja case, which was given considerable national media attention and celebrated by the ANCYL, the ANC found itself in a similar predicament to the DA. Journalists had exposed the unflattering story of 1,600 unenclosed toilets in Rammulotsi township near Viljoenskroon in the ANC-controlled Free State Province. These open toilets, which had been erected in 2003, were a massive embarrassment to the ANC which immediately dispatched a high profile delegation to Rammulotsi which included ANCYL President Julius Malema and Sports Minister Fikile Mbalula.

From the statements and perspectives of the media, the courts, activists and politicians, it would seem that by 2011, toilets and sanitation had indeed become 'properly' political matters involving questions of dignity, privacy and human rights. Alongside these technical, legalistic and human rights concerns related to juridical interpretations of dignity and privacy, the open toilets also made it very difficult for politicians, state officials and citizens to reconcile their vision of a progressive, rights-based constitutional democracy and transitional social justice with the idea of citizens having to defecate in public. But there were still other twists and turns to this tale of toilets.

THE TOILET WARS GO VIRTUAL AND VIRAL

For the ANCYL in the Western Cape, the open toilets in Makhaza were a gift from the gods, and they quickly became the core theme of the ANC's campaign speeches in the run-up to the 2011 local government elections. For the ANCYL in particular, the High Court judgement seemed to confirm its assertions that the open toilets were clear evidence of the inherent racism of the DA-controlled Municipality and its refusal to recognize the dignity of black people. Responding to the open toilets in Makhaza, the ANCYL called for the youth to vandalize Cape Town to protest against the DA's 'poor service delivery' record. As ANCYL leader Loyiso Nkohle put it, 'We are going to destroy everything and make the city ungovernable . . . We are calling on all youth to do this, especially those living in informal settlements' (*Mail & Guardian*, 2010). Nkohle's deputy Chumile Sali stated that the ANCYL was embarking on these actions to expose what was happening in parts of Cape Town where the DA had failed to deliver services: 'The African people's dignity has been undermined by the DA. It is time to take action' (ibid.). In a press statement in May 2011, ANCYL regional treasurer

Andile Lili acknowledged being at the forefront of the protests against the open toilets: 'I led all those protests and I will continue to do so until the issue is resolved. Our people are suffering and definitely the city is racist to leave us living like this with no toilets... What do they think of us if they can leave us here like this, with many residents having to go into the bush?' (Underhill, 2011). In 2010, Lili's ANCYL branch had written an open letter to Human Settlements Minister Tokyo Sexwale calling on him to intervene: 'Our complaint is based on the reality that African people residing in Makhaza, Khayelitsha, are forced to shit in full view of the public... This satanic action by the [Democratic Alliance] city council is tantamount to gross human rights violations and undermines the people's right for their dignity to be protected as stipulated in Section 10 of the Constitution' (*Mail & Guardian*, 2010). Although this ANCYL polemic against the DA Municipality imploded when journalists uncovered the 1,600 open toilets in the ANC-controlled Free State Province, this did not stop Lili and Nkohle from becoming the lead figures in the June 2013 protests against portable toilets.

Social movements such as SJC and Abahlali baseMjondolo had spent a number of years attempting to place issues such as toilets and poor sanitation in informal settlements on the national agenda, but it was the dramatic media image of the open toilet that was the catalyst for political parties and the state to claim that they too were now taking sanitation matters seriously. The political elite and ordinary South Africans citizens, including the middle classes who tend to be indifferent towards or ignorant of the daily conditions of poor sanitation in informal settlements, expressed shock and outrage that citizens had to carry out their ablutions in the open in full view of passers-by. During an interview a month before the May 2011 local government elections, Mandla Majola, a veteran activist of the Treatment Action Campaign (TAC) who had recently joined the SJC, told me that even residents of the formal housing sections of Khayelitsha expressed shock when they found out about the condition of toilets and sanitation in the adjacent informal settlements in their township. Majola referred to the SJC's decision to hold a 'toilet queue protest' in Khayelitsha on 26 April 2011, on the day before Freedom Day,[11] in order to 'educate' residents about the dismal sanitation conditions in the township's informal settlements: 'On the

11. Freedom Day is a national holiday that celebrates the day in April 1994 when South Africans voted in the first post-apartheid democratic elections. The toilet queue protest scheduled for this symbolically important holiday resulted in hundreds of SJC activists converging on government buildings and facilities and queuing to use the toilets. This form of protest is part of the repertoire of activist strategies for drawing attention to sanitation conditions in the global South. In 2010, over 300 SJC activists converged on toilets in Sea Point in the shadow of the nearby World Cup Soccer Stadium in order to convey the a sense of outrage at the massive disparities between local government spending on toilets and sanitation in middle class areas compared to informal settlements.

27th April [1994] there was a long queue for votes and we got the freedom, and we got the so called democracy. *Now we are queuing for sanitation, for toilets,* and there are many people without access to toilets and they are really struggling. We need to open people's eyes to see' (interview, Mandla Majola, April 2011).

There are of course many possible reasons why the images of the open toilets were able to trigger such powerful shock effects. One of the many sites for the public expression of shock and outrage was the blogosphere. In July 2010, 'Thomas Mjiva', a *Mail & Guardian* blogger, attacked DA-supporting bloggers for making excuses for the DA-controlled City of Cape Town's open toilets 'blunder'. He also pointed out that open defecation along the N2 highway was a routine practice for people living in informal settlements such as Makhaza:

> Please visit the area [Makhaza] for at least 2 days and nights and you will realise that when you say people are not forced to defecate in public you are insulting many. By the way don't you see these people doing the act next to the fences by the N2. If not just go there and you will see for yourself the leftovers (Evidence).[12]

Most of the expressions of public outrage failed to acknowledge that many informal settlement residents endure even greater indignities on a daily basis by having to relieve themselves in the open. Whereas the modern toilet without walls shocked most bloggers because of assumptions about the inherent privacy of defecation, 'Thomas Mjiva' noted in his blog contribution on the *Mail & Guardian* website that open defecation was an everyday practice in many informal settlements in Cape Town. Although open defecation is indeed very widespread in many poor communities throughout South Africa, it was the open toilets that profoundly unsettled the understandings of politicians and citizens regarding the democratic transition and basic rights to dignity in a modern state. These developments raised the troubling question: what kind of democracy are we talking about when these kinds of injustices and indignities still occur?

In response to this growing public outrage, the City drew on technicist arguments that its provision of toilets in the area met the national norms and standards of one toilet per five households. However, the City's problems escalated once the media began reporting on the fact that 55 of the 225 toilets erected in Makhaza remained unenclosed, either because residents refused or could not afford to enclose the toilets, or because they were too ill or infirm to do so. Even the Office of the City Manager's own Forensic Report on 'alleged irregular construction of toilets' — referred to in the document as the 'loo with a view' — questioned the basis of the City's claim that

---

12. See comments section below the article at: http://mg.co.za/article/2010--07--05-zille-anc-youth-league-behind-toilets-saga

a binding agreement had been reached between the City and the residents about self-enclosing the toilets:

> The community accepted the offer of a 'loo with a view' as they had made use of the 'bucket system' for the past twenty years and they were concerned that should they not agree with the 'loo with a view' they would be left with the 'bucket system' of sanitation. Our view is that the community was given a 'Hobson's choice' in this regard.[13]

THE SOCIAL JUSTICE COALITION AND ITS GRASSROOTS POLITICS OF JUSTICE AND TRANSITION

While walking through RR Section, an informal settlement in Khayelitsha, 'AP', a Social Justice Coalition activist and resident from a nearby township, talked of the difficulties she encountered when trying to convince residents that allowing children to play in water contaminated by raw sewage was abnormal and unacceptable. She told me that these conditions were so much part of everyday life in places like RR Section that residents could not imagine anything different. She also spoke of residents whose children are sick with diarrhoea on a weekly basis. For AP the task was to create community-based forms of 'sanitation literacy' whereby residents could begin to question the normalization of these conditions. She also spoke of how residents, especially those who worked outside of RR Section, claimed that they only came home to eat and sleep, and that they had gotten used to the conditions. AP also spoke about the normalization of everyday violence, the high rates of child rape in the settlement, and how women and children were routinely attacked at night when they went outside to relieve themselves. Young girls from RR Section had told her that they entered into sexual relationships with local gangsters in order to secure protection from sexual assault. She herself had been attacked at gunpoint when she returned from taking her child to an outside toilet. It was these experiences and testimonies of residents of RR Section that alerted SJC activists to the salience of the intersection between sanitation and safety in informal settlements. It also alerted them to the need to develop ways to 'conscientize' residents about the intolerable nature of the situation. Rather than simply relying on the authority of scientific studies and statistics on sanitation conditions in informal settlements, SJC activists routinely drew on dramatic personal testimonies in meetings with officials as well as at public gatherings in Khayelitsha where SJC activists sought to convince local residents of the gravity of the sanitation crisis.

The SJC's aim — to address these inextricably intertwined sanitation and safety issues — required strategic engagement with questions of technical

---

13. Office of the City Manager, Forensic Services Department Forensic Report, Forensic Investigation into Alleged Irregular Construction of Toilets in the Silvertown Housing Project, 30 July 2010. Case No: FSD167/09–10.

Figure 7. A poster produced in 2011 by the Social Justice Coalition (SJC), a social movement working on sanitation issues in the informal settlements of Khayelitisha. It was designed for a toilet queue protest that sought to draw attention to the stark disparities between sanitation resources in affluent and poor parts of the city. The media coverage of the protests and persistent activism ultimately convinced the city government to establish a janitorial system to monitor and maintain toilets in Cape Town's informal settlements.

expertise as well as the 'politics of the spectacle'. For instance, in an effort to render the conditions legible to the state and the wider public, as well as those who suffer them on a daily basis, the SJC commissioned, translated and disseminated scientific research that documented E.coli levels in RR Section and demonstrated the high risk of disease from exposure to water contaminated by raw sewage.[14] The SJC employed a repertoire of tactics that included the use of statistics, litigation, the media, personal testimonies and protests. Mass petitions and media spectacles such as toilet queue protests outside government buildings in Khayelitsha, as well as outside public toilets in affluent neighbourhoods, sought to blame and shame government for not providing adequate budgets for the monitoring and maintenance of toilets and sanitation in informal settlements. For example, on 27 April 2011, an estimated 2,500 Khayelitsha residents queued behind a toilet outside the Mayor's office to hand over a petition signed by 10,000 residents. The media played a central role in these 'Queue for Clean & Safe Sanitation' campaigns. In a series of articles for the *Cape Times*, the well-known health journalist, Anso Thom, drew on the personal testimonies of residents living in Khayelitsha to dramatize their daily experiences.

> Her shack and yard is [sic] regularly flooded with raw sewage from a nearby pipe which blocks and then floods its contents into her surroundings. [Nozakhe] Thethafuthi claims that sewage first started flowing out from two manholes around her home in the winter of 2006. She has been forced to build a moat around her house in an attempt to relay the sewage to the swamp behind her shack. The effluent in the swamp is channeled to the ocean. The stench is sickening, her living conditions inhumane. Thethafuthi nods her head when asked if the stinking sewage flows into the shack. 'Yes, it often happens right throughout the year', she says, pushing the black beanie away from her forehead. 'My daughter is at the clinic right now with one of my grandchildren because he has diarrhoea. The babies have had diarrhoea episodes every week since their birth (a year ago)', says Thethafuthi. (Thom, 2010)

Thom also writes about Makhosandile 'Scarre' Qezo, a resident of RR Section who was viciously attacked when he crossed Landsdowne Road to relieve himself in the early hours of the morning. He was attacked in the open veld adjacent to the N2 highway, a place that is used daily by hundreds of community members who do not have access to toilets. These testimonies are repeated at SJC gatherings and disseminated in press releases, and these accounts have become part of the emerging historical narrative of SJC. In a *Cape Times* feature article published in November 2011, Gavin Silber, the Coordinator of SJC, narrated Zanele's story; a few days earlier he had told the same story to a Khayelitsha audience of about 100 local residents:

> On a dark, wintry evening in June 2009, Zanele [Xaki] undertook her usual walk to an empty clearing alongside the N2 — a waste-ridden desolate expanse where criminals frequently

---

14. Memorandum on the results of the water sampling in RR Section taken on 8 September 2010 and sent to SJC by Dr J.M. Barnes, Division of Community Health on 30 September 2010.

attack vulnerable residents attempting to relieve themselves. The stench is unbearable, and those who make use of it often complain of contracting worms, gastroenteritis or diarrhea. While attempting to cross Landsdowne Road, Zanele was hit by a car. She was hospitalized for three weeks with a broken pelvis and missed several months of school. Today she is too scared to make this trip, and instead uses a toilet belonging to a shopkeeper five minutes away. (Silber, 2011)[15]

These dramatic narratives and testimonies feature in the SJC's engagement with officials and policy makers as well as grassroots pedagogical campaigns that seek to 'visibilize' and politicize structurally determined sanitation conditions and practices, such as open defecation, for those residents of informal settlements who have normalized the daily realities of chronic poverty. Newspaper articles on RR Section by journalists such as Anso Thom also draw on the SJC's archive of personal testimonies which are often performed at public meetings in Khayelitsha. These testimonies graphically capture and render legible the conditions of structural violence that characterize informal settlements in Cape Town and other South African cities. Thom's accounts of health problems and structural inequality, which she writes about in close collaboration with SJC activists, make connections between a variety of actors and institutions, brought together in these stories of toilets, sanitation, violence, indignity and social suffering. In the *Cape Times* article referred to above, she writes about the scientists and medical researchers who measure E.coli levels and infant mortality rates; a public health official who acknowledges that poor sanitation is responsible for the 'extremely high incidences of diarrhoea and death rates' in RR Section; the City and Provincial officials who blame the problem on 'vandalism'; and the hypothetical middle class Rondebosch family who, unlike RR Section residents, would never agree to share a toilet with twelve other families (Thom, 2010). It is through these kinds of media representations of daily life in places like RR Section that SJC has been able to render sanitation matters politically legible.

SJC's engagement with scientific expertise, statistical data, testimonials, journalists and researchers[16] to lobby and pressure the state for resources, mirrors the tactics of TAC's particular brand of AIDS activism (see Robins, 2008). This approach has also shaped SJC's attempts to make the City of Cape Town more accountable and transparent in its delivery of policing services in these poorer communities. Just as TAC has engaged with health professionals, medical scientists and researchers from a variety of disciplines, SJC has mobilized technical expertise to analyse crime statistics in order to identify the distribution of different forms of crime in

15. The article is an edited version of Silber's contribution to the 2011 Irene Grootboom Memorial Lecture Series dialogues in Khayelitsha.
16. A number of medical researchers and professors of public health and medicine, as well as social scientists such as the author, have written feature articles in the local and national press on SJC and on conditions in Cape Town's informal settlements.

Khayelitsha. For instance, an analysis of statistics from RR Section revealed that crime figures relating to gender-based violence were being dramatically underreported. This was attributed to the fact that courts and police were overburdened, and only homicide was being routinely reported to the police. This structural invisibility with respect to gender-based violence was identified as a serious problem that SJC activists decided to prioritize. The statistics also revealed that the number of road accidents and fires in RR Section were the highest in Cape Town. SJC members began using aerial photographs and satellite maps to show the overlay and concentration of all these problems in particular areas in Khayelitsha.[17] In other words, SJC's tactical use of data collection sought to render visible the extent of social and economic problems, state service delivery inefficiencies, and 'structural violence' in Khayelitisha, and in RR Section in particular. This 'politics of legibility' was strategically deployed by SJC to name, blame and shame the state into responding to specific sanitation and crime related problems. Through these activist practices, the SJC has expanded public understandings of what I refer to in this chapter as 'transitional social justice'. In 2014, the SJC and its civil society partners succeeded in their efforts to lobby for the establishment of the Pikoli-O'Regan Commission of Inquiry into Policing in Khayelitsha. This official state investigation into the conditions of everyday violence, crime, policing and the workings of the criminal justice system in Khayelitsha took place despite concerted opposition from the national Minister of Police, who had applied unsuccessfully to the Constitutional Court to prevent the DA Premier Helen Zille from setting up the Commission.

SLOW VIOLENCE, 'SLOW ACTIVISM' AND TRANSITIONAL SOCIAL JUSTICE

In 2011 the SJC released a press statement expressing concern that the open toilet scandal had deteriorated into political point scoring between the ANC and the DA. The SJC statement called for an end to the 'battle of brinkmanship' between the ANC and DA. Rather than fixating on the open toilet saga, the SJC statement drew attention to the more mundane realities of everyday life for the '10.5 million people in South Africa [who] continue to live without access to basic sanitation'. From the perspective of SJC, the spectacle of the open toilet obscured these daily conditions of racialized

---

17. The interpretation of these data also led the SJC leadership to conclude that deploying more police to the area would not necessarily be the answer, and neither would more ambulances solve the problems. This was due to the fact that RR Section had no roads but only paths, making vehicle accessibility a serious problem. These kinds of analyses sought to influence the ways in which local government intervened in the area.

poverty and structural violence.[18] For the SJC, these were the real challenges for transitional social justice. The SJC attempted to render these everyday realities visible to the state and the wider public by organizing 'walks of witness' whereby religious leaders and journalists were taken to some of the poorest informal settlements in Khayelitsha. In July 2011, Muslim, Jewish and Christian religious leaders, including the Anglican Archbishop of Cape Town, Thabo Makgoba, joined SJC activists on a walk of witness to RR Section in order to get firsthand experience of the daily conditions in these shantytowns. *Cape Times* journalist Zara Nicholson (2011) reported on how shocked and devastated the religious leaders were to find 'unhygienic toilets, no running water, refuse in pathways and exposed electricity lines'.

By the end of 2011 it appeared that the Cape Town Mayor's Office was finally starting to respond to the SJC's persistent demands for a budget for the maintenance, cleaning and repair of communal toilets in the city's informal settlements. It is not clear to what degree these SJC campaigns were aided by the media coverage of the open toilets scandal and the court ruling. SJC activists pointed out that behind the open toilet spectacle lay the daily realities of raw sewage, sanitation-related illnesses, and practices of open defecation. To address the kinds of systemic problems associated with chronic poverty required slow, sustained modes of activism rather than relying on hyper-transient mass mediated spectacles such as the Toilet Wars. These SJC activists seemed acutely aware that practices such as open defecation were concealed beneath layers of stigma and shame. Activists such as AP also encountered the normalization of these abject conditions by residents themselves. It would seem that the Toilet Wars of 2011 only partially succeeded in rendering the sanitation crisis in poor communities more visible to the state and the wider public.

CONCLUDING REFLECTIONS

The open toilet scandal was not only a catalyst for talk and debate about privacy and dignity, issues that featured centrally in the mainstream media, blogs, the High Court and Human Rights Commission findings, and party political rhetoric. The controversy can also be understood as a lens onto the specific character of South Africa's modernist state and its particular brand of developmentalism and liberal democracy. The representatives of the South African state routinely proclaim its accomplishments in terms of 'rolling out' massive programmes involving welfare grants, housing, electricity, water and sanitation — including modern, porcelain toilets — in order to create 'a better life for all'. This high modernist vision is very evident, for instance,

---

18. Social Justice Coalition memorandum in response to the Toilet Wars of 2010 and 2011; http://www.sjc.org.za/.

Figure 8. Portable flush toilet protests in June 2014 in Kosovo informal settlement in Cape Town, where residents destroyed "porta potty" toilets that they claimed violated their human rights and dignity.

PORTA-POTTY PROTEST

BREAKDOWN: Residents of Kosovo informal settlement destroyed 14 'porta-potties' yesterday PICTURE: CINDY WAXA

Residents smash portable toilets seen as 'health risk'

in the posters that line Cape Town's N2 highway boldly proclaiming that 'Slums shall be abolished' and that shacks will be replaced by dignified 'proper housing'. It is also visible in the legal charters of the post-apartheid state. For instance, the Constitution promises the 'progressive realization' of socio-economic rights for all its citizens. However, these expressions of constitutional utopianism and state commitment to transitional justice and modernist development routinely run up against limits and barriers that result from a lack of financial resources and institutional capacity. In the light of this, it is tempting to interpret the image of the modern toilet without walls as yet another dispiriting indicator of the limits and unfulfilled promises of national liberation, state service delivery and modern citizenship. For state officials and politicians, the unenclosed, 'anti-dignity' toilets brought into sharp relief the elusiveness of these modernist visions and aspirations.

It is precisely in this gap between 'the modern' and the 'not quite modern' that a proliferation of new social movements has emerged to pressure the state to meet its obligations with regard to health, housing, land, sanitation and so on (see Robins, 2008). Responding to the limitations and failures of the democratic transition, social movements of the urban poor such Abahlali baseMjondodo and Social Justice Coalition have sought to create the conditions for the emergence of new understandings of transitional social justice and what it means to be a citizen in a democratic state with much unfinished business.

There are of course other ways of interpreting why the open toilet acquired such potent symbolic currency, why it came to be seen as such an affront to black dignity, and how it became *the* key campaign issue in the run-up to the 2011 elections. One possible explanation already mentioned is that there was obvious party political mileage to be gained by drawing attention to this open toilet scandal in the hotly contested Western Cape Province. For the ANCYL, the open toilets saga was framed as a direct attack on black dignity and a clear sign of the DA's historically embedded racism. But this alone does not account for the symbolic and political impact of the open toilets. A historically produced association of the spectacular imagery of the open toilets with apartheid's assault on the dignity of black South Africans is surely one compelling reason why this image 'went viral' and why it provided such potent political capital for the ANCYL. This association was evident in the Beja High Court ruling cited above. From this perspective, the open toilets could be read as the spectre of a disturbing return of the racism, injustices and indignities of the apartheid past; a condensation of the fear that post-apartheid democracy had failed to significantly transform structural inequality, racism, and the everyday conditions of chronic poverty. In summary, the open toilets could be seen as an indictment of the serious limits of post-apartheid transitional justice mechanisms, and the democratic transition in general. This reading suggests that the open toilets of 2011 came to signify the stark limits of the democratic transition as manifested through the persistence of massive unemployment, racialized inequalities, deep poverty, the AIDS pandemic, crime, everyday violence, corruption and so on (Marais, 2011; Robins, 2005). Images of open toilets seventeen years after the arrival of democracy clearly troubled and unsettled the post-revolutionary state's linear and progressive narrative of transitional justice: the progressive realization of 'a better life for all'. Matters of dignity and privacy, so central to South Africa's Constitution and its post-apartheid political culture, seemed to be rendered meaningless by these images of toilets without walls.

Finally, this case study has suggested that the politicization of issues such as sanitation in the post-apartheid period reveals that narrowly conceived transitional justice mechanisms such as the TRC are no longer at the centre of political life in South Africa. In fact, the TRC had a relatively short shelf life as a national political programme of action. Its mandate was to facilitate a smooth democratic transition and once this was more or less achieved, in 1994, it lost its rationale. The dwindling significance of the TRC was inevitable given that its conception of transitional justice was narrowly confined in terms of 'gross human rights violations'. With this mandate, it could not address the more systemic problems of structural violence, chronic poverty and racialized inequality. But it is precisely these issues that have continued to animate popular politics in the post-TRC period. The escalation of service delivery protests and labour strikes in recent years is testimony to this political reality. It would seem that as early as the late 1990s, the TRC had already run its course, and was increasingly being overshadowed by a vibrant, and at times violent, popular politics that honed in on economic injustices and the politics of everyday life in poor communities. Issues such as service delivery, housing, sanitation, public health and labour conditions have become matters of transitional social justice that go well beyond the parameters of the TRC's brief. The TRC and other conventional transitional justice mechanisms have generally been unable to capture the imagination of the wider population, largely because they have tended to be confined to narrowly circumscribed conceptions of transitional justice and human rights. The Toilet Wars and the SJC's style of slow activism draw attention to the limits of this transitional justice model as well as signalling new possibilities for imagining social justice activism that resonates with everyday experiences in poor and working class communities. This case study of the Toilet Wars has shown how the political logic of the exception underlying both 'transitional justice' concepts and mechanisms and the politics of the spectacle, took on forms that contrasted starkly with the logic of 'the ordinary' which characterized the structural violence of everyday life that SJC activists challenged through their practices of slow activism and transitional social justice.

REFERENCES

Anders, G. and O. Zenker (2014) 'Transition and Justice: An Introduction', *Development and Change* 45(3): 395–414.

Appadurai, A. (2002) 'Deep Democracy: Urban Governmentality and the Horizon of Politics', *Public Culture* 14(1): 21–47.

Arendt, H. (1958) *The Human Condition*. Chicago, IL: University of Chicago Press.

Bayart, J-F. (1993) *The State in Africa: Politics of the Belly*. New York: Longman.

Boltanski, L. (1999) *Distant Suffering: Morality, Media and Politics*. Cambridge: Cambridge University Press.

Business Day (2011) 'Sexwale Appoints Team to Sort Out Open Toilet Mess', 7 September.

Calhoun, C. (ed.) (1993) *Habermas and the Public Sphere*. Cambridge, MA: MIT Press.

Cape Argus (2013) 'ANC Blasts Faeces Protest. Crackdown: Party to Discipline Members after "Poo Attack" on Zille Convoy', 5 June, p.1.

Cape Times (2013) 'Faeces Flung at Zille Convoy', 5 June, p.1.

Chalfin, B. (2014) 'Public Things, Excremental Politics, and the Infrastructure of Bare Life in Ghana's City of Tema', *American Ethnologist* 1(1): 92–109.

Coogan, T.P. (2002) *On the Blanket: The Inside Story of the IRA Prisoners' 'Dirty' Protest*. New York and Basingstoke: Palgrave Macmillan.

Feldman, A. (1991) *Formations of Violence: The Narrative of the Body and Political Terror in Northern Ireland*. Chicago, IL, and London: University of Chicago Press.

Habermas, J. (1989) *The Structural Transformation of the Public Sphere: An Inquiry into a Category of Bourgeois Society*. Cambridge: Polity Press.

Laporte, D. (2000) *History of Shit*. Cambridge, MA, and London: MIT Press.

Mail & Guardian (2010) 'ANC Youth League Calls for Trashing of Cape Town', May 25.

Marais, H. (2011) *South Africa Pushed to the Limit: The Political Economy of Change*. Cape Town: University of Cape Town Press.

Mbembe, A. (2001) *On the Postcolony*. Berkeley and Los Angeles, CA: University of California Press.

Mehta, L. and S. Movik (eds) (2011) *Shit Matters: The Potential of Community-led Total Sanitation*. Warwickshire, UK: Practical Action Publishing.

Morgan, M. (2002) 'The Plumbing of Modern Life', *Postcolonial Studies* 5(2): 171–95.

Municipal Outreach Project (2009) 'The Bucket System in 2009'. Newsletter 16, 9 April.

Nicholson, Z. (2011) 'Tour Witnesses Grim Reality for Khayelitsha Residents: Religious Leaders Shown Squalor', *Cape Times* 1 July p. 6.

Nixon, R. (2006) 'Slow Violence, Gender, and the Environmentalism of the Poor', *Journal of Commonwealth and Postcolonial Studies* 13(2)–14(1): 14–37.

Nixon, R. (2011) *Slow Violence and the Environmentalism of the Poor*. Cambridge, MA and London: Harvard University Press.

Penner, B. (2010) 'Flush with Inequality: Sanitation in South Africa'. http://places. designobserver.com/feature/flush-with-inequality-sanitation-in-south-africa/21619/

Robins, S. (ed.) (2005) *Limits of Liberation after Apartheid: Citizenship, Governance and Culture*. Oxford: James Currey; Athens, OH: Ohio University Press; Cape Town: David Philip.

Robins, S. (2008) *From Revolution to Rights in South Africa: Social Movements, NGOs and Popular Politics*. London: James Currey; Pietermaritzburg, South Africa: University of KwaZulu-Natal Press.

Robins, S. (2013a) 'The Toilet Wars: Politicisation of Human Waste', *Cape Times* 27 September.

Robins, S. (2013b) 'How Poo Became a Political Issue: Sanitation is an Old Global Issue', *Cape Times* 2 July.

Silber, Gavin (2011) 'We Must Recognize Communities Exist before We Can Deliver Basic Services: Like it or Not, "Temporary" Settlements Are Here to Stay', *Cape Times* 10 November.

SJC (2011) 'SJC Welcomes Significant Shift in Cape Town's Sanitation Policy'. Press statement, 3 October. http://www.sjc.org.za/posts/sjc-welcomes-significant-shift-in-cape-towns-sanitation-policy

Thom, A. (2010) 'Deathly Effects of No Toilets: Diarrhoea, Death, Disability. Anso Thom Uncovers the Indignity of Living without Sanitation', *Cape Times* 10 June.

Underhill, G. (2011) 'Big Stink over Makhaza Loos Lingers On', *Mail & Guardian* 6 May.

6

New Law against an Old State: Land Restitution as a Transition to Justice in Post-Apartheid South Africa?

Olaf Zenker

INTRODUCTION

One morning in October 2010, I was sitting in the living room of a farmhouse near the settlement of Stoffberg, northeast of Pretoria, South Africa. My hosts were the Botha family who had been party to the legal dispute regarding the so-called 'Kafferskraal' land claim.[1] At the time, I was collecting data for a research project about the ongoing South African land restitution process, through which the state compensates former victims of land dispossession on racial grounds. For this research, I selected a number of exemplary land claim cases, talked to representatives of all parties involved, checked court files and engaged in participant observation on the farms and in the Land Claims Court. Since the 'Kafferskraal' case was one of them, I had arranged to meet the Botha family on that day, and we discussed their experiences regarding this particular restitution case. Portion 3 of the 'Kafferskraal' farm had been owned by the Botha family since the late nineteenth century, as was proven when I was shown their historical title deed and cadastral map, dating back to 1893. As a matter of fact, the farm had already been in possession of the family since it was first granted in private ownership in 1872, as the

---

The research on which this text is based has been financially supported by the Berne University Research Foundation (2009–2011) as well as by an Ambizione Research Fellowship of the Swiss National Science Foundation (2012–2014). During my stays in South Africa, the Departments of Anthropology at the University of the Witwatersrand, Johannesburg, and the University of South Africa (UNISA), Pretoria, provided me with welcoming and inspiring research environments. This chapter benefitted greatly from engaged discussions around its presentation at various occasions, notably our ECAS 2011 panel Transition and Justice: Negotiating the Terms of New Beginnings in Africa, held in Uppsala. I am particularly grateful to my co-convener and co-editor Gerhard Anders as well as Laurens Bakker, Keebet von Benda-Beckmann, Ben Cousins, Julia Eckert, Marion Fresia, Vinodh Jaichand, Steffen Jensen, Tim Kelsall, Hanri Mostert, Johanna Mugler, David O'Kane, Julia Pauli, Mats Utas, Julia Zenker and the anonymous referees of Development and Change for their critical engagements.

1. The name of this farm has appeared on successive title deeds since 1872. The word *kaffer* is an offensive term for African people and *kraal* refers to an enclosure for cattle within an African homestead. As we will see below, however, this fact was recently used to positive effect by the claimants in court. Given that this name is consistently used in state proceedings such as court files and judgments, oscillating uncannily between being a seemingly neutral signifier and representing precisely the racial discrimination which lies at the heart of land restitution, I stick to it, placing it in quotation marks to highlight its problematic nature.

Transition and Justice: Negotiating the Terms of New Beginnings in Africa, First Edition.
Edited by Gerhard Anders and Olaf Zenker.
Chapters © 2015 by The Institute of Social Studies. Book compilation © 2015 John Wiley & Sons, Ltd.

Bothas were also matrilaterally related to the first white[2] owner, Abraham Johannes Korf.

While the Bothas agreed that land which had been taken unlawfully in the past should now be restituted to the former owner, they questioned the validity of the 'Kafferskraal' land claim, since South African land restitution (as we will see below) only deals with dispossessions after 1913. So how could anybody have been dispossessed in terms of current restitution legislation, I was rhetorically asked, if their portion 3 had continuously been in the family's possession long before 1913? Therefore, the Botha family, together with the Prinsloo family owning portion 2 of 'Kafferskraal', had legally challenged the validity of the land claim in the Land Claims Court and, subsequently, in the Supreme Court of Appeal. However, on both occasions, they lost. By the time of our meeting, the state had already bought the respective portions from both families and handed them over to the claimant community. The Bothas stressed forcefully that they still felt the judgments neither to be just nor to follow what they regarded as 'the law'. Mr Botha Jnr expressed this strong sense of injustice by claiming that the state is 'creating a situation for me, in fifty years' time, to be the next land claimant, because I've been treated unfairly now. So in fifty years' time, whatever might happen, it's not impossible that I'll be the next land claimant! ... You cannot fix a mistake with a mistake'.[3]

Based on a case study of the 'Kafferskraal' land claim, this chapter scrutinizes South African land restitution with regard to its capacity to provide a transition to justice in the post-apartheid era. I thereby consciously refrain from studying this process with reference to an analytical concept of 'justice' — be it in terms of utilitarianism, libertarianism, fairness, capabilities, participatory parity, etc.[4] Instead, my focus is exclusively on 'justice' as it is emically understood, and constructed, by the actors themselves. 'Justice' is thus interpreted in a broad sense as an evolving co-production involving various actors engaged in negotiating, and putting into practice, the concrete terms of South Africa's new beginning with regard to its moral rightness. The chapter is premised on the assumption that these discursive and practical negotiations of justice, as exemplified in land restitution, are strongly influenced by divergent evocations of logics of exceptionality and logics of the ordinary. Reference to logics of the exception seems inevitably to arouse associations with the recently somewhat popular Agambian paradigm of 'sovereignty' and its foundational 'state of exception' (Agamben, 1998, 2005), which builds on the earlier works of Carl Schmitt (1985) and Walter

---

2. I use the conventions of African, Indian, coloured, black (as inclusive of the previous three categories) and white to describe the different social groups that were identified as 'distinct' under the apartheid system. At the same time, I acknowledge the dilemma the usage of these socially constructed terms entail, in that they might reinforce notions of their alleged 'reality' as being biologically predetermined.
3. Interview with members of the Botha family, 11 October 2010.
4. For an overview of different theories of justice, see Brighouse (2004) and Sandel (2010).

Benjamin (1996). Given the massive scope of social scientific engagements with Giorgio Agamben's state of exception, and the somewhat divergent focus on exceptionality in this text, I will refrain from discussing Agamben's critique of sovereignty as such.[5] For present purposes, it suffices to say that Agamben's exception seems to simultaneously offer too much and too little. It offers (and asks for) too much in that it ultimately proclaims the state of exception to be the paradigm of modern government, and the camp, populated by citizens reduced to 'bare life', to be the modern predicament. Thus downplaying, among others, the difference between liberal democracy and totalitarian dictatorship — once described by Adorno (2000: 155) as 'a total difference'[6] — Agamben's homogenizing and unitary exception also arguably offers too little. It lets the highly divergent logics of exceptionality pass unnoticed, which are only possibly and not necessarily centred on law and the state, and not exclusively evoked by 'the sovereign'.

By contrast, the notion of variable logics of exceptionality in this chapter propagates a more empirically open conception, accommodating a whole variety of modes, which, from the actor's point of view, insist on some profound break with normality, the familiar and the mundane — in short, the ordinary — that demands and justifies extraordinary measures in exceptional times. Correspondingly, proponents of logics of the ordinary insist on some profound continuity with normality and the mundane which, in turn, allows reading, and motivating, behaviour in all too familiar terms — whatever such behaviour may say of itself (see Anders and Zenker, 2014, reprinted as the Introduction to this volume). Seen in this light, singular events may acquire a different selectivity and connectivity, that is, different pasts and potential futures (Luhmann, 1995: 215), depending on the peculiar logic(s) through which they are contextualized. In this way, South African land restitution can be interpreted as evolving through crisscrossing pathways of agency which — based on divergent logics of exceptionality and the ordinary — bring forth the peculiar nature of any potential transition to 'justice' in post-apartheid South Africa.

In order to approach the possible justice of South African land restitution in such terms, the chapter first sketches the concrete institutional set-up with reference to the Restitution of Land Rights Act (Act 22 of 1994) and the constitutional provision for both the protection of private property and the restitution of land rights. Against this backdrop, 'the justice' of the actual land restitution process is explored with regard to conflicting interpretations by various sets of actors involved in the 'Kafferskraal' land claim, using data generated in the course of an ongoing research project on South African land restitution (see Zenker, 2012a, 2012b, forthcoming-a, forthcoming-b,

---

5. For an extensive enumeration of recent scholarship on Agambian sovereignty as well as a critical engagement with the genealogy, and consequences, of Agamben's approach, see Jennings (2011).

6. I am indebted to Heins (2005: 860) for this observation.

forthcoming-c). This chapter focuses on divergent understandings of what
historically constituted valid rights in land and corresponding forms of
compensation in the past. These understandings account for the continuing
discrepancies regarding the legitimacy of various property regimes which, in
turn, inform different evaluations of 'the justice' of the final outcome in this
land claim. As is shown, these differences are ultimately rooted in incompat-
ible logics of exceptionality and the ordinary, which conceive land restitution
either in terms of 'law-making' or 'law-preserving violence' (Benjamin,
1996). The chapter concludes by discussing the implications of this overall
configuration for land restitution as a measure of 'transitional justice'.

THE RESTITUTION ACT WITHIN THE LEGAL RECONSTITUTION OF SOUTH AFRICA

South African land restitution was mandated both by the Interim Constitution
of the Republic of South Africa (Act 200 of 1993) and by the current Constitution of the Republic of South Africa (Act 108 of 1996) as an extraordinary
measure, placing the state under a duty to redress land dispossessions as a
result of past racially discriminatory laws or practices. The basic criteria and
procedures for the restitution process were provided for by the Restitution
of Land Rights Act (Act 22 of 1994). Section 2(1) of the act provides a set of
criteria according to which claimants are entitled to restitution in the form of
either restoration of a right in land or equitable redress. The claimant could
be an individual (or a direct descendant) or a community (or part of a community) whose rights in land were derived from shared rules determining access
to land held in common by such a group. Claims of dispossession of land
rights through racially discriminatory laws and practices could not pre-date
19 June 1913.[7] Finally, claimants may not have received just and equitable
compensation (as stipulated in the constitution) for the dispossession at
issue and had to lodge their claim before 31 December 1998.[8] Significantly,
restitution was explicitly not limited to former freehold ownership of
land. Instead, the right in land to be restituted was defined quite broadly
in section 1 of the Restitution Act, including 'any right in land whether
registered or unregistered, and may include the interest of a labour tenant
and sharecropper, a customary law interest, the interest of a beneficiary
under a trust arrangement and beneficial occupation for a continuous period

---

7. This was the date of the proclamation of the Natives Land Act (Act 27 of 1913), first legalizing massive dispossessions country-wide by introducing racial zones of possible landownership and by restricting black reserves to only 7 per cent of South African land (later to be extended to 13 per cent).
8. On 29 June 2014, President Jacob Zuma signed the Restitution of Land Rights Amendment Act (Act 15 of 2014) into law reopening the lodgement of land restitution claims until 30 June 2019.

of not less than 10 years prior to the dispossession in question'. As we will see in the so-called 'Kafferskraal' case, this had profound consequences for the perceived justice of restitution outcomes.

The Restitution Act further established the Commission on Restitution of Land Rights, including the Chief Land Claims Commissioner and the Regional Land Claims Commissioners, as well as the Land Claims Court (LCC), as its key players. The subsequent examination by the Commission of lodged claims ultimately validated about 80,000 claims as legitimate and in need of resolution.[9] Since then, commission bureaucrats have mediated between claimants and usually white landowners in order to settle on a largely market-oriented agreement, where the state buys the land and, based on certain conditions, hands it over to the claimants. The minister and, by delegation, the land claims commissioners, have the power to facilitate and conclude settlements by agreement. Only claims that cannot be resolved this way take the judicial route through the LCC. This also entails the possibility of expropriation — an option that is also constitutionally enshrined (Hall, 2010: 21–32). Based on figures from 2011, about 5 per cent of restitution claims (that is, 3,673 cases) remain outstanding (Department of Rural Development and Land Reform, 2011: 40). These cases are typically quite complex and face numerous challenges for their resolution. Yet, not only the outstanding restitution claims, but also the officially 'resolved' cases continue to be haunted by many problems (see James, 2007; Walker, 2008; Walker et al., 2010; Zenker, 2012b, forthcoming-a).

The history of race-based land dispossession had always occupied an important position in the African National Congress's (ANC) understanding of the liberation struggle (Walker, 2008: 50–1). Political protests, legal battles and the meticulous documentation of the racially based land dispossessions and forced removals involving an estimated 3.5 million black people between 1960 and 1983 (Platzky and Walker, 1985: 10), had constituted key areas of land activism in and around the ANC for many decades. However, despite a political rhetoric highlighting the land question, towards the late 1980s rural issues occupied a rather low priority on the ANC's political agenda (Klug, 2000: 125). Given the ANC's general preoccupation with urban–industrial issues and the strong emphasis on property rights by the still ruling National Party (NP), especially concerning agricultural land, land reform became a matter of strategic compromise (Walker, 2008: 54). This resulted in a balanced constitutional protection of both property rights and the right to redress for race-based violations of past rights in land; first, in the Interim Constitution of 1993 (Chaskalson, 1994: 131–2), and then in the Constitution of the Republic of South Africa of 1996 (Klug, 2000: 124–36;

9. See Zenker (2012a, forthcoming-b) for extensive discussions of the shifting figures within restitution statistics as well as their recent transformation into explicit performance indicators of South African land restitution.

Walker, 2008: 50–69). The institutional framework for land restitution needs to be seen within this context of the profound reconstitution of the overall South African legal order during the transitional negotiations (Zenker, 2012b).

As Ruth Hall points out, however, both the 1998 deadline for lodging claims and the 1913 cut-off date, categorically excluding all prior colonial dispossessions, have been hotly contested (Hall, 2010: 23). Yet until very recently, the government consistently opposed accepting new claims, not least because this would entail an explosion in costs (ibid.: 24). With regard to the 1913 cut-off date, the ANC government provided an ex-post rationalization in 1997: it pointed out that given the numerous conflicts between African groupings prior to 1913, as well as the massive growth and scattered distribution of the overall African population thereafter, there would be a high risk of endless inter-ethnic conflict among the dispossessed, were pre-1913 claims to be admitted (Department of Land Affairs, 1997: section 4.14.2); by contrast post-1913 dispossessions evidently favoured white supremacy. A further reason for the 1913 deadline can be found in the necessity for political compromise during the constitutional negotiations, as described above.[10]

While the 1913 cut-off date has indeed continued to categorically exclude claims to restitution for pre-1913 dispossessions, it is important to emphasize that two factors have decisively broadened the scope for land restitution to actually include cases often assumed in both public debates and the academic literature to fall outside the jurisdiction of land restitution. First, according to the above-mentioned broad definition of 'rights in land', much more than merely a loss of freehold land ownership qualifies victims of post-1913 dispossessions for an entitlement of restitution. Second, the largely overlooked jurisprudential role of the courts (Mostert, 2010) has substantially broadened the scope of restitution through redefining ownership in such a way that many dispossessions are actually conceived as having, indeed, occurred post-1913. These two aspects constitute core elements underlying the divergent understandings of justice as instantiated by the 'Kafferskraal' land claim.

THE CASE OF THE SO-CALLED 'KAFFERSKRAAL' LAND CLAIM: A HISTORY OF REPOSSESSION

The farm 'Kafferskraal' is situated on the edge of the highveld escarpment, approximately 200 km to the northeast of Pretoria and situated within the

---

10. However, during the State of the Nation Address on 14 February 2013, President Jacob Zuma announced that the government would re-open the lodgement of land claims and allow limited exceptions to the 19 June 1913 cut-off date to accommodate claims by the descendants of the Khoi and San. On 29 June, the Restitution of Land Rights Amendment Act (Act 15 of 2014) was signed by President Zuma, extending the deadline for lodging new land claims until 30 June 2019. In an Explanatory Memorandum the government declared its intention to deal separately with pre-1913 land dispossessions as a result of state action.

Greater Groblersdal Local Municipality, Mpumalanga Province.[11] The name of this farm, measuring about 4,200 hectares, has appeared on successive title deeds since 1 December 1872, when the Zuid-Afrikaansche Republiek (ZAR), also known as the 'Transvaal Republic', first granted the land in private ownership to the white farmer Abraham Johannes Korf. While the farm name is pejorative, as mentioned above (footnote 1), it signified a fact which was used in court to positive effect by the claimant community. They argued that the land had long been settled by black people and that this fact, and related land rights, survived the superimposition of white registered title.[12]

The settlement history of the farm and surrounding areas is both crucial for an understanding of this restitution case and highly contested. For this reason, I will restrict myself to those historical elements that were more or less taken for granted by all parties and hence formed the backdrop for the subsequent legal dispute. In this spirit, a history of this area can be summarized as follows. During the first half of the nineteenth century, intense competition characterized the region, as three powerful South African kingdoms — the Pedi, the Swazi and the Zulu — struggled for dominance. The interplay of colonial penetration, especially in the form of arriving Boer Voortrekkers in the 1840s, and the emergence of new African kingdoms, wars and migration in the aftermath of the Difaqane[13] sent further shock waves throughout the region (Delius, 2007: 137). In 1852, Boer settlers established the ZAR in what later became known as the South African province of 'Transvaal', encompassing the area at issue as its eastern part. In the early decades, 'the ZAR was weak and poor and as an administrative, judicial and executive body it was inefficient' (Delius and Hay, 2009: 51). The Boers wanted to own and control the land and further distribute it to white settlers. They attempted to buy land from various kings and chiefs, occupied pockets of land that did not fall under the control of any particular chief and subordinated smaller African chiefdoms and communities. In this process, the ZAR issued title deeds for what it regarded as its land to the growing number of immigrating white *burghers* (citizens) (ibid.: 51–2).

Within this overall context, the Ndebele[14] was one local group among others. Much earlier in their history, they had divided into the two kingdoms

---

11. This local municipality was meanwhile renamed and rezoned into the bordering Limpopo Province. However, as the farm was still situated in Mpumalanga at the time this claim was processed, I continue to refer to Mpumalanga Province.
12. See the judgment of the Supreme Court of Appeal, reported as Prinsloo & Another v. Ndebele-Ndzundza Community & Others 2005 (6) SA 144 (SCA), section 1.
13. The Difaqane, also called Mfecane, refers to a period, caused by colonial conquest and tensions within and among indigenous groups, of warfare, migration and political change within African society during the first half of the nineteenth century (see Delius, 2007: 107–111).
14. The overall Ndebele have been classified into Northern and Southern sections, of which the Northern Ndebele subsequently came to be substantially influenced by Northern Sotho language and cultural forms. Thus, the name 'Ndebele' is often used as shorthand only for the Southern section, as is the case in this text (see Delius, 1989: 228–29).

of Manala and Ndzundza (Delius, 1989: 229). While both sections suffered heavily in the course of the Difaqane, the Ndzundza Ndebele recovered better, and by the 1840s had re-emerged as a significant kingdom under King Mabhoko, with various fortified mountain strongholds. The coexistence with the Boers proved conflictual, 'with the Ndzundza refusing Boer demands for labour and denying their claims to ownership of the land' (ibid.). Against a number of failed Boer attempts to subjugate the kingdom, Ndzundza power reached its heights in the late 1860s and 1870s. However, substantial changes were on the way:

> The British annexation of the Transvaal in 1877 resulted in a restructuring and strengthening of the state, and in 1879 a British-led army (with Swazi and Ndzundza assistance) finally defeated the Pedi paramountcy (i.e. the most powerful African kingdom in the area). As the balance of power swung away from the African states in the region, landowners and speculators started to press claims to formerly unoccupied farms and to those which had been worked only on sufferance of the Ndzundza rulers. Shortly after retrocession (i.e. the restoration of ZAR independence from Britain in 1881), the Ndzundza and the restored Republican administration found themselves at loggerheads over competing land claims and over whether the chiefdom fell under the authority of the Zuid-Afrikaansche Republiek (ZAR). In 1882 the Pedi pretender Mampuru sought refuge amongst the Ndzundza after having murdered his brother Sekhukhune. Nyabela's refusal to hand him over to the ZAR brought the wider conflicts to a head. (ibid.: 231)

The protracted Mapoch War that followed ended in 1883, when the Ndzundza were forced to capitulate. Their tribal leadership was disrupted with the imprisonment of King Nyabela and other members of the royal family. The land around the royal stronghold, situated on the farm 'Mapochs-gronden' — named after the above-mentioned Ndzundza King Mabhoko — was confiscated, subdivided and handed over to Boers who had fought in the war (van Vuuren, 2010: 10–11). The population of the kingdom was dispersed among the ZAR burghers — 'in the interests of order, safety and humanity', as the ZAR government decreed — and indentured for a period of five years (1883–88) (Delius, 1989: 232). This led to much arbitrary displacement of Ndzundza Ndebele within the ZAR territory and ensured that the Ndzundza, subsequently working mainly as labour tenants on white-owned farms, would never officially regain their pre-colonial territory (van Vuuren, 2010: 10). The incarceration of the royal family and the dispersal of the population constituted a severe blow to the Ndzundza Ndebele, but their imprisoned leadership managed to organize the escape of Nyabela's brother. Matsitsi was sent to the farm 'Kafferskraal' to re-establish chiefly guidance and the male initiation ritual (*ingoma*), an important Ndebele institution until today (Delius, 1989: 241; van Vuuren, 2010: 11–12).

As mentioned above, the farm 'Kafferskraal' had been in white titled ownership since 1872 and subdivided into three separate portions with changing owners from at least 1902. White owners never actually lived on the farm, while generations of Ndzundza Ndebele resided and worked on 'Kafferskraal', including Matsitsi and his chiefly successors who regularly organized male initiation schools on the farm and exercised judicial functions there. At various points in the 1920s and 1930s, Ndzundza leaders also attempted to buy a portion of 'Kafferskraal' from willing white sellers but were prevented from doing so by various racially discriminatory laws (see below). Against this backdrop, and after some changes in white ownership of 'Kafferskraal', most members of the local Ndebele community were finally evicted by the late 1930s and removed to the north to the state-owned farm Goedgedacht and surrounding areas in the Nebo district (today Limpopo Province) which, as reserve land, later became part of the Lebowa homeland.

This final removal constituted the end point in a long process of cumulative dispossession that had started in the nineteenth century. At that time, divergent property regimes of arriving white settlers and competing African chiefdoms under their respective 'customary laws' had uneasily co-existed until the latter's dispossession 'by right of conquest' (Bundy, 1972: 379). After the establishment of the Union of South Africa in 1910, the Natives Land Act (Act 27 of 1913) unified the somewhat divergent regulations for African reserves and landed property in the four provinces of the Union. It introduced racial zones of exclusive landownership and restricted black reserves to only 7 per cent of South African land. Furthermore, it reduced legal occupation by blacks on white farms to labour tenancy or wage labour, thereby effectively abolishing squatting and sharecropping as successful strategies for relatively independent African peasant farmers, thus ensuring the supply of cheap labour to white farmers (Bundy, 1972: 384). While the implementation of the Natives Land Act was slow and uneven, allowing the Ndzundza Ndebele to continue living on 'Kafferskraal' into the 1930s, it still prevented them from buying a portion of 'Kafferskraal', as this farm fell outside the areas designated as African reserves.

The Native Trust and Land Act (Act 18 of 1936) released additional land for black reserves, expanding the total amount of land officially set aside for the majority African population to (still only) 13 per cent of South African land. The act also established the 'South African Native Trust' to control the administration and acquisition of land (with public funds). The trust became the registered owner of almost all the reserves, as a title was usually not vested in the people who lived there (Platzky and Walker, 1985: 89). It was in the wake of these acts that the Ndzundza Ndebele community on 'Kafferskraal' was eventually removed in the late 1930s to several trust farms in the Nebo district.

Meanwhile, a parallel system of administration for the African population had been established. The Native Administration Act (Act 38 of 1927) modified and consolidated the system of chiefly rule and 'customary law', placing all chiefs under the Governor-General as the white 'supreme chief'. While the powers of chiefs were thereby to some extent restricted, their authority in local African administration was also officially recognized, for instance, their continuous right to control land allocation in the reserves. Through this process, a dominant property regime in the reserves emerged under apartheid in which *de jure* trust-owned land *de facto* turned into the chief's 'property' through his control of access to the land. This laid the foundation for many post-apartheid conflicts with chiefs (as the case of the Ndzundza Ndebele shows below), who insist that they are the true owners of the land.

Within this overall framework, a proclamation was published in the government gazette on 2 August 1957 that defined the trust farms in Nebo, to which the Ndzundza Ndebele had been removed, as their 'tribal area' and established a 'Bantu Tribal Authority' for this Ndebele tribe under the then Chief Poni Mahlangu, called 'Ndebele Tribal Authority'. However, these trust farms in Nebo became the relocation site for successive waves of removals from the late 1930s, in which both Ndebele- and Pedi-speaking people, mainly ex-labour tenants, were relocated from nearby white farms. While the earlier arrivals, like the Ndzundza Ndebele who moved in at the beginning of this period, usually managed to establish some rights to land for ploughing, later arrivals, especially from the late 1960s onwards, were only able to acquire residential stands (James, 1988: 36). As in other reserves, the South African government also subjected the area to agricultural 'Betterment planning', that is, schemes introduced since the 1930s and 1940s in an attempt to control land usage and thus improve and rationalize reserve agriculture (Platzky and Walker, 1985: ix). However, the Betterment schemes in Nebo had the adverse effect of actually reducing the size and viability of these plots: 'In attempting to provide land for the waves of more recent settlers, the planners took land away from earlier settlers, rendering them unable to produce more than a supplement to migrant wages' (James, 1988: 36).

The growing land shortage on the trust farms contributed to local impoverishment and increased the dependence on the wider South African system of labour migration, thus stabilizing the reproduction of cheap labour, upon which South African capitalism depended (Wolpe, 1995). At the same time, the continued expansion of both labour migration and forced removals into the homelands led to processes of political cross-fertilization and a growing interaction of township and rural youth from the 1970s onwards. This effected an increasing politicization also of rural areas, and youth involvement in rebellions such as the 1986 uprisings in Sekhukhuneland/Lebowa (Delius, 1996) and the revolt in 1986 against political independence in KwaNdebele (Phatlane, 2002).

With the demise of apartheid, different Ndzundza Ndebele groups and individuals lodged restitution claims for 'Kafferskraal'. After establishing *prima facie* validity, the proscribed notice concerning the restitution claim of the three portions of 'Kafferskraal' was published by the Regional Land Claims Commissioner in the government gazette on 2 January 1998. The validity of the claim was researched and the various valid claims — mostly by individuals or nuclear families from the Ndzundza Ndebele community under then Chief M.J. Mahlangu of the Ndebele Tribal Authority — were consolidated. For that purpose, a land claims committee called Sibuyela

Ekhaya (We Return Home) was formed in cooperation with the chief and his council to represent the entire Ndzundza Ndebele community with a valid claim on 'Kafferskraal', on whose behalf Chief M.J. Mahlangu had also lodged a separate land claim on 18 September 1995 regarding 'Kafferskraal' and sixteen neighbouring farms along the Stoffberg-Groblersdal corridor (see also van Vuuren, 2010: 10). In the course of various stakeholder meetings, organized by commission officers with representatives of the claimant community and the three sets of white landowners, it became clear that while the owner of portion 1 agreed after initial opposition to sell his portion (as he subsequently did), the Prinsloo and Botha families, owning portions 2 and 3 respectively, continued to contest the validity of the claim. The Regional Land Claims Commissioner thus referred the case to the Land Claims Court (LCC) on 19 January 2000, since no agreement could be reached.

On the basis of extensive submissions and court hearings on 7–10 October, 1 November and 9 December 2002, the LCC gave a judgment on 23 December 2002 with regard to the validity of the claim by answering five questions: first, whether there had been a community on 'Kafferskraal' as contemplated in the restitution act; second, if so, whether the community had rights in land falling under the Restitution Act; third, whether, if such rights had existed, they had been dispossessed as a result of past discriminatory laws and practices; fourth, whether there had been substantial compliance with the procedure prescribed for lodgement of claims; and fifth, whether the claim was not excluded on the basis of a just and equitable compensation in the past.[15]

In its judgment, the LCC answered all these questions in favour of the claimant community. First, it found that although the Ndundza had been scattered over the area after the Mapoch War, they had retained their identity as a distinct group, lived on the farm under tribal conditions ruled by various chiefs, and maintained rights in land derived from shared rules determining access to land held in common. Furthermore, they left as a community in 1939 and letters from various government authorities over a prolonged period recognized the claimants as a community.[16] Second, given that the community had lived on the farm from at least 1883 until the late 1930s, cultivated the soil, kept livestock and shared the land as a community without any white owners occupying the farm or consistently exercising ownership rights (except for two decades of demanding an annual rent), the court found that the community had a restorable right in land in the form of beneficial occupation of no less than ten years prior to dispossession.[17] Third, the court

---

15. See the judgment of the LCC, sections 4–7, reported as Ndebele-Ndzundza Community v. Farm Kafferskraal NO 181 JS2003 (5) SA 375 (LCC).
16. Ndebele-Ndzundza Community v. Farm Kafferskraal NO 181 JS2003 (5) SA 375 (LCC), sections 17–18.
17. Ndebele-Ndzundza Community v. Farm Kafferskraal NO 181 JS 2003 (5) SA 375 (LCC), section 19.

decided that the community had been dispossessed by the cumulative effect
of a number of racially discriminatory laws and practices, first turning them
into labour tenants on their own land, then preventing them from purchas-
ing the land and finally allowing for their eviction. Furthermore, the record
shows the involvement of the government in the actual relocation.[18] Fourth,
the court found that, on the whole, the claim had been lodged substantially
in compliance with the legal requirements.[19] Last but not least, the court
found that the relocation farm, Goedgedacht, could not have been intended
as compensation at the time, since it was explicitly declared by the government as only a temporary solution. The court found additional merit in
the argument by the claimants' advocate that 'in any case, Goedgedacht,
having been provided as part of homeland consolidation, a discriminatory
act in itself, cannot now be accepted as compensation for past discriminatory acts.... To accept as compensation, land given in furtherance of such
policies would be tantamount to buttressing the very acts the Constitution
and the Act are intended to undo'.[20] Correspondingly, the LCC found that
the claimants were entitled to restitution and granted them leave to set the
matter down for a hearing of the remaining issues that had been excluded
pending the outcome of the trial.[21]

An application by the Prinsloo and Botha families for leave to appeal
against the whole of the LCC judgment was granted on 17 February 2004
by the Supreme Court of Appeal (SCA). In its judgment on 31 May 2005,
the SCA dealt with four issues: first, whether the claimants were a community as contemplated in the act; second, if so, whether the community had
restorable rights in land; third, whether the community was dispossessed as
contemplated in the act; and fourth, whether the claim was not excluded on
the basis of a just and equitable compensation in the past.[22]

The SCA, again, principally confirmed the validity of the claim. First, it
found that the claimants constituted a community as defined in the restitution act since these Ndzundza Ndebele continuously lived and worked
on the farm for at least fifty years under tribal authority, held the land
in common with each other, occupied the farm exclusively without immediate supervision or direct control of the white landowners, and did so
under Ndzundza Ndebele traditions, as the telling fact shows that Matsitsi was explicitly sent back to 'Kafferskraal' in the 1880s in order to

18. Ndebele-Ndzundza Community v. Farm Kafferskraal NO 181 JS 2003 (5) SA 375 (LCC),
    sections 20–22.
19. Ndebele-Ndzundza Community v. Farm Kafferskraal NO 181 JS 2003 (5) SA 375 (LCC),
    sections 23–28.
20. Ndebele-Ndzundza Community v. Farm Kafferskraal NO 181 JS 2003 (5) SA 375 (LCC),
    section 29.
21. Ndebele-Ndzundza Community v. Farm Kafferskraal NO 181 JS 2003 (5) SA 375 (LCC),
    section 36.
22. Prinsloo & Another v. Ndebele-Ndzundza Community & Others 2005 (6) SA 144 (SCA).

re-establish male initiation rites.[23] Second, the court emphasized that the restitution act put forward a broad definition of 'rights in land', going far beyond formal ownership and including customary law interests and rights of labour tenants and sharecroppers. Without further specifying the exact nature of their former land rights, the SCA found that the claimants had certainly exercised rights no less than those recognized in the act.[24] Third, the court confirmed that there had been a dispossession as contemplated in the act, emphasizing that the absence of a physically forced removal did not mean that there was no dispossession. The court stated that the community was not given a real choice, as people had to relocate and live and work under changed conditions there or stay on the farm as labour tenants under significantly changed conditions.[25]

However, regarding the fourth question, whether the claim was excluded due to just and equitable compensation in the past, the SCA found that the LCC had erred. The SCA noted that the LCC had argued that no just and equitable compensation had occurred, since the relocation farm had been intended only as a temporary measure (while *de facto* becoming permanent) and, since being part of the racially discriminatory practice of homeland consolidation, could not now be accepted as a legitimate compensation in the past. The SCA found that neither the Restitution Act nor the constitution provided any basis for excluding past compensation on such grounds. The SCA thus ordered that the issue of past compensation be remitted to the LCC for further consideration, when dealing with the remaining issues that had been excluded from the original LCC trial.[26]

In light of having lost their overall appeal, the Prinsloo and the Botha families decided not to pursue the case further to the level of the Constitutional Court. Instead, they reached a settlement with the claimants that was made an order by the LCC on 21 August 2006, in which all parties consented to the transfer of the two remaining 'Kafferskraal' portions on the following principal condition: 'that the value of the rights in land that the community had in respect of the farm "Kafferskraal" 181 JS prior to dispossession, and the compensation, if any, that the community received as a result of the dispossession of such rights, shall be taken into account'[27] when the outstanding claims by the same community regarding the above-mentioned

---

23. Prinsloo & Another v. Ndebele-Ndzundza Community & Others 2005 (6) SA 144 (SCA), sections 11–31.
24. Prinsloo & Another v. Ndebele-Ndzundza Community & Others 2005 (6) SA 144 (SCA), sections 32–40.
25. Prinsloo & Another v. Ndebele-Ndzundza Community & Others 2005 (6) SA 144 (SCA), sections 41–49.
26. Prinsloo & Another v. Ndebele-Ndzundza Community & Others 2005 (6) SA 144 (SCA), sections 51–56.
27. See section 2.3 in the settlement agreement, attached as Annexure X to the unreported judgment of the LCC, in re Ndebele-Ndzundza Community regarding the farm Kafferskraal 181 JS, Case No. LCC 03/2000, 21 August 2006.

sixteen neighbouring farms (several portions of which are also owned by the two families) are adjudicated by the LCC. On this basis, the remaining two portions of 'Kafferskraal' were subsequently bought for the claimant community. However, when I last researched this case (February 2012) the outstanding sixteen claims were still being processed by the Regional Land Claims Commissioner and had not yet reached the LCC. It remains to be seen how the contested issue over just and equitable compensation in the past will be dealt with by the court.

THE CONTESTED JUSTICE OF THE 'KAFFERSKRAAL' LAND CLAIM

When I talked to different members of the Sibuyela Ekhaya committee, they evidently felt that finally justice had been done in restoring their former right in land and upgrading it to full ownership in order to redress the injustice of their dispossession in the past. However, some procedural injustices remained. As claimants complained, despite the LCC order in 2006, the official transfer of the remaining two portions of 'Kafferskraal' was further delayed until 2010 by protracted negotiations between the former white owners and the state regarding the price for the acquisition of the land. And while the state finally bought the remaining two portions in 2010, the claimants still did not know (when I last spoke to them in February 2012), when they would receive the new title deeds. As Mr Shabangu, the committee chairman, explained to me, these delays unduly prolonged the claimants' insecure tenure and precarious situation, as they continued to be unable, for instance, to prove to banks or private investors that the land actually belonged to them. Mr Shabangu further complained about the insufficient post-settlement support, which the Department of Land Affairs is supposed to offer all restitution beneficiaries in order to enable them to turn their restored land into sustainable sources of income.

Major problems have also persisted with the royal council of the Ndzundza Ndebele Chief Poni II Mahlangu in Nebo, whose predecessor, the late M.J. Mahlangu, had lodged a separate claim for 'Kafferskraal' and sixteen neighbouring farms.[28] As I learnt in interviews and conversations with members of the Ndebele Tribal Authority, they felt that the Sibuyela Ekhaya committee had 'stolen' their claim on 'Kafferskraal' and the other sixteen farms within the restitution process. Against the backdrop of the above-mentioned dominant property regime in the reserves under apartheid — when the chief, as the state-backed allocator of reserve land, had acted as its *de facto* owner — members of the royal council further demanded, in conflict with current state law such as the Communal Property Associations Act (Act 28

---

28. Interviews with various members of the Sibuyela Ekhaya committee on 7 September 2010,
    5 November 2010, 25 August 2011, 2 September 2011, 13–14 February 2012.

of 1996), that the land should in any case be owned and managed directly by the chief, as he was 'the true owner' of the land under 'customary law'.[29] Therefore, intra-communal strife was much more prevalent in my encounters with the various claimants than the still rather abstract problem that the issue of past compensation might (at least partly) undermine *all* Ndzundza Ndebele claims on the other sixteen farms in the future.

By contrast, the former white owners — that is, members of the Prinsloo and Botha families — were rather bitter about what they saw as the injustice that the trial had done them. As illustrated by the introductory vignette, I learnt in various conversations that land restitution as such was seen as morally right, but only when landowners with title deed had been dispossessed, as was the case in the infamous 'black spot removals' of black titled landowners. All over the world, it was claimed, ownership existed only with proper title deed, yet in South African restitution, people could claim a right in land simply because they had lived on the land for longer than ten years. In the case of 'Kafferskraal', the outcome was perceived as profoundly unjust, as the farm had been in white titled ownership since 1872 and, in the case of the Botha family, even in direct family ownership long before the 1913 cut-off date. Generally speaking, it was argued, local African people had lost their rights in land long before the 1913 cut-off date during the nineteenth century wars of conquest. The white government had still compensated them subsequently by setting aside land in the reserves, and yet new farms were nevertheless claimed in recent years. Furthermore, as Mr Botha Snr explained:

> When the claim was made, at the first meeting, we were told 'the claim is not against you as a person, it is against the state'. But when it came to the case, I had to pay my own lawyers, while the state was on the side of the claimants. So I do not understand how it is not against us, if we have to pay our costs! I had to prove against the state that the portion of Kafferskraal is my property. I thought that this wasn't fair. We had to prove out of our own pockets that it was our own land, for which we had title deeds and everything.[30]

This evidently showed, it was argued, that South African land restitution was neither a just process nor based on a just law; instead it was a political process and a political court, as it was not about giving land back to the rightful owners, who had been dispossessed, but exclusively about handing over land to Africans for political reasons. Only the fact that the SCA had ordered to take past compensation into account when adjudicating the claim on the remaining sixteen farms was seen as, at last, constituting some form of justice.[31]

---

29. Interviews with the royal council of the Ndebele Tribal Authority in Nebo, and its various members, on 30 August, 6 September, 25 October 2010, 24 August 2011, 31 January and 15 February 2012.
30. Interview with members of the Botha family, 11 October 2010.
31. Interviews with members of the Prinsloo and Botha families, 2 February, 11 September and 11 October 2010.

This diametrical opposition in the evaluation of the in/justice of the outcome in the 'Kafferskraal' case can be traced back to a fundamental difference in opinion regarding the legitimacy of alternative property regimes. The former white landowners continued to propagate a narrow conception of exclusive, formal ownership that is unified, hegemonic and elevated above other less comprehensive rights, which has until recently largely been supported by South African property law (Mostert, 2010: 69–70). In this interpretation, earlier African 'owners' of 'Kafferskraal' had been dispossessed long before 1913, therefore the restitution claim fell well outside the scope of the Restitution Act. In keeping with their conception of ownership, these former white owners advocated a broader understanding of past compensations, in which Africans with no ownership rights were 'compensated' in the course of their removal with rights in land regarding the relocation farms.

By contrast, the claimant community put forward a broad conception of their right in land regarding 'Kafferskraal' — framed as 'beneficial occupation' (rather than 'a customary law interest') by their lawyers in terms of the restitution act — which they had retained despite the superimposition of both the white registered title and state-backed property regime in the reserves. Their ultimate dispossession therefore occurred after the 1913 cut-off date and was thus clearly within the ambit of the restitution process. It follows that to describe their removal to the trust farms as a form of compensation was at best cynical, and at worst an impertinence. In the claimants' narrower understanding of past compensation (informed by their broad conception of land rights), relocating them made final their dispossession as opposed to constituting compensation.

As discussed above, the LCC followed the claimants in their interpretation of their former rights in land and their subsequent dispossession, while also rejecting an interpretation of the relocation farms as a form of past compensation. The SCA overruled this judgment concerning past compensations, yet upheld the LCC's decision to interpret rights in land broadly. As Hanri Mostert shows with reference to recent case law, especially regarding the Richtersveld land claim,[32] but also 'Kafferskraal', decisions by the LCC, the SCA and the Constitutional Court have significantly transformed and broadened core concepts of land ownership, representing 'a major turn in South African jurisprudence on land rights' (Mostert, 2010: 62–4, 67, 76). This may be illustrated by two core statements in the SCA judgment on 'Kafferskraal', which declare that 'the fact that registered title exists neither necessarily extinguishes the rights in land that the statute [the restitution act] contemplates, nor prevents them from arising' and that '[t]he statute

---

32. See Richtersveld Community and Others v. Alexkor (Pty) Ltd and Another 2001 (3) SA 1293 (LCC); Richtersveld Community and Others v. Alexkor (Pty) Ltd and Another 2003 (2) All SA 27 (SCA); and Alexkor (Pty) Ltd and Another v. Richtersveld Community and Others 2004 (5) SA 460 (CC).

also recognises the significance of registered title. But it does not afford it unblemished primacy'.[33]

In view of the massive racially motivated land dispossessions of the past, these extraordinary transformations in the conception of South African landownership are seen as a restoration of justice by state officials in the commission and the courts, and land claimants alike. In other words, these actors invoke a logic of exceptionality that highlights a massive break with humane, desirable normality which demands and justifies the extraordinary measures of land restitution in exceptional times. Given that the former government is responsible for past dispossessions through its own laws, they cannot easily be redressed in terms of the former legal categories of 'property' and 'ownership', since these made dispossession possible in the first place. Thus sometimes referred to as 'transformation legislation' (Walker, 2008: 5), land restitution is seen as constituting a transformative legal counter-violence or 'law-making violence', to borrow Walter Benjamin's term, which establishes new property law that remains necessarily and intimately bound to violence under the title of state power (Benjamin, 1996: 248).

However, from the point of view of former white landowners, who insist on an earlier and unchanged conception of exclusive formal ownership, such legal transformations and the judicial outcomes they make possible seem illegitimate and deeply unjust. In other words, far from making restitution's law-making logic of exceptionality their own, these former owners believe they have unmasked land restitution as actually following the perfectly ordinary logic of 'victor's justice'. For them, land restitution represents a redistribution of goods based on political considerations rather than a remedy based on the manifest victimhood of individual beneficiaries. On the one hand, these former owners thus advocate a logic of the ordinary with regard to the 'true' nature of land restitution, which implies a continuity of an alleged political bias of the former anti-apartheid movement against white farmers. On the other hand, this 'unmasking' is intimately linked to another logic of the ordinary, which insists on the rightfulness and hence legal continuation of the former conception of exclusive formal ownership that prevailed under apartheid. Taken together, these two logics of the ordinary combine in a 'law-preserving violence' (Benjamin, 1996) which is concerned with the protection of the legal principles, and the still skewed patterns of landownership made possible by them, underpinning the former state of landed property.

In short, the continuing discrepancies regarding the legitimacy of the various property regimes which inform the different evaluations of 'the justice' of this land claim are ultimately rooted in an incompatibility between the law-making logic of exceptionality that drives the restitution process

---

33. See Prinsloo & Another v. Ndebele-Ndzundza Community & Others 2005 (6) SA 144 (SCA), sections 36 and 38.

and the law-preserving logics of the ordinary, as accentuated by former landowners. Hence, a transition to justice does not take place for all, because some actors involved cannot agree that land restitution should ultimately bring about a truly 'new law against an old state'.

CONCLUSION: NEW LAW AGAINST AN OLD STATE

South African land restitution conforms closely to Ruti Teitel's definition of 'transitional justice', which is concerned with a 'conception of justice associated with periods of political change, characterized by legal responses to confront the wrongdoings of repressive predecessor regimes' (Teitel, 2003: 69). South Africa's post-1994 land restitution process can thus be discussed as a form of transitional justice, even though research and public debate on the topic with regard to South Africa has focused almost exclusively on the Truth and Reconciliation Commission (TRC) (Zenker, 2011: 2–3).

Taking into account the result of this case, and rethinking South African land restitution in terms of transitional justice, it becomes possible to throw into sharper relief the potential and limitations of land restitution to facilitate a transition towards a more just South Africa. As shown, land restitution is based on a law-making logic of exceptionality which is invoked and enacted by the state. While being similar to Agamben's state of exception declared by the sovereign, there are two important differences. First, as a transitional justice measure, land restitution consciously marks a threshold between two substantially different regimes, while explicitly addressing an old state of injustice (in both senses of the phrase) through developing *new law* within an equally transformed framework of legality (such as a new constitution) rather than merely *suspending the law*. Land restitution thus differs from the paradigmatic 'state of exception', given that it is by necessity concerned with establishing 'new law against an old state'.[34]

Second, in order to achieve the transitional justice goals of justice and reconciliation, land restitution's law-making logic of exceptionality must succeed in winning over broad societal support for its project. However, a *de facto* sovereign, in its successful enforcement of the state of exception, is not truly dependent upon legitimacy. This highlights the importance of not only focusing on the inner logic of transitional justice. Instead, it is crucial to situate concrete transitional justice measures within wider local, that is, 'place-based' (Shaw et al., 2010), debates on various logics of exceptionality

---

34. The most concise example of this principle can possibly be found in subsection (3)(b) of the equality clause (section 8) of the Interim Constitution of 1993: 'Every person or community dispossessed of rights in land before the commencement of this Constitution under any law which would have been inconsistent with subsection (2) [of this equality clause prohibiting unfair discrimination] had that subsection been in operation at the time of the dispossession, shall be entitled to claim restitution of such rights ....'

and the ordinary that are seen as being 'really' behind these measures (see the Introduction to this volume). Put differently, given the multiple logics of exceptionality and the ordinary with which transitional justice measures locally co-exist and often conflict, the relative success of 'transitional justice' also crucially depends on its capacity, over time, to win over a broad majority of actors to share its definitions of 'justice' and 'reconciliation'.

As the case study of the 'Kafferskraal' land claim showed, South African land restitution clearly succeeded with regard to the first point, developing a significantly transformed (property) law against an old state of landed injustice. However, regarding the second point of securing broad support for its law-making logic of exceptionality, land restitution, relatively speaking, failed — at least in this case. It did not succeed in bringing about a transition towards a situation that was widely interpreted as exhibiting more justice than before, since the former landowners stuck to their own law-preserving logics of the ordinary. While such broad-based support is admittedly always difficult to establish, I will end with a brief reflection upon one peculiar feature of South African land restitution that makes this support-building endeavour even more difficult, namely the absence of any explicit requirement for a face-to-face interaction and reconciliation between current owner and claimant.

This is not to say, of course, that the interested parties do not meet during the restitution process. Stakeholder meetings with all interested parties do take place, and also happened in the 'Kafferskraal' case. However, their purpose is to inform parties about the existence of a land claim and to attempt to settle the claim by agreement. Their aim is not to explain the law-making logic of exceptionality that informs land restitution. Much discontent regarding the in/justice of restitution outcomes possibly springs from the fact that white landowners often expect restitution to operate as an ordinary process within an unchanged property system, whereas, in fact, it is driven by an exceptional process of a new transformative property regime. The likelihood of achieving a more congruent and widely shared understanding of this process would be considerably improved if restitution institutionalized a much more substantive engagement between current owner and claimant. In this way, a mutual sharing of histories of possession and dispossession could lead to greater understanding and more 'common sense' — that is, more consensual understandings of history and justice, and thus, ultimately, to more reconciliation.

There is no guarantee, of course, that such an approach would always succeed. The divergent sense of entitlement of African claimants and white owners might prove to be irreconcilable. African claimants may completely reject any sense of legitimate white ownership, thus possibly dismissing the latter's constitutional right to just and equitable compensation when the state returns the land. Similarly, the families of current owners may have lived on or farmed the claimed lands for several generations and may have developed an equal sense of belonging and entitlement, which could make it difficult to transcend their earlier conception of exclusive formal ownership. Furthermore, given the judicialized nature of the restitution process, an open exchange about what the different parties regard as historical fact may be unlikely when parties are in actual dispute and little incentive exists to reveal such 'evidence' to their opponents.

Although it might be difficult to achieve 'common sense' between parties under such judicialized conditions, a process that incorporates a much stronger element of face-to-face interaction between the different parties, in which the existence and legitimacy of property regimes other than those formerly accepted by the colonial state are made explicit, would still stand a better chance of achieving reconciliation and more consensual understandings of justice than is currently the case. Such a shared understanding and support for a 'new law against an old state' — which ultimately summarizes the transitional justice project of restitution's law-making logic of exceptionality — is crucial for South African land restitution in order to better achieve a transition to a state of more justice for all.

REFERENCES

Adorno, T.W. (2000) 'Über Mitbestimmung, Regelverstösse und Verwandtes. Diskussion im Rahmen der Vorlesung am 5.12.1967' ['On Participation, Rule Violations and Related Matters. Discussion during the Lecture on 05.12.1967'], in R. Tiedemann (ed.) *Frankfurter Adorno Blätter VI [Frankfurt Adorno Notes VI]*, pp. 155–68. München: Edition Text + Kritik.

Agamben, G. (1998) *Homo Sacer: Sovereign Power and Bare Life*. Stanford, CA: Stanford University Press.

Agamben, G. (2005) *State of Exception*. Chicago, IL: University of Chicago Press.

Anders, G. and O. Zenker (2014) 'Transition and Justice: An Introduction', *Development and Change* 45(3): 395–414.

Benjamin, W. (1996) 'Critique of Violence', in M. Bullock and M.W. Jennings (eds) *Walter Benjamin: Selected Writings Volume 1: 1913–1926*, pp. 236–52. Cambridge, MA: Belknap Press.

Brighouse, H. (2004) *Justice*. Cambridge: Polity Press.

Bundy, C. (1972) 'The Emergence and Decline of a South African Peasantry', *African Affairs* 71(285): 369–88.

Chaskalson, M. (1994) 'The Property Clause: Section 28 of the Constitution', *South African Journal on Human Rights* 10: 131–39.

Delius, P. (1989) 'The Ndzundza Ndebele: Indenture and the Making of Ethnic Identity', in P. Bonner, I. Hofmeyr, D. James and T. Lodge (eds) *Holding Their Ground: Class, Locality and Culture in 19th and 20th Century South Africa*, pp. 227–58. Johannesburg: Witwatersrand University Press/Ravan Press.

Delius, P. (1996) *A Lion Amongst the Cattle: Reconstruction and Resistance in the Northern Transvaal*. Oxford: James Currey.

Delius, P. (2007) *Mpumalanga: History and Heritage*. Scottsville: University of Kwazulu-Natal Press.

Delius, P. and M.A. Hay (2009) *Mpumalanga: An Illustrated History*. Johannesburg: Highveld.

Department of Land Affairs (1997) 'White Paper on South African Land Policy'. Pretoria: Government Printers.

Department of Rural Development and Land Reform (2011) 'Strategic Plan 2011–2014'. Pretoria: Department of Rural Development and Land Reform.

Hall, R. (2010) 'Reconciling the Past, Present, and Future: The Parameters and Practices of Land Restitution in South Africa', in C. Walker, A. Bohlin, R. Hall and T. Kepe (eds) *Land, Memory, Reconstruction, and Justice: Perspectives on Land Claims in South Africa*, pp. 17–40. Athens, OH: Ohio University Press.

Heins, V. (2005) 'Giorgio Agamben and the Current State of Affairs in Humanitarian Law and Human Rights Policy', *German Law Journal* 6(5): 845–60.

James, D. (1988) 'Land Shortage and Inheritance in a Lebowa Village', *Social Dynamics* 14(2): 36–51.

James, D. (2007) *Gaining Ground? 'Rights' and 'Property' in South African Land Reform*. Abingdon: Routledge; New York: Cavendish.

Jennings, R.C. (2011) 'Sovereignty and Political Modernity: A Genealogy of Agamben's Critique of Sovereignty', *Anthropological Theory* 11(1): 23–61.

Klug, H. (2000) *Constituting Democracy: Law, Globalism, and South Africa's Political Reconstruction*. Cambridge: Cambridge University Press.

Luhmann, N. (1995) *Social Systems*. Stanford, CA: Stanford University Press.

Mostert, H. (2010) 'Change through Jurisprudence: The Role of the Courts in Broadening the Scope of Restitution', in C. Walker, A. Bohlin, R. Hall and T. Kepe (eds) *Land, Memory, Reconstruction, and Justice: Perspectives on Land Claims in South Africa*, pp. 61–79. Athens, OH: Ohio University Press.

Phatlane, S.N. (2002) 'The Farce of Homeland Independence: Kwandebele, the Untold Story', *Journal of Asian and African Studies* 37(3–5): 401–21.

Platzky, L. and C. Walker (1985) *The Surplus People: Forced Removals in South Africa*. Johannesburg: Ravan Press.

Sandel, M.J. (2010) *Justice: What's the Right Thing to Do?* New York: Farrar, Straus and Giroux.

Schmitt, C. (1985) *Political Theology: Four Chapters on the Concept of Sovereignty*. Cambridge, MA: MIT Press.

Shaw, R., L. Waldorf and P. Hazan (eds) (2010) *Localizing Transitional Justice: Interventions and Priorities after Mass Violence*. Stanford, CA: Stanford University Press.

Teitel, R.G. (2003) 'Transitional Justice Genealogy', *Harvard Human Rights Journal* 13: 69–94.

van Vuuren, C.J. (2010) 'Memory, Landscape and Event: How Ndebele Labour Tenants Interpret and Reclaim the Past', *Anthropology Southern Africa* 33(1&2): 9–18.

Walker, C. (2008) *Landmarked: Land Claims and Land Restitution in South Africa*. Athens, OH: Ohio University Press.

Walker, C., A. Bohlin, R. Hall and T. Kepe (eds) (2010) *Land, Memory, Reconstruction, and Justice: Perspectives on Land Claims in South Africa*. Athens, OH: Ohio University Press.

Wolpe, H. (1995) 'Capitalism and Cheap Labour Power in South Africa: From Segregation to Apartheid', in W. Beinart and S. Dubow (eds) *Segregation and Apartheid in Twentieth-Century South Africa*, pp. 60–90. London: Routledge.

Zenker, O. (2011) 'Land Restitution and Transitional Justice in Post-Apartheid South Africa'. Working Paper No. 134. Halle: Max Planck Institute for Social Anthropology.

Zenker, O. (2012a) 'The Indicatorisation of South African Land Restitution'. Working Paper 2012:01. Basel: Basler Afrika Bibliographien (BAB).

Zenker, O. (2012b) 'The Juridification of Political Protest and the Politicisation of Legalism in South African Land Restitution', in J. Eckert, B. Donahoe, C. Strümpell and Z.Ö. Biner (eds) *Law against the State: Ethnographic Forays into Law's Transformations*, pp. 118–46. Cambridge: Cambridge University Press.

Zenker, O. (forthcoming-a) 'Bush-Level Bureaucrats in South African Land Restitution: Implementing State Law under Chiefly Rule', in O. Zenker and M. Hoehne (eds) *The State and the Paradox of Customary Law in Africa*. Aldershot: Ashgate.

Zenker, O. (forthcoming-b) 'Failure by the Numbers? Settlement Statistics as Indicators of State Performance in South African Land Restitution', in R. Rottenburg, S.E. Merry, S.-J. Park

and J. Mugler (eds) *A World of Indicators: The Making of Governmental Knowledge through Quantification*. Cambridge: Cambridge University Press.
Zenker, O. (forthcoming-c) 'Legal Pluralism, Communal Land Tenure and Multiple Livelihoods in South Africa's Countryside', *Journal of Legal Pluralism*.

STATUTES

Natives Land Act (Act 27 of 1913)
Native Administration Act (Act 38 of 1927)
Native Trust and Land Act (Act 18 of 1936)
(Interim) Constitution of the Republic of South Africa (Act 200 of 1993)
Restitution of Land Rights Act (Act 22 of 1994)
Communal Property Associations Act (Act 28 of 1996)
Constitution of the Republic of South Africa (Act 108 of 1996)
Restitution of Land Rights Amendment Act (Act 15 of 2014)

7

Transitional Justice, States of Emergency and Business as Usual in Sierra Leone

Gerhard Anders

EXCEPTIONAL MEASURES: 'OPERATION JUSTICE'

On 10 March 2003, investigators of the UN-backed Special Court for Sierra Leone and Sierra Leonean police officers carried out several arrests under the codename 'Operation Justice'. They arrested the Minister for Internal Affairs, Sam Hinga Norman, who had led a pro-government militia, the Civil Defence Forces (CDF), during the civil war, and two former leaders of the Revolutionary United Front (RUF), the main rebel group fighting against successive governments and the CDF during the 1990s. More arrests were made in Pademba Road Prison in Freetown, where the former RUF leader Foday Sankoh and Alex Tamba Brima, a commander of the renegade soldiers who had formed the Armed Forces Revolutionary Council (AFRC) in May 1997, were transferred into the custody of the Special Court. Later that day, the five detainees were flown by helicopter to the Special Court's detention facility on Bonthe Island, about 200 miles south-east of Freetown. Over the following months five more former commanders from the CDF, the RUF and the AFRC joined them. That left just three indicted men at large. One of them, the Liberian president Charles Taylor, was eventually arrested in March 2006.[1] The second, the former RUF-commander Sam 'Maskita' Bockarie, was killed in May 2003 in Liberia, where he had moved in December 1999. The third, the former AFRC leader Johnny Paul Koroma,

---

This chapter is based on fieldwork funded by the Swiss National Science Foundation. It greatly benefited from discussions with my co-editor Olaf Zenker and the participants in our panel at the AEGIS European Conference on African Studies in Uppsala. I would like to thank the anonymous reviewers for their helpful comments. Of course, any remaining errors or omissions are entirely my responsibility.

1. The indictment against Charles Taylor is beyond the scope of this analysis, which only deals with the situation in Sierra Leone between 1999 and 2004. Taylor was indicted on 7 March 2003 and the indictment was unsealed in June 2003. Taylor left Liberia in August 2003 and went into exile in Nigeria where he remained until his arrest at the border with Cameroon in late March 2006. The trial against him lasted from June 2007 until March 2011; he was found guilty and sentenced to fifty years in prison in April 2012. The judgment was confirmed by the Appeals Chamber on 26 September 2013 and Taylor was transferred to the United Kingdom where he serves his sentence in Her Majesty's Prison Frankland in County Durham.

Transition and Justice: Negotiating the Terms of New Beginnings in Africa, First Edition.
Edited by Gerhard Anders and Olaf Zenker.

went into hiding in January 2003 after he was accused of involvement in a botched attack on an armoury in Freetown.

According to the Special Court's prosecutor, the former US Department of Defence lawyer David Crane, these men held 'greatest responsibility' for war crimes and crimes against humanity committed during the civil war in Sierra Leone. The Special Court had the mandate to try leaders of the various armed factions who were responsible for the atrocities committed against the civilian population. Prosecutions centred on charges of terrorizing the civilian population, enslavement, pillage, systematic killings, atrocities such as the amputation of limbs, sexual violence, the recruitment of child soldiers and violence against peacekeepers, hundreds of whom had been taken hostage by the RUF in May 2000. These crimes had attracted most attention both internationally and in Sierra Leone, where the RUF and AFRC committed many atrocities during their attack on Freetown in January 1999.

With 'Operation Justice' the Special Court signalled that 'we mean business' and that 'no one is above the law', according to Crane.[2] From his perspective, the Special Court made a crucial contribution to a new beginning in Sierra Leone. In another interview Crane stated: 'in order for this country to move forward and have long-term peace, we have to stop impunity'.[3] Other representatives of the court echoed Crane's view. Geoffrey Robertson, the court's first president, highlighted that the Special Court was unique as it was 'established in the country where the crimes were committed and where its work can count as part of the reconciliation process' (SCSL, 2003: 3). From the perspective of the UN, the establishment of the Special Court was necessary to address a 'situation of impunity'[4] in Sierra Leone, which justified this extraordinary measure. This view reflects the retributive vision of justice driving the promotion of international criminal tribunals; it has proved to be at odds with the ideas about reconciliation advanced by the Truth and Reconciliation Commission (TRC) in Sierra Leone, a tension examined in more detail below. According to Resolution 1315 adopted by the UN Security Council in August 2000, 'a credible system of justice and accountability . . . would contribute to the process of national reconciliation and to the restoration and maintenance of peace'. But what was the court's impact on Sierra Leone's social and political topography? Did it indeed send out the message that no one is above the law and contribute to a new beginning by charging a dozen men with war crimes and crimes against humanity?

Kelsall's (2009) study of the Special Court for Sierra Leone disputes this claim by advancing a cultural relativist argument. According to Kelsall, cultural differences made 'the application of international justice a fraught affair' (ibid.: 17). The present analysis shares Kelsall's critical perspective

---

2. Interviews given by David Crane in March 2003: www.sierra-leone.org/Archives/slnews0303.html.
3. Interview, David Crane with the author in Utrecht, The Netherlands, 11 June 2008.
4. Preamble of the Agreement between the UN and the Government of Sierra Leone on the Establishment of a Special Court for Sierra Leone.

but adopts a more comprehensive approach that situates transitional justice mechanisms in wider debates and conflicts about transition and justice (see the Introduction). It focuses on the Special Court's position in the context of the political economy of the transition phase rather than cultural differences in the courtroom. Instead of limiting its scope to a particular institution, the chapter aims at elucidating the contradictions that characterized the transition period between 1999 and 2004. It shows that the official announcements issued by representatives of the UN, the Special Court and political leaders in Sierra Leone were in stark contrast to what actually happened during this period. Taking its cue from Shaw's (2010) perceptive study of continuities and contradictions between the TRC and the Disarmament, Demobilization and Reintegration (DDR) programme in Sierra Leone, this analysis explores the intersections between related events and processes during the transition period. The Special Court's attempts to realize its promise of justice cannot be isolated from the political conflicts and violent clashes at the turn of the 21st century.

The court was established during a time characterized by intense power struggles and attempts of former military leaders to establish themselves in the post-conflict social and political order. Whilst it thwarted the ambitions of a few to convert their military exploits into political office or material benefits, it is open to debate whether the court actually contributed to a new beginning after the end of the civil war. In fact, the Special Court constituted just one of the influences shaping the reconfiguration of Sierra Leone's social and political order between 1999 and 2004. The analysis presented here traces the frantic jockeying for influence and security in the context of bitter and violent political conflicts that were at odds with the official commitments to justice and peace espoused by politicians and former military leaders. Some succeeded in converting their position into political and economic capital but others were less successful.

It is striking that when the Lomé Peace Agreement between the government and the RUF disintegrated in May 2000, several hundred former rebels of the RUF and the AFRC were arrested by the national authorities. Spending years in detention, more than eighty of them were eventually charged with treason, murder and related charges in the national courts. By contrast, the Special Court only charged thirteen individuals of which ten eventually stood trial. This discrepancy highlights the importance of the national arena for a comprehensive understanding of Sierra Leone's transition after the end of the civil war and underlines the need to examine a whole range of related events and developments in Sierra Leone between 1999 and 2004. Drawing on Fassin and Pandolfi (2010), this analysis shows that the exceptional circumstances that justified the interventions of the UN and the Special Court were, in fact, not extraordinary from the perspective of political and military leaders who were doing business as usual, trying to outmanoeuvre their rivals in spite of grand announcements of a new beginning.

The chapter will first situate the Special Court's establishment within the context of the massive state-building exercise spearheaded by the UN mission to Sierra Leone, and the debate about how to come to terms with the violent past after the end of the war. This debate revolved around several contentious issues including the blanket amnesty granted in the Lomé Peace Agreement, which had been signed by President Kabbah and RUF leader Foday Sankoh under intense international pressure, and the parallel operation of two transitional justice mechanisms. The second part of the chapter focuses on the bitter political conflicts between 1999 and 2003 and the violent clashes in May 2000 that triggered the establishment of the Special Court. These conflicts were characterized by the attempts of former commanders to convert their military strength into political, economic and social capital. After declaring a state of emergency, the government arrested hundreds of former rebels and conducted a number of criminal trials against RUF members and renegade soldiers. Finally, the third part of the chapter situates the men arrested by the Special Court in 2003 in the context of the strategies and tactics employed by former military leaders and commanders to carve out a niche for themselves in the post-conflict order. It shows that the Special Court's impact remained relatively limited even though it thwarted the attempts of these men to conduct business as usual.

A NEW BEGINNING AND TRANSITIONAL JUSTICE

On 18 January 2002, then President Ahmad Tejan Kabbah officially declared the end of the civil war that had plagued Sierra Leone for more than a decade. Kabbah's announcement came a few days after the UN had reported the completion of the disarmament of 45,000 combatants belonging to the RUF, the AFRC and the pro-government CDF. At the time, the United Nations Mission in Sierra Leone (UNAMSIL) was at its peak with 17,500 military personnel deployed all over the country, providing security and overseeing the implementation of the disarmament, demobilization and reintegration programme. A few months later, on 14 May 2002, general elections were held with incumbent president Kabbah and the Sierra Leone People's Party (SLPP) winning a landslide victory with over 70 per cent of the vote.

In a nutshell, these events tell the story of a war-ravaged country slowly returning to normality with the assistance of UN peacekeepers who provided security and disarmed tens of thousands of fighters. It is a narrative of rebuilding a nation after the descent into chaos and violence had necessitated the intervention of the international community to stop the bloodshed and restore order. This transition from chaos to order features a sequence of steps beginning with the restoration of security, followed by the disarmament and reintegration of combatants, eventually culminating in democratic elections. This sequence is presented in terms of depoliticized technologies deployed to address technical challenges (Fassin and Pandolfi, 2010). In Sierra Leone, the stabilization and rebuilding of the country were supplemented by two transitional justice mechanisms, the UN-backed Special Court for Sierra

Leone and the national TRC, both established in 2002. Coming to terms with the violent past by holding accountable those who committed crimes and establishing a historical record were seen as key to national reconciliation and creating the conditions for political and social stability — a veritable new beginning.

However, the transition period was much messier than this simplistic account suggests. Fierce and often violent political battles shaped the new beginning in Sierra Leone in contradictory and contested ways which were not reflected in the sequence from humanitarian intervention to transitional justice and eventually democratization and economic development. In July 1999, representatives of Kabbah's government and the RUF, the main rebel group, signed the Lomé Peace Agreement providing for the inclusion of the RUF in a government of national unity, a blanket amnesty for crimes committed during the civil war and the establishment of a Truth and Reconciliation Commission. But the peace process soon stalled. Parts of the RUF resisted disarmament and took 500 peacekeepers hostage in May 2000 (see below). During that month, the government of national unity unravelled. Foday Sankoh, the RUF leader, and hundreds of RUF members were arrested after several protesters were killed during a demonstration at Sankoh's residence in Freetown. Immediately after the arrest of the RUF members, Kabbah's government requested the establishment of an international criminal tribunal to try Sankoh and the RUF leaders 'for crimes against the people of Sierra Leone and for taking of UN peacekeepers as hostages'.[5] In August 2000, the UN Security Council authorized the establishment of an international criminal tribunal in Freetown with the mandate to hold accountable those 'bearing greatest responsibility' for war crimes and crimes against humanity (Resolution 1315). On 16 January 2002, the UN and the government of Sierra Leone signed an agreement to establish the Special Court,[6] and in August 2002 the first registrar, the chief of the court's administration, and the first chief prosecutor, the Pentagon lawyer David Crane, arrived in Freetown, 'hitting the ground running', as Crane put it. Only seven months later Crane ordered 'Operation Justice'.[7]

The establishment of the Special Court resulted in the parallel operation of two transitional justice mechanism following different logics. The Special Court was built on the principle of retributive justice, the idea that a sense of closure depended on the punishment of those responsible for crimes, whereas the TRC was based on the notion that truth-telling and the establishment of an historical record would contribute to national reconciliation. In March 2002, the commissioners of the TRC were sworn in, and in November 2002

5. Letter dated 9 August 2000 from the Permanent Representative of Sierra Leone to the UN, addressed to the President of the Security Council (S/2000/786: Annex).
6. Agreement between the United Nations and the Government of Sierra Leone on the Establishment of a Special Court.
7. Interview, David Crane, Utrecht, 11 June 2008.

statement takers fanned out over the country to document the civil war. The TRC held public hearings between April and August 2003 and published its final report, including a set of recommendations for the government, in October 2004 (TRC, 2004).

The parallel operation of these two very different transitional justice institutions proved to be difficult and their relationship was often characterized by tension and competition. There were two main reasons for this. First, both institutions relied on voluntary contributions and competed for the limited funding made available by the Western donor countries for transitional justice in Sierra Leone. In the end, the Special Court was more successful in absolute terms, attracting initial funding of US\$ 56 million, less than half of what had originally been budgeted, whereas the TRC eventually received pledges of US\$ 4 million, also less than half of what had initially been budgeted (Schabas, 2003: 1039–40). Second, because of their parallel operation and debates about the scope of the amnesty granted under the Lomé Agreement, many people in Sierra Leone did not perceive the two institutions as separate entities with complementary mandates and therefore were not sure where the line would be drawn between those who would be granted amnesty and those facing prosecution (Coulter, 2009; Shaw, 2005, 2010: 118–23).

Officially, the representatives of the Special Court denied that there were difficulties between the two institutions. According to the court's first annual report, 'both organisations recognised their respective roles and objectives and, overall, the relationship proved to be cordial' (SCSL, 2003: 6). From a legal perspective, there was no conflict, according to the architects of the Special Court, as the amnesty did not apply to crimes committed under international criminal law. Hence, the prosecution for war crimes and crimes against humanity did not contradict the amnesty granted under the Lomé Agreement.

The TRC was more candid about difficulties that were admitted by representatives of the Special Court only in private. According to the TRC report, the parallel existence of the two organizations 'highlighted the need for harmonisation and an operational model designed to mitigate inherent tensions and avoid potential pitfalls in future instances where a TRC and criminal court work are supposed to work in tandem' (TRC, 2004: 17). The TRC report highlighted the problems of the simultaneous operation in a context where a peace agreement provided for a blanket amnesty and the establishment of a truth commission. In fact, the establishment of the Special Court rescinded the amnesty for those accused of 'bearing greatest responsibility' for the crimes committed during the civil war. From the TRC's perspective, this was highly problematic since the commission 'was proposed as a substitute for criminal justice in order to establish accountability for the atrocities that had been committed during the conflict' and the creation of the Special Court 'signalled to combatants in future wars that peace agreements containing amnesty clauses ought not to be trusted and, in so doing, has undermined the legitimacy of such national and regional peace initiatives' (TRC, 2004: 18).

The TRC report was also highly critical of the government led by President Kabbah who had declared a state of emergency and arrested hundreds of suspected RUF members in May 2000. Many of them remained in detention without charge for years (TRC, 2004: 448–51). The next section will examine in more detail these arrests and the criminal trials carried out by the national authorities during Sierra Leone's volatile transition period.

THE STATE OF EMERGENCY AND POLITICAL CONFLICTS

The justification given for the massive humanitarian-military intervention after 1999 and the establishment of two transitional justice mechanisms was the chaos of civil war that had been affecting Sierra Leone since 1991. From the perspective of diplomats and policymakers in New York, Washington and London, the situation in Sierra Leone constituted a threat to regional and global security. This concern added urgency to the diplomatic pressure exercised on the Sierra Leonean government to enter negotiations with the RUF and the renegade soldiers of the AFRC.

In May 1997, a group of junior soldiers in the AFRC, under the leadership of Major Johnny Paul Koroma, staged a coup against President Kabbah, forcing him into exile in Guinea for almost a year. The AFRC was eventually driven out of Freetown in February 1998; President Kabbah returned on 10 March, and immediately declared a state of emergency, which allowed the government to detain suspects without charge and to suspend civil rights. It did exactly that, arresting 1,600 suspected supporters of the RUF and AFRC.[8] Most of them were soon released but at the end of March 1998 the Attorney-General charged fifty-nine of them with treason in connection with the 1997 coup. Among them was the RUF leader Foday Sankoh, who had been extradited from Nigeria where he had been under house arrest since March 1997. Then, in July 1998, a court martial was held for a group of thirty-eight soldiers who had allegedly participated in the coup. Punishments handed down in the two trials were draconian. Thirty-two of those charged in the High Court, including Foday Sankoh, were found guilty and thirty-one of them received the death sentence. In the court martial, thirty-four were found guilty and received the death sentence. As the court martial did not provide for an appeal these executions were carried out one week after the judgment: on 19 October 1998, twenty-four soldiers were executed by firing squad on a beach near Freetown and the sentences of the remaining ten were commuted to life imprisonment. The appeals in the High Court cases were still pending when all the accused escaped during an assault by the AFRC and RUF on Freetown in January 1999 (Kandeh, 2004: 174; TRC, 2004: 307–16).

8. News reports for 26 March 1998: see www.sierra-leone.org/Archives/slnews0398.html

According to some observers (Bangura, 2000: 560; Kandeh, 2004: 175; Keen, 2005: 220), the treason trials against alleged AFRC supporters and the execution of the twenty-four soldiers were perceived as deepening ethnic and political divisions between northerners, who dominated the army, and people from the southeast, where the SLPP government enjoyed most support. The TRC report suggests that the execution of the soldiers alienated the RUF and the AFRC leadership from the government in Freetown and contributed to their decision to launch a counter-offensive in December 1998 that culminated in the attack on Freetown in January 1999 (TRC, 2004: 315–16).

This offensive finally grabbed international headlines and after the ECOMOG[9] peacekeeping troops led by Nigeria had repulsed the rebels of the AFRC and the RUF, international pressure on the government and the rebels to negotiate a peace agreement grew. The signing of the Lomé Agreement in June 1999 appeared to usher in a new spirit of cooperation and reconciliation between government and rebels. The state of emergency remained in force but the RUF transformed itself into a political party, the Revolutionary United Front Party (RUFP), and joined the SLPP in a government of national unity. The combatants of all armed groups were to participate in a DDR programme. UN peacekeepers arrived in the country to oversee the implementation of the Lomé Agreement.

In October 1999, some of the more educated RUF leaders — the 'political wing' (TRC, 2004: 335) — joined the government headed by President Kabbah as cabinet ministers and deputy ministers. RUF leader Foday Sankoh was appointed Chairman of the grandly named Commission for the Management of Strategic Resources, National Reconstruction and Development (CMMRD), a position with the status of Vice-President (ibid.: 349). The RUFP received four cabinet positions and four deputy minister positions. This was short of the promises made in Lomé, where the RUF had been promised a senior ministry such as Finance, Foreign Affairs or Justice (ibid.: 349). Meanwhile, the RUF field commanders who controlled large swathes of the north and east of the country were reluctant to disarm the forces under their command (ibid.: 337–9, 352–3). At this point, their relationship with the political leadership of the RUFP in Freetown was strained and communications were poor (ibid.: 353–5). The political leaders around Foday Sankoh, in turn, had an interest in keeping the armed cadres as an alternative option and for political leverage (ibid.: 362–4).

The reluctance of the RUF leadership to disarm led, at the beginning of May 2000, to several attacks by RUF combatants on UN peacekeepers who were tasked with disarming the RUF. Within a week more than 500 UN peacekeepers had been taken hostage by the RUF. These attacks on the peacekeepers were widely seen as a violation of the Lomé Peace Agreement

---

9. The Economic Community of West African States Monitoring Group.

and, on 8 May 2000, thousands of people gathered at Sankoh's residence in Freetown in a peaceful protest. During the demonstration Sankoh's bodyguards opened fire and killed twenty-two demonstrators. Former AFRC soldiers loyal to Major Johnny Paul Koroma and CDF fighters who had joined the demonstration then attacked Sankoh's compound. Fifteen people in the compound were killed, but Sankoh and the senior RUF cadres present were able to escape. After nine days in hiding, Sankoh was arrested on 17 May 2000 (ibid.: 331–447).

In response to the violation of the Lomé Agreement, President Kabbah and his inner circle used a two-pronged strategy against the RUF. In August 2000, he sent a letter to the UN Security Council, urging it to establish a special court 'to try and bring to credible justice those members of the RUF and their accomplices responsible for committing crimes against the people of Sierra Leone and for taking of UN peacekeepers as hostages'.[10] In Resolution 1315, the UN Security Council decided that the Special Court should have jurisdiction over members of all warring factions but limited it to those bearing 'greatest responsibility' for the crimes committed during the war. Earlier, however, on 7 and 8 May 2000, President Kabbah had used the state of emergency to order the arrest of almost 200 suspected members of the RUF. The TRC report criticizes Kabbah's government for using the violent incident as a pretext to end the RUF's participation in government. The TRC report concludes that several RUF ministers and some of Sankoh's bodyguards had already been arrested before the demonstration, on 7 May 2000, in a pre-emptive move authorized by the SLPP majority in parliament. In effect, this move dissolved the government of national unity even before the violent incident on 8 May 2000 (ibid.: 390–91). By the end of May 2000, the police had arrested several hundred suspected members of the RUF under the state of emergency (AI USA, 2001).[11]

These arrests neutralized the RUF/RUFP political leadership and effectively thwarted the attempts of some of its elements to convert their wartime exploits into political office. It also revealed a split between the RUF's political elite in Freetown and the 'military wing' — the field commanders who occupied large parts of the north and who did not seek to free the arrested RUF members. After three weeks, and after negotiations with the Liberian President Charles Taylor, they released the UN peacekeepers. Issa Sesay emerged as the RUF's interim leader in May 2000; under his leadership, the RUF eventually agreed to resume disarmament in an agreement between the government and the RUF which was signed in May 2001 (ibid.: 461).

---

10. UN Security Council S/2000/786 Letter dated 9 August 2000 from the permanent representative of Sierra Leone to the UN addressed to the President of the Security Council.
11. After keeping them for almost two years in detention, the public prosecutor's office charged Sankoh and sixty RUF members with the murder of the protesters who were killed on 8 May 2000 at Sankoh's compound in Freetown; the other detainees were released.

The arrests under the state of emergency not only targeted the RUF. Between 2000 and 2003, the Sierra Leonean authorities arrested dozens of renegade soldiers who had belonged to the AFRC. Most of them were associated with a group of former AFRC members, the West Side Boys. These arrests came in two waves. In September 2000, a group of West Side Boys were arrested in the wake of a British commando raid to free British soldiers who had been taken hostage. Thirty-eight of them were charged with murder, conspiracy to murder and aggravated robbery. The second wave followed the attempted attack on an armoury near Freetown in January 2003 when about eighty individuals, mainly former members of the AFRC and West Side Boys, were arrested. Among them were Alex Tamba Brima, Bazzy Kamara and Santigie Borbor Kanu, who were later indicted for war crimes by the Special Court. The public prosecutor charged seventeen individuals with treason (AI USA, 2004). In December 2004, the High Court found eleven of them guilty, passing ten death sentences and one sentence of ten years' imprisonment. In March 2006, the trials of the former RUF members were eventually concluded. The High Court acquitted forty-two of the accused and found twenty-six guilty, passing prison sentences of up to ten years. In the trial against the West Side Boys, twenty-five accused were acquitted and six were sentenced to life imprisonment (AI USA, 2007). The eleven verdicts of treason passed in December 2004 were eventually overturned in December 2008, when the Court of Appeals acquitted the accused because of lack of evidence, and released them.

The manner in which the government handled the detentions and trials provoked protests from Amnesty International and other human rights groups (AI USA, 2003). The TRC report also formulated a scathing critique of the use of the emergency powers to detain former RUF and AFRC members in 'safe custody' and to imprison them for years without trial (TRC, 2004: 72–4). Referring to the arrest of twenty-five members of the RUF in May 2000, who were held under emergency regulations for two years, the report concluded that:

> The 25 men arrested on 7 May 2000 stand as living examples of the abuse of the justice system that persists in Sierra Leone. Their continued detention beyond the morning of 8 May 2000 dealt a crushing blow to the causes of truth and reconciliation in Sierra Leone ... There has been no transparency whatsoever in the disposal of 'justice' against these men. (ibid.: 397)

Based on these findings, the commission recommended the 'immediate release of all persons held in "safe custody detention"' (ibid.: 127) and the protection of fundamental human rights even under emergency regulations (ibid.: 129). It is noteworthy that the TRC translated this critique of Kabbah's government into 'imperative recommendations' (ibid.: 129) but the commission's critique of the arrest of the RUF members was never acknowledged by the government and President Kabbah never accepted any limitation of the emergency powers vested in him by the constitution (although he did refrain from using them after 2002).

The account of these arrests and detentions under a state of emergency undermine the official narrative of the country's slow emergence from civil war and chaos with the help of the 'international community' and the Special Court for Sierra Leone. It also raises doubts about the image of Kabbah's government as a champion of peace and reconciliation. The TRC report sketches a much more ambivalent picture in which President Kabbah and the SLPP used the emergency powers and the government's international legitimacy in a deliberate attempt to marginalize the leaders of the RUF and the AFRC who continued to threaten Sierra Leone's new beginning — although they tried to conceal their plans behind the lofty language of peace, justice and national reconciliation. This language had been espoused by all leaders of the warring factions. Even Foday Sankoh called for forgiveness when he said 'we are ready to give peace a chance' after signing the Lomé Agreement, although many in Sierra Leone and abroad found it difficult to take this statement seriously.[12] By comparison, President Kabbah's commitment to peace seemed more credible and as legitimate head of state, elected in the 1996 elections, he enjoyed the support of the international community. It can be argued that, after the Lomé Peace Agreement unravelled, he used the emergency powers against the RUF and the AFRC because they were perceived to be a threat to the fragile peace agreement. These arrests and trials, however, were eclipsed by the trials at the Special Court involving the men charged with 'bearing greatest responsibility' for the crimes committed during the civil war.

ARRESTED DEVELOPMENTS: THE SPECIAL COURT INDICTEES

In terms of sheer numbers, the thirteen indictments of the Special Court were dwarfed by the arrests of hundreds of members of the RUF, AFRC and West Side Boys between 2000 and 2003 and the trials of more than eighty of them accused of murder, treason and other serious crimes. Symbolically, however, the Special Court indictments played a central role in the official narrative of Sierra Leone's new beginning. President Kabbah and the country's political establishment, as well as representatives of the UN, the UK, the US and the Special Court, highlighted the importance of the court for the country's transition from a violent past to a peaceful future. They were endorsed by international activist organizations such as No Peace Without Justice and Human Rights Watch. The Special Court not only symbolized a national new beginning but was also hailed as an important step in the development of international justice. By contrast, the arrests and trials carried out by the national authorities had the nature of ordinary criminal trials against political opponents accused of treason that have been a feature of Sierra Leonean politics since independence (cf. Kandeh, 2004).

---

12. Sankoh's statement was made on 7 July 1999 during the signing ceremony in Lomé (www.sierra-leone.org/Archives/slnews0799.html).

The exceptional and highly symbolical character of the Special Court indictments warrants closer analysis. This section examines the attempts of the men arrested in 2003 to carve out a niche for themselves in post-war Sierra Leone; it does so by comparing them with similar attempts by former commanders of the various armed factions.[13] It shows that the efforts of the Special Court indictees to establish new livelihoods after the end of the war did not differ substantially from those of former combatants in general; all of them tried to gain social and economic autonomy, although the indictees did so at a much grander scale and with much more success than their followers — until their arrests (Bürge, 2011; Coulter, 2009; Peters, 2005; 2011; Shaw, 2010). After Foday Sankoh died in the custody of the Special Court in July 2003, Sam Hinga Norman, Minister of Internal Affairs at the time of his arrest, and Major Johnny Paul Koroma were the only indictees in Sierra Leone who had political ambitions at the national level.

The three former RUF commanders who remained in the Special Court's detention facility after Sankoh's death had much more modest ambitions. After the arrests of the RUF's political wing in May 2000, the RUF field commanders — the 'military wing' — in the north and the east concentrated on the benefits offered by the DDR programme. The Special Court indictees Issa Sesay, Morris Kallon and Augustine Gbao were no exception: at the time of their arrest in March 2003, Sesay and Kallon were in the process of setting up fisheries projects as part of community development initiatives, while Gbao was running an agricultural development project in his home village in Kenema district.[14]

Before he was arrested at the Special Court's behest, Sesay was apparently also in negotiation with Oluyemi Adeniji, Special Representative of the UN Secretary General, for a scholarship abroad.[15] In Sierra Leone, various leaders of armed factions have used this strategy to go abroad. The leaders of the National Provisional Ruling Council (NPRC) received scholarships to study in Britain and the US. Valentine Strasser, the former head of state (1992–96), studied at the University of Warwick; former NPRC strongman SAJ Musa received a UN grant to study at Birmingham University; and Tom Nyuma, a former regional NPRC commander, attended college in the US before returning to Sierra Leone where he joined the SLPP in 2007 (Christensen, 2012). Compared to the more ambitious attempts of the RUF political leadership to convert the RUF's military strength into government positions after signing the Lomé Agreement in 1999, the efforts of Sesay and his co-accused to carve out a niche for themselves in the post-conflict order were very limited in scope. Nevertheless, had they succeeded in getting a

---

13. The indictment against Charles Taylor, former president of Liberia, is beyond the scope of this analysis; see footnote 1.
14. News reports of 12 March 2003: www.sierra-leone.org/archives/slnews0303.html (accessed 2 August 2010).
15. Interview, David Crane, Utrecht, 11 June 2008.

sponsorship or leading local development projects, they would have turned from rebel commanders into respected community members with a relatively secure livelihood — no small achievement in a society characterized by abject poverty and few economic opportunities.

The three former soldiers who stood trial at the Special Court had been members of the AFRC and later the West Side Boys. As noted above, the AFRC was formed under the leadership of Major Johnny Paul Koroma after mutinous soldiers had toppled the democratically elected government in May 1997. When they were pushed out of Freetown in February 1998 by Nigerian-led ECOMOG forces, they regrouped in the northern part of Sierra Leone. They then attacked Freetown in January 1999 with the explicit objective of being reinstated into the Sierra Leone Army (SLA).[16] According to the TRC report, reintegration into the army continued to be their primary objective after the Lomé Agreement (TRC, 2004: 330, 387). In a surprising move, Kabbah appointed Johnny Paul Koroma as Chairman of the Commission for the Consolidation of Peace (CCP), the body charged with overseeing the implementation of the Agreement, in a bid to 'engage Koroma in the peace process in the interests of national reconciliation' (ibid.: 343–4).

Many former AFRC fighters succeeded in filtering back into the SLA, which was being trained by the British, but many others — including former commanders — were less lucky. The largest organized group of former soldiers were the West Side Boys in the Okra Hills east of Freetown. They consisted of former AFRC combatants who had established a base there after their attack on Freetown was repulsed by Nigerian troops in February 1999.[17] The West Side Boys were led by Bazzy Kamara (a Special Court indictee) and Hassan Bangura (aka Bombblast). They professed allegiance to Johnny Paul Koroma and after Koroma was appointed Chairman of the CCP, many of them joined him in Freetown where they acted as his bodyguards. In May 2000, this group acted as an auxiliary force to government troops fighting against the RUF (TRC, 2004: 384–9, 428, 459; Utas and Jörgel, 2008: 503). The West Side Boys' support for the government was rewarded and their leaders rejoined the army or continued to work as Koroma's bodyguards (TRC, 2004: 330–1; Utas and Jörgel, 2008: 504).[18]

Major Johnny Paul Koroma had been instrumental in neutralizing the RUF as a political force during the events in the beginning of May 2000 and he

---

16. Trial Chamber Judgment 20 June 2007 Prosecutor v. Brima, Kamara and Kanu, SCSL-04–16-T-613: 72.
17. Trial Chamber Judgment 20 June 2007 Prosecutor v. Brima, Kamara and Kanu, SCSL-04–16-T-613: 79.
18. A remnant group stayed in the Okra Hills and abducted a group of British soldiers in August 2000. This group was largely destroyed during a British commando raid to free the hostages: at least twenty-five fighters were killed and eighteen others, including their leader Foday Kallay, were arrested (Telegraph 17 September 2000: www.telegraph.co.uk/news/worldnews/europe/1355809/Fire-fight-in-the-Occra-Hills.html).

emerged as a key player in the period between 2000 and 2003. In August 2000, he officially disbanded the AFRC and formed a political party, the Peace and Liberation Party (PLP). He was elected as a Member of Parliament for Wilberforce in Freetown, an area where many soldiers live, in the general elections of May 2002. In January 2003, some of his followers — including Alex Tamba Brima and Santigie Bobor Kanu, who were later indicted by the Special Court for war crimes — were arrested after a failed attack on an armoury in Freetown. Koroma was able to escape and allegedly fled to Liberia. Rumours that he was killed on the orders of Charles Taylor have been vehemently disputed by Taylor's defence lawyers.[19] Koroma's escape came just weeks before his indictment by the Special Court and in spite of the rumours about his death he is officially considered to be still at large. His indictment by the Special Court could have been anticipated: as the leader of the AFRC he was one of the principal suspects and among the first nine persons indicted by the court on 7 March 2003.

By contrast, the leader of the Civil Defence Forces, Sam Hinga Norman, then Minister of Internal Affairs, was very surprised when he was arrested on 10 March 2003 since he had not expected to be indicted.[20] With the exception of Charles Taylor, who was arrested in 2006, Norman was the most high profile military-political leader to be arrested by the Special Court. The CDF was a pro-government militia that had fought against the rebels of the RUF and the renegade soldiers of the AFRC (Hoffman, 2007), and which was committed to re-establishing the democratically elected government of President Kabbah. CDF was actually an umbrella term for several ethnic militias that had emerged during the early and mid-1990s to defend local communities from attacks by the RUF rebels and marauding government soldiers. The CDF mainly consisted of the Mende ethnic militias known as *kamajors*, the Mende word for traditional hunters (Hoffman, 2007: 642). After the Mende-dominated Sierra Leone People's Party won the general elections in 1996, Norman emerged as leader of the *kamajors* and was appointed deputy Minister of Defence. In 2002, he was appointed Minister of Internal Affairs. According to some observers, Norman claimed a leadership role in the SLPP and was perceived by other SLPP leaders as a threat to their interests (Abraham, 2003). His arrest effectively thwarted any plans he might have had of playing a leading role in national politics.

During the civil war, the CDF had fought against the RUF and AFRC and sometimes served as an auxiliary force for the West African peacekeeping force, ECOMOG. After disarmament in 2002 many of its commanders set up development projects and NGOs or joined local politics as SLPP functionaries. Others sought office in the chiefdom administrations with which the *kamajors* and the other ethnic militias had been in close contact during

19. Special Court for Sierra Leone, Defence Motion for Disclosure of Exculpatory Information relating to DCT-032, 24 September 2010.
20. Interview, David Crane, Utrecht, 11 June 2008.

the war (Hoffman, 2007: 660). Moinina Fofana, former 'Director of War' of the CDF, for example, was appointed Chiefdom Speaker, i.e. head of the Paramount Chief's administration, in his native chiefdom. His attempt to convert his high position in the CDF into political office was thwarted by the prosecutors of the Special Court for Sierra Leone who ordered his arrest in June 2003. Another of the accused, Allieu Kondewa, former *kamajor* 'High Priest', had returned to his home area in Bonthe district where he operated as herbalist until his arrest in June 2003.

This account of the Special Court's indictees reveals a complex and volatile political landscape in which the former commanders and leaders worked hard to find a position which would provide them with political influence, material security or at least safety from their political opponents. It juxtaposes the struggles of the men who were presented as the main culprits, with the lofty promises of justice made by the Special Court for Sierra Leone. The arrests of the leaders of the three groups led to three separate trials at the Special Court's compound in the capital. The trial against Sesay, Kallon and Gbao, the so-called RUF trial, began in July 2004 and concluded on 25 February 2009, when the trial chamber found Sesay and Kallon guilty on sixteen counts and Gbao on fourteen counts. Sesay was sentenced to fifty-two years' imprisonment, Kallon to forty years and Gbao to twenty-five years, minus the time served since their arrest. In a decision delivered on 26 October 2009, the Appeals Chamber upheld these convictions. The trial against three leaders of the AFRC, Alex Tamba Brima, Brima Bazzy Kamara and Santigie Borbor Kanu, started in March 2005. The trial chamber delivered its judgment on 20 June 2007 and convicted the accused on eleven counts. Brima was sentenced to fifty years, Kamara to forty-five years and Kanu to fifty years, minus time served. These convictions, too, were upheld by the court's Appeals Chamber. The trial against three CDF leaders, Sam Hinga Norman, Moinina Fofana and Allieu Kondewa, began in June 2004. Norman died in February 2007 while undergoing medical treatment in Dakar, Senegal (SCSL, 2007). On 2 August 2007 the trial chamber found the remaining two accused guilty on four counts and sentenced them to six and eight years, including time served. The Appeals Chamber overturned these sentences, and sentenced Fofana to fifteen years and Kondewa to twenty years, minus time served.[21]

CONCLUSIONS

Regardless of the concept of justice one adheres to, the Special Court for Sierra Leone largely failed to deliver its lofty promises. Supporters of a

---

21. On 31 October 2009, the eight convicted men were transferred to a prison in Rwanda where they are currently serving their sentences. This decision was taken because the prisons in Sierra Leone do not meet international standards, while Rwanda had capacity in a prison in which convicts of the International Criminal Tribunal for Rwanda were supposed to be detained (SCSL, 2009).

retributive vision of justice were disappointed that only thirteen individuals were indicted for bearing 'greatest responsibility' for the war crimes and crimes against humanity committed during the civil war. Amnesty International criticized the indictment of only a 'small number of the persons responsible for the numerous crimes committed' (AI, 2008). On the other hand, proponents of more holistic approaches such as the TRC, failed to see how the symbolical punishment of a few men could contribute to coming to terms with the country's violent past. In the TRC's opinion, the Special Court's emphasis on punishment undermined the TRC's 'restorative and healing objectives' (TRC, 2004: 18).

The evidence presented in this chapter casts doubt on the claims to justice advanced by both organizations and suggests that Sierra Leone's experiment with transitional justice had a much more mixed outcome. The Special Court has been presented as standing above the national legal framework and outside the national political landscape, but in fact it was the product of a violent conflict in which the RUF, and later the AFRC/West Side Boys, were marginalized and ceased to play a decisive role in national politics. The arrests, detentions and trials were one of the means employed by the government led by President Kabbah in this conflict between the political establishment and the rebels who sought to convert their wartime exploits into political office and material security. The TRC, in turn, delivered a damning verdict on the human rights record of Kabbah's government and the extensive use of the state of emergency, although its recommendations in this regard have never been implemented or even acknowledged by the government.

Both organizations were part of the national political arena and have to be seen in the context of the multi-faceted and contested new beginning that was characterized by the attempts of politico-military leaders and commanders to convert their military strength into political and economic capital after the end of the war. The transition period was contradictory and by no means the linear progression from war to democracy suggested by the official narratives. Behind the façade of official commitments to peace and justice, the leaders of the various factions were engaged in a bitter power struggle over the terms of the new beginning. In the meantime, tens of thousands of their followers went through the DDR process and tried to make a life for themselves under conditions of abject poverty and with little prospect of improvement. For the hundreds of members of the RUF and West Side Boys who were detained at Pademba Road Prison for up to six years the situation has been even more difficult: they were cut off from society during their detention and now carry the stigma of ex-detainees. In this sense, the new beginning in Sierra Leone displays many features of the pattern of doing politics or 'politricks' (Christensen and Utas, 2008) that has characterized Sierra Leone since independence.

The discrepancy between the official narrative of a new beginning — effected by means of handing down justice and holding accountable the perpetrators of violence according to the strict principles of international rule of law — and the messy reality of post-conflict politricks, mass arrests under a state of emergency and protracted trials in the national courts, is exemplified in the urban topography of Freetown. From a strictly legal perspective, the Special Court's narrow and compartmentalized approach was arguably justified, but the fact that its representatives ignored the detainees in Pademba Road Prison, just a few hundred metres down the road from the court's compound, raises doubts about its wider contribution to national reconciliation and justice in Sierra Leone. In fact, several men indicted by the Special Court were transferred from Pademba Road Prison, but the court's representatives refused to address the contradiction between their promise to deliver justice and the detention of hundreds of people under a state of emergency in a prison failing to meet international standards.

REFERENCES

Abraham, A. (2003) 'Sierra Leone: Post-conflict Transition or Business as Usual?'. News from NAI series. Uppsala: The Nordic Africa Institute. http://www.nai.uu.se/publications/news/archives/033abraham/

AI (2008) *The Implementation of Key Recommendations: Priorities in 2008 and Beyond.* London: Amnesty International Secretariat.

AI USA (2001) *Annual Report: Sierra Leone.* New York: Amnesty International USA.

AI USA (2003) *Annual Report: Sierra Leone.* New York: Amnesty International USA.

AI USA (2004) *Annual Report: Sierra Leone.* New York: Amnesty International USA.

AI USA (2007) *Annual Report: Sierra Leone.* New York: Amnesty International USA.

Bangura, Y. (2000) 'Strategic Policy Failure and Governance in Sierra Leone', *Journal of Modern African Studies* 38(4): 551–77.

Bürge, M. (2011) 'Riding the Narrow Tracks of Moral Life: Commercial Motorbike Riders in Makeni, Sierra Leone', *Africa Today* 58(2): 59–95.

Christensen, M. (2012) 'Big Man Business in the Borderland of Sierra Leone', in M. Utas (ed.) *African Conflicts and Informal Power: Big Men and Networks*, pp. 60–77. London: Zed Books.

Christensen, M. and M. Utas (2008) 'Mercenaries of Democracy: The "Politricks" of Remobilized Combatants in the 2007 General Elections, Sierra Leone', *African Affairs* 107(429): 1–25.

Coulter, C. (2009) *Bush Wives and Girl Soldiers: Women's Lives through War and Peace in Sierra Leone.* Ithaca, NY: Cornell University Press.

Fassin, D. and M. Pandolfi (eds) (2010) *Contemporary States of Emergency: The Politics of Military and Humanitarian Interventions.* New York: Zone Books.

Hoffman, D. (2007) 'The Meaning of a Militia: Understanding the Civil Defence Forces of Sierra Leone', *African Affairs* 106(425): 639–62.

Kandeh, J.D. (2004) 'Unmaking the Second Republic: Democracy on Trial', in I. Abdullah (ed.) *Between Democracy and Terror: The Sierra Leone Civil War*, pp. 164–79. Dakar: CODESRIA.

Keen, D. (2005) *Conflict and Collusion in Sierra Leone.* Oxford: James Currey.

Kelsall, T. (2009) *Culture under Cross-examination: International Justice and the Special Court for Sierra Leone.* Cambridge: Cambridge University Press.

Peters, K. (2005) 'Reintegrating Young Combatants in Sierra Leone: Accommodating Indigenous and Wartime Value Systems', in J. Abbink and I. van Kessel (eds) *Vanguard or Vandals: Youth, Politics and Conflict*, pp. 267–96. Leiden: Brill.

Peters, K. (2011) *War and the Crisis of Youth in Sierra Leone*. Cambridge: Cambridge University Press.

Schabas, W. (2003) 'The Relationship between Truth and Reconciliation Commissions and International Courts: The Case of Sierra Leone', *Human Rights Quarterly* 25(4): 1035–66.

SCSL (2003) 'First Annual Report of the President of the Special Court for Sierra Leone for the Period 2 December 2002 – 1 December 2003'. Freetown: Special Court for Sierra Leone.

SCSL (2007) 'Autopsy Shows Sam Hinga Norman Died of Natural Causes'. Press Release, 28 March. Freetown: Special Court for Sierra Leone.

SCSL (2009) 'Special Court Prisoners Transferred to Rwanda to Serve their Sentences'. Press Release, 31 October. Freetown: Special Court for Sierra Leone.

Shaw, R. (2005) 'Rethinking Truth and Reconciliation Commissions: Lessons from Sierra Leone'. Special Report No. 130. Washington, DC: United States Institute of Peace.

Shaw, R. (2010) 'Linking Justice with Reintegration? Ex-combatants and the Sierra Leone Experiment', in R. Shaw, L. Waldorf and P. Hazan (eds) *Localizing Transitional Justice: Interventions and Priorities after Mass Violence*, pp. 111–32. Stanford, CA: Stanford University Press.

TRC (Sierra Leone Truth and Reconciliation Commission) (2004) *Witness to Truth: Report of the Sierra Leone Truth and Reconciliation Commission*. Accra: GPL Press.

Utas, M. and M. Jörgel (2008) 'The West Side Boys: Military Navigation in the Sierra Leone Civil War', *Journal of Modern African Studies* 46: 487–511.

8

'When we Walk Out, What was it all About?': Views on New Beginnings from within the International Criminal Tribunal for Rwanda

Nigel Eltringham

INTRODUCTION

Arusha

It's my first day at the International Criminal Tribunal for Rwanda (ICTR), Arusha, Tanzania. I meet with an External Relations officer. 'I haven't sold my soul to the devil yet', he tells me, 'but there are plenty of people willing to raise the flag and let it flutter in the wind'. He hands me a pamphlet entitled 'ICTR: Challenging Impunity'. 'Here's the propaganda', he says, telling me to go and speak to a particular prosecutor, who'll give me the 'official line'. 'He claims that a purpose of the ICTR is deterrence. But just look what's happening in Darfur', waving his hand northwards. 'This place is a salve for the conscience of an organization that could have done something in 1994'.

A few days later, I meet two defence lawyers in a hotel bar. 'It's a victor's court, a persecution of Hutus', one begins, 'a way of concealing the responsibility of the International Community'. 'Will it contribute to reconciliation?', I ask. 'The claim for reconciliation is puzzling. The Tribunal is actually a persecution of Hutus. No Tutsi have been brought here. This is a victor's court. That is how the Hutu in Rwanda and in the diaspora see it, as persecution'. 'But', the other defence lawyer interjects, 'the accused persons say, and keep saying, we shouldn't give up. We are putting everything on record for history. The truth will come out one way or another. "Put everything on the record", they say "and then later our children will decide on the truth"'.

I am grateful to the Nuffield Foundation (SGS/32034) and British Academy (SG-47168) for supporting research conducted under COSTECH (Tanzanian Commission for Science and Technology) Research Permit No. 2006–304-CC-2006–122. Part of the chapter was written while a Visiting Researcher at the School of Global Studies, University of Gothenburg. I am grateful to the school, especially Marita Eastmond and Joakim Öjendal, and to comments from those who attended the Global Studies Lecture at which an earlier version of the paper was presented. I am also grateful to Gerhard Anders and Olaf Zenker for organizing the panel 'Transition and Justice: Negotiating the Terms of New Beginnings in Africa' at the 4th European Conference on African Studies (Uppsala, 15–18 June 2011) at which an earlier version of the chapter was presented and to Mats Utas for his comments. I am also grateful to the anonymous reviewers who commented on earlier drafts.

Transition and Justice: Negotiating the Terms of New Beginnings in Africa, First Edition.
Edited by Gerhard Anders and Olaf Zenker.
Chapters © 2015 by The Institute of Social Studies. Book compilation © 2015 John Wiley & Sons, Ltd.

A few days later, I meet with a judge in his office. Our conversation begins with a discussion of how the accused were selected. He picks up a ring-bound document on his coffee table and reads from the Tribunal's Statute contained in a November 1994 UN Security Council Resolution: "'Upon a determination that a prima facie case exists, the Prosecutor shall prepare an indictment" — that's in Article 17'. I then ask about the Preamble to the Resolution which states that one of the purposes of the Tribunal is to 'contribute to the process of national reconciliation'. The judge replies, 'If the Tribunal does its work properly it will contribute to reconciliation. But we judges simply evaluate the credibility of evidence and relate it to the crimes alleged. The introduction of political objectives like reconciliation would undermine the quality of justice. My thoughts are governed by my judicial function. If I go into the court thinking about "purposes", then I would not be a judge'.

That afternoon, I finally meet the prosecutor recommended to me on my first day. I explain that I'm interested in knowing what those who work at the Tribunal think its purpose is. 'Let's take a look at the resolution', he says as he goes across to his desk and picks up the same bound set of documents consulted by the judge. He reads directly from the preamble "'will contribute to ensuring that such violations are halted and effectively redressed" — will end the cycle of impunity — and make a "contribution to peace and reconciliation". Therefore, we are making peace. This is a fundamental part of what we do'.

So ended my first two weeks in Arusha.

The ICTR

'When we walk out, what was it all about?' a prosecution lawyer once asked, posing the question as much to himself as to me. The comments above demonstrate that those who worked at the ICTR answered that question in diverse ways. In contrast to this diversity and nuance, the Registrar of the Tribunal wrote in the first edition of the *ICTR Newsletter* in 2003:

> As you all know, the Tribunal is striving to effectively discharge its mandate of trying persons accused of being responsible for genocide and other serious violations of humanitarian law committed in Rwanda in 1994. By so doing, the Tribunal is playing an effective role in promoting international peace and security and putting to an end such crimes. The Tribunal is also sending a strong message, regionally and internationally, that the international community is determined to put to an end the culture of impunity, which is a hallmark of such crimes. Also, by discharging its mandate, the Tribunal is contributing to the national reconciliation and unity in Rwanda. Unfortunately, little is known about how the daily activities of the ICTR are conducted. (Dieng, 2003: 1)

On one hand, this statement reflects positions noted in the Introduction to this volume (see also Anders and Zenker, 2014). As one of a number of transitional justice interventions in Africa, the ICTR was an exceptional response to the 1994 genocide and, as such, marked a 'new beginning' internationally, regionally and nationally as it tried to terminate an abiding 'culture of impunity'. And yet, the reference to hidden 'daily activities' raises questions about how those immersed in the quotidian activities of international criminal justice related to the Tribunal's purported exceptionality and its role as a 'new beginning'.

Recent scholarship has emphasized the need to attend to the way in which the supposedly universal mechanisms of 'transitional justice' are 'localized' (see Shaw et al., 2010). As a consequence of this research, scholars have argued that transitional justice institutions, including international tribunals, should be more attuned to the specificities of the contexts in which they operate (see Betts, 2005). This emphasis on the localization of transitional justice has concentrated on the affected 'locals' and has, on the whole, not concerned itself with those who work for these institutions (Baylis, 2008: 364). When they are considered, they tend to be homogenized. Madlingozi (2010: 225), for example, speaks of 'transitional justice entrepreneurs' whom he describes as 'a well-travelled international cadre of actors [who] theorize the field; set the agenda; legitimize what constitute appropriate transitional justice norms and mechanisms'. McEvoy (2007: 424–6) similarly states of transitional justice institutions that 'actors within such institutions develop a self-image of serving higher goals' and notes 'the tendency of international lawyers to eulogize the glory and majesty of international law'. However, in her critique of the 'rule of law' aspect of 'transitional justice' discourses, Clarke (2009: 64) says of the 'cosmopolitan elite' that implements international criminal justice that the 'interests that tie these individuals to their elite enterprise are varied — shaped by professional ambitions, corporate economic interests, a personal desire for travel, idealistic aspirations for world peace, a commitment to the moral project of human rights through rule of law mechanisms, or a combination of these'. I certainly encountered this diversity at the ICTR.

The specific sites occupied by this diverse group, in which their varied interests are played out, must also be recognized as *localities*; there is no such place as the 'international' divorced from the messiness of quotidian practice. As I have argued elsewhere (Eltringham, 2010: 208) international tribunals must be seen as sites of local 'vernacularization' (see Merry, 2006), where assumptions and claims regarding 'transitional justice' are mediated, appropriated, translated, modified, misunderstood or ignored by (cosmopolitan) 'locals' just as they are in the villages of Sierra Leone (Shaw, 2007); of East Timor (Kent, 2011) or Bosnia (Selimovic, 2010). This chapter, therefore, explores the messy realities of the ICTR as experienced by the (cosmopolitan) locals who worked there, who both invoked and challenged official claims that the ICTR was an exceptional response that marked a 'new beginning'. The chapter will gain entry to these divergent opinions by focusing on the lack of indictments of members of the Rwandan Patriotic Army for alleged massacres in Rwanda in 1994. First, following a brief introduction to the Tribunal, the chapter considers the claim that the Tribunal marked a 'new beginning'. Assessments of the ICTR by lawyers and judges are then explored through the accusations that the Tribunal enacted 'victor's justice'. All quotes are taken from interviews conducted in Arusha, 2005–2007.[1]

CONTEXT

Between 7 April and mid–July 1994 an estimated 937,000 Rwandans, the vast majority of whom were Tutsi, were murdered in massacres committed by militia, the *gendarmerie* and elements of the army, often with the participation of the local population (see Des Forges, 1999; Eltringham, 2004; IRIN, 2001). As de facto custodian of the term 'genocide', the United Nations was slow to designate the events as such. Only in his report of 31 May 1994, did the UN Secretary General declare genocide had been committed (UN, 1994b: para 36). In a letter to the President of the UN Security Council on 28 September 1994, the post-genocide Rwandan government requested that an international tribunal be established (UN, 1994c). This suggestion was supported on 4 October by a UN Commission of Experts appointed by the Secretary General (UN, 1994b: paras 133–42); on 6 October by the President of Rwanda (UN 1994a: 5); and, on 13 October, by the Special Rapporteur of the Commission on Human Rights on the situation of human rights in Rwanda (Degni-Ségui, 1994: 19). UN Security Council Resolution 955 (UN, 1994e),[2] initially sponsored by the United States and New Zealand, mentions the following purposes for the ICTR: to bring to justice those responsible for violations of international humanitarian law (referring to genocide, crimes against humanity and war crimes); to 'contribute to the process of national reconciliation and to the restoration and maintenance of peace'; and to halt violations of international humanitarian law (deterrence). Trials began in 1996 and lasted an average of four years (one lasted nine years) (GADH, 2009a: 76).

---

1. None of those interviewed are Rwandan. There have been no Rwandan judges at the ICTR and no Rwandan defence lawyers. Rwandans have acted as investigators for defence teams, as interpreters and in witness protection.
2. Rwanda voted against the Security Council resolution because it believed that the temporal jurisdiction should have been broader (from 1990–1994); that the ICTR should have had its own prosecutor and appeals chamber; that the judges should have had recourse to the death penalty; and that the tribunal should have been located in Rwanda (UN, 1994f: 13–16).

The organs of the Tribunal investigated, and put on trial, *any person* accused of committing the following in Rwanda in 1994: genocide (as defined by the 1948 UN Convention for the Prevention and Punishment of the Crime of Genocide); crimes against humanity (a widespread or systematic attack on a civilian population); and 'war crimes' (Article 3 common to the 1949 Geneva Conventions). The Tribunal's four courtrooms and offices were located in two rented wings of the Arusha International Conference Centre. The Tribunal had three principal organs: the Office of the Prosecutor (which investigated allegations, issued indictments and prosecuted the case in court); the Registry (administration); and three 'Trial Chambers' composed of sixteen permanent and nine *ad litem* judges. There was no jury; the three judges who sat in each trial assessed the evidence and issued a judgment. At the time of writing, seventy-five cases have been completed (including twelve acquittals), sixteen cases are on appeal and nine indictees remain 'at large'. The Tribunal has been the subject of sustained criticism regarding the selection of the accused; the cost (US$ 1.5 billion); and length of trials (see ICG, 2003; Peskin, 2008: 151–234). In 2009, the Security Council called on the Tribunal to complete all its work by the end of 2012 (UN, 2009b). On 20 December 2012, the Tribunal's judges issued their final sentence (apart from appeals), sentencing Augustin Ngirabatware (Minister of Planning during the genocide) to thirty-five years of imprisonment for genocide and crimes against humanity.

THE ICTR AS 'NEW BEGINNING'

UN Security Council Resolution 955 that brought the Tribunal into existence in November 1994 (UN, 1994e) would suggest a primary focus on the national level (bring to justice those responsible, deter future crimes and 'contribute to the process of national reconciliation and to the restoration and maintenance of peace'). But even in the Security Council debate immediately following the resolution's adoption it was clear that the relative weight given to these purposes, and their relationship to one another, was a matter of perspective. Although some members reiterated that the Tribunal would be an 'instrument of national reconciliation' (UN, 1994f: 6) others were less certain, commenting that 'The Tribunal might become a vehicle of justice, but it is hardly designed as a vehicle of reconciliation' (ibid.: 7).

There were also more subtle divergences. While for some members the ICTR would ensure that 'normality is restored to the country' (ibid.: 12), for others it would end Rwanda's *normal* 'cycle of violence' (ibid.: 5), characterized by some members as a 'culture of impunity' (ibid.: 7). Rather than 'the restoration and maintenance of peace', the fight against 'impunity' implied a radical 'new beginning' which, in the words of the Rwandan member, would require Rwandans to 'learn new values' and required the 'construction of a new society' (ibid.: 14). However, in addition to this national new beginning, hopes were expressed that the ICTR would play a role in the new beginning for the *global* project of international criminal justice. Members hoped the ICTR would 'provide international penal experience which will be useful for the establishment of the future permanent court [the International Criminal Court]' (ibid.: 4) and 'signify a breakthrough in creating mechanisms that would impose international criminal law' (ibid.: 7). Rather than a new beginning specific to Rwanda, the ICTR was perceived as a mechanism to further resuscitate the project of international criminal justice that had stalled after the International Military Tribunal (Major War Criminals) at Nuremberg (1945–46) and the International Military Tribunal for the Far East (1946–48). Even at this early stage, the ICTR was heralded as a new beginning, but the level at which that novelty applied (national or international) was unclear.

Given that such diverse positions on the purposes of the Tribunal were present in the first hours after its creation, it is no surprise that those whom I met in Arusha held equally varied perspectives on whether the Tribunal was an exceptional intervention marking a new beginning, or business as usual. As part of the recent resuscitation of the project of international criminal justice (beginning with the creation in 1993 of the International Criminal Tribunal for the Former Yugoslavia, ICTY), there was no established cadre of international criminal lawyers and judges to populate the ICTR courtrooms (Eltringham, 2010). In addition, none of the lawyers or judges I spoke with recalled a prior, burning commitment to international criminal justice. A prosecution lawyer, for example, explained that, 'through a friend', he had been a defence lawyer at another international criminal tribunal, had 'got a taste for this' and did not feel like going back to 'burglary or bank robbery'. A defence lawyer recalled how he received an e-mail from a friend who 'wanted someone with a bit of French and I thought it sounded interesting'. A prosecution lawyer, having been a banking lawyer for seventeen years, simply 'wanted to do something different'. Another defence lawyer told me how it appeared to be an 'interesting case and involved overseas travel, but I don't have any burning interest in International Criminal Law', while a judge told me how he was nominated by his State 'without prior consultation' and that 'It was not something I wanted to do'.

The apparent lack of previous investment or experience in the project of international criminal justice means that lawyers and judges lacked a priori expectations. The assessment of international criminal justice they held when I spoke to them, while not pre-determined by the institutional location they occupied, was forged by the specific power(lessness) that accompanied their institutional location whether judiciary, prosecution or defence. Judges have the power to judge, but they cannot choose who is indicted; defence lawyers have the power to 'preserve history', but they consider the ICTR to be a 'victor's court'. As a consequence of these different institutional locations and the relative power individuals possess, the claim that the ICTR marks a new beginning was interpreted in different ways. As will be discussed below, some who worked at the Tribunal reiterated the position found in the UN Security Council resolution and debate that, in ending impunity, the Tribunal was a new beginning for Rwanda as well as a new beginning for international criminal justice. However, certain defence lawyers, described as 'political' by their colleagues, saw the Tribunal as simply a new mode of long-established colonial domination and as the revivification of 'victor's justice' first encountered at the Nuremberg and Tokyo Tribunals. For them, the ICTR was 'business as usual' (see introduction to this volume; see also Anders and Zenker, 2014). I also encountered judges and defence lawyers who argued that the ICTR courtroom was no different from any other courtroom they had worked in and that defending/judging someone accused of genocide was no different from defending/judging someone accused of stealing a car or burglary. As the judge says in the opening section 'we judges simply evaluate the credibility of evidence and relate it to the crimes alleged'. Both these positions downplayed (in different ways) claims to exceptionality: 'political' defence lawyers bemoan the 'business as usual' of 'victor's justice' while judges and certain defence lawyers actively promote 'business as usual' in the courtroom.

When I first arrived at the Tribunal, a national new beginning for Rwanda consisting of 'peace' and 'reconciliation' permeated the ICTR's public presentation. The Tribunal's website reproduced part of a speech made in September 1998 by the then Secretary General, Kofi Annan: 'For there can be no healing without peace; there can be no peace without justice; and there can be no justice without respect for human rights and rule of law'. Over my first few days at the Tribunal, I became aware of other allusions to the Preamble. Pinned to a notice board outside the library there was a list of 'New Acquisitions & Highlights' the header of which read 'Information for Justice and Reconciliation'. On my first day, I was handed a twenty-six minute video produced in 2005 entitled 'Towards Reconciliation' and a leaflet entitled 'The ICTR at a Glance' (ICTR, n.d.) which stated that the ICTR was created 'to contribute to the process of national reconciliation in Rwanda and to the maintenance of peace in the region, replacing an existing culture of impunity with one of accountability'.

For me, such claims resonated with Falk-Moore's (2000: 2) observation that while 'ordinary experience' suggests law and legal institutions can only 'effect a degree of intentional control of society', this 'limited degree of control and predictability is daily inflated in the folk models of lawyers and politicians all over the world ... as if there were no possible uncertainties in the results'. As time went by, however, I became aware that rather than foreground the (intangible) national new beginning for Rwanda (reconciliation, peace), ICTR officials foregrounded the strictly quantifiable (number of arrests, number of convictions) *and* the tangible contributions to the *global* new beginning for international criminal justice (jurisprudence). Under the heading 'The Achievements of the ICTR', the leaflet 'The ICTR at a Glance' (ICTR, n.d.) provided the following list:

> Obtained the cooperation of the international community in the arrest of suspects, the travel of witnesses to Arusha, and the detention of convicted persons and, in general, support for its aims and activities.

> Secured the arrest of about 70 individuals accused of involvement in the 1994 genocide in Rwanda. Completed trials of several of those arrested ...

> Laid down principles of international law, which will serve as precedents for other International Criminal Tribunals and for courts all over the world. ...

> Established a complex international institution based in Arusha and Kigali. The institution includes four modern fully equipped Courtrooms and the first ever Detention Facility to be set up and run by a United Nations body.

I also became aware that this public emphasis on the global ('Laid down principles of international law') was replicated in internal documents. Of the nine 'accomplishments' outlined in an internal discussion paper on the 'legacy' of the ICTR and ICTY (ICTR, 2005), only two were concerned with Rwanda ('improved the chances of reconciliation between Rwanda's ethnic groups'; 'impact of the rule of law in Rwanda'); the remaining seven were concerned with the 'unique and innovative' legal decisions and judgments, the new beginning for international criminal justice (ibid.: 14).

Such emphases can, in part, be explained by the audit regime under which the ICTR operated. Since the introduction of a 'Completion Strategy' in 2003 (UN, 2003) the Tribunal's President and Prosecutor were required to present reports to the UN Security Council every six months (UN, 2004: para 6).[3] The oral reports occasionally referred to 'our contribution to justice and reconciliation in Rwanda', but the bulk of information was the strictly tangible (number of arrests, judgments, new trials started). The vast majority of those who worked at the Tribunal were not, however, subject to an audit regime. When they asked themselves, 'When we walk out, what was it all about?', a number of possibilities presented themselves. Some are tangible (number of arrests/completed trials, jurisprudence), some are speculative (national reconciliation, peace, deterrence). Some fulfil aspirations found in the Preamble to the 1994 Resolution (number of arrests/completed trials, national reconciliation, peace, deterrence) and some do not (ending the 'culture of impunity', jurisprudence). But there is a third, tripartite way in which these possibilities can be parsed: those that simply fulfil a formal requirement of the Tribunal as a court of law (number of arrests, completed trials); those that signal a new beginning for Rwanda (ending the 'culture of impunity', national reconciliation, peace, deterrence); and those that signal a new beginning, not for Rwanda, but for the project of international criminal justice (jurisprudence).

---

3. Oral reports are at http://ictr-archive09.library.cornell.edu/ENGLISH/speeches/index.html

I will take two prosecution lawyers as an illustration of the different ways individuals related to these different possibilities. The prosecutor quoted at the start of the chapter invested in the Rwanda-specific promises of the Preamble ('we are making peace'). Within minutes, however, he told me that the ICTR's 'legacy' was its global contribution to the new beginning of the project of international criminal law:

> We think of it as stitching together a fabric. The Tribunal, its law, its definitions of crimes, these are now all available to other institutions. This Tribunal has made an enormous contribution to the international legal regime. The Tribunal was not explicitly created for the purpose of knitting the fabric together, but these definitional achievements are consistent with that defining statute. We see our legacy as our jurisprudence.

For this prosecution lawyer, the legacy was straightforward: an 'enormous contribution to the international legal regime'. However, his use of the inclusive first person plural ('We see our legacy as our jurisprudence') is deceptive. Five days later I met with another prosecution lawyer. I began by asking him whether he thought that lawyers, on first arriving at the ICTR, believed it could achieve the promises of the Preamble. He responded with a far less celebratory tone than that of his colleague, 'We operatives of international justice assumed it would be simple, we would come and dispense justice, end the culture of impunity, establish peace and then go away. But it didn't happen that way'. He then employed the quantifiable: 'At Nuremberg only twenty-two tried, even at the Special Court for Sierra Leone [SCSL, established 2002], with all the gruesome acts there, only thirteen persons on trial. But in Rwanda, on the contrary, we have tried fifty people. So, what are we doing wrong? But nobody makes a good comparison between the ICTR and Sierra Leone or Nuremberg'.

Sensing he was reverting to the script I had encountered elsewhere, I asked him whether he considered ICTR jurisprudence (the precedents established by the trials) to be an 'achievement'. 'Jurisprudence is not an excuse', he replied, 'It's one of the complexities that we argue with; it's part of our legacy'. 'What do you mean', I asked, 'that jurisprudence is "not an excuse?"'. Talking first about the failure of the ICTR statute to provide compensation to victims he then spoke of his worries about how the ICTR was perceived in Rwanda:

> To a Rwandese who knows that the Akayesu trial[4] cost the International Community US$ 600,000 and victims are dying by their hundreds every day, can we say that we are delivering justice as a legacy? Victims continue to die while those detainees who would have died of AIDS have been kept alive. Therefore, when we go we will say that we have 'delivered justice', but would that resonate with the victims? Our legacy will be measured by how we improve the lives of Rwandese and stopped impunity.

---

4. In September 1998, Jean Paul Akayesu (mayor of Taba commune from April 1993 until June 1994) was the first person to be found guilty of the crime of genocide.

Compared to his colleague, he has a very different idea of what constitutes the ICTR's legacy and, by extension, how he understands the work he does. He does not contradict his colleague's assessment ('We see our legacy as our jurisprudence'), but global jurisprudence is not 'an excuse' for local failure. The two lawyers (located in the same organ) propose different ways in which the ICTR can be assessed; simply as a court of law ('we have tried fifty people'); as a new beginning for Rwanda ('improve the lives of Rwandese and stopped impunity'); or as a new beginning for the project of international criminal justice ('we see our legacy as our jurisprudence'). These nuanced differences of opinion become even more evident if one explores how different actors in the Tribunal related to accusations of 'victor's justice'.

'VICTOR'S JUSTICE' AND ALLEGATIONS AGAINST THE RWANDAN PATRIOTIC FRONT

As already indicated, the ICTR was created in response to the interim report (4 October 1994) of a UN Commission of Experts which concluded that Tutsi had been victims of genocide between 6 April and 15 July 1994 (UN, 1994b: paras 44, 124, 33, 48). The report stated that 'on the basis of ample evidence ... individuals from both sides to the armed conflict' had committed war crimes and crimes against humanity (ibid.: para 146); and that there were 'substantial grounds' to conclude that 'Tutsi elements' had committed 'mass assassinations, summary executions, breaches of international humanitarian law [i.e. war crimes] and crimes against humanity' (ibid.: para 82). The Commission stated that it had received from the UN High Commissioner for Refugees (UNHCR) 'extensive evidence of systematic killings and persecution ... of Hutu individuals by the [Rwandan Patriotic Front] army' (ibid.: 30). This would appear to be a reference to a report sent to the High Commissioner for Refugees by Robert Gersony who had led a UNHCR mission in Rwanda (1 August to 5 September 1994) to investigate the repatriation of refugees. On 19 September 1994, Gersony presented evidence to UN officials in Kigali of 'calculated, pre-planned, systematic atrocities and genocide against Hutus by the RPA', claiming that 30,000 had been massacred, that the 'methodology and scale' suggested a 'plan implemented as a policy from the highest echelons of the government', and that 'these were not individual cases of revenge and summary trials but a pre-planned, systematic genocide against the Hutus' (ICTR, 2006a: para 4; see also Khan, 2000: 51–4).[5] Although the UNHCR subsequently denied the existence of this report (Des Forges, 1999: 726), it appears that Gersony also briefed US diplomats in Kigali on 17 September 1994 (ICTR, 2006c) and that based on

---

5. UN officials rejected Gersony's findings (ICTR, 2006a: paras 6, 7; see Eltringham, 2004: 105–6).

this briefing and other reports (ICTR, 2006d), a US State Department memo (dated 21 September 1994) anticipated that the UN Secretary General would announce that there is 'evidence that the RPA is involved in ethnic cleansing, acts of genocide, or war crimes' (ICTR, 2006b). On 10 October 1994, the Commission of Experts met with UNHCR officials including Gersony (UN, 1994d: para 20) and in its final report (9 December 1994) recommended that 'an investigation of violations of international humanitarian law and of human rights law attributed to the [RPF] be continued by the Prosecutor for the International Tribunal for Rwanda' and that it would hand over 'all relevant files' to the UN Secretary General (UN, 1994d: para 100; see Sunga, 1995: 124).

That the ICTR would prosecute 'both sides' (those responsible for the genocide and the RPA for war crimes and crimes against humanity) remained the public intention in the early years of the Tribunal's operation. In February 1995, the UN Secretary General justified the choice of Arusha (Tanzania) as the seat of the ICTR by saying that it would ensure 'complete impartiality and objectivity in the prosecution of persons responsible for crimes committed by both sides to the conflict' (UN, 1995: para 42). Judge Laity Kama (then President of the ICTR) stated, in September 1998, that 'All parties, including the RPF, who have committed crimes against humanity must be prosecuted. It is a simple question of equality. The credibility of international justice demands it' (quoted in Hazan, 1998). 'Special investigations' into alleged crimes committed by the RPA/F were opened by the ICTR Prosecutor in February 1999 (Cruvellier, 2010: 240–41) and made public by Carla Del Ponte (the ICTR's third Prosecutor) in December 2000 (IRIN, 2000). Obstruction by the Rwandan government (dominated by the RPF), which prevented prosecution witnesses from travelling to Arusha, was interpreted, at the time, as a response to the threat of indictments (ICTY, 2002; UN Wire, 2002). Although both the ICTR President (ICTR, 2002) and Prosecutor (ICTY, 2002) registered formal complaints to the UN Security Council (in July and October 2002 respectively) it was only in August 2003 that the UN Security Council issued a resolution calling on Rwanda to 'render all necessary assistance to the ICTR, including on investigations of the Rwandan Patriotic Army' (UN, 2003: para 3).[6] Del Ponte was removed from her position as ICTR Prosecutor in September 2003. Although the new prosecutor, Hassan Bubacar Jallow, revived the 'Special Investigations' in 2004 (GADH, 2009b: 45), the prosecutorial strategy outlined in the ICTR President's 'Completion Strategy' (May 2004) indicated that only genocide cases would be prosecuted (ICTR, 2004a). No indictments against members of the RPA were forthcoming, and in 2009 the Prosecutor indicated that he had no intention of issuing indictments before the ICTR closed (UN, 2009a: 33).

---

6. A call repeated in a UN Security Council resolution on 26 March 2004 (UN, 2004).

At the time of Del Ponte's removal, it was suspected that this was due to her pursuit of the 'Special Investigation' and that she had been about to issue RPF indictments (Reydams, 2005: 978; see also HRW, 2003). Del Ponte herself indicated that she believed 'pressure from Rwanda contributed to the non-renewal of my mandate' (Hirondelle News Agency, 2003). In 2007, Florence Hartmann, Del Ponte's former spokesperson (2000–06), published a book in which she alleged that US diplomats had pressured Del Ponte not to indict the RPF and had, ultimately, been instrumental in removing her as ICTR Prosecutor (Hartmann, 2007: 261–79).[7] Del Ponte confirmed these allegations in her autobiography published in 2009 (Del Ponte and Sudetic, 2009: 234–39).[8]

Commentators have persistently accused the ICTR of 'victor's justice' (HRW, 2002; HRW and FIDH, 2006; Reydams, 2005) and allegations against the RPF are part of the judicial record (as indicated by the references to trial exhibits above).[9] As a consequence, rather than a new beginning for international criminal justice, the ICTR, it has been argued, was business as usual, marking a 'return to the Nuremberg paradigm of international criminal justice' (Reydams, 2005: 981), the paradigm of 'victor's justice'.

Hidden Views on 'Victor's Justice'

I found that the accusation of 'victor's justice' was a ubiquitous, if often private, concern among those with whom I spoke at the ICTR. Among the members of the Office of the Prosecutor, none dismissed allegations against the RPF. A number were adamant that there should be RPF indictments, while others argued that the genocide, as the 'major crime base', must remain the priority to ensure the rights of defendants who had been in custody for up to ten years. When, for example, I asked a prosecution lawyer whether he was concerned about the accusations of 'victor's justice', he replied:

> We are required to investigate RPF crimes because they are under our jurisdiction. But it needs to be approached diplomatically. We are accused of 'victor's justice', but our major crime base is the genocide. We still have people in detention awaiting trial. This must be the priority. How can we take on new cases when people have been in detention for four to five years and we are accused of violating their rights to a fair trial? There is a potential for the Rwandan government to disrupt trials. We are never sure that if we take up the issue what will happen.

---

7. Regarding US and UK support for the RPF dominated Rwandan Government, see CHRI (2009).
8. This explanation is challenged by others (Moghalu, 2005: 133).
9. All of these exhibits are available at http://trim.unictr.org

When I asked another prosecution lawyer about the ability of the Rwandan government to disrupt trials if RPF indictments were raised (as occurred in 2001–02), he replied, 'It would be possible for us [the prosecution] to do our cases without any one from Rwanda, but the defence would cry blue murder because all of their best witnesses are there'. Whether propelled by a sincere commitment to the rights of the accused or because infractions of the accused's rights can disrupt the prosecution's case, prosecution lawyers were keenly aware that the power of the Prosecutor was curtailed by the Rwandan government. Rather than a *principled* opposition to RPF indictments, this gave rise to a prevalent, pragmatic *resignation*. As a prosecution lawyer explained to me:

> Like Nuremberg, we are accused of enacting 'victor's justice'. Given that the RPF committed atrocities, although not genocide, the fact that the Prosecutor is unable to provide justice for those from the other side of the conflict continues to haunt us. The dilemma we face is that the Rwandan government can disrupt our trials. When we close, that is one of the criticisms we will face. We cannot complete trials without the help of the RPF. We want international justice, but we cannot avoid dilemmas.

What I found surprising was defence lawyers' understanding of the prosecution's dilemma, for example, a defence lawyer told me: 'The prosecution are tying themselves to the Rwandan government in order to get access to witnesses. It's not that the prosecutors are bad, but they're concerned with institutional survival. They're people who care'. Another defence lawyer observed that 'You can't charge the RPF, because Kagame [commander of the RPF in 1994 and President of Rwanda since 2000] would close down the Tribunal'. Even when a defence lawyer began by criticizing the prosecution, he still acknowledged this dilemma, 'The Prosecution has an attitude that taints all things because they are only prosecuting one side. But the witnesses all come from Rwanda. Therefore, the Prosecutor is stuck in this and cannot manoeuvre. The Rwandan government can close the doors and the Tribunal at a functional level will not operate'.

The revelations by Hartmann in 2007 regarding US pressure further enhanced defence 'sympathy' for the prosecution's position. While in 2005 a defence lawyer told me that 'When Del Ponte said on 13 December 2000 she would indict the RPF, she had the powers and the evidence, but no intention', by 2007 defence lawyers were distributing copies of the relevant sections of Hartmann's book (effectively exonerating Del Ponte) at a workshop organized to reflect on the Tribunal's 'legacy' (Eltringham, 2008). Yet, such sympathy always had a strategic edge with defence lawyers using an appreciation for the Prosecutor's 'dilemma' to imply that all the convictions were in doubt, that if 'the Tribunal was created to combat impunity' then one-sided convictions questioned 'the legitimacy of all judgements'.

This was not, however, a uniform position held by all defence lawyers. One described the use of RPF crimes as a defence as 'OK, I killed my wife because he did' (the *tu quoque* defence),[10] adding that because 'people have been here for a long time, they build up personal relations with the defendants which can lead them to a loss of objectivity'. This reflects a division I encountered among defence lawyers. While at the 2007 'legacy' workshop representatives of ADAD (Association des Avocats de la Defense) distributed a 109-page dossier entitled 'Avoiding a "Legacy" of Victor's Justice and Institutional Impunity: Challenges for the ICTR and the United Nations Security Council' (including excerpts from Hartmann's book), another defence lawyer described ADAD as being 'full of politically-motivated and self-promoting nitwits', complaining that there was an 'inordinate proportion of defence lawyers who are politically motivated'. Another defence lawyer observed how a colleague 'is so political. The clients all love it because he says what they want to hear, but his fellow defence lawyers hate him for it because it doesn't help their case'. A third defence lawyer summed up this position:

> Our job is no different from a plumber. There's a legal leak, you need a technician to fix it. We'd rather do interesting work and if the client isn't a sleaze ball, all the better. But it's a technical exercise. The process at the Tribunal should be focused on the resolution of a dispute, both sides should argue as hard as possible. But there's a lot of highly politically motivated people there.

This position among defence lawyers was that the Tribunal should be an *unexceptional* place in which politics (principally 'victor's justice') should be avoided in favour of technical 'business as usual'.

Those defence lawyers described as 'political' also considered the ICTR to be *unexceptional*, but for entirely different reasons. For them, as 'victor's justice', it amounted to 'business as usual' that could be traced back to Nuremberg. Yet, this was only one element of their complex evaluation of the ICTR. One defence lawyer (among those described as 'politically motivated' by colleagues) told me that that the ICTR was a 'political institution' and that 'it's just a bunch of white people condemning Africans to show what will happen if they do not toe the line'. The lawyer appealed to an 'alternative logic of the ordinary' in seeing a 'neo-colonial agenda ... behind the rhetoric of exception' and a 'new beginning' (see introduction to this volume; see also Anders and Zenker, 2014). Despite this denunciation, the lawyer still conceded that 'because the trials are adversarial it means that we can present to the public some reality in some small way, more and more stuff has come out'.

This position, that although the ICTR was a 'Victor's court' there were elements of the trials that were redeemable, was something I encountered with other defence lawyers. To return to the two defence lawyers quoted in

---

10. Meaning 'you, too' or 'you, also'; that is, 'Since you committed the same crime, why is it only me who is being prosecuted?'.

the opening section: although they described the ICTR as a 'victor's court' and 'a persecution of Hutus', they tempered their assessment by describing the trials as a mechanism to preserve history (see Eltringham, 2009):

> The accused persons say, and keep saying, we shouldn't give up. We are putting everything on record for history. The truth will come out one way or another. Put everything on the record and then later our children will decide on the truth. People will be able to read and make their own decisions in the future. We have all the records. The judgement is not made now; the judgement will be made in the future.

Like their colleague ('more and more stuff has come out'), these defence lawyers saw trials as a mechanism to establish the 'true' history of the 1994 genocide. But *unlike* their colleague, they did not reject the wider project of international criminal justice. Regarding the SCSL, for example, one of the two defence lawyers observed that 'In Sierra Leone, all the parties in the conflict were indicted'. Although condemning the ICTR as a 'victor's court', these defence lawyers *also* spoke of their clients' commitment to the trial; that the trial provided an opportunity for creating a 'record for history' and that failures at the ICTR did not mean that the project of international criminal justice was universally moribund.

The idea that ICTR trials, whatever their shortcomings, were redeemable as a mechanism to record 'history' was conveyed by other defence lawyers. One noted that a client had told his lawyer, 'We appreciate what you have done, that our children's children will know the truth, that truth was spoken and that truth cannot be hidden forever'. Another defence lawyer observed that the 'semblance of an equality of arms' enabled the disclosure and publication of documents related to alleged RPF crimes, thus an opportunity to tell 'the untold story of the Rwanda War'. While on one hand these defence lawyers denounced the ICTR as an *unexceptional* continuation of 'victor's justice' traced back to Nuremberg and Tokyo, they simultaneously acknowledged that the ICTR provided an *extra-ordinary* opportunity to collate and disseminate a counter-narrative.

So what of the judges? When I first met the judge quoted in the opening comments at the start of this chapter, I asked not about allegations against the RPF, but simply how 'the Tribunal' had chosen to put certain people on trial.[11] The judge responded, 'I don't have a direct answer, but I can say two things. First, the Prosecutor is an independent organ of the Tribunal. The decision to prosecute is made by the Prosecutor without any influence. Therefore, it is not "the Tribunal" which selects the accused'. In this way, the judge swiftly disaggregated 'the Tribunal', delineating the power of the Prosecutor in order to demarcate his own power(lessness). To further emphasize this, the judge reached for a binder of the ICTR's key legal documents resting on

---

11. For the prosecution's stated criteria for prosecution, see ICTR (2004b).

his coffee table and read to me the article of the 1994 Statute which declares the Prosecutor's independence (UN, 1994e: Art. 17). By exhibiting the 'cult of the text' (Bourdieu, 1987: 851) and deferring to an immutable text that assigns roles and power, the judge was making clear to me that while judges must approve an indictment prepared by the prosecution (UN, 1994e: Art 18[1]), they cannot order the indictment of anyone or review the Prosecutor's decision not to indict someone who has been investigated. Unprompted, he continued:

> Selective prosecution has been a judicial question, that we only prosecute Hutu people when Tutsi people also committed crimes against humanity ... you know, this idea of 'victor's justice' that has been around since Nuremberg and that it is no different here. I, from a judicial point of view, I would not describe it as this, but judiciary are not involved in the selection of who to prosecute.

It is worthy of note that it was the judge who introduced the issue of 'victor's justice' and the 'business as usual' reference back to Nuremberg. In this light, his initial emphasis on the independence of the judiciary and reference to the Statute suggests 'victor's justice' is a constant accusation from which the judge was seeking to pre-emptively insulate himself.

While abdicating responsibility was one response I encountered among judges, I also encountered other positions. One judge, for example, told me (in 2007) that 'It's essential that the RPF is put on trial. UN Security Council Resolutions 1503 and 1504 include the RPF'. When, later in the conversation, I asked him whether he thought one of the objectives of the ICTR was to create an 'historical record', he replied that if it 'established facts in an unemotional, detached way', it would 'contribute to reconciliation'. He continued, however, in a more cryptic fashion:

> There are small contributions here and there. The acquittals, for example, or those who have been convicted, but acquitted on some counts, demonstrate that reality is not black and white, but a mixture. Asking questions such as who shot the plane down, etc.? The important thing is that it's perceived as being fair and not short-sighted. At the same time we've included references to books, the testimony of experts, etc. But they cannot take over, it's a court. There are negatives, but also blaming it for what it didn't do.

The phrase 'there are small contributions here and there' resonates in a surprising way with the ('politically motivated') defence lawyer who suggested that ICTR trials have enabled 'more and more stuff' to come out. In addition, the judge chooses as an example the attack on 6 April 1994 of the plane carrying the Presidents of Rwanda and Burundi which signalled the start of the genocide, an attack blamed by some on the RPF (see Oosterlinck et al., 2012; Thalmann, 2008). His reference to the twelve acquittals and part-acquittals suggests balance while his comment that 'reality is not black and white' suggests the weakness of the duality of Hutu perpetrators vs Tutsi victims. Perhaps it is 'books, testimony of experts' that refer to alleged crimes of the RPF that he has in mind. And by 'negatives' does he mean the failure to indict members of the RPF? Again, the judge responded to a question I had not posed. Having indicated that he believes the RPF should be indicted, he appears to be arguing that RPF culpability has been acknowledged as far as possible *within the trials the Prosecutor has given him to adjudicate*.

The judge was evidently aware of criticism of the ICTR and fears that what it had accomplished would be ignored and that critics were 'blaming it for what it didn't do'. Comments by judges' Assistant Legal Officers (ALOs) perhaps give some insight into judges' fear of blame. An ALO told me (in 2006) that the Prosecutor was just waiting to finish presenting evidence in two prominent cases, for which he needed 'the co-operation of the Rwandan authorities', but that 'I bet my bottom dollar that when these are over there will be RPF indictments'. A year later, however, the Prosecutor had made public the last 'sealed indictments' which, it transpired, were not for members of the RPF. Commenting on this, another ALO told me (in 2007) that 'everyone had thought that the three sealed indictments were RPF and everyone, including judges, were shocked when they discovered they weren't'. In a similar vein another ALO told me (also in 2007) that 'Up until four months ago everyone thought they were the RPF, that at the eleventh hour they were finally going to put things right. I think some of the judges were convinced they were and were disappointed'.

While judges impressed on me that that they were not responsible for who was indicted ('the prosecutor exercises independent judgement') or that the allegations against members of the RPF had been acknowledged as far as was possible ('there are small contributions here and there'), reports from ALOs that judges hoped the Prosecutor would 'put things right' and that judges were 'shocked' and 'disappointed' when this did not happen suggests that judges feared such considerations would not insulate them from criticism of the ICTR in the *longue durée*. This would appear all the more likely given that detractors were already criticizing 'the Tribunal' (rather than the Prosecutor) for failing to indict the RPF (HRW, 2009).

CONCLUSION

There can be no doubt that the ICTR was promoted by its spokespersons as a 'new beginning', an exceptional, temporary ad hoc response that would dismantle a long-standing 'culture of impunity'. The current critique of transitional justice suggests that it is to Rwanda that one should look to assess this promise. Surveys conducted in Rwanda, however, suggest that Rwandans have very little knowledge of the institution (Longman et al., 2004).

Yet, seeking affirmation or rejection of the ICTR solely in Rwanda would obscure another site of assessment. As noted, the current critique of transitional justice tends to portray the 'local' as a place of endless colourful variation in which the hopelessly simplistic prescriptions and logics of international criminal justice and human rights are bound to come unstuck. Such an analysis tends to portray 'transitional justice' as a disembodied, unified set of discourses and related practices. The analysis above, however, demonstrates that unanimity within transitional justice (even within a single organ of the Tribunal such as the prosecution) is illusory and we must attend to an interstitial locality: the transitional justice institution itself and those who inhabit it.

One of the obstacles to such exploration is that those who speak on behalf of transitional justice institutions actively promote a notion of unanimity and unity (see Baylis, 2008: 368). For example, discussing the choice of those who have been indicted, the Tribunal's registrar has written 'The Tribunal has followed a thematic and geographical approach to its work based on the patterns of involvement of leading individuals in several sectors of society — politicians, military, civil administrators, media, and clergy — and the locations of the crimes alleged' (Dieng, 2001). It is not, however, 'the Tribunal' that has followed this approach, but *the Prosecutor*, for it is neither the registrar, the judges nor, obviously, defence lawyers who choose who is indicted. As the judge forcefully corrected me when I asked him why the Tribunal has chosen to indict certain people: 'The decision to prosecute is made by the Prosecutor without any influence. Therefore, it is not "the Tribunal" which selects the accused'. In another example, the former spokesman of the ICTR writes 'When the Tribunal's judges handed down two path-breaking judgments in late 1998 ... the Tribunal regained its confidence in full' (Moghalu, 2005: 66). Such a statement also collapses the discrete organs and associated power designated by the Tribunal's statute. By designating 'independent' organs 'the Chambers' (judges), 'the Prosecutor', 'registry', and defence lawyers, the 1994 Statute (United Nations, 1994e: Art 10: 20) assigns and circumscribes power. It is this differentiation, combined with the diverse biographies of lawyers and judges, that generates the diverse, messy perspectives that have been the subject of this chapter.

By attending to hidden views generated by this system of relations one can begin a 'public engagement with powerful institutions whose knowledge systems constantly organize attention away from the contradictions and contingencies of practice and the plurality of perspectives' (Mosse, 2006: 938). What emerges is a complex critique of the ICTR as an exceptional 'new beginning'. Just as the judgment of a precursor institution (the Nuremberg Tribunal) stated that 'Crimes against international law are committed by men, not by abstract entities' (IMT, 1947: 233) so, in turn, there is a need to distinguish between the image of the ICTR as a disembodied 'abstract entity' that did or did not mark a national or global new beginning, and the ICTR as what it actually was, a collection of situated persons negotiating their simultaneous empowerment and disempowerment, and the different assessments of the institution this generated.

REFERENCES

Anders, G. and O. Zenker (2014) 'Transition and Justice: An Introduction', *Development and Change* 45(3): 395–414.

Baylis, E. (2008) 'Tribunal-hopping with the Post-conflict Justice Junkies', *Oregon Review of International Law* 10: 361–90.

Betts, A. (2005) 'Should Approaches to Post-conflict Justice and Reconciliation be Determined Globally, Nationally or Locally?', *European Journal of Development Research* 17(4): 735–52.

Bourdieu, P. (1987) 'The Force of Law: Toward a Sociology of the Juridical Field', *Hastings Journal of Law* 38(5): 814–53.

CHRI (2009) 'Rwanda's Application for Membership in the Commonwealth'. New Delhi: Commonwealth Human Rights Initiative.

Clarke, K.M. (2009) *Fictions of Justice: The International Criminal Court and the Challenge of Legal Pluralism in Sub-Saharan Africa*. Cambridge: Cambridge University Press.

Cruvellier, T. (2010) *Court of Remorse Inside the International Criminal Tribunal for Rwanda*. Madison, WI: University of Wisconsin Press.

Degni-Ségui, R. (1994) 'Situation of Human Rights in Rwanda'. New York: United Nations.

Del Ponte, C. and C. Sudetic (2009) *Madame Prosecutor: Confrontations with Humanity's Worst Criminals and the Culture of Impunity*. New York: Other Press.

Des Forges, A.L. (1999) '"Leave None to Tell the Story": Genocide in Rwanda'. New York: Human Rights Watch.

Dieng, A. (2001) 'Africa and the Globalization of Justice: Contributions and Lessons from the International Criminal Tribunal for Rwanda'. Paper presented at conference Justice in Africa, Wilton Park, Sussex, England (30 July – 2 August).

Dieng, A. (2003) 'Registrar's Note', *ICTR Newsletter* June.

Eltringham, N. (2004) *Accounting for Horror: Post-Genocide Debates in Rwanda*. London: Pluto.

Eltringham, N. (2008) '"A War Crimes Community": The Legacy of the International Criminal Tribunal for Rwanda Beyond Jurisprudence', *New England Journal of International and Comparative Law* 14(2): 309–18.

Eltringham, N. (2009) '"We are not a Truth Commission": Fragmented Narratives and the Historical Record at the International Criminal Tribunal for Rwanda', *Journal of Genocide Research* 11(1): 55–79.

Eltringham, N. (2010) 'Judging the "Crime of Crimes": Continuity and Improvisation at the International Criminal Tribunal for Rwanda', in A. Hinton (ed.) *Transitional Justice: Global Mechanisms and Local Realities in the Aftermath of Genocide and Mass Violence*, pp. 206–26. New Brunswick, NJ: Rutgers University Press.

Falk-Moore, S. (2000) *Law as Process: An Anthropological Approach*. Oxford: James Currey.

GADH (2009a) 'International Criminal Tribunal for Rwanda: Model or Counter Model for International Criminal Justice?'. Geneva: Geneva Academy of International Humanitarian Law and Human Rights.

GADH (2009b) 'International Criminal Tribunal for Rwanda: Model or Counter Model for International Criminal Justice? Session 5 Debates with Prosecutors'. Geneva: Geneva Academy of International Humanitarian Law and Human Rights.

Hartmann, F. (2007) *Paix et châtiment, Les guerres secrètes de la politique et de la justice internationals* [*Peace and Retribution: The Secret Wars of International Politics and Justice*]. Paris: Flammarion.

Hazan, P. (1998) 'Les crimes commis contre les Hutus ne doivent pas demeurer impunis' ['The Crimes Committed against the Hutu Should not Remain Unpunished'], *Le Temps* 18 September.

Hirondelle News Agency (2003) 'ICTR/Prosecutor – Interview with Carla Del Ponte'. Arusha 16 September.

HRW (2002) 'Rwanda: Deliver Justice for Victims of Both Sides'. New York: Human Rights Watch.

HRW (2003) 'Leading Rights Groups Urge Security Council to Ensure Management Reforms do not Undermine Rwanda Tribunal'. New York: Human Rights Watch.

HRW (2009) 'Rwanda: Tribunal Risks Supporting "Victor's Justice": Tribunal Should Vigorously Pursue Crimes of Rwandan Patriotic Front'. New York: Human Rights Watch.

HRW and FIDH (2006) 'Letter to Council Members on Eve of Meeting with Lead Prosecutor'. New York: Human Rights Watch and Fédération Internationale des Ligues des Droits de l'Homme.

ICG (2003) *Tribunal Penal International Pour le Rwanda: Pragmatisme de Rigueur* [*The International Criminal Tribunal for Rwanda: Time for Pragmatism*]. Brussels: International Crisis Group.

ICTR (2002) 'ICTR President Seizes Security Council', ICTR Bulletin. Arusha: International Criminal Tribunal for Rwanda.

ICTR (2004a) 'Letter dated 30 April 2004 from the President of the ICTR addressed to the President of the Security Council'. Arusha: International Criminal Tribunal for Rwanda.

ICTR (2004b) 'Statement by Justice Hassan B. Jallow, Prosecutor of the International Criminal Tribunal for Rwanda to the United Nations Security Council. 29 June'. Arusha: International Criminal Tribunal for Rwanda.

ICTR (2005) 'International Justice: The Legacy of the United Nations International Criminal Tribunal for the Former Yugoslavia and of the International Criminal Tribunal for Rwanda: Discussion Paper (Draft)'. Arusha: International Criminal Tribunal for Rwanda.

ICTR (2006a) 'Military I – Defence Exhibit DK112 – UN Code Cable "The Gersoni Report Rwanda"'. Arusha: International Criminal Tribunal for Rwanda.

ICTR (2006b) 'Military I – Defence Exhibit DNT257 – US Document from US Secretary of State to US Mission to UN Dated 22/09/94'. Arusha: International Criminal Tribunal for Rwanda.

ICTR (2006c) 'Military I – Defence Exhibit DNT264 – US Document from George E. Moose to the US Secretary of State; 12/09/94; Subject: New Human Rights Abuses in Rwanda'. Arusha: International Criminal Tribunal for Rwanda.

ICTR (2006d) 'Military I – Defence Exhibit DNT261 – Human Rights Watch, Absence of Prosecution, Continued Killings, Sept. 1994'. Arusha: International Criminal Tribunal for Rwanda.

ICTR (n.d.) 'The ICTR at a Glance'. Arusha: International Criminal Tribunal for Rwanda.

ICTY (2002) 'Address by the Prosecutor of the International Criminal Tribunals for the former Yugoslavia and Rwanda, Mrs Carla del Ponte to the United Nations Security Council, 29 October'. The Hague: International Criminal Tribunal for the Former Yugoslavia.

IMT (1947) *Trial of the Major War Criminals Before the International Military Tribunal*. Nuremberg: International Military Tribunal.

IRIN (2000) 'Del Ponte Addresses Alleged RPF Massacres with Kagame'. Integrated Regional Information Network for Central and Eastern Africa (14 December).

IRIN (2001) 'Government Puts Genocide Victims at 1.07 Million'. Integrated Regional Information Network for Central and Eastern Africa (19 December).

Kent, L. (2011) 'Local Memory Practices in East Timor: Disrupting Transitional Justice Narratives', *International Journal of Transitional Justice* 5(3): 434–55.

Khan, S.M. (2000) *The Shallow Graves of Rwanda*. London: I.B. Tauris.

Longman, T., P. Pham and H. M. Weinstein (2004) 'Connecting Justice to Human Experience: Attitudes toward Accountability and Reconciliation in Rwanda', in E. Stover and H.M.

Weinstein (eds) *My Neighbour, My Enemy: Justice and Community in the Aftermath of Mass Atrocity*, pp. 206–25. Cambridge: Cambridge University Press.

Madlingozi, T. (2010) 'On Transitional Justice Entrepreneurs and the Production of Victims', *Journal of Human Rights Practice* 2(2): 208–28.

McEvoy, K. (2007) 'Beyond Legalism: Towards a Thicker Understanding of Transitional Justice', *Journal of Law and Society* 34(4): 411–40.

Merry, S.E. (2006) 'Transnational Human Rights and Local Activism: Mapping the Middle', *American Anthropologist* 108(1): 38–51.

Moghalu, K.C. (2005) *Rwanda's Genocide: The Politics of Global Justice*. New York: Palgrave Macmillan.

Mosse, D. (2006) 'Anti-social Anthropology? Objectivity, Objection, and the Ethnography of Public Policy and Professional Communities', *Journal of the Royal Anthropological Institute* 12(4): 935–56.

Oosterlinck, C., D. Van Schendel, J. Huon, J. Sompayrac and O. Chavanis (2012) 'Rapport D'expertise: Destruction En Vol Du Falcon 50 Kigali (Rwanda)' ['Expert Report: Destruction in Flight of the Falcon 50 Kigali (Rwanda)']. Paris: Cour d'appel de Paris Tribunal de Grande Instance de Paris.

Peskin, V. (2008) *International Justice in Rwanda and the Balkans: Virtual Trials and the Struggle for State Cooperation*. Cambridge: Cambridge University Press.

Reydams, L. (2005) 'The ICTR Ten Years On: Back to the Nuremberg Paradigm?', *Journal of International Criminal Justice* 3(4): 977–88.

Selimovic, J.M. (2010) 'Perpetrators and Victims: Local Responses to the International Criminal Tribunal for the Former Yugoslavia', *Focaal* 57: 50–61.

Shaw, R. (2007) 'Memory Frictions: Localizing the Truth and Reconciliation Commission in Sierra Leone', *The International Journal of Transitional Justice* 1(2): 183–207.

Shaw, R., L. Waldorf and P. Hazan (2010) *Localizing Transitional Justice: Interventions and Priorities after Mass Violence*. Stanford, CA: Stanford University Press.

Sunga, L.S. (1995) 'The Commission of Experts on Rwanda and the Creation of the International Tribunal for Rwanda', *Human Rights Law Journal* 16(1–3): 121–24.

Thalmann, V. (2008) 'French Justice's Endeavours to Substitute for the ICTR', *Journal of International Criminal Justice* 6(5): 995–1002.

UN (1994a) 'General Assembly Official Records Forty-ninth Session 21st Meeting'. New York: United Nations General Assembly.

UN (1994b) 'Letter dated 1 October 1994 from the Secretary General to the President of the Security Council Transmitting the Interim Report of Commission of Experts on the Evidence of Grave Violations of International Humanitarian Law in Rwanda, including Possible Acts of Genocide (Annex: Preliminary Report of the Independent Commission of Experts established in accordance with Security Council resolution 935 [1994])'. New York: United Nations.

UN (1994c) 'Letter dated 28 September 1994 from the Permanent Representative of Rwanda to the United Nations'. New York: United Nations.

UN (1994d) 'Letter from the Secretary-General to the President of the Security Council transmitting the final report of the Commission of Experts (Annex: Final Report of the Commission of Experts established pursuant to Security Council resolution 935 [1994])'. New York: United Nations.

UN (1994e) 'Resolution 955 (1994) Adopted by the Security Council at its 3453rd Meeting'. New York: United Nations Security Council.

UN (1994f) 'Transcript of the 3453rd Meeting of the United Nations Security Council'. New York: United Nations.

UN (1995) 'Report of The Secretary-General Pursuant to Paragraph 5 of Security Council Resolution 955 (1994)'. New York: United Nations.

UN (2003) 'Security Council Resolution 1503 (2003) Adopted by the Security Council at its 4817th Meeting'. New York: United Nations.

UN (2004) 'Security Council Resolution 1534 (2004) Adopted by the Security Council at its 4935th Meeting'. New York: United Nations Security Council.

UN (2009a) 'Address to the United Nations General Assembly by the Prosecutor of the ICTR'. New York: United Nations General Assembly.

UN (2009b) 'Security Council Resolution 1901 (2009) Adopted by the Security Council at its 6243rd Meeting'. New York: United Nations Security Council.

UN Wire (2002) 'Del Ponte Protests to Security Council that Rwanda is not Co-operating', UN Wire/United Nations Foundation.

9

New Start or False Start? The ICC and Electoral Violence in Kenya

Sabine Höhn

INTRODUCTION

International criminal trials have been heralded as helping the transition from armed conflict to post-conflict societies (Akhavan, 2001; Almquist and Eposito, 2011; Gegout, 2013; Robinson, 2003, Teitel, 2003). Recently criminal justice has taken on a different form of political conflict: the International Criminal Court's cases of post-election violence in Kenya and Côte d'Ivoire indicate a new route for the international response to electoral violence. In Kenya the ICC stepped in after it became apparent that the Kenyan police were not investigating attacks that had occurred after the contested 2007 elections. The ICC intervention speaks to the dialectics of exception that characterizes international justice. On the one hand prosecution is the ordinary and ordered response to mass violence. Prosecuting those most responsible is presented as the expected reaction to any kind of violence, domestic or international. The Kenyan case not only testifies to the new importance of the judicial in the international reaction to violence, it also demonstrates the tension between the rhetoric of exception and ideals of order that are at the heart of international criminal justice. Prosecution is framed as the technical response to political violence that can be referred to international courts if domestic prosecution is not initiated. This is why ICC Chief Prosecutor Luis Moreno-Ocampo could declare that the ICC formed part of Kenya's judiciary system.[1] International criminal trials are represented as one-off interventions that help states to cope with violence that is seen as exceptional enough to evoke international concerns and justify external intervention, as argued in the Introduction to this volume (see also Anders and Zenker, 2014; Fassin and Pandolfi, 2010).

At the same time the ICC involvement is represented as an exceptional step in dealing with Kenya's electoral violence. No one had ever been brought

---

This research was made possible by a British Academy post-doctoral fellowship. Thanks to Gerhard Anders and Olaf Zenker for helpful and constructive feedback throughout, and to the anonymous referees for comments on an earlier version of the paper.

1. Luis Moreno-Ocampo, press conference 26 November 2009 in Nairobi: http://www.icc-cpi.int/NR/rdonlyres/AC13413D-D097--4527-B0AE-60CF6DBB1B68/281313/LMOINTRO statement26112009_2_2.pdf

Transition and Justice: Negotiating the Terms of New Beginnings in Africa, First Edition.
Edited by Gerhard Anders and Olaf Zenker.

before a Kenyan court for instigating electoral violence. Moreno-Ocampo stated that the ICC process was an 'example of how to do justice' that could 'rebuild Kenya on new foundations',[2] thus reiterating the argument that international justice facilitates the transition to a more democratic political order (Olsen et al., 2010; Turner, 2008). The investigations were not only a novelty for Kenya, but also for the ICC. Although the ICC is tasked with enforcing international law by prosecuting crimes against humanity, irrespective of their contexts, until the prosecution started to investigate the situation in Kenya it had never taken on large-scale and systematic violence in connection with multiparty elections and outside of an ongoing conflict. Treating the violent contention of electoral results first and foremost as a criminal act projected a particular idea of how political disputes ought to be fought out and how 'proper' democratic consolidation ought to work.

This chapter examines how far the ICC's involvement in Kenya represents a new beginning for international criminal justice in Africa, for Kenya and for the international response to electoral violence and political conflict in multiparty regimes more broadly. International criminal justice is expected to effectively end impunity and thus deter future warmongers. However, these promises have to be seen in the context of the rather limited possibilities of international justice in practice (Anders and Zenker, 2014). Trials are bound by their own legal imperatives (Wilson, 2011a: 113). The specific nature of the charges and a particular trajectory of jurisprudence make trials genuinely unable to address the long-term socio-political causes of violent conflict. The Kenyan case thus illustrates the tension between the high promises and the limited and often messy realities of international justice.

Although trials are unlikely to address the root causes of violence, they have gained widespread support from Western donor states, not least due to the idea that in functioning democracies electoral results are challenged in courts and not on the streets (Turner, 2008). Representing the 2007 attacks as extraordinary ignores the fact that electoral violence in Kenya is hardly exceptional (Branch, 2013; ICG, 2012; Mugo, 2013; Pflanz, 2012). It was arguably the recognition that violence had become the standard reaction to contested elections that motivated structural domestic reforms to prevent a repetition of the 2007/8 violence in 2013. Indeed, the relative calm of the 2013 elections was due less to the ICC process deterring instigators of violence than to the new constitution, fundamental institutional reforms and a profound public wish to avoid another bloodbath (Dersso, 2013; Kimenyi, 2013; Onyango-Obbo, 2013).

This chapter is organized as follows. First, it provides an overview of the factors that contributed to the post-electoral violence in 2007/8. It then examines how far international court cases could represent a new beginning for Kenya's electoral politics. The third section situates the ICC Kenya case

---

2. Ibid.

in the global shift towards a juridification of international affairs and argues that the case represents a new beginning for the international response to electoral violence. The final section discusses two key aspects of international criminal law: the law's focus on individual responsibility, and the need for international justice to represent its intervention as exceptional.

POST-ELECTORAL VIOLENCE IN KENYA

Just before the end of 2007, Kenya's president Mwai Kibaki was declared winner of a contested presidential election. This came as a surprise, as the opposition Orange Democratic Movement (ODM) had won a comfortable parliamentary majority in the preceding parliamentary elections, securing ninety-nine seats against the governing party's forty-three seats. Until shortly before the official announcement of the presidential results, Kibaki's opponent, ODM's Raila Odinga, had led by a considerable margin. According to an International Crisis Group report this was an obvious case of electoral fraud, and vote rigging appeared to have happened both at constituency and central level (ICG, 2008). When the contested results were announced on 30 December 2007, the ODM refused to accept the result but declined to take the case to court as it claimed that the judiciary was firmly under the control of the current government and any court ruling would be heavily biased.

The announcement of the election result immediately triggered large-scale violence; it was widespread and in some areas was planned and systematic (Brown, 2011; HRW, 2008; Waki Commission, 2008). Supporters of Raila Odinga, who were predominantly Luo, targeted Kibaki's Kikuyu followers, driving them from their land and their homes and shops. Kikuyu youth gangs retaliated, with the help of the outlawed Mungiki sect, and attacked Luo and Kalenjin settlements and houses. The police were allegedly involved in the attacks, or at least stood by as the violence unfolded (KNCHR, 2008; OHCHR, 2008; Waki Commission, 2008: 285). Especially hard hit were towns like Kisumu, Nairobi and Eldoret and the Rift Valley province. Approximately 1,000 people died and over 300,000 people were displaced. The spread and intensity of the violence were completely unexpected: electoral violence on that scale had not erupted in Kenya for over a decade. In the run-up to the elections, hopes for a peaceful ballot had been high as the tone of both parties had been conciliatory. Additionally, the experience of both the 2002 election and the 2005 constitutional referendum had been encouraging (Cheeseman, 2008): in both instances the ruling party had lost and had accepted defeat. There was also general confidence in the impartiality of the electoral commission that had overseen the previous presidential election, which had ended KANU's thirty-two year rule in 2002 (ICG, 2008: 6; Kagwanja and Southall, 2009; Kiai, 2008).

Hopes of a peaceful vote might have been unrealistic, however, since several signs pointed to a contested election. The build-up to the election was marked by considerable violence, which resulted in 200 deaths and 70,000 displaced (HRW, 2008: 19). The presidential vote especially was expected to be a close call (Waki Commission, 2008) and close elections had never been particularly peaceful in the past. Although Kenya had experienced electoral violence since the early 1960s (Rutten and Owuor, 2009), it became especially intense with political liberalization and the advent of multiparty elections in 1992 (Kagwanja and Southall, 2009; Rutten and Owuor, 2009; Steeves, 2011). The elections of 1992 and 1997 were both accompanied by significant violence, with the Rift Valley and the Western Province being especially targeted, as they were again in 2007 (Article 19, 1998; HRW, 1993; KHRC, 1998). Violence in the wake of the first multiparty election in 1992 had killed over 1,500 people and displaced at least 300,000 (Brown, 2011; HRW, 1993: 1, 90) — a similar number to the casualties in 2007/8. In 1997 the state's security forces repressed peaceful demonstrations in the run-up to the election. After the elections, ethnic groups associated with the opposition were targeted for supporting the 'wrong side' (Brown, 2011). Between 70 and 100 people died and up to 200,000 people were displaced (Akiwumi, 1999).

The relative calm of the 2002 elections and the 2005 constitutional referendum were believed to signify the end of the era of electoral violence and to indicate that electoral defeat would now be peacefully accepted by the losing party (Branch and Cheeseman, 2009; Harneit-Sievers and Peters, 2008; Mueller, 2011). With hindsight it appears that the calm elections had more to do with party politics and the unequivocal defeat of one side at the polls than signalling structural changes that could prevent post-election violence for good. In 2002, the opposition National Rainbow Coalition (NARC) under Mwai Kibaki defeated KANU by such a margin that the ruling party of thirty-two years was unable to challenge the outcome. Several senior KANU politicians had defected to other parties before the election, or had left KANU to found their own parties, often taking their constituencies with them (de Smedt, 2009). In a political system where personal loyalty trumps party ties (Mueller, 2008, 2011) this meant that the ruling party lost its majority in parliament and a coalition of influential politicians, united in Kibaki's NARC, won the election. Although individuals had moved in and out of KANU's inner circle before,[3] the exodus of senior politicians before the 2002 election was especially high, triggered in part by Moi's contentious choice of successor, the inexperienced Uhuru Kenyatta (Steeves, 2006). The resulting electoral defeat was accepted by KANU; similarly, Kibaki had to accept the clear rejection of his draft constitution three years later.[4]

---

3. Kibaki had been minister in Moi's Cabinet and Raila Odinga had also held a high position in KANU before both left to found their own parties (Steeves, 2006).
4. The 'no' campaign against the new constitution was led by Raila Odinga, Kibaki's challenger in the presidential election in 2007 (ICG, 2008: 2).

In 2007, however, the electoral results were less clear and vote rigging seemed to have made the key difference that kept Kibaki in power; in the eyes of Odinga's supporters, the real winner was deprived of his rightful claim to the presidency (HRW, 2008; ICG, 2008: 9). Violence was the immediate response to electoral fraud. Alternative routes for addressing vote rigging — like recourse to domestic courts — had proven ineffective in the past and were widely mistrusted. Violence was easy to organize through senior politicians' extended networks of patronage. Political support in exchange for material reward provided the infrastructure to organize both electoral support and — after the fraud became apparent — electoral violence (Mueller, 2011; de Smedt, 2009). Furthermore, there were already militarized groups in society. The state had long lost its monopoly over the legitimate means of violence as more and more politicians used youth gangs, age groups and sects to intimidate and weaken opponents (Brown, 2011; HRW, 1993). Neighbourhood groups took the law in their own hands in the face of a corrupt and inefficient police and judiciary, thus contributing further to the militarization of society (Mueller, 2008). Violence became a common way to intimidate political opponents; with ever fewer material benefits at their disposal, it was much easier for politicians to reward youth groups for literally whipping up support (de Smedt, 2009). In 2007 youth gangs were the main perpetrators of electoral violence in Kenya (Githongo, 2010); ordinary citizens joined in for fear of being seen as opponents of the gangs and thus becoming targets themselves (de Smedt, 2009).

Violence was not only easy to organize and deploy; it also seemed for the opposition to be the only way to challenge rigged results since the courts could not be trusted to arbitrate independently (Machuka, 2008). Violence had become the normal — and recourse to courts the exceptional — reaction to electoral rigging in Kenya, thus inverting the relation between the ordinary and the extraordinary response. This is because state institutions had been deliberately weakened over decades and were not trusted to redress electoral fraud (Mueller, 2008, 2011; Smith, 2009): Kenya's institutional checks and balances had often been overridden by politicians with entirely different sets of incentives (Mueller, 2011), and the advent of multiparty elections in the 1990s had not led to a subsequent strengthening of other democratic institutions like the judiciary. In fact the dominance of the executive over the courts had remained a highly guarded privilege of every government as it gave the incumbents a critical advantage in contested elections. Since courts have regularly failed to arbitrate in cases of electoral fraud, public trust in the regulatory power of the judiciary has declined. Widespread protests after elections indicate a growing dissatisfaction with purely electoral democracy and a demand for meaningful constitutional and institutional reforms that would make political leaders more accountable to voters (Smith, 2009). This is why the ICC process, with its promises to end impunity and strengthen the rule of law, was so well received in Kenya, raising hopes for future elections.

In the context of weakened state institutions and in a militarized society, violence was easy to organize but very difficult to stop. Only the mediation of Kofi Annan and several other senior African politicians brought about a negotiated power-sharing agreement, which ended the violence in spring 2008. The new government mandated a commission of inquiry to examine the root causes of violence and identify those most responsible. The Waki Commission (named after its chairman, Judge Philip Waki) found evidence of spontaneous violence, but also of violence that was planned, with considerable logistics going into travelling to locations in order to maim, kill and displace (Waki Commission, 2008). It found substantial involvement on the part of politicians and businesspeople, and stated that the violence was made possible by the collapse of state institutions. The commission identified a number of people deemed to be most responsible for planning the violence and handed a sealed envelope with their names to Kofi Annan. That the envelope was not given to the government (Rice, 2009) was a strong indication of the lack of public trust in the government's intention to prosecute those responsible (Mueller, 2011).

Establishing the Waki Commission appeared to be a sincere attempt to identify those most responsible for the violence. However, Kenya has a tradition of setting up commissions of inquiry after atrocities but failing to implement their recommendations. Commissions of inquiry after the murder of a popular MP in the 1970s, after the death of a former Foreign Affairs minister in 1990 and after post-election violence in the 1990s all remained without political consequences. The number of such commissions and the constant lack of follow-up has further eroded public confidence in Kenya's ability to carry through with respect to matters of justice. Expectations were therefore not particularly high when the Waki Commission published its recommendations, including the call for a Special Tribunal to try those deemed most responsible. When parliament indeed vetoed the constitutional change necessary to establish the Tribunal, Kofi Annan forwarded the envelope, together with six boxes of collected evidence, to the Prosecutor at the International Criminal Court in The Hague. The ICC's involvement promised a new beginning in addressing electoral violence and official impunity (Leebaw, 2008; Teitel, 2000). Investigations by its prosecutors may have represented the international standard reaction to violence, but they were exceptional in Kenya where previous measures had never been able to bring the instigators to court.

A NEW BEGINNING FOR KENYA'S ELECTORAL POLITICS?

In some senses, then, the ICC intervention was indeed a new beginning. It marked a turn away from corrupt and inefficient domestic courts and a different approach to electoral violence than the ubiquitous but inconsequential commissions of inquiry. In Kenya, the ICC is often represented as an independent and effective international court and contrasted with politically motivated trials at home (ICPC, 2011; KHRC and FIDH, 2009; Okwara, 2011).[5] The implication is that the ICC hearings should mark the end of impunity for violence. Nevertheless, arguments that a mere summons to the ICC would be enough to end political careers (Ndegwa, 2011) proved to be false, as Kenyatta and Ruto won the 2013 presidential elections, despite — or maybe even because of — their impending trial in The Hague (Mamdani, 2013). This illustrates a tension between the lofty promise of international trials to deter future warmongers and the sobering reality that proceedings in The Hague have not prevented suspects from gaining the highest office in their home country.

Even proponents of international criminal justice have doubts about the deterrent effect and the courts' efficiency in preventing further violence. Richard Wilson points out that deterrence is often used to sell tribunals to the international community as an effective policy, not because their proponents believe in it (cited in Vinjamuri, 2010: 209, note 23). Deterrence is virtually impossible to prove because it requires a clear causal link between court proceedings and the end of violence. International criminal courts prosecute so few suspects that perpetrators of violence are likely to assume that they will not be targeted (Wippmann, 1999).[6] Since the Kenya trials have started, allegations of witness bribery[7] and a motion in the Kenyan parliament to withdraw from the Rome Statute (by which the ICC was established) have shown that those in high office have multiple ways of derailing proceedings, even if the cases are not being heard in a domestic court. Additionally, if international criminal cases collapse due to insufficient evidence this is often erroneously taken as evidence of a suspect's innocence (Bueno, 2013; IRIN, 2012). The ICC proceedings therefore might or might not make individuals think twice before instigating violence in the future; but even if deterrence works at the individual level, it will not increase the domestic judiciary's independence. The root causes of Kenya's electoral violence were systematic, located in long-term grievances and a weak judiciary. These could not be addressed by prosecuting individual perpetrators of violence, however high ranking. Actual court proceedings were therefore ill suited to fulfilling the court's lofty promise of helping societies to come to terms with past violence and master the transition to a peaceful order (Ambos et al., 2009; Anders and Zenker, 2014; Teitel, 2000).

---

5. Contrasting the independence of international courts with corrupt and politicized trials at national level has been a general tendency since the arrival of international criminal justice. For a critical discussion of this trend see Anders (2009: 137); Höhn (2010).
6. For the debate on the promise and effectiveness of deterrence see, amongst others, Aukermann (2002); Drumbl (2003); Gustafson (1998); Vinjamuri (2010); Wippman (1999).
7. On 2 October 2013 the ICC issued its first arrest warrant for obstructing the course of justice against Kenyan journalist Walter Barasa, charging him with 'corruptly influencing' witnesses to withdraw their testimonies (BBC, 2013).

The ICC proceedings individualized the guilt for electoral violence and neglected the socio-political roots of this violence. Framing the electoral violence as exceptional ignored the fact that the attacks were based on long-term grievances over land and access to political opportunities often framed in terms of ethnic privileges and distilled in elections that pitted candidates from different ethnic groups against each other (Branch and Cheeseman, 2009; HRW, 2008; Mueller, 2011; Rutton and Owuor, 2009; de Smedt, 2009). Access to resources and political opportunities had long been channelled through loyalty to individual politicians. Falling public revenues in the 1980s, coupled with political and economic liberalization, led to a shrinking of these resources and thus of the inner circle of influential politicians. Those trends were intensified under the Kibaki administration from 2002, which halted constitutional reforms in order to maintain the executive's hold over public institutions (Branch, 2011; Branch and Cheeseman, 2009).

Ethnic divisions were a readily accessible and widely understood idiom which was used to articulate a host of other tensions including contestations over land, access to political and economic power and memory of dispossession and violence in the past (Branch and Cheeseman, 2009). These divisions were important drivers of the violence but could not be negotiated in court. That is why the ICC intervention seems to have played only a minor role in preventing violence in the 2013 elections. More important were domestic factors like the coalition between Kenyatta and Ruto (Dersso, 2013; Taylor 2013), a genuine fear of a repetition of the violence, the new constitution and the reform of the electoral law (Mamdani, 2013). The coalition of Kenyatta and Ruto — a Kikuyu and a Kalenjin — was particularly important in keeping the elections peaceful because ethnicity had always been at the forefront of electoral contestations. The systematic weakening of the state meant that when violence erupted the state was incapable of controlling it. Underlying the violence was thus a crisis of the state, which necessitated political reform rather than judicial prosecution alone. The socio-political root causes of the violence explain why the violence erupted, why the state was unable to stop it and why court trials were unlikely to address it.

A NEW BEGINNING FOR INTERNATIONAL RESPONSES TO POLITICAL VIOLENCE: BRINGING POLITICAL CONFLICT TO COURT

After the 2007 post-electoral violence had been ended by a mediated power-sharing agreement, more and more voices demanded a criminal investigation into who was to blame for the widespread killing and displacement. Referring the attacks to court was a new kind of response to electoral violence. In 1993 electoral violence had killed and displaced a similar number of people as in 2007/8. Donors then supported social reconciliation programmes and humanitarian assistance to the displaced, but did not call for criminal investigations of those most responsible for the violence (Brown, 2011).

The new prominence of criminal justice indicates a new beginning for the international response to political conflicts — what Ruti Teitel, with regard to the Milosovic and Saddam trials, called the 'juridicization of international affairs' (2005: 838). Similarly Leslie Vinjamuri identified several trends that contributed to the new prominence of international justice and its lofty promises, including the tendency of the UN Security Council to combine justice and military force in reacting to demands for intervention (Vinjamuri, 2010: 199), and pressure by lobby groups for international justice to deal with conflicts through the courts. Judgements about the responsibility and guilt for mass violence thus seemed promising not only for Kenyans seeking solace for their suffering, but also for international policy makers trying to find a sustainable, independent, widely acceptable and effective way to deal with political violence. As the EU's External Service's Managing Director for Africa put it:

> If there are no rules, and no accountability, people will sooner or later take the law into their own hands .... The international community and international justice can help avoid such situations by setting norms and providing mechanisms to ensure that justice can be done, even in the most lawless environments, and that even the most powerful can be held to account. If the ICC did not exist, we would have to invent it. (Westcott, 2011)

Arguments for international criminal justice have been transformed, from the notion that it merits support because it is good in principle, to the claim that it should be promoted because it brings peace and deters future crimes (Vinjamuri, 2010: 200). This has raised the stakes considerably. International justice is seen as a precondition for peace and development,[8] but the Kenya case at the ICC has already highlighted the difficulties that international criminal justice faces in coming to terms with electoral violence. Its focus on individual guilt failed to address the root causes of conflict and its representation of the violence as democratic transition gone wrong further detached the violence from its structural causes. Representing the violence as a means to advance the political ambitions of a few individuals disassociated the attacks from the broader history of electoral contestations and made it impossible to examine why electoral violence had become so normal in Kenya.

Criminal prosecution seemed to provide a promising and widely supported mechanism to break with the past and promote a new beginning in the response to political violence. When a criminal trial was first mentioned in the Waki Commission report, the Kenyan government supported the suggestion. Three Cabinet members met with the ICC Chief Prosecutor Moreno-Ocampo in July 2009 and underlined the government's commitment to establishing the recommended Special Tribunal to hold the hearings in

---

8. See for example the Security and Justice Section of the Department for International Development website: http://www.dfid.gov.uk/What-we-do/Key-Issues/Governance-and-conflict/Justice-and-security/ (accessed 7 February 2012).

Kenya. They promised to refer the case to The Hague if the Kenyan parliament did not approve the constitutional amendment necessary to establish the Tribunal. However, when the parliament vetoed the amendment, the government made no move to refer the case to the ICC. In November 2009 the ICC Prosecutor took the unprecedented step of investigating the violence in Kenya without a referral from a member state or the Security Council. In a hearing a few months later, two of the three ICC Pre-Trial Chamber judges were convinced that there was sufficient basis to proceed with the investigation. The six suspects who were subsequently summoned to The Hague included representatives of both the government and the opposition. On the government's side were Kenya's deputy Prime Minister, Uhuru Kenyatta, the secretary to the cabinet, Francis Kirimi Muthaura, and the former police chief, Mohammed Hussein Ali. On the opposition's side the Court summoned the Minister for Industrialization, Henry Kosgey, the suspended Education Minister, William Ruto, and the radio executive, Joshua Arap Sang. All six were charged with murder, forcible transfer and persecution. The government's suspects were additionally charged with rape and other inhuman acts. All were accused under Article 25 (3)(a) of the 1998 Rome Statute that determined that a person can be liable if that person commits a crime through another person regardless of whether that other person is criminally responsible.[9]

Although several Kenyan MPs supported the ICC hearings, the government tried to delay the proceedings from the start. During the Pre-Trial process, the government challenged the admissibility of the case at the ICC on the grounds that Kenya was willing and able to investigate the suspects itself.[10] In its challenge Kenya argued that new legislation strengthened domestic courts and empowered them to try the suspects under Kenya's 2009 International Crimes Act.[11] However, the Pre-Trial judges remained unconvinced that Kenya was investigating the so-called 'Ocampo 6' for the same charges as the ICC, and rejected the application. Domestic authorities had not followed the internationally expected course in reacting to the violence and had not initiated criminal investigations. The 2009 Crimes Act could only deal with future atrocities and did not cover past violence. Even if the authorities had started investigations it remained doubtful whether high-ranking Kenyan officials would have been targeted. The Kenyan International

---

9. Court Transcript ICC-01/09–01/11-T-1-ENG ET WT 07–04–2011 1–24 PV PT; ICC-01–09–02-11-T-1-ENG ET WT 08–04–2011 1–23 PV PT.

10. Pre-Trial Chamber II 'Decision on the Application by the Government of Kenya Challenging the Admissibility of the Case Pursuant to Article 19(2)(b) of the Statute ICC -01/09–01/11–19', para 48. Article 17 of the Rome Statute determines that a case is admissible at the ICC if a state is not investigating the same suspects for the same crimes or if the authorities are investigating but not prosecuting the suspects.

11. Pre-Trial Chamber II 'Application on behalf of the Government of The Republic of Kenya pursuant to Article 19 of the ICC Statute', ICC-01/09–02/11–26 31–03–2011, para 23, 57).

Crimes Act is modelled on the ICC Statute, but it does not include its Article 27, which states that official capacity is irrelevant for criminal prosecution and thus that even high-ranking officials can be prosecuted (Okuta, 2009: 1073).

National efforts to deal with the 2007/8 violence therefore seemed deeply flawed from the beginning and aroused scepticism as to whether Kenyan authorities were indeed preparing to investigate and try the Ocampo 6.[12] A day after the six suspects appeared for the first time before the Pre-Trial Chamber in The Hague, in April 2011, Kenya failed in its application to the United Nations Security Council to defer the case (Mutiga, 2011; Reuters, 2011). The Security Council has the power to postpone ICC cases for up to a year if it deems that criminal investigations endanger regional peace and stability. However, the Security Council argued that the hearings in the Kenya case did not pose such a threat.[13] The 'confirmation of charges' hearing took place in September 2011 and the Pre-Trial Chamber decided with a majority vote in January 2012 to commit four of the six suspects to trial, dismissing the charges against Henry Kosgey and Mohammed Hussein Ali.[14] The first trial against William Ruto and Joshua Arap Sang started in September 2013. It appears that public support in Kenya for the ICC trials has decreased sharply in the intervening period and a majority of Kenya's parliamentarians have openly criticized the ICC for infringing the country's sovereignty. Although this criticism is not unanimously supported in Kenya, it has attracted unprecedented African and international solidarity (e.g. Citizennews, 2010; Karimi, 2013; News24 Kenya, 2013).

TRIAL IMPERATIVES AND THE LIMITS OF LAW'S POTENTIAL AS NEW BEGINNING

Individual Guilt vs Collective Planning

It is unlikely that trials can effectively end political violence because criminal investigations are ill fitted to deal with political contestations. Gerry Simpson has argued that judicial inquiries attempt to rise above politics. Their attempt to depoliticize conflict cannot succeed because in some areas of dispute there is only politics (Simpson, 2007: 140) and political decisions do not fit readily

---

12. Pre-Trial Chamber II 'Decision on the Application by the Government of Kenya Challenging the Admissibility of the Case Pursuant to Article 19(2)(b) of the Statute', para 44.
13. In November 2013 another attempt was made at the Security Council to get the Kenyan cases deferred. Again it was defeated, but this time the vote was remarkably close and the application missed the required quorum by only two votes (Reuters, 2013).
14. Pre-Trial Chamber II 'Decision on the Confirmation of Charges Pursuant to Article 61(7)(a) and (b) of the Rome Statute', ICC-01/09–02/11–382-Red 26–01–2012, para 430. In March 2013 the prosecution also dropped the charges against Francis Muthaura, leaving only three of the original six suspects facing trial.

into a legal matrix (ibid.: 148). Although they overlap to a considerable degree, the criminal and the political follow different logics (Simpson, 2007). The criminal focuses on the individual, is bound by set rules of evidence and is determined by trial imperatives, whereas the political emphasizes the collective, systematic and long-term roots of conflict. The differences between the two logics are already apparent in the Kenya hearings.

From the outset, negotiations in the ICC Kenya hearings were determined by trial imperatives. The nature of the specific charges determines prosecution and defence strategies and shapes what is discussed in the courtroom, as Richard Wilson has shown (Wilson, 2011a: 106).[15] The main charge in the Kenya investigation was crimes against humanity, which necessitated proof that the individuals involved were pursuing an 'organizational policy'.[16] The six suspects did not belong to the same side of the electoral contest and there were no clear connections between any of them. The most contested question, which dominated prosecution and defence strategies in the early stages, was whether individual acts indeed amounted to a coherent policy. Unlike the challenge to the admissibility of the case, the tension between individual guilt and the necessity to prove the systematic nature of the attacks almost stopped the proceedings. The different opinions about the organizational policy point to a traditionally contested point in international criminal justice. As the individual has become the central unit for sanctioning violence (Fletcher, 2005: 1031), the connection to collective responsibility has become particularly difficult to make.

Previous international tribunals have grappled with this as well. The International Criminal Tribunal for Rwanda had difficulties establishing the existence of different ethnic groups and a genocidal mind-set of perpetrators in Rwanda despite the fact that trials for genocide had been the reason to establish the Tribunal in the first place (Wilson, 2011b: Ch. 7). It has been argued that a trial's sole function ought to be to determine individual guilt, not to re-evaluate history or judge the crime's context (Arendt, 1965: 253). However, the nature of international criminal justice charges requires a link between individual acts and larger strategies to systematically kill, displace and inflict harm. Although individuals appear before international courts, it is the connection between their acts and broader political strategies, as well as the link between key decision makers, that renders their cases admissible

---

15. In an example from another trial, Kamari Clarke shows that in the ICC's case against Thomas Lubanga Dyilo, the charges of conscripting children determined the Prosecution's strategy to represent Lubanga's militia not as perpetrators of violence, but as child victims, in order to prove Lubanga's culpability (Clarke, 2009: 105).
16. Article 7 (2)(a) of the Rome Statute. There is a difference here between the English and other language versions of the Rome Statute. Whereas the English version requires an 'organizational policy', the other versions speak of a 'policy of an organization'. This difference allows for a broader definition of what counts as a 'crime against humanity' in the English version.

before an international court.[17] International criminal trials therefore always make claims about the context and meaning of those violent acts and in doing so re-interpret socio-historical narratives presented in the courtroom (Wilson, 2011b). Bridging the gap between the concrete evidence of individual acts and the intangible nature of collective criminality has been a central difficulty for international courts ever since their establishment.

In the Kenya hearings the collective was particularly difficult to establish as no armed group exercised any state-like functions.[18] The specific link between the attacks and an overall plan remained contested and the judges differed in their evaluation of whether the attacks followed a particular pattern. Two of the three Pre-Trial Chamber judges were convinced that any private group capable of performing acts infringing on basic human values qualified as an organization in the sense of the Rome Statute. The majority of Pre-Trial Chamber judges allowed the prosecutor to formally open investigation into the situation in Kenya, stating that the 'formal nature of a group and the level of its organization should not be the defining criterion'.[19] They argued that the attacks appeared systematic and that this sufficed to prove such a policy. In their decision they cited previous ICC jurisprudence:

> the attack .... must be conducted in furtherance of a common policy involving public or private resources. Such a policy may be made either by groups of persons who govern a specific territory or by any organization with the capacity to commit a widespread or systematic attack against a civilian population. The policy need not be explicitly defined by the organizational group. Indeed, an attack which is planned, directed or organized — as opposed to spontaneous or isolated acts of violence — will satisfy this criterion.[20]

Using such a generous definition of organization renders many crimes admissible at the International Criminal Court. Since any systematic attack can qualify as a crime against humanity, the state disappears as central perpetrator of this crime. However, one judge remained unconvinced that there was reasonable basis to believe that crimes against humanity had been committed. Judge Kaul questioned the precedent character of the previous ICC ruling as the Pre-Trial Chamber at that time had referred to acts of military-like

---

17. The necessary link between individuals might prove to be a difficult requirement for the prosecution's case against Uhuru Kenyatta after it dropped its charges against alleged co-perpetrator Francis Muthaura in March 2013. Trial judge Ozaki has already enquired how Kenyatta could be accused of a common policy if he was the only suspect. At the time of writing, the prosecution remained confident that it could present enough evidence against Kenyatta in trial, although it had to drop the charges against his co-accused.

18. Pre-Trial Chamber II 'Dissenting Opinion of Judge Kaul', ICC-01/09–19 31–03–2010, para 52.

19. Pre-Trial Chamber II 'Decision Pursuant to Article 15 of the Rome Statute on the Authorization of an Investigation into the Situation in the Republic of Kenya', ICC-01/09–19-Corr. 31–03–2010, para 90.

20. Pre-Trial Chamber I 'Decision on the confirmation of charges against Katanga and Ngudjolo', ICC 01/04–01/07–717, para 396.

organizations. Referring to other language versions of the Rome Statute he concluded that an organization had to have some state-like abilities such as a common purpose, a hierarchical command structure, the capacity to sanction members, and the means available to attack civilians on a large scale. He concluded: 'The general argument that any kind of non-state actors may be qualified as an "organization" within the meaning of article 7 (2)(a) of the statute on the grounds that it "has the capability to perform acts which infringe on basic human values" without any further specification seems unconvincing to me'.[21]

Neither the Pre-Trial Chamber's debate around crimes against humanity, nor Kenya's challenge to the case's admissibility, mentioned Kenya's weak institutions. The proceedings represented the attacks as exceptional criminal acts which called for prosecution as the routine response that could restore order. When Kenya challenged the admissibility of the case, the Pre-Trial Chamber pointed to Kenya's inaction with regard to the six suspects and noted that Kenya had failed to prove that it was investigating the same persons for the same charges.[22] However, the Chamber could not address the question of why Kenya had failed to do so and thus could not raise the issues of the corrupt judiciary and the wide public mistrust in the state's weak institutions. As the judges made clear:

> In considering whether a case is inadmissible under article 17(1)(a) and (b) the initial questions to ask are (1) whether there are ongoing investigations or prosecutions or (2) whether there have been investigations in the past and the State having jurisdiction has decided not to prosecute the person concerned. It is only when the answers to these questions are in the affirmative that one has to look at the second halves of the sub para (a) and (b) and to examine the question of unwillingness and inability. To do otherwise would be to put the cart before the horse. It follows that in case of inaction, the questions of unwillingness or inability does not arise; inaction on the part of the State having jurisdiction renders a case admissible before the court.[23]

The proceedings made it very clear that according to the ICC, Kenyan authorities ought to have investigated the Ocampo 6. In a state with a functioning rule of law the authorities would have reacted to the recommendations of the Waki Commission. The electoral violence and the subsequent state inaction were a clear sign that the rule of law was weak and that democratic consolidation had gone wrong. Beyond this, the ICC hearing was incapable of asking why courts failed to prosecute the suspects or of assessing why the

21. Pre-Trial Chamber II 'Dissenting Opinion of Judge Kaul', ICC-01/09–19 31–03–2010, para 53.
22. Pre-Trial Chamber II 'Decision on the Application by the Government of Kenya Challenging the Admissibility of the Case Pursuant to Article 19(2)(b) of the Statute', ICC-01/09–01/11–19, para 32.
23. Pre-Trial Chamber II 'Decision on the Application by the Government of Kenya Challenging the Admissibility of the Case Pursuant to Article 19(2)(b) of the Statute', ICC-01/09–01/11, para 48, citing Katanga Appeals Chamber ICC-01/04–01/07–1497, para 78.

state institutions had been so weak. The ICC proceedings did not examine the root causes of Kenya's electoral violence and could not investigate the political motivations behind the systematic weakening of domestic courts. The promise of the ICC's Prosecutor that the ICC intervention represented a new beginning for Kenya might have been premature. The proceedings in The Hague marked a clear break with the tradition of state inaction and impunity for large-scale violence and thus fulfilled a key function of a transitional justice mechanism (Aukerman, 2002; Elster, 2004: 240). However, the inability to address the structural causes of the violence rendered the proceedings incapable of contributing to a truly new beginning for state–society relations in Kenya. Despite this inability to discuss the root causes of violence, international criminal justice has become a major form of international response to political conflict.

The Democratic Order and the Criminal Exception

The increasing prominence of international tribunals and the ICC points to an increasing judicialization of political violence (Simpson, 2007). Since the mid-1990s prosecution appears to have become one of the international community's favourite responses to political conflict. What is new in the Kenya case is that the violent contestation of multiparty elections is treated as criminal behaviour and as a sign that the democratic transition has gone wrong, necessitating extraordinary measures like the intervention of an international court. This conceals to some degree the fact that in Kenya violence after elections had been the norm and independent court action completely absent. Incapable of recognizing the structural causes of the violence and unable to reflect on the role of specific ideals of democratic order in its own intervention, international criminal justice could not fulfil its promise to represent a truly new beginning for Kenya.

There is an inherent tension between ideas of the orderly and narratives of the exceptional that underlie the criminalization of post-electoral violence. Gerry Simpson has pointed out that often ideologies stand trial at international criminal courts — Nazism in Nuremberg, nationalism at the International Criminal Tribunal for Former Yugoslavia, racism at the International Criminal Tribunal for Rwanda (Simpson, 2007: 13). In the Kenya case it is the lack of an orderly democracy that is on trial. The ICC hearings presented the lack of an orderly democratic transition as a state of exception that required a criminal prosecution, and the lack of a judicial investigation in Kenya rendered the case admissible at the ICC. Ideals of an orderly democratic transition include that the defeated party accepts the results of a ballot, and that any doubt about the regularity of procedures is taken to independent courts where the results can be challenged and those responsible for electoral fraud held accountable. None of this happened in Kenya.

Criminalizing the lack of orderly electoral contestation points to a particular idea of how political conflict ought to be carried out and how democracies ought to function. Peaceful multiparty elections that bring a change of power and in which the losing party accepts defeat are often presented as a hallmark of successful democratic regimes and as an indicator of consolidated democracies (Campbell and Harwood, 2011; Kuenzi and Lambright, 2005; Schedler, 1998). Sceptics have argued that competitive multiparty elections do not necessarily help to strengthen democracies if state institutions are still weak and the rule of law has not been established (Mansfield and Snyder, 2007). However, the general agreement holds that in orderly democracies peaceful and free elections should function to turn over power. In contrast, electoral rigging and the violent reaction it triggers are taken as signs that a democracy is not consolidated and that the democratic transition remains incomplete.

The ICC case presented the attacks as an exceptional event, which should have triggered domestic criminal prosecution as the regular response to violence. When the domestic judiciary remained inactive the ICC's prosecution stepped in with the promise that its criminal investigations would help to put democracy back on track in Kenya. In 2009 Moreno-Ocampo spoke of the ICC proceedings as 'opportunities to rebuild Kenya on new foundations',[24] and in 2013 he reiterated that the prosecution was a game-changer in the country's electoral history and paved the way for the predominantly peaceful 2013 elections.[25] The international character of the criminal proceedings was presented as a one-off intervention that should ideally result in a regular reaction by domestic courts. This expectation is shared by Kenyans and Western donor states. As Brownyn Anne Leebaw (2008: 100) has argued, international criminal justice establishes its claim to legitimacy by minimizing the challenges that international courts present to the dominant political order. To do this, international courts present their interventions as singular which enables them to maintain order while helping the transition in extraordinary periods of political upheaval (Teitel, 2000: 6).

The ICC does what the international community would expect domestic courts to do: initiate prosecution after extraordinary levels of violence. Mark Drumbl (2004) has argued that the dominant meta-narrative of international criminal law represents mass violence as something transgressive of universal norms. These extraordinary acts of criminality thus necessitate thorough investigation, effective prosecution, and retributive punishment; they are marked out by special categories of criminality that recognize the extraordinary nature of the crimes. This, in turn, gives rise to proscriptions concerning

---

24. Luis Moreno-Ocampo, press conference 26 November 2009 in Nairobi: http://www.icc-cpi. int/NR/rdonlyres/AC13413D-D097-4527-B0AE-60CF6DBB1B68/281313/LMOINTRO statement26112009_2_2.pdf.
25. *The Star* (2013). However, his claims can be contested, as analyses so far suggest other explanations for the peaceful elections of 2013, including the decisive influence of Kenya's new constitution, its legal reforms and the general will to avoid another outbreak of violence (Dersso, 2013).

genocide, crimes against humanity and war crimes. The criminalization of post-electoral violence marked it out as an exceptional reaction to electoral fraud in Kenya. The violence had to be framed as exceptional crime against humanity in the Pre-Trial proceedings to make the case admissible and to justify international criminal intervention. The criminalization of violence has largely separated it from the overall political process of contested multiparty elections and has prevented an inquiry into the root causes of the violence. Past electoral violence had not been less intense or widespread but had triggered a different kind of response. The novelty in the 2007/8 attacks did not therefore lie in the extent or the intensity of the violence, but in the international response to it.

International responses to electoral violence traditionally called for long-term socio-political solutions, voter education, mediation and power sharing which in the end terminated the violence in Kenya. Those immediate measures were usually combined with efforts to initiate substantial long-term political and legal reforms. Even in February 2008 the International Crisis Group's recommended responses to the violence were essentially political and long-term. They included a detailed programme of power sharing, constitutional and legal reform and economic policies that would convince the drivers of violence to disarm and prevent future violence (ICG, 2008). This is in line with the previously dominant approach that identified structural processes leading to violence, such as economic liberalization, youth mobilization and the systematic marginalization of particular social groups (Laakso, 2007). Previous policy had thus seen electoral violence as part of the wider political conflict to be addressed through political mediation between contenders together with long-term socio-political interventions such as addressing marginalization and voter education. Prosecuting electoral violence in court presents the attacks as criminal behaviour by a few individuals. Prosecution thus promises a rather quick solution to political violence by maintaining that prosecuting key figures will be a deterrent and stop future violence. If international criminal tribunals and courts are an indication that the law has become the standard way to think about war (Simpson, 2007), then the recent venture into electoral violence shows that the law has increasingly become the dominant way to think about political conflict more broadly. In this view, violence ceases to be the outcome of collective grievances and is instead seen as a strategy of individuals to attain political advantages. Consequently violence can be stopped by prosecuting those individuals.

International criminal justice administers a response to political violence from afar. It stands aloof from the power struggles that triggered the violence and that mark post-conflict societies. Many Kenyans regard this as its greatest advantage and some have argued that the distance allows the courts to be independent and less easily corrupted by individual powerful politicians (Anders, 2009: 137; Wilson, 2005: 921). Sceptics, however, have pointed out that it is exactly that distance that makes courts unaware of structures of power and unable to address the grievances that underlie the conflict (Finnström, 2011; Kelsall, 2009).

Court trials are not only ill-suited to take into account questions of culture (Kelsall, 2009) and power (Clarke, 2009). Their focus on individual command responsibilities also systematically masks questions of the role and capability of the state — questions that are often central to the possibility of widespread violence. This points to an increasing reluctance on the part of Western donor states to engage with the link between state capacity and sovereignty and a tendency to separate the issue of weak state institutions from questions about the appropriate redress for violence. Trials are unable to address the systematic erosion of state functions and the decreasing ability of the state to contain violence, and lack the mechanisms to examine the reasons why state institutions are weak.

CONCLUSION

The ICC investigations into post-electoral violence in Kenya mark a new beginning in several respects. For international criminal justice in Africa, the Kenya hearing is the first instance in which an international criminal court has started to investigate violence in a consolidated democracy rather than in connection with ongoing armed conflict. This indicates an expanded definition of political contestation that the international community is willing to refer to courts. Although it is still too early to say whether this represents a new trend, the fact that two of the most recent investigations at the ICC concern post-electoral violence indicates that international criminal law is increasingly being applied to violence associated with the democratic process and that the international community is more prepared to provide the expected response to extraordinary levels of violence if the domestic judiciary is unwilling or unable to do so.

For Kenya, the ICC case, together with the new constitution and a reformed electoral law, may be a factor in the process of strengthening the judiciary and may signal an end to ineffective commissions of inquiry. It could also potentially shake up the traditional belief that office automatically brings immunity from criminal investigation. However, for the ICC hearing to mark a truly new beginning for Kenya's judiciary, it needs to be accompanied by substantial domestic political and judicial reform — something that international criminal justice cannot administer. It is also highly unlikely that the ICC intervention will end political conflict or represent a solution for electoral fraud. Multiparty politics marked a new beginning for Kenya in the 1990s but relied too heavily on old structures of political power to represent a clear break with the past. The ICC case might represent an exceptional response to electoral fraud, but the domestic judiciary is still structurally dependent on the executive and needs to gain more independence if courts are to effectively address electoral fraud in the future.

The new beginning that international criminal justice marks for the international engagement in post-conflict violence is more pronounced. It indicates a less patient response to political conflict, one that individualizes guilt rather than addresses the long-term social causes of violence. Criminal justice promises a more results-based and clear-cut response than the traditional long-term socio-political responses to electoral violence. International court cases are so attractive because they can be limited in terms of their duration and expenses and still have a potentially high political impact as they testify to the international will to act on violent conflict. Their new prominence in international relations contributes to the juridification of politics (Andrieu, 2010; Habermas, 2006; Silverstein, 2009; Tambakaki, 2009), the tendency to 'rely on legal processes and legal arguments, using legal language, substituting or replacing ordinary politics with judicial decisions and legal formality' (Silverstein, 2009: 5). It is also indicative of the international trend to criminalize state actions in breach of particular interests (Simpson, 2004: 290). However, two central aspects of international criminal law limit the extent to which it can really facilitate a new beginning after political violence. The first is the law's focus on individual responsibility, which excludes any considerations of systematic causes for violence. The second is the need for international justice to represent its intervention as exceptional, thereby eschewing discussions about the deliberate weakening of domestic courts that had made the international intervention necessary in the first place.

The ICC hearings do not necessarily facilitate the transition to a new political system, but they represent a new international approach to violence in an existing political order. In this they differ from other criminal justice cases in Africa that have often been part of broader strategies to transform the political system of particular states. The ICC Kenya hearing seeks to modulate the existing political order and points to the tension between the ideal of how democracies ought to function and the reality of political violence and illiberal mechanisms of political contestations. The internationalization of criminal prosecution is conceptualized as exceptional, an extraordinary measure to help the transition from electoral violence as state of exception to a peaceful ideal. It promises a new beginning for Kenya, but its representation of the violence as exceptional obfuscates the fact that violence has long been the common reaction to alleged electoral fraud in Kenya. The return to normality that the ICC intervention promised was therefore not a 'return' at all. Kenya's history of elections and electoral violence has shown that new beginnings have too often relied on old structures: it is only if those structures are reformed that the beginning can be truly new.

REFERENCES

Akhavan, P. (2001) 'Beyond Impunity: Can International Criminal Justice Prevent Future Atrocities?', *The American Journal of International Law* 95(1): 7–31.

Akiwumi, A.M. (1999) 'Report of the Judicial Commission Appointed to Inquire into Tribal Clashes in Kenya'. Nairobi: Government of Kenya.

Almqvist, J. and C. Espósito Massicci (eds) (2011) *The Role of Courts in Transitional Justice: Voices from Latin America and Spain.* London: Routledge.

Ambos, K., J. Large and M. Wierda (eds) (2009) *Building a Future on Peace and Justice. Studies on Transitional Justice, Peace and Development: The Nuremberg Declaration on Peace and Justice.* Berlin: Springer.

Anders, G. (2009) 'The New Global Legal Order as Local Phenomenon: The Special Court for Sierra Leone', in F. Benda-Beckman, K. Benda-Beckman and A. Griffiths (eds) *Spatializing Law: An Anthropological Geography of Law in Society*, pp. 137–57. Burlington, VT: Ashgate.

Anders, G. and O. Zenker (2014) 'Transition and Justice: An Introduction', *Development and Change* 45(3): 395–414.

Andrieu, K. (2010) 'Transitional Justice: A New Discipline in Human Rights', in *Online Encyclopedia of Mass Violence*. http://www.massviolence.org/Transitional-Justice-A-New-Discipline-in-Human-Rights, ISSN 1961–9898

Arendt, H. (1965) *Eichmann in Jerusalem: A Report on the Banality of Evil.* New York: Viking Press.

Article 19 (1998) *Kenya: Post-Election Political Violence.* London and Nairobi: Article 19.

Aukerman, M. (2002) 'Extraordinary Evil, Ordinary Crime: A Framework for Understanding Transitional Justice', *Harv. Hum. Rts. J.* 15: 39–97.

BBC (2013) 'ICC seeks Walter Barasa Arrest for Kenya "Witness Tampering"'. BBC News 2 October 2013. http://www.bbc.co.uk/news/world-africa-24364778 (accessed 9 December 2013).

Branch, D. (2011) *Kenya: Between Hope and Despair, 1963–2011.* New Haven, CT: Yale University Press.

Branch, D. (2013) 'Kenya between Hope and Despair. Again'. African Arguments. http://africanarguments.org/2013/02/28/kenya-between-hope-and-despair-again/

Branch, D. and N. Cheeseman (2009) 'Democratization, Sequencing, and State Failure in Africa: Lessons from Kenya', *African Affairs* 108(430): 1–26.

Brown, S. (2011) 'Lessons Learned and Forgotten: The International Community and Electoral Conflict Management in Kenya', in D. Gillies (ed.) *Elections in Dangerous Places: Democracy and the Paradoxes of Peacebuilding*, pp. 127–43. Montreal: McGill-Queen's University Press.

Bueno, O. (2013) 'Reactions to the Ngudjolo Decision: Divisions among Iturian Communities', 2 January. New York: Open Foundations. http://www.katangatrial.org/2013/01/reactions-to-the-ngudjolo-decision-divisions-among-iturian-communities/

Campbell, J. and A. Harwood (2011) 'African Democracy: Elections Despite Divisions'. Council on Foreign Relations Expert Brief, October. http://www.cfr.org/world/african-democracy-elections-despite-divisions/p26288

Cheeseman, N. (2008) 'The Kenyan Elections of 2007: An Introduction', *Journal of Eastern African Studies* 2(2): 166–84.

Citizennews (2012) 'Respect Kenya's Sovereignty, Leaders Tell ICC'. http://www.citizennews.co.ke/news/2012/local/item/14771-respect-kenyas-sovereignty-leaders-tell-icc (accessed 14 November 2013).

Clarke, K.M. (2009) *Fictions of Justice: The International Criminal Court and the Challenge of Legal Pluralism in Sub-Sahara Africa.* Cambridge: Cambridge University Press.

Dersso, S.A. (2013) 'Kenya: How Kenya Delivered Its Peaceful General Elections'. Addis Ababa: Institute for Security Studies. http://www.polity.org.za/article/how-kenya-delivered-its-peaceful-general-elections-2013-03-25

Drumbl, M. (2003) 'Toward a Criminology of International Crime'. Washington and Lee Public Law and Legal Theory Research Paper Series 03–07. Lexington, VA: Washington and Lee University School of Law.

Drumbl, M. (2004) 'Pluralizing International Criminal Justice', *Mich. L. Rev.* 103: 1295–1328.

Elster, J. (2004) *Closing the Books: Transitional Justice in Historical Perspective*. Cambridge: Cambridge University Press.

Fassin, D. and M. Pandolfi (2010) 'Introduction', in D. Fassin and M. Pandolfi (eds) *Contemporary States of Emergency: The Politics of Military and Humanitarian Interventions*, pp. 9–29. New York: Zone Books.

Finnström, S. (2010) 'Reconciliation Grown Bitter? War, Retribution and Ritual Action in Northern Uganda', in R. Shaw and L. Waldorf (eds) *Localizing Transitional Justice*, pp. 135–57. Stanford, CA: Stanford University Press.

Fletcher, L. (2005) 'From Indifference to Engagement: Bystanders and International Criminal Justice', *Michigan Journal of International Law* 26: 1013–95.

Gegout, C. (2013) 'The International Criminal Court: Limits, Potential and Conditions for the Promotion of Justice and Peace', *Third World Quarterly* 34(5): 800–18.

Githongo, J. (2010) 'Fear and Loathing in Nairobi: The Challenge of Reconciliation in Kenya', *Foreign Affairs* 89 (July/August): 2–9. http://www.foreignaffairs.com/articles/66470/john-githongo/fear-and-loathing-in-nairobi

Gustafson, C. (1998) 'International Criminal Courts: Some Dissident Views on the Continuation of War by Penal Means', *Houston Journal of International Law* 21: 51–84.

Habermas, J. (2006) *The Divided West*. Cambridge: Polity Press.

Harneit-Sievers, A. and R. Peters (2008) 'Kenya's 2007 General Election and Its Aftershocks', *Afrika Spectrum* 43: 133–44.

Höhn, S. (2010) 'International Justice and Reconciliation in Namibia: The ICC Submission and Public Memory', *African Affairs* 109: 471–88.

HRW (1993) 'Kenya – Divide and Rule: State Sponsored Ethnic Violence in Kenya'. New York: Human Rights Watch.

HRW (2008) 'Ballots to Bullets: Organized Political Violence and Kenya's Crisis of Governance'. New York: Human Rights Watch.

ICG (2008) 'Kenya in Crisis'. Africa Report No. 137. International Crisis Group.

ICG (2012) 'Kenya: Impact of the ICC Proceedings'. Policy Briefing No. 84. International Crisis Group.

ICPC (2011) 'Building Sustainable Peace through Ending the Cycle of Impunity in Kenya'. Nairobi: International Center for Policy and Conflict.

IRIN (2012) 'Reactions from the DRC to ICC Acquittal of Militia Leader 19 December 2012'. IRIN News. http://www.irinnews.org/report/97079/ (accessed 9 December 2013).

Kagwanja, P. and R. Southall (2009) 'Introduction: Kenya — A Democracy in Retreat?', *Journal of Contemporary African Studies* 27(3): 259–77.

Karimi, F. (2013) 'African Union Accuses ICC of Bias, Seeks Delay of Cases against Sitting Leaders'. CNN 12 October. http://edition.cnn.com/2013/10/12/world/africa/ethiopia-au-icc-summit/ (accessed 9 December 2013).

Kelsall, T. (2009) *Culture under Cross-Examination: International Justice and the Special Court for Sierra Leone*. Cambridge: Cambridge University Press.

KHRC (1998) 'Killing the Vote: State Sponsored Violence and Flawed Elections in Kenya'. Nairobi: Kenya Human Rights Commission.

KHRC and FIDH (2009) 'ICC Prosecutor Targets Unpunished Crimes in Kenya'. Nairobi: Kenya Human Rights Commission and International Federation for Human Rights.

Kiai, M. (2008) 'The Crisis in Kenya', *Journal of Democracy* 19(3): 162–8.

Kimenyi, M. (2013) 'Kenya: A Country Redeemed after a Peaceful Election'. Washington, DC: Brookings Institution. http://www.brookings.edu/blogs/up-front/posts/2013/04/02-kenya-peaceful-elections-kimenyi

KNCHR (2008) 'On the Brink of the Precipice: A Human Rights Account of Kenya's Post-2007 Election Violence. Final Report'. Nairobi: Kenya National Commission for Human Rights.

Kuenzi, M. and G. Lambright (2005) 'Party Systems and Democratic Consolidation in Africa's Electoral Regimes', *Party Politics* 11(4): 423–46.

Laakso, L. (2007) 'Insights into Electoral Violence in Africa', in M. Basedau, G. Erdmann and A. Mehler (eds) *Votes, Money and Violence: Political Parties and Elections in Sub-Saharan Africa*, pp. 224–53. Uppsala: Nordiska Afrikainstitutet.

Leebaw, B.A. (2008) 'The Irreconcilable Goals of Transitional Justice', *Human Rights Quarterly* 30(1): 95–118.

Machuka, M. (2008) 'Seek Court Action, PNU Leaders Tell Raila', *The Standard* 3 January. http://allafrica.com/stories/200801021298.html (accessed 2 February 2012).

Mamdani, M. (2013) 'Mamdani on Why Raila Lost', *Daily Monitor* 10 March. http://www.monitor.co.ug/Magazines/ThoughtIdeas/Kenya-2013–The-ICC-election/-/689844/1715440/-/mplnfd/-/index.html (accessed 9 December 2013).

Mansfield, E.D. and J.L. Snyder (2007) 'The Sequencing "Fallacy"', *Journal of Democracy* 18(3): 5–10.

Mueller, S.D. (2008) 'The Political Economy of Kenya's Crisis', *Journal of Eastern African Studies* 2(2): 185–210.

Mueller, S.D. (2011) 'Dying to Win: Elections, Political Violence, and Institutional Decay in Kenya', *Journal of Contemporary African Studies* 29(1): 99–117.

Mugo, P. (2013) 'Rising Violence and Insecurity as Kenya's General Elections Approach'. Peace and Conflict Monitor. http://www.monitor.upeace.org/archive.cfm?id_article=954

Mutiga, M. (2011) 'Security Council Rejects Kenya's ICC Deferral Bid', *African Review* 19 March. http://www.africareview.com/News/-/979180/1129084/-/hqdtjdz/-/index.html (accessed 9 December 2013)

Ndegwa, A. (2011) 'Outcome Could Make or Break Uhuru Career', *The Standard* 6 October. http://www.standardmedia.co.ke/?id=2000044232&cid=653&articleID=2000044232 (accessed 9 December 2013).

News24 Kenya (2013) 'Duale: ICC Pull Out Will Protect Kenya's Sovereignty'. http://www.news24.co.ke/Politics/Duale-says-ICC-pull-out-will-protect-Kenyas-sovereignty-20130904 (accessed 14 November 2013).

OHCHR (2008) 'Report from OHCHR Fact-finding Mission to Kenya, 6–28 February 2008'. Geneva: Office of the High Commissioner for Human Rights.

Okuta, A (2009) 'National Legislation for Prosecution of International Crimes in Kenya', *Journal of International Criminal Justice* 7: 1063–76.

Okwara, E. (2001) 'The International Criminal Court and Kenya's Post-election Violence: National Justice through Global Mechanisms?'. GGI Analysis 2/2011. Brussels: Global Governance Institute.

Olsen, T.D., L.A. Payne and A.G. Reiter (2010) 'The Justice Balance: When Transitional Justice Improves Human Rights and Democracy', *Human Rights Quarterly* 32(4): 980–1007.

Onyango-Obbo, C. (2013) 'Why Kenyans Didn't Run Berserk after the Tense March 4 Elections', *Daily Nation Kenya* 13 March.

Pflanz, M. (2012) 'Victims of Kenya Violence Shrug at ICC Effort'. Christian Science Monitor. http://www.csmonitor.com/World/Africa/2012/0124/Victims-of-Kenya-violence-shrug-at-ICC-effort

Reuters (2011) 'UN Council Shelves Kenya Request to Defer ICC Case', Reuters 9 April. http://af.reuters.com/article/topNews/idAFJOE73801I20110409 (accessed 17 February 2012).

Reuters (2013) 'Africa Fails to Get ICC Kenya Trials Deferred at United Nations', Reuters 15 November. http://www.reuters.com/article/2013/11/15/us-kenya-icc-un-idUSBRE9AE0S420131115 (accessed 9 December 2013).

Rice, X. (2009) 'Annan Hands ICC List of Perpetrators of Post-election Violence in Kenya', *The Guardian* 9 July. http://www.theguardian.com/world/2009/jul/09/international-criminal-court-kofi-annan (accessed 9 December 2013).

Robinson, D. (2003) 'Serving the Interests of Justice: Amnesties, Truth Commissions and the International Criminal Court', *European Journal of International Law* 14(3): 481–505.

Rutten, M. and S. Owuor (2009) 'Weapons of Mass Destruction: Land, Ethnicity and the 2007 Elections in Kenya', *Journal of Contemporary African Studies* 27(3): 305–24.

Schedler, A. (1998) 'What is Democratic Consolidation?', *Journal of Democracy* 9(2): 91–107.

Silverstein, G. (2009) *Law's Allure: How Law Shapes, Constrains, Saves, and Kills Politics.* Berkeley, CA: University of California Press.

Simpson, G. (2004) *Great Powers and Outlaw States: Unequal Sovereigns in the International Legal Order.* Cambridge: Cambridge University Press.

Simpson, G. (2007) *Law, War and Crime: War Crimes Trials and the Reinvention of International Law.* Cambridge: Polity Press.

de Smedt, J. (2009) '"No Raila, No Peace!" Big Man Politics and Election Violence at the Kibera Grassroots', *African Affairs* 108(433): 581–98.

Smith, L. (2009) 'Explaining Violence after Recent Elections in Ethiopia and Kenya', *Democratization* 16(5): 867–97.

The Star (2013) 'I Brought Peace to Kenya, Says Ocampo', *The Star* 16 March. http://www.the-star.co.ke/news/article-112363/i-brought-peace-kenya-says-ocampo

Steeves, J. (2006) 'Presidential Succession in Kenya: The Transition from Moi to Kibaki', *Commonwealth & Comparative Politics* 44(2): 211–33.

Steeves, J. (2011) 'Democracy Unravelled in Kenya: Multi-party Competition and Ethnic Targeting', *African Identities* 9(4): 455–64.

Tambakaki, P. (2009) 'Cosmopolitanism or Agonism? Alternative Visions of World Order', *Critical Review of International Social and Political Philosophy* 12(1): 101–16.

Taylor, M. (2013) 'Kenya 2013: The Power of Nightmares'. African Arguments. http://africanarguments.org/2013/03/10/kenya-2013-the-power-of-nightmares-%E2%80%93-by-magnus-taylor/

Teitel, R.G. (2000) *Transitional Justice*. Oxford: Oxford University Press.

Teitel, R.G. (2003) 'Transitional Justice Genealogy', *Harvard Human Rights Journal* 16: 69–94.

Teitel, R.G. (2005) 'The Law and Politics of Contemporary Transitional Justice', *Cornell International Law Journal* 38: 837–62.

Turner, C. (2008) 'Delivering Lasting Peace, Democracy and Human Rights in Times of Transition: The Role of International Law', *The International Journal of Transitional Justice* 2(2): 126–51.

Vinjamuri, L. (2010) 'Deterrence, Democracy, and the Pursuit of International Justice', *Ethics & International Affairs* 24(2): 191–211.

Waki Commission (2008) 'Final Report of the Commission of Inquiry on Post-Election Violence'. Nairobi: Government of Kenya.

Westcott, N. (2011) 'International Justice, Peace and Crisis Management: The European Union and Africa'. Speech delivered at Conference on Experiences and Reflections from Africa and the EU 50 Years after Dag Hamerskjold, The Hague (9 November).

Wilson, R. (2005) 'Judging History: The Historical Record of the International Criminal Tribunal for the Former Yugoslavia', *Human Rights Quarterly* 27(3): 908–42.

Wilson, R. (2011a) 'Through the Lens of International Criminal Law: Comprehending the African Context of Crimes at the International Criminal Court', *Studies in Ethnicity and Nationalism* 11(1): 106–15.

Wilson, R. (2011b) *Writing History in International Criminal Trials*. Cambridge: Cambridge University Press.

Wippman, D. (1999) 'Atrocities, Deterrence, and the Limits of International Justice', *Fordham International Law Journal* 23(2): 473–88.

10

Justice without Peace? International Justice and Conflict Resolution in Northern Uganda

Kimberley Armstrong

INTRODUCTION

The decision of the International Criminal Court (ICC) in late 2003 to open an investigation into events of the conflict between the Lord's Resistance Army (LRA/M) and the Government of Uganda was a momentous occasion. It represented an important step forward for the newly established International Court in its efforts to render itself a relevant institution in global politics and a key purveyor of international justice.[1] For Uganda, it also marked a critical turning point in a seemingly unending conflict that had involved forced conscriptions, brutal killings and the mass displacement of the majority of the population in northern Uganda, the region where the conflict has had its most devastating effects. The decision, however, also became notable for the controversy it ignited, as local reaction to the decision of the Court to investigate the conflict was decidedly unenthusiastic. Many politicians, religious leaders and traditional leaders of the Acholi — the ethnic group residing in the most affected areas and also one of the key players in the LRA hierarchy — were very vocal in their opposition to the decision of the Court.

The local leaders, along with a number of humanitarian organizations, opposed the ICC intervention based on a number of concerns. The primary concern was that the potential indictments of rebel leaders would render ongoing attempts to renew peace talks between the LRA and the government impossible. For some time, local leaders in the Acholi region had worked to challenge the central government in Uganda regarding the best way to resolve the conflict which had raged for almost two decades. The intervention of the ICC at the request of the central government was a new twist to the ongoing political struggle and it threatened the efforts made by local

Funding for this research was generously provided by the International Development Research Centre (IDRC) Doctoral Research Grant, the Social Sciences and Humanities Research Council (SSHRC) doctoral fellowship and Fonds québécois de la recherche sur la société et la culture (FQRSC) doctoral fellowship. The author is grateful to the referees for comments on an earlier version.

1. The term 'international justice' as I use it here refers both to international legal systems set up to address violations of human rights and international law, as well as moral and philosophical frameworks often associated with such institutions. This term is sometimes interchangeable with 'global justice' (cf. Dembour and Kelly, 2007: 3).

Transition and Justice: Negotiating the Terms of New Beginnings in Africa, First Edition.
Edited by Gerhard Anders and Olaf Zenker.
Chapters © 2015 by The Institute of Social Studies. Book compilation © 2015 John Wiley & Sons, Ltd.

leaders to seek conflict resolution through peace talks and amnesty of former rebels. The preference for peaceful solutions to the conflict was premised on the principle that the government had failed in previous attempts to end the conflict militarily. In each case, military operations had actually served to increase rather than allay the suffering of the population. There was also considerable distrust of the government among the Acholi. Most believed that the government did little to end the conflict and even considered the government as party to their suffering through its policy of forced displacement into camps that were poorly provisioned and largely unprotected (ARLPI, 2001). Caught between the government and the LRA, local leaders in the region had been lobbying international organizations and foreign governments to support their attempts to pressurize the Ugandan government to enter into peace talks with the LRA and finally bring peace to northern Uganda.[2] Peace was, after all, considered paramount to end the suffering and enable the population to return to their homes and begin the process of rebuilding their lives.

The decision of the ICC to investigate, therefore, was considered a direct challenge to local peace efforts and the intervention of the ICC into the affairs of northern Uganda was quickly characterized as a contest between peace and justice. Debate over the Court's decision to investigate the LRA/M conflict occurred in the news media, in reports published by interested local, national and international organizations, and in academic discussions at conferences, in journals and books.[3] However, for most of the general public, the news media was particularly important in framing and presenting the debate and, by and large, the media focused on the apparent dilemma between peace and justice (see, for example, Perkins, 2008; Thomasson, 2008).

The characterization of the dilemma as one of peace versus justice, however, tended to mask a much more complex political struggle. In particular, it moved attention away from a struggle of power over who should bear the right to determine the way forward for northern Uganda. In her analysis of the justice debate in Uganda, anthropologist Kamari Maxine Clarke has pointed to the competing sovereignties of the victims, the state and international institutions. Drawing on Agamben's notion of the 'state of exception',[4] she notes that:

> The state of exception is also reflected in the power of individuals working through global institutions to manage international justice mechanisms and suspend national-level processes.

---

2. Negotiations between the government and the LRA had occurred before; for closer analyses of these negotiations, see Obita (2002); Simonse (1998).
3. A few examples include: Allen (2006); Branch (2004); Hovil and Quinn (2005); Pham et al. (2005).
4. Agamben (1998) argues that sovereign power lies in the ability of the sovereign to determine the state of exception. In a state of exception, law is suspended, but not violated. A state of exception allows for the extension of power by the sovereign power. In this case, according to Clarke (2007), international organizations are imposing their sovereign power over nation states on the basis of a state of exception.

This is directly relevant to the competition between the ICC and national-level strategies for justice in Uganda, as it relates to the power to decide when and with respect to whom the law does or does not apply. (Clarke, 2007: 153)

While Clarke is referring more specifically to the power to define the exact application of international justice in specific situations, the logic of exception was raised in more general ways as well. The initial decision of the ICC to accept the referral of the Ugandan government rested explicitly on the state of exception, as the basis for intervention implies the inability or unwillingness of the sovereign nation to deal with the crimes themselves. However, once the government began to cast doubt over its own support for the ICC intervention, claims of sovereignty over the Ugandan case needed to be constantly reproduced by the ICC. This doubt was raised since, despite the fact that the Ugandan government had initially referred the case to the ICC, the same government eventually agreed to participate in the Juba Peace Talks with the LRA that began in 2006, and assured the rebel leaders they would not be arrested if they presented themselves for the talks. Furthermore, in the formal agreement drawn up between the rebels and the government, the rebel leaders were assured that their cases would be heard by special courts in Uganda rather than by the ICC.[5]

ICC officials responded not only by reminding the Ugandan government of their legal obligation, but also, as peace talks progressed, by continuing to formulate very specific versions of peace as singularly capable of providing a solution to the Ugandan crisis. A new beginning for Uganda, so the Court would have it, could never be achieved without addressing issues of justice and impunity. After all, much was at stake for the newly founded Court. The Court itself had been built upon the promise of a break with the past as illustrated in the comments of the Chairman of the Drafting Committee for the Rome Statute, Cherif Bassiouni, who claimed that 'the world will never be the same after the adoption of the Statute of the International Criminal Court' (United Nations, 1998). As Anders and Zenker note in the Introduction of this volume, debates about new beginnings have increasingly been framed in terms of transitional justice. In the case of northern Uganda, this configuration was particularly critical as the legitimacy of the Court and, more specifically, its ability to deal with situations of ongoing conflict, was at risk. Key to this formulation of a new beginning was the postulation that it would not be possible to break with the past and obtain a fresh start if justice was not delivered.

In contrast, the local leaders in northern Uganda were put on the defensive as their struggle for peace was now being complicated by international demands for justice. Not unlike the international community, local leaders

---

5. For in-depth analyses of the Juba Peace Talks, see Atkinson (2010); Schomerus and Ogwaro (2010).

also made claims to sovereignty by raising the spectre of exception. They argued that the Ugandan case was unique given that many of the rebels were themselves victims. Moreover, the victims perceived themselves as caught between two offenders, the government and the rebels. Local leaders considered peace the number one priority and the foundation upon which a new beginning could be achieved, since the greatest offence against the population was thought to be the way the conflict had been allowed to cripple the population economically and socially. Finally, local leaders argued that local forms of justice, in particular a process known as *mato oput*, were more culturally appropriate for the Acholi people.[6]

Each side of the debate mobilized discursive constructions in order to legitimize their own claims to sovereignty and therefore to the right to determine how a new beginning in northern Uganda could be achieved and what it should look like. Within the framework of peace versus justice that was prevalent in the media, both sides made lofty claims about their particular pathway to a new beginning. Proponents of the ICC promised an 'end to impunity' and 'sustainable peace', while those opposed to the ICC intervention spoke of 'reconciliatory justice' that could offer a more holistic version of justice and healing. Neither of these claims, however, was capable of standing up to sustained scrutiny.

The purpose of this chapter, therefore, is to analyse more closely the lofty claims made by ICC officials as well as the local leaders who opposed the ICC intervention, and to attempt a better understanding of what was really at stake and of those motivations and objectives that were rarely exposed for public consumption. By bringing these issues to light, one can illustrate the manner in which the public imagination is manipulated through media while differential distributions of power and preconceived notions of relevant concepts are left mainly undisturbed.[7]

---

6. *Mato oput* is a traditional process of conflict resolution that requires the offender to take responsibility for his or her actions and for reparations to be made to the victims before a ritual is performed to heal divisions between offenders and victims. Historically, these divisions would usually be at the level of the clan. For more detailed descriptions of the practice, see Allen (2010); Baines (2005); Finnström (2008).
7. This chapter examines the debate as it developed following the public announcement of the ICC decision in early 2004 until the period following the final collapse of peace talks in late 2008. It is based on research carried out for my PhD dissertation and includes periods of fieldwork in northern Uganda in 2005 and 2007, as well as analyses of news articles, press releases, reports and academic writing. During fieldwork, more than 100 interviews were conducted with residents in IDP camps and with various religious, political and cultural leaders. At the time of writing this chapter, the people of northern Uganda are enjoying a kind of peace, but the same cannot be said of communities in neighbouring countries where members of the LRA are believed to be in hiding. Since the collapse of the peace talks, more than 1,000 people have been killed by the LRA and many more abducted or tortured. Most recently, the United States has promised to assist the Ugandan military in their operations to kill or capture the LRA command.

INTERNATIONAL JUSTICE

One would assume that by highlighting the dilemma between peace and justice, Court officials would be called to task on the possibility that the intervention of the ICC could be prolonging the suffering of people in northern Uganda and pushing the conflict toward intractability if the rebels refused to surrender without the removal of the indictments set out by the Court. However, in most cases, when officials of the Court were questioned on this topic, their response has consistently been that the intervention of the Court in Uganda has actually assisted and not hindered the peace process. In particular, ICC officials took credit for the commencement of peace talks, known as the Juba Peace Talks, between the LRA and government that began in 2006. Fatou Bensouda, then ICC Deputy Prosecutor, was quoted as saying to the French press that the 'ICC is not an impediment to peace . . . . I think the warrants that have been issued by the ICC have contributed tremendously to making the perpetrators of these crimes come to, even negotiate with the government' (Bosire, 2007). Similarly, Maria Mabinty, the ICC outreach officer in Kampala, was quoted as saying, 'I don't believe that the ICC has blocked the process in any way, in fact, it's the presence of the ICC and its activities that have seen this process come this far' (BBC News, 2004). Such statements, repeated in a number of interviews and analyses, construct the ICC indictments against the rebels as the main catalyst for the Juba Peace Talks and an expected peace. However, not only do these constructions tend to ignore a number of other factors that likely played a critical role in establishing the environment for negotiations between the government and the LRA/M, they also overlook altogether the fact that the ICC remained the most critical impediment to an agreed solution.

Certainly, the indictments against the rebels had an impact on the LRA/M leadership and influenced their decisions. Nonetheless, it would be naïve to believe that the ICC intervention was the only or even necessarily the most important factor which led the LRA/M leaders to make public demands for negotiations with the government. The Nairobi Agreement signed in 1999 between the Ugandan and Sudanese governments required both governments to cease support to rebels in their respective countries. Though support to the LRA/M continued even after the Agreement was signed, this event marked the beginning of increased tensions between the Khartoum government and the LRA/M as well as a decrease in financial and material support. The public acknowledgment that the Khartoum government had been supporting the LRA/M also worked to increase international attention and political pressure on the Sudanese to end their relations with the rebels. In 2002, the Sudanese government even gave permission to the Ugandan military to enter their territory to fight the LRA. By 2005, when the Sudanese government signed a Comprehensive Peace Agreement with the Sudan People's Liberation Army/Movement (SPLA/M), Sudanese support for the LRA/M is believed to have been almost completely cut off. It also meant that the

LRA/M would be vulnerable if they remained in Southern Sudan since they would no longer enjoy the protection of the Khartoum government forces. Certainly, the decline in funding and the souring of relations between the Khartoum government and the LRA/M leadership intensified following the unprecedented attention brought to the conflict after the ICC intervention. However, it also leads one to question why such diplomatic pressure and international attention was not brought to the situation much earlier. Had such financial, technical and diplomatic resources been available to the people of northern Uganda in the years prior to the establishment of the ICC, the war may have been brought to an end much earlier, suggesting that international concern for the conflict was more a show of support for the ICC than a desire to see an end to conflict in northern Uganda.

The degree to which many of the actors now interested in resolving the two-decade long conflict also came with a predetermined agenda is evidenced in an article submitted to a Ugandan newspaper by Human Rights Watch in May 2007. The article states that:

> Last month we spoke with people who were victims of the massive displacement that occurred in the north due to the conflict. Nearly all those we met in displaced camps expressed an intense desire to return to their homes. A number conveyed real concern that prosecution of LRA/M leaders could further delay their departure and therefore saw the ICC as an obstacle. A distinct vocal minority, however, declared a desire to see those most responsible brought to trial, although they questioned how the ICC could arrest those it had charged. (Keppler and Dicker, 2007)

The article is interesting in that it first notes that through its own consultations with the population in northern Uganda, only a 'vocal minority' were interested in justice and even then with certain reservations. Yet, the authors of the article still go on to suggest that, 'those with an interest in seeing a lasting end to the conflict in northern Uganda should insist on an outcome that includes peace and justice. Anything less would be abandonment of the victims, international principle, and won't last long' (ibid.). The statement not only sets out to define what kind of peace is necessary for Ugandans, it also substitutes the priorities stated by 'a number' of the victims for those stated by the 'vocal minority'. Such statements from a number of organizations, particularly human rights organizations and INGOs promoting the ICC, became commonplace after the announcement of the investigation, bringing attention to the conflict while simultaneously working to define what a reasonable path to peace should look like.

Whether or not the ICC indictments contributed to bringing the different parties to the table, this was the argument made by the supporters of the ICC intervention. And, typically, the claim that the ICC had contributed to the peace process was accepted at face value by the news media. Press releases and statements by ICC officials tended to highlight the necessity of justice for durable peace and stress that without the indictments it is uncertain whether the rebels would have been motivated to become involved in a peace process. But, by not confronting or admitting that the indictments were potentially the biggest stumbling block to a final peace agreement, the ICC appeared to be avoiding any direct inquiries regarding its own agenda and set of priorities.

The attempt to divert attention away from challenges to peace in northern Uganda, along with other cases underway in Democratic Republic of Congo (DRC), Sudan and the Central African Republic (CAR), could well have been part of a utilitarian calculation whereby it was hoped that if the Court could make an example of a few cases, it would deter the possibility of future crimes. In this utilitarian equation, officials of the Court may have been gambling that early Court successes would result in fewer violations of humanitarian law in the future and would therefore have an overall positive outcome for humanity. However, in such an equation, many lives are put at risk or sacrificed for long-term goals that may never be realized. Indications that this was the actual, if understated, goal of the Court are revealed in statements made by the ICC Registrar Sylvana Arbia following the first failed attempt at obtaining LRA Commander Joseph Kony's signature on the peace agreement. Responding to the question of whether the ICC's refusal to remove the indictment was the reason behind Kony's decision not to sign the peace agreement, Arbia stated, 'though the agreement would bring peace, ICC does not think lasting peace should be brokered this way where impunity is a relevant factor. The intention of the ICC is to deter such acts where people expect to rebel and commit crimes then go free because a peace agreement was signed' (Muyanja, 2008). Another example is the comment made by the former ICC President Philippe Kirsch that 'the pursuit of justice isn't necessarily synonymous with the interests of peace' (*Ottawa Citizen*, 2008). The comments provide rare insight into the philosophy of the Court and the willingness to allow peace to be forfeited in the name of justice.

At a theoretical level, such revelations are more commonly and easily made. In a description of different phases of transitional justice, the legal scholar Ruti Teitel, for instance, laments the incorporation of discourses of ethics and religion into transitional justice and holds that 'a dynamic discourse that juxtaposed and even sacrificed the aim of justice for the more modest goal of peace emerged in Phase II' (Teitel, 2003). The ease with which Teitel is able to make the evaluative judgement that peace is a more modest goal than justice can be somewhat attributed to the fact that her comments are not attached to any particular conflict. For ICC officials answering to the case of northern Uganda, it would be necessary to attach that evaluation directly to the lives lost when peace is forfeited. Therefore, most officials have tended to avoid such statements.

Even after the failure of the peace talks in late 2008, most officials continued to cast blame elsewhere, pointing the finger at States Parties for not carrying out the arrests. In an important address made by Chief Prosecutor Luis Moreno-Ocampo at an international conference, he argued that:

> The tension I see in Uganda or Darfur is not between Peace and Justice. It is not the decisions of the International Criminal Court which undermine the peace processes and conflict resolution initiatives . . . . It is the lack of enforcement of the Court's decisions which is the real threat to enduring Peace. Allowed to remain at large, the criminals exposed are continuing to threaten

the victims, those who took tremendous risks to tell their stories; allowed to remain at large, the criminals ask immunity under one form or another as a condition to stopping the violence. They threaten to attack more victims. I call this extortion, I call it blackmail. We cannot yield. (Moreno-Ocampo, 2007)

The Prosecutor's statement, once again, denies the possibility that the Court's intervention could prevent peace and lays responsibility for the continuation of conflict and failure to capture the rebels on the shoulders of various governments and international actors. But this analysis sidesteps the real challenges that continue to exist in implementing these arrests. Without the possibility of a negotiated solution, the only feasible means to end the conflict is by killing or capturing the rebel leaders, an objective that has proven near impossible to achieve for over twenty years, and one which is likely to involve the killing and displacement of many more civilians. While such a dilemma may be characterized as blackmail, the risks faced by civilians in the region must be acknowledged and factored into the debate on peace and justice. There must be recognition that a utilitarian calculation that places justice as a priority over peace may cost thousands of human lives in the short term, all while the long-term outcomes are speculative at best.

The peace versus justice characterization has also been strategically beneficial to supporters of the Court since 'peace' has easily been reconceived as 'impunity'. The apparent interchangeability of these terms is the result of the belief that all alternatives to international criminal justice lead to impunity. Thus, any efforts to prioritize peace are rewritten as strategies for impunity. Once 'peace' becomes replaced with 'impunity', the arguments against justice become increasingly hard to make. The ability to render all alternatives to international penal justice as impunity is realized through the countless descriptions of LRA/M commanders escaping justice if they are made to submit themselves to local forms of justice and even on many occasions if they are allowed to be tried in front of a national court set up for the purpose of judging war crimes. For example, one Ugandan international law expert, commenting on the Agreement signed between the LRA/M and the Ugandan government that covers accountability, notes that:

> Until the charges the Ugandan state intends to bring against the LRA/M leadership are known, the fear must be that they will not address the human rights abuses for which the ICC wants them tried, while the traditional justice offered to lesser perpetrators is not justice at all, but a shield against it — and a violation of the victim's right to see the perpetrator punished. The whole system of amnesty, he warns, 'promotes a culture of impunity where violence is the norm' — the very thing the ICC was intended to overcome. (Quoted in Perkins, 2008)

Though local mechanisms of seeking justice may merit some reservation, the outright disregard for national or local processes should also be questioned. All systems of justice have limitations and require scrutiny, but writing off traditional mechanisms as nothing more than a form of impunity discounts outright the social value and meaning these processes can have within the community and the role they can play in reconciliation.

The assumption that only criminal law, and in a number of arguments only *international* criminal law, is capable of rendering justice is an indication of how quickly international justice discourse has become normalized in the imagination of the global public. Equating other forms of justice with impunity and presenting international justice as the only means to ending impunity raises the status of the ICC in relation to national governments and other judicial or quasi-judicial processes. This relative status imparts the ICC with important influence and legitimacy in international relations and with the general public, allowing the interests of international justice to take precedence over other interests. The ability to define legitimate forms of peace and justice are representative of an important means by which supporters of international justice have managed to control the agenda and characterize the Court as an important tool in conflict resolution.

While for many, the claim that the ICC is uniquely capable of imparting justice may ring true, this assumes a universally accepted notion of justice. In northern Uganda, such an assumption would be very misplaced. When individuals in northern Uganda were asked to define justice during interviews I held in 2005 and 2007, a variety of responses were given. Some individuals said people being allowed to return to their homes would be justice; others said that justice would entail the return of the rebels so that everyone could live in harmony; still another said justice would come from a reconciliation that takes all history into account. One man said that justice is when those who are knowledgeable make someone who doesn't know anything understand what he did wrong — that is, making someone who doesn't understand, understand. He also noted that justice should come from the side of government, since most of the rebels did not willingly enter the conflict.

Significantly, a common theme was that justice cannot be achieved; lives lost cannot be repaid. As one man said, 'neither the government nor Kony can pay for all that they have done' (interview, March 2007). Jacques Derrida, among others, has argued that law can never completely arrive at justice. This is the case because 'law is organized around the demand for universality' and therefore must provide strict and replicable guidelines; whereas justice must answer to the 'absolutely singular' and is therefore infinite in possibilities (Derrida, 2003 cited in Haslam, 2007: 59). Based on the definitions of justice imparted to me, it would certainly seem true that law is unlikely to provide justice in the case of northern Uganda. Justice for most people I spoke to entailed the restoration of their former lives and at least some recognition and reparation for the lives that have been indelibly altered or lost. In spite of this, supporters of the ICC have readily presented and equated justice as uniquely pertaining to the outcome of criminal trials, providing a powerful testament to the normative effect of law.

In most cases, the obstacles to peace presented by the ICC intervention have never been fully investigated; instead, it is the positions of those opposing the ICC which are put under scrutiny. The general assumption underlying the debate, therefore, is that international justice is the correct and natural solution and that opposition to it must be explained. In general, supporters of international justice have been allowed to assert that peace without justice is not really peace at all. In doing so, they disregard the fact that there are many examples in the history books of countries that have realized sustainable peace without seeking justice, South Africa being one of the better known and recent examples. Moreover, there is no concrete evidence that justice is necessary for sustainable peace. In fact, in the few cases where the relations of justice and peace have been examined, the evidence is ambivalent at best (see, for example, Fletcher et al., 2009; International Center for Transitional Justice, 2007). Nonetheless, the claim that peace must include justice has prevailed in international circles, with the exception perhaps of the Middle East and Afghanistan cases, where it is unlikely that peace would be sacrificed for the sake of justice. At the time of the debate, however, many in northern Uganda were asking: if the ICC cannot bring peace, can it really make claims to providing justice?

LOCAL PEACE

On the other side of the debate, opponents of the ICC intervention in Uganda tended to form their arguments around two collections of principles. The first set of arguments focused on the pragmatic concerns that the ICC investigation raised among those who had been struggling for peace in the region. This approach was widely supported by all who opposed the Court's involvement, including many officials from international organizations who had invested in bringing peace to the region and who had become familiar with the historical and political situation. Though the UN never officially opposed the Court's involvement, many individuals working for the UN in northern Uganda during the early days of the ICC announcement expressed their displeasure during informal discussions or interviews, and they also tended to highlight the challenge the intervention posed to peace. The second set of arguments incorporated fundamental points of the first arguments, but took opposition to the ICC a step further, basing the argument against ICC intervention on cultural and religious principles. This approach was taken mainly by local leaders, though some international actors also supported aspects of the arguments. The mobilization of discourses of cultural relativism and national reconciliation followed a historical trajectory of local leaders resisting government domination of both the representation of events and the nature of the conflict, as well as decision making on what policy to adopt to end the war. However, from a strategic perspective, the mobilization of such discourses—particularly a cultural relativist discourse—in a struggle against the imposition of the International Court, tended to divert attention away from the challenges the Court presented to peace and towards questions of cultural authenticity. Arguments against the ICC based on the pragmatic concern of peace tended to be more successful at the international level than relativist arguments which moved the discussion from a peace versus justice debate to one of tradition versus modernity or justice versus impunity. This is not to suggest that a cultural relativist argument does not have its own merits, but given the rather challenging objective of gaining international support for a withdrawal of the ICC from Uganda, the result, more often than not, was to make the Acholi themselves the object of scrutiny, rather than the ICC.

Following the announcement of the ICC decision to investigate the conflict, reaction from the Acholi region of northern Uganda was swift. Many leaders publicly challenged the timing of the ICC intervention and argued that the ICC could prove to be an impediment to peace; and peace, according to the local leaders, was the priority for northern Ugandans. Then vice-president of the Acholi Religious Leaders Peace Initiative (ARLPI), the Right Reverend Macleord Ochola, was quoted as saying, 'this kind of approach is going to destroy all efforts for peace. People want this war to stop. If we follow the ICC in branding the LRA/M criminals, it won't stop'. He went on to say, 'we're not saying impunity should be encouraged, we're saying this is poor timing. Let us not forget that UPDF [Uganda People's Defence Forces] have also committed atrocities which will at some stage need to be investigated' (*IRIN News*, 2004). The words of the religious leader highlight key points that opponents of the ICC investigation have emphasized throughout their campaign against ICC intervention. First, they do not argue that justice is unnecessary, only that it does not take precedence over peace; second, they felt that both sides of the conflict should be held accountable.

However, it was not only the local leaders who opposed the Court's intrusion into events. A coalition of local and international NGOs, known as CSOPNU, which includes well-known organizations such as Norwegian Refugee Council, Save the Children and CARE International, also publicly opposed the move. In a letter written to Chief Prosecutor Moreno-Ocampo, the coalition of civil society organizations voiced five areas of concerns over the decision of the ICC to intervene in the conflict: the timing of the investigation; issues of complementarity; the scope of the investigations; security and protection; and public relations (CSOPNU, 2004). In all, the communication to the Prosecutor demonstrates a strong coalition of local and international actors, all of whom are situated in northern Uganda and intimately familiar with the historical and political context. The arguments against the ICC intervention are largely pragmatic in nature, that is, they do not question the value of the ICC or of international justice, but lay out practical reasons why the Court may not be the best instrument to achieve justice. This is not only because it threatens peace but also because it does not have jurisdiction over all elements of the conflict and therefore cannot provide complete justice. This particular framing of arguments against the ICC was prevalent in the period following the announcement and was articulated through reports and more formal types of communication such as policy briefs or press releases.[8]

Despite the shared objectives of some international and local actors in their bid to resist ICC involvement and to support local institutions, there were some subtle shifts in the general message of arguments emanating largely from local religious, traditional and some political leaders. In fact it was not so much a shift in the position of the leaders, it was more accurately a position based on pragmatic arguments, but over time, it took attention away from certain elements of the pragmatic arguments. Many of the local leaders drew on cultural relativist and national reconciliation discourses in an attempt to strengthen and justify their opposition to international criminal trials.

The instrumentalization of 'culture' and 'religion' as arguments against ICC intervention has to be understood in the wider historical context. Discourses of cultural relativism and national reconciliation had been utilized by local leaders as they resisted what they perceived to be government oppression and domination during the war as well as negative stereotypes of the Acholi people. Dominant narratives of the conflict had painted the Acholi as violent and uncivilized, placing responsibility for the conflict on the Acholi themselves. In order to counter these dominant representations and resist government control, Acholi leaders had fought to rewrite the foundations of Acholi identity and narratives of the conflict. This process drew upon the experiences of many Native American societies and African Americans in the 1960s and 1970s who were 'revalorizing ethnic or racial markers of a despised distinctiveness' (Cowan et al., 2001: 2). It was part of a social project to re-instil pride and a positive sense of ethnic (or tribal) identity in a context of breakdown.

Thus, arguments against the ICC intervention generally followed a logic of exception that emphasized discourses of cultural relativism, religious appropriateness and popular demand. Peace was presented as the absolute priority of the people in the Acholi districts and the only way to bring about a new beginning. Peace could best be obtained by offering amnesty to the rebels in order to lure them from the bush and through peace negotiations at the higher levels. Forgiveness was considered appropriate both in cultural and religious terms, since Acholi systems of justice were said to promote reconciliation and not retribution, which was also consistent with religious frameworks that highlight forgiveness and mercy. For example, one INGO official stated, 'it's the tension between retributive and restorative justice. The people of the North would prefer restorative justice. That is rooted in their culture and they would argue that the ICC have no grounding with what is going on in the region if it thinks the answer is to pull out a whole lot of rebels' (Volqvartz, 2005). Traditional systems of justice were promoted

---

8. For example, Hovil and Quinn (2005); Human Rights Watch (2004); *IRIN News* (2004).

as better suited than Western legal systems at bringing about reconciliation on a number of bases, including the fact that they can aim at attaining the truth about events and promote the reparation of relationships between individuals and groups. Furthermore, the Acholi felt that the system of justice or reconciliation that was to be adopted should include some form of compensation as many victims believed that to be an important component of justice.

The ICC brought with it a great deal of legitimacy and authority within the international community and as such it presented a formidable challenge. The legitimacy of the Court is largely built on discourses of human rights and international justice that have gained power by being naturalized in many areas of global relations and philosophy. The response to the ICC, therefore, also drew on influential discourses in order to destabilize the hegemony of the global discourse of international justice. In a continuation of arguments made in support of a peaceful solution through amnesty and peace talks, arguments against the ICC drew on discourses of cultural relativism, religious principles of mercy and political discourses on national reconciliation, for example, those provided by post-apartheid South Africa. A report published by Refugee Law Project, a Kampala-based organization seeking to understand the impact of the Amnesty Act, provides an example of how a relativist argument was used to explain the appropriateness of local solutions. It argues that amnesty is more in keeping with the cultural framework of the Acholi: 'Furthermore, numerous respondents emphasised the fact that it [Amnesty Law] resonates with specific cultural understandings of justice: amnesty is taking place within societies in which the possibility of legal and social pardon is seen to better address the requirements for long-term reconciliation than more tangible forms of punishment meted out within the legal structures' (Hovil and Lomo, 2004: 1).

Arguments against the ICC from a relativist perspective were also common in discussions held with individuals from the region. For example, a local NGO official explained that 'Western legal systems are not restorative. For the Acholi, murder and other crimes are not individual acts, they involve the whole clan. So, restoration must involve the whole clan'. He also said that 'people prefer peace over justice', and 'justice is a long process' (interview, September 2005). In Kampala, Zachary Lomo, the co-author of a number of reports on northern Uganda and then director of Refugee Law Project, described his experiences speaking with people in the Acholi region about justice. He explained that most people he spoke to longed for peace and were willing to forgo justice, at least in the short term, in order to attain peace and to return to their normal lives. He described an interaction with one woman in a camp for the displaced. She said to him, 'Let there be peace, let the Konys and the Ottis have amnesty'. He then asked, 'But what about all that they have done?'. She replied, 'Do you think I love evil? But I am here with my last child and no means of giving him a proper life. Let there be peace and then we will deal with those who have committed evil . . . in our own way' (interview, November 2005). The desire to deal with the conflict 'in our own way' then, was emphasized as a counter-argument to the powerful lobbies for criminal justice. Forgiveness, amnesty and reconciliation were key concepts that were all related back upon the cultural dynamics of the Acholi.

Although such arguments were deeply felt by many in northern Uganda, when interpreted through international media, the focus of the debate drifted away from important issues surrounding the Court and became increasingly focused on Acholi culture and practices. Religious foundations of forgiveness often rang hollow when juxtaposed with the list of atrocities committed by the rebels, while cultural relativist arguments tended to be reduced to romantic revisionism. In a discussion of the relations between 'culture' and 'rights', Cowan et al. (2001: 9) point out that '"culturalist claims" — claims which invoke notions of culture, tradition, language, religion, ethnicity, locality, tribe or race — have become a familiar rhetorical element in contemporary rights processes'. While the authors note that culturalist claims have political weight, they also note that they can be a double-edged sword. They go on to say that culturalist claims can 'represent what has been called "strategic-essentialism". Activists from, or working on behalf of, communities making claims are often well aware that they are essentializing something which is, in fact, much more fluid and contradictory, but they do so in order that their claims be heard' (ibid.:10). Nonetheless, the need to oversimplify and essentialize culture in relativist arguments can ultimately make those arguments vulnerable. This certainly appeared to be the case in northern Uganda, as it diverted attention away from crucial gaps in ICC policy and practice, and towards questions of cultural authenticity and the nature of Acholi society.

While some international organizations continued to show support for the views of the local leaders, the strength of discourses of cultural relativism and reconciliation tended to fall flat when they were translated through the international media. International news reports tended to present the case as a straightforward dichotomy between modernity and tradition. Even in articles intended to display the subtleties of the arguments on both sides, the position of the Acholi often came off as an incredibly archaic alternative to a well-established and respected legal system. For example, in the International section of the *New York Times,* a fairly detailed article attempting to clarify the logic behind the opposition to the ICC indictments of LRA/M members still managed to present the traditional systems in an overly simplified manner that ultimately ridiculed them. Generally due to a journalistic style intended to captivate rather than inform, the report lost the opportunity to more sensitively present its subject. The opening paragraph of the article sets the general tone: 'The International Criminal Court at The Hague represents one way of holding those who commit atrocities responsible for their crimes. The raw eggs, twigs and livestock that the Acholi people of northern Uganda use in their traditional reconciliation ceremonies represent another'

(Lacey, 2005). The reduction of traditional systems in northern Uganda to component parts serves to shock the audience and sensationalize the supposed gap between the Western and the African systems. The description is more of a caricature than an explanation that would open the minds of the readers. The article continues in this theme with a description of the LRA/M and the conflict:

> The fighting features rebels who call themselves the Lord's Resistance Army and who speak earnestly of the import of the Ten Commandments, but who routinely hack up civilians who get in their way. To add to their numbers, the rebels abduct children in the night, brainwash them in the bush, indoctrinate them by forcing them to kill, and then turn them — 20,000 over the last two decades — into the next wave of ferocious fighters seeking to topple the government. Girls as young as 12 are assigned as rebel commanders' wives. Anyone who does not toe the line is brutally killed. (ibid.)

Such a description, juxtaposed against a ritual involving raw eggs and twigs and relying heavily on the forgiveness of the community, could hardly be expected to stir the sympathies of most audiences in the West for whom the article is intended. Not surprisingly, therefore, most outside observers respond with absolute disbelief when they are told of the general resistance to the ICC in northern Uganda. More importantly, the idea of letting people like Joseph Kony 'off the hook' for the kind of atrocities he has committed is considered by many observers as utterly appalling and is presented as a clear example of Africans not able to know what is in their own best interest. Articles such as these raised considerable doubt about the Acholi's capacity for forgiveness and the possibility for traditional practices to bring reconciliation. In this way, attention was diverted from more significant questions about the relationship of peace and justice to questions of cultural incommensurability. In effect, Acholi culture, rather than the practices of the ICC, became the major points of dispute.

Discussions of the dilemma often hovered over questions of whether or not the Acholi were actually as forgiving as proclaimed by local leaders or whether rituals such as *mato oput* were really useful (Allen, 2006; Pham et al., 2005; Pham et al., 2007). These questions are important and worthy of investigation, but they are also evidence of the pitfalls of instrumentalizing culture in struggles of power. Once the leaders made claims that forgiveness and reconciliation are central to Acholi culture, and traditional mechanisms more aligned with the Acholi worldview, they opened themselves up to close scrutiny of these statements. The essentializing nature of culturalist claims forced representatives of this position to speak about Acholi culture as a fixed and closed system and not as a dynamic, interconnected and continually evolving set of practices and beliefs that encompass contradictory and paradoxical relations as much as consistent and harmonious ones. This situation produces false presentations of absolutes that are easy to challenge. In order to scrutinize whether Acholi are forgiving, one need only find some individuals who hold different views; one is not necessarily required to prove that all or even most Acholi are not willing to forgive.

Proving whether or not the Acholi are actually willing to forgive and whether forgiveness and reconciliation are fundamental aspects of Acholi culture is not the objective of this contribution. However, it is worth noting that my research suggests that while a number of people were uncertain whether they would be able to forgive or live alongside the rebel leaders, the vast majority expressed a willingness to put aside their anger and live with the rebels if this would bring them peace. This is not, however, to argue that the Acholi embrace a culture of forgiveness or that they are inherently more peaceful or categorically different from other populations. It is to argue that societies can draw on certain elements, flawed or otherwise, of their culture, history or beliefs, in order to strategize certain future outcomes or organizations of their society. All societies innovate, reinvent and transform. It is not because a direct and undisrupted historical trajectory cannot be drawn between current strategies and an ancient past that these strategies must be considered illegitimate.

Ultimately, a cultural relativist position tended to diminish rather than strengthen the position of the opponents of the ICC intervention. A relativist position also served to alienate some international actors who were otherwise supportive of resistance to the ICC intervention. As advocates of criminal trials engaged in the debate, 'justice' became ever more limited to the processes of prosecution and punishment. Over time, it became increasingly difficult for international actors to support traditional mechanisms as alternatives to justice, especially since the efficacy of traditional mechanisms had been called into doubt and the arguments for traditional justice as an alternative to criminal justice had been characterized as romanticized versions of an imaginary past.

CONCLUSION

As a site of negotiation between local and global priorities, the debate in northern Uganda has far-reaching consequences. Though the situation remains without a conclusion, important questions have been tabled regarding the relationship between peace and justice. These questions will have to be answered. For the moment, the ICC and the principles of international justice retain considerable support from the international community, particularly when the Court's attention is focused on corners of the world considered remote and volatile. In such cases, the unequal relations of power become especially evident.

The close examination of the Ugandan case demonstrates how the debate became more about controlling public opinion through lofty claims of ending impunity and resolving conflict, rather than examining the best way forward for Ugandans. Though not completely successful, the debate provided a platform for ICC supporters to construct particular representations of the Court that were critical to making the Court relevant in situations of ongoing conflict and reproducing the Court as a key component of transitional justice. Many of the claims made by Court officials, though not empirically substantiated, tended to correspond with preconceived notions about the role of justice, and what can be described as a generalized aspiration that problematic and violent regions of the world could be tamed by applying legal solutions. At the same time, culturalist arguments used by local leaders to oppose the ICC intervention often served only to bolster the case of ICC supporters. In the end, the agenda to support international justice and the newly established International Court overtook the agenda for peace in northern Uganda, all the while leaving unasked the question of whether justice can be achieved without peace.

REFERENCES

Agamben, G. (1998) *Homo Sacer: Sovereign Power and Bare Life*. D. Heller-Roazen, transl. Stanford, CA: Stanford University Press.

Allen, T. (2006) *Trial Justice: The International Criminal Court and the Lord's Resistance Army*. London: Zed Books in association with International African Institute.

Allen, T. (2010) 'Bitter Roots: The "Invention" of Acholi Traditional Justice', in T. Allen and K. Vlassenroot (eds) *The Lord's Resistance Army: Myth and Reality*, pp. 242–61. London: Zed Books.

Atkinson, R.R. (2010) 'The Realists in Juba? An Analysis of the Juba Peace Talks', in T. Allen and K. Vlassenroot (eds) *The Lord's Resistance Army: Myth and Reality*, pp. 205–22. London: Zed Books.

ARLPI (2001) 'Let My People Go: The Forgotten Plight of the People in Displaced Camps in Acholi'. Gulu: Acholi Religious Leaders Peace Initiative and the Justice and Peace Commission of Gulu Archdiocese.

Baines, E. (2005) 'Roco Wat I Acoli: Traditional Approaches to Reintegration and Justice'. Vancouver, BC: Liu Institute for Global Issues; Gulu: Gulu District NGO Forum.

BBC News (2004) 'Ugandans Seek "Massacre Revenge"', BBC World News 25 February. http://news.bbc.co.uk/2/hi/africa/3485092.stm

Bosire, B. (2007) 'ICC Rules Out Lifting Ugandan Rebels' Arrest Warrants. Agence France-Presse (AFP) 22 November. http://www.reliefweb.int/rw/RWB.NSF/db900SID/SODA-7979QY?OpenDocument

Branch, A. (2004) 'International Justice, Local Injustice: The International Criminal Court in Northern Uganda', *Dissent Magazine* 51(3): 22–26.

Clarke, K.M. (2007) 'Global Justice, Local Controversies: The International Criminal Court', in M.-B. Dembour and T. Kelly (eds) *Paths to International Justice: Social and Legal Perspectives*, pp. 134–60. Cambridge: Cambridge University Press.

Cowan, J.K., M.-B. Dembour and R.A. Wilson (2001) 'Introduction', in J.K. Cowan, M.-B. Dembour and R.A. Wilson (eds) *Culture and Rights: Anthropological Perspectives*, pp. 1–26. Cambridge: Cambridge University Press.

CSOPNU (2004) 'Letter to the Prosecutor of the International Criminal Court Regarding Investigations in Northern Uganda', 1 April. Kampala: Civil Society Organisations for Peace in Northern Uganda.

Dembour, M.-B. and T. Kelly (2007) 'Introduction: The Social Lives of International Justice', in M.-B. Dembour and T. Kelly (eds) *Paths to International Justice: Social and Legal Perspectives*, pp. 1–25. Cambridge: Cambridge University Press.

Derrida, J. (2003) 'Autoimmunity: Real and Symbolic Suicides. A Dialogue with Jacques Derrida', in G. Borradori (ed.) *Philosophy in a Time of Terror: Dialogues with Jurgen Habermas and Jacques Derrida*, pp. 85–136. Chicago, IL: University of Chicago Press.

Finnström, S. (2008) *Living with Bad Surroundings: War, History, and Everyday Moments in Northern Uganda*. Durham, NC: Duke University Press.

Fletcher, L.E., H.M. Weinstein and J. Rowen (2009) 'Context, Timing and the Dynamics of Transitional Justice: A Historical Perspective', *Human Rights Quarterly* 31(1):163–220.

Haslam, E. (2007) 'Law, Civil Society and Contested Justice at the International Criminal Tribunal for Rwanda', in M.-B. Dembour and T. Kelly (eds) *Paths to International Justice: Social and Legal Perspectives*, pp. 57–82. Cambridge: Cambridge University Press.

Hovil, L. and Z. Lomo (2004) 'Whose Justice? Perceptions of Uganda's Amnesty Act 2000: The Potential for Conflict Resolution and Long-term Reconciliation'. Working Paper No. 15. Kampala: Refugee Law Project.

Hovil, L. and J.R. Quinn (2005) 'Peace First, Justice Later: Traditional Justice in Northern Uganda'. Working Paper No. 17. Kampala: Refugee Law Project.

Human Rights Watch (2004) 'ICC: Investigate All Sides in Uganda'. News Release 4 February. http://www.hrw.org/en/news/2004/02/04/icc-investigate-all-sides-uganda

International Center for Transitional Justice (2007) 'Pursuing Justice in Ongoing Conflict: A Discussion of Current Practice'. Paper presented at Building a Future on Peace and Justice Conference, Nuremburg (24–25 June). http://www.peace-justice-conference. info/download/WS%202-pursuing_Justice_in_Ongoing_Conflict_ICTJ_FINAL.pdf

IRIN News (2004) 'Uganda: Peace Groups and Government Officials Worried about ICC Probe into LRA', 30 January. www.irinnews.org/report.asp?ReportID=39225

Keppler, E. and R. Dicker (2007) 'Trading Justice for Peace in Uganda Won't Work. Human Rights Watch, 5 February. http://hrw.org/english/docs/2007/05/02/uganda15832.htm

Lacey, M. (2005) 'Atrocity Victims in Uganda Choose to Forgive', *New York Times* 18 April. http://www.nytimes.com/2005/04/18/international/africa/18uganda.html

Moreno-Ocampo, L. (2007) 'Address by Luis Moreno-Ocampo, Prosecutor of the International Criminal Court'. Speech delivered at Building a Future on Peace and Justice Conference, Nuremburg (24–25 June). http://www.peace-justice-conference.info/download/ speech%20moreno.pdf

Muyanja, R. (2008) 'Uganda: Interview with ICC Registrar, Silvana Arbia', *Bukedde* 6 June.

Obita, J.A. (2002) 'First International Peace Efforts 1996–1998. Protracted Conflict, Elusive Peace: Initiatives to End the Violence in Northern Uganda'. http://www.c-r.org/our-work/accord/northern-uganda/contents.php

Ottawa Citizen (2008) 'War-Crimes Court Won't Bend to Political Pressure: Canadian Head', 11 August. http://www.canada.com/topics/news/world/story.html?id=fcc9a95a-5acf-43e6-a58b-950f3c79a3aa

Perkins, A. (2008) 'Justice for War Criminals — or Peace for Northern Uganda?', *The Guardian* 20 March. http://www.guardian.co.uk/society/katineblog/2008/mar/20/justicefor warcriminalsorp

Pham, P., P. Vinck, E. Stover, A. Moss, M. Wierda and R. Bailey (2007) 'When the War Ends: A Population-Based Survey on Attitudes about Peace, Justice and Social Reconstruction in Northern Uganda'. Berkeley, CA: Human Rights Center; New Orleans, LA: Payson Center for International Development; New York: ICTJ.

Pham, P., P. Vinck, M. Wierda, E. Stover and A.D. Giovanni (2005) 'Forgotten Voices: A Population-Based Survey of Attitudes about Peace and Justice in Northern Uganda'. Berkeley, CA: International Center for Transitional Justice and Human Rights Center at the University of California, Berkeley.

Schomerus, M. and B.A. Ogwaro (2010) 'Searching for Solutions in Juba: An Overview'. http://www.c-r.org/our-work/accord/northern-uganda-update/solutions_in_juba.php

Simonse, S. (1998) 'Steps Towards Peace and Reconcilation in Northern Uganda: An Analysis of Initiatives to End the Armed Conflict between the Government of Uganda and the Lord's Resistance Army 1987–1998'. Utrecht: Pax Christi Netherlands.

Teitel, R.G. (2003) 'Transitional Justice Genealogy', *Harvard Human Rights Journal* 16: 69–94.
Thomasson, E. (2008) 'Analysis — Uganda Highlights Tension between Peace, Justice. Reliefweb, 4 March. http://www.reliefweb.int/rw/RWB.NSF/db900SID/EVOD-7CEJQ3? OpenDocument&Click=
United Nations (1998) 'Secretary General Says Establishment of International Criminal Court is Major Step in March Towards Universal Human Rights, Rule of Law'. Press Release L/ROM/23, 18 July. http://www.un.org/icc/pressrel/lrom23.htm
Volqvartz, J. (2005) 'ICC Under Fire Over Uganda Probe', CNN 23 February. http:// www.cnn.com/2005/WORLD/africa/02/23/uganda.volqvartz/index.html?iref=allsearch

11

The Violence of Peace: Ethnojustice in Northern Uganda

Adam Branch

INTRODUCTION

The guns have fallen silent, and peace has returned to northern Uganda after two decades of vicious war between the Ugandan government and the Lord's Resistance Army (LRA). With the rebels' reign of brutality a thing of the past, the Acholi have left the squalid camps where they lived for years and returned to their land, and the long process of reconstruction and reconciliation has begun. Instead of war and humanitarianism, peace and justice — often combined within 'transitional justice' — are the signs under which interventions can now occur. Or so the official narrative proclaims — just as it had proclaimed the war to be a black-and-white struggle in which the Ugandan government, together with their Western partners, sought to rescue the civilian population from the terrorist Lord's Resistance Army.

However, given the gulf between the official narrative about the war and the actual course of the war, it may not be surprising that today's declared peace is rife with violence. Fighter jets roar overhead almost every day. The political protests in the wake of the 2011 presidential elections — for which the military had deployed extensively — were met with extreme force, as they were in other areas of Uganda. Strange diseases erupt among the rural population, for whom the state has disavowed almost all responsibility, as it did during the war. Land, the only thing left to most people, is being lost through often violent dispossession. Paramilitaries occupy rural schools, game wardens have killed farmers, and the military is staking out land for its own use. The main town in the region, Gulu, is seeing rapid urbanization into slums, increasing poverty, inequality and crime. The Uganda People's Defence Force (UPDF) is spread throughout the region in the name of hunting the remnants of the LRA as American military contractors fly reconnaissance missions overhead and US Special Forces carry out operations on the ground. Rumours circulate of new rebel groups and there is widespread talk of another war.

How do we make sense of the fact that today's peace is shot through with violence and that a regime of transitional justice is accompanied by the emergence of new — and not so new — forms of injustice? I argue that

The author would like to thank the faculty and students at MISR and SDSU where previous versions of this paper have been discussed, as well as the editors of this volume for their encouragement and the anonymous referees for their suggestions.

Transition and Justice: Negotiating the Terms of New Beginnings in Africa, First Edition.
Edited by Gerhard Anders and Olaf Zenker.

this peace-time violence should not be seen as a vestige of the war or as a product of social breakdown caused by the war, which could be solved through the consolidation of peace and more extensive transitional justice and reconstruction. Instead, I argue that violence is a central element in the re-constitution of structures of power and inequality in post-war northern Uganda. Violence and peace are not antithetical: the violence of peace is not residual, destructive and non-political, but rather is productive political violence, pushing towards specific possible futures, while cutting off others.

The irony is that some forms of today's political violence and the injustices they support are legitimated and put into practice through transitional justice itself. This is the central paradox explored by this chapter: how practices of justice that claim to enable the transition from war to peace can instead violently entrench the very forms of domination and inequality that gave rise to war in the first place. The chapter focuses on one particular modality of transitional justice that has risen to prominence in northern Uganda: traditional justice promotion or what I call, drawing on Paulin Hountondji's critique of ethnophilosophy, 'ethnojustice' (Hountondji, 1996). Today, numerous state- and donor-driven ethnojustice projects can be found, ranging from discovering lost chiefs, to building a palace for the so-called Acholi paramount chief, providing development funds for redistribution by the Acholi council of chiefs, and providing money for reconciliation rituals. Before discussing ethnojustice itself, I will first critically examine the discourse of transitional justice more broadly in order to show how ethnojustice, although conceived of as a reaction against the limitations of orthodox liberal transitional justice, embodies the same political logic as the latter and can lead to similarly counterproductive results.

TRANSITIONAL JUSTICE IN QUESTION: VIOLENCE AND POLITICAL ORDER

Hannah Arendt provides a seminal account of the paradoxical relation between founding violence and political order, as the editors to this volume point out (Anders and Zenker, 2014). In her words, 'violence was the beginning and, by the same token, no beginning could be made without using violence, without violating' (Arendt, 1990: 20). Founding violence, of course, is a long-standing problematic in political theory, one reflected upon by thinkers ranging from Machiavelli to Walter Benjamin. A common point of entry is the dilemma posed by the fact that every normal political–legal order must rely on extra-legal, exceptional violence for its own foundation. Founding violence thus cannot be assimilated within the order that it, *de facto*, founds, because it is antithetical to the very norms and laws that, *de jure*, underpin that order. It is the violence of fratricide, parricide, extermination, primitive accumulation or mass expulsion. It can be revolutionary violence in which the forms of domination and inequality that upheld one order are destroyed and new forms of power and modes of distribution are established. The problem of founding violence can be dealt with by placing that violence in the unspeakable past; however, that past can always return to haunt the present and its pretension to non-coercive, ordinary legality.

Transitional justice denotes a different relationship between founding violence and post-violence political order.[1] Instead of founding violence being relegated to the unspeakable past, it is incessantly invoked in the present, whether for the purpose of redress or forgiveness. Instead of attempting to forget the past, it is used to provide the present order with legitimacy, derived from this order's claim to deal justly with the past through legal, political and social mechanisms. The ideals and norms informing transitional justice for past wrongs are thus advanced as the legitimate framework of today's political community. In short, today's political order establishes its legitimacy by claiming to justly assimilate the violence of the past to the present.

In its claim to remedy the injustice of the past through justice today, transitional justice has a certain resonance with notions of revolutionary justice. Revolutionary justice is given a classic formulation in Lenin's *State and Revolution*: subsequent to a violent revolution, the state, which was the '"special coercive force" for the suppression of the proletariat by the bourgeoisie, of millions of working people by handfuls of rich, must be replaced by a "special coercive force" for the suppression of the bourgeoisie by the proletariat (the dictatorship of the proletariat)' (Lenin, 1964: 397). The new order, brought to power through revolutionary violence, will continue to carry that revolution to completion using the coercive instruments of the state in the name of revolutionary justice. In the legal terrain, this can be seen as 'victor's justice' without the bad conscience that often afflicts liberal legalists when faced with post-transition trials.[2]

Similar to revolutionary justice, transitional justice claims to rectify past injustices through political institutions today. It, too, may use coercion to effect this justice, whether by preventing attempts at extra-legal remedy or by punishing those who cannot be forgiven. The difference is the commitment of orthodox transitional justice to a specific normative order: a liberal-legalist, human rights-based order to be founded in a 'responsible' sovereign

---

1. My use of the phrase 'transitional justice' refers to a specific discourse, set of practices and institutions that have emerged as a coherent framework in the last twenty years. Even if there are practices that today's scholars of transitional justice might place under that rubric (Teitel, 2003), I am interested in those practices and institutions that understand themselves specifically as 'transitional justice'. As I argue, these have a specific normative underpinning, with specific political consequences. See Huyse (1995) for a reminder of how recent the phrase 'transitional justice' is.

2. For an illumination of this bad conscience, it is useful to compare, for example, Merleau-Ponty's (1980) description of the show trials in *Humanism and Terror*, or the Soviet jurists' position at Nuremberg, with the discomfort that trials from Nuremberg to Tadic have created in liberal jurists. For seminal, critical contributions to the debate, see Kirchheimer (1961), Koskenniemi (2002), Shklar (1964) and Simpson (2007).

state — what some have termed the model of 'liberal peace' (Chandler, 2006; Duffield, 2001; Paris, 2004). This order's supposed universal validity means that transitional justice will represent itself not as a radical transformation, but as establishing or re-establishing a proper, legitimate, liberal order which is presumed to enjoy consent from all proper, modern, liberal subjects. Thus, while transitional justice can proceed from many starting points — 'rogue states', 'failed states', crimes against humanity, civil wars, insurgencies, or other situations that are presented as violating liberal norms — it all leads to the same end point, that of liberal peace.

The consequence is that the necessary link between transitional justice and actual political transition is severed. Transitional justice can be called upon to rectify any declared threat to liberal norms, past or present, as its instruments are even used to actively *promote* the transition to a liberal order (Teitel, 2003), for example, when the International Criminal Court (ICC) is deployed as a complement to Western military intervention. Transitional justice becomes a set of technical instruments that can be employed by states, donors or international organizations in the name of ending or rectifying declared transgressions of liberal norms. There is no requirement that transitional justice grows from or responds to a social demand in order to be valid, as transitional justice is divorced from any necessary connection to social or democratic forces. Thus, when transitional justice invokes forgiveness in the name of reconciliation and peace, it is forgiveness for those who are deemed to be aligned with the liberal framework or redeemable within it. When it invokes punishment in the name of accountability, ending impunity, and peace, that is for those who are accused of having irredeemably violated the liberal order.

The politics of transitional justice are thus determined from two directions. First, the range of harms from the past that can be designated as injustices, and thus deserving of rectification, is limited by the liberal transitional justice framework. Certain forms of power or inequality that are deemed unjust, even by the majority, may be placed off-limits from remedy or transformation by those states, donors or experts who claim to put transitional justice into practice. Robert Meister argues that the South African Truth and Reconciliation Commission (TRC) did precisely this by providing a guarantee for whites to retain the economic benefits they gained under apartheid (Meister, 2011). The tools or modes of action that can be used legitimately to realize justice are also limited by the transitional justice framework. Long, expensive and risky court proceedings displace more immediate and clear forms of retribution; or a revolutionary upsurge that drove the political transition is demobilized and forced to abandon its more radical demands in the name of a just, inclusive political order. Additionally, the statist orientation of transitional justice, in which the end goal is to build 'responsible' states, can give it an anti-popular dimension. In short, the internal logic of transitional justice can define and restrict what can be done in the name of justice and how it can be done, rendering it a disciplining process.

A second set of political effects stem not from the disciplinary internal logic of transitional justice, but from its potential for instrumentalization. Given the inherent ambiguity of the liberal human rights framework and its capacity for polyvalent invocation and strategic manipulation, decisions about who is aligned with liberal order and who is a threat to it will be politically determined (Douzinas, 2007). Similarly, decisions determining which parties to forgive and which to punish can easily be steered by the interests of the politically powerful, nationally or internationally. Thus, for example, the ICC decides to prosecute the LRA, aligned with Khartoum, but to grant effective immunity to the Ugandan government, aligned with the US and Western donors. Or, the siege on Benghazi is responded to through an R2P military intervention and criminal prosecution, while the siege on Sirte is ignored (Grovogui, 2011).

Through these two routes — discipline and instrumentalization — transitional justice can end up reinforcing the injustices of the past instead of remedying them. Moreover, this reinforcement may itself be violent when it needs to overcome resistance by those whose demands for justice are silenced or not met. Forgiveness can mean protecting certain privileged groups or individuals from demands for substantive justice and may also be effected through coercion. Punishment can mean using violence to enforce sanctions against those deemed irredeemably criminal — usually the losers of the conflict, which may further perpetuate grievances. Transitional justice can be counter-revolutionary when it silences demands for justice that transgress the liberal framework (Meister, 2011). It can be conservative when it re-enforces structures of domination and inequality in the name of reconciliation and forgiveness. It can also be vengeful when it is the victors continuing war by legal means in the name of ending impunity and ensuring accountability — the accusation levelled by liberal legalist Hans Kelsen at the Nuremberg trials (Zolo, 2009).

Thus, transitional justice can end up reinforcing the very injustices and modes of domination and inequality that gave rise to episodes of violence in the first place. This tendency goes beyond what the editors of this volume refer to as 'tensions and contradictions between the often lofty and abstract ideals of (transitional) justice and their actual enactments and realizations in practice' (Anders and Zenker, 2014). The problem faced by transitional justice is more fundamental than a disjuncture between rhetoric and reality. The tendency of transitional justice to employ violence to help establish unjust political order is not due to the messiness of reality — it is inherent to transitional justice and has a specific political valence.

While the orthodox liberal transitional justice discourse and practice has occupied a significant place in Uganda, perhaps the most prominent demand within the scope of transitional justice has been for a different, non-liberal form of justice — so-called traditional justice, what I refer to as ethnojustice. However, as I explain, the same political tendencies that are found in liberal transitional justice — the way in which its disciplinary internal logic and its instrumentalization create the possibility to violently reinforce the very forms of domination and inequality that gave rise to upheaval in the first place — are also found in ethnojustice.

THE TURN TO TRADITION

Interventions claiming to promote traditional reconciliation and justice are found throughout Africa, and the increasing interest in African tradition as part of the transitional justice agenda can be seen as part of a broader cultural turn in development, justice, state building and counterinsurgency (Gregory, 2008). In the words of one proponent of this new embrace of tradition, there has been a beneficial 'renaissance in the concept of "the indigenous" and the concepts of "traditional" and "indigenous" . . . offer possible advantages of sustainability and participation, the "elixir" that orthodox approaches to peace-making seek to attain' (MacGinty, 2008: 140).

The logic informing traditional reconciliation and justice interventions is a familiar one that derives from the broader field of peace building. Violence is seen as emerging from the breakdown of war-affected societies, the etiology of which is located in the collapse of traditional values and social harmony, the disappearance of ritual practices that ensured such harmony, and the loss of authority among elders and other traditional leaders. Thus, the breakdown of war-affected society, where that society is defined as traditional, is cause and consequence of violence. Traditional reconciliation and justice interventions are to help rebuild this lost authority structure so that it can preside over reconstructed traditional societies, as Africans are to be 'empowered' as tribes, under customary chiefs. This is the ethnojustice agenda, in which the fulfilment of justice is equated with the establishment of what is considered a traditional social order.

This turn to traditional culture represents a radicalized attempt to institute more genuine 'participation' in peace building with a view to improving the legitimacy and efficacy of Western intervention. It follows the logic of the liberal understanding of transitional justice, namely that there is an absolute and legitimate social-political order that needs to be re-established in the wake of violence. However, this absolute order that is to be re-established, instead of being based in a universal human rights framework, is based in a particular cultural framework. This switch is grounded in the idea that in certain parts of the world, the most important, authentic identities are cultural identities, particularly traditional, customary or tribal identities. Participation should thus take place within this cultural framework or risk being rejected as an alien imposition (Chopra and Hohe, 2004; Richmond, 2008; Zartman, 2000). The West has long conceived of Africa in tribal terms, thus it comes as small surprise that Africa finds itself at the cutting edge of this multifaceted turn toward cultural intervention.

The invocation of culture and tradition in the service of peace and justice also reflects a deeper mistrust among interveners regarding the extent to which Africans are prepared for modernity. It represents an effort to transcend the problems they see as arising from the attempt to impose liberal Western models on supposedly 'illiberal' places like Africa. From this perspective, violence in Africa is most fundamentally derived from the disruption caused by the clash between a timeless, still-present and ineradicable African tradition and an imposed Western modernity. It follows that the promotion of liberal peace would exacerbate the underlying causes of conflict by intensifying modernity's disruptive force and by marginalizing those whose participation is needed to successfully promote peace and justice. Ethnojustice thus appeals to Western audiences by basing its legitimacy on claims to represent and work with authentic African identity and difference, treat Africans with dignity as Africans and avoid imposing Western ideas and models.

However, because ethnojustice conceives of Africans as possessing an unspoken unanimous worldview, it cannot but impose a Western imagination of African institutions. During the colonial period the instrumental identification and use of African tradition was based upon the notion that a too-fast transition to modernity would introduce destructive upheaval into African cultures. Today, the idea of an eternal African tradition is again imagined and deployed instrumentally. The history of Western instrumentalization of imagined notions of African tradition as the basis of indirect-rule colonialism should itself give pause to those promoting this new phase of transitional justice intervention. In this sense, ethnojustice represents the revival, not of African tradition, but of the British tradition of indirect rule in Africa under which African tribes were to be civilized. As Tim Allen puts it, 'efforts were made to do the same thing rather more systematically in the past, when "tribal" customs were incorporated into the indirect administration of the British protectorate through government-appointed chiefs and other local agents' (Allen, 2010: 253).

Not all calls for traditional justice come from Westerners seeking better purchase for intervention in Africa, however. African critics of Western involvement in Africa have also made clear the need to go beyond orthodox transitional justice in seeking futures of peace, development and justice (Lekha Sriram and Pillay, 2009). As the Zimbabwean human rights activist Brian Kagoro argues, transitional justice needs to be divorced 'from its neo-liberal and neo-imperial hue to guarantee its success in Africa' (Kagoro, 2012: 15). In its place, he continues, African activists should advance 'a self-sustaining Afro-centric transitional justice that takes on board the historiography of African conflicts as well as the broader geo-political and geo-economic contexts of such conflicts' (ibid.: 9). Despite the often wide-ranging and radical statements calling for an African transitional justice that recognizes the continent's particular historical experience, this literature tends to reduce what is specifically 'African' to the cultural. It fails to problematize the tradition–modernity dichotomy that underlies both ortho-dox transitional justice (which values the modern) and ethnojustice (which values the traditional). The literature tends to assume that a particularly 'African' transitional justice would lead to 'a healthy balance between tradition and modernity when it comes to the strategies deployed to promote justice and reconciliation' (Murithi, 2012: 214). Creating such a balance would require a complementary merger of formal legal mechanisms and traditional mechanisms, whereby each corrects the shortcomings of the other. This approach begs the question of why the concept of 'transitional justice' should be retained at all, and why other, less ideologically burdened political concepts aren't employed instead.

My argument will be that, despite its self-proclaimed distance from the liberal peace model, the political consequences of so-called Africanized interventions can end up hewing closely to the outcomes of so-called liberal transitional justice interventions. First, both forms can be effectively instrumentalized by states. The instrumentalization of liberal transitional justice enables states to deploy violence in the name of human rights at the national and international level. Likewise, the instrumentalization of ethnojustice enables states to insulate themselves from demands for accountability or justice after periods of conflict. Second, the internal logic of both can lead to reinforcing forms of inequality or domination through discipline. Liberal transitional justice puts private property and the capitalist market economy off-limits and consolidates a liberal political and economic order. Similarly, the internal logic of ethnojustice insulates gender and age-based structures of domination from challenge and can thus consolidate a patriarchal, geron-tocratic social order. The remainder of this chapter provides a critique of the theory and practice of ethnojustice as it has been instantiated in the response to the war in northern Uganda.

TRANSITIONAL JUSTICE IN UGANDA

Civil war began in the Acholi region of northern Uganda soon after Yoweri Museveni, the commander of the southern-based National Resistance Army (NRA), seized power from a principally northern government in 1986. Museveni's NRA proceeded to occupy the Acholi region of northern Uganda and launched a violent campaign there against the civilian population, partly in a misguided attempt to prevent the eruption of insurgency, partly in revenge for the atrocities for which the south held northerners responsible during the civil war of 1981–86. Instead of preventing a rebellion, this state violence provoked that very rebellion, as a series of primarily Acholi rebel movements emerged in 1986–88, including the Uganda People's Democratic Army and the Holy Spirit Movement (HSM), which led to a further escalation of government violence against Acholi civilians. After the failure of those early movements, by the end of the decade a new rebel group, which combined orthodox guerrilla tactics with a blend of political and spiritual orientations, the LRA, had arisen as the most potent rebel force.

By that time, the support that previous rebel groups had enjoyed among the Acholi peasantry had diminished due to the rebels' military failures and the government's brutal counterinsurgency. In that atmosphere, the LRA interpreted reduced popular support as Acholi civilian support for the government and directed their violence at suspected government collaborators. The LRA soon became infamous for its massacres, maiming, and the forced recruitment of tens of thousands of Acholi, many of them children. The Ugandan government's counterinsurgency was also brutal, focused on destroying suspected popular rebel support. Hundreds, if not thousands, of Acholi were killed by direct state violence. The most devastating aspect of the government's counterinsurgency was its policy of mass forced displacement and internment. Starting in 1996, the government forcibly displaced the entire rural Acholi population, over a million people, driving them out of their homes and into internment camps through a campaign of threats, murder and bombing and burning down entire villages. Once in the camps, the government failed to provide adequate relief aid or protection, which led to a massive humanitarian crisis with excess mortality levels reaching approximately 1,000 people per week. The violence did not end until 2006, when the LRA departed from Uganda, apparently for good, and the dominant discourse concerning the north shifted to one of reconstruction and justice.

The broader structural conditions that gave rise to and prolonged the war were twofold. First and foremost were national political issues which centred around grievances the Acholi community held against the post-1986 Museveni-led government. The Acholi were largely excluded from the new government, and their political leaders were subject to state violence and repression. Economically, the Acholi demanded compensation for the massive looting of cattle, one of their main sources of livelihood, which was carried out by the NRA troops soon after their arrival in the north. And then there was the massive violence of the counterinsurgency itself, especially forced displacement, which the Acholi demanded be brought to an end and for which they demanded compensation.

Second were social upheavals within the Acholi community. These comprised everyday, and not-so-everyday, forms of resistance, primarily by women and youth, against the assertion of patriarchal, gerontocratic power within clan and household structures. Resistance to the power of older men helped to give rise to phenomena such as spirit possession, manifesting largely among young women, which provided a space of authority beyond the control of older men. This resistance can also be seen in the social composition of the rebel groups, especially the HSM and LRA. The former was led by a young woman spirit medium and the latter by a young male spirit medium, both drawing their support largely from young men and women. The war was the result of a confluence of national and internal political crises which were further exacerbated during the course of the war (Branch,

2011). Thus, any form of justice in the post-war period would have to address both the domination and inequality imposed by the state against the Acholi as a community, and the domination and inequality imposed by older men against youth and women within the Acholi community. I will argue that ethnojustice tends to worsen these two forms of injustice instead of remedying them.

Debates over justice were triggered by the intervention of the ICC, which commenced its investigation in July 2004 in response to a referral from the Ugandan government in late 2003. With the ICC's intervention, the international transitional justice industry quickly got involved as well. In the debate that followed, a number of divergent demands were heard: that the ICC prosecute all parties involved, that the ICC leave Uganda, that a blanket amnesty be guaranteed, that a combination of national and international trials be used, or that a truth commission be established. But the position that received the most attention was voiced by Acholi activists and political leaders who, with increasing support from international donors, demanded that legal procedures be replaced by Acholi traditional justice. Controversy has raged since then, with supporters of the ICC accusing proponents of traditional justice of condoning impunity, and supporters of traditional justice accusing the ICC of prolonging the war and destructively imposing Western ideas of justice upon the Acholi. Both sides comprise alliances between local, national and international political actors; both can locate consent within Acholiland; and each accuses the other of being promoted by foreign donors (Allen, 2006; Branch, 2007). Since the end of the war in 2006, traditional justice has received further institutional support at the Juba Peace Talks, in particular in Agenda Item 3, and in the Peace, Recovery and Development Plan (Komakech, 2012: 67). It is to the early articulations of traditional justice that I turn next.

ETHNOJUSTICE IN THEORY[3]

Ethnojustice is a discourse that combines elements from ethnography and from the study of law and ethics to describe what it claims are traditional systems of justice of non-Western cultures. In describing a traditional system of justice, ethnojustice purports to present a single, coherent, positive system that is consensually and spontaneously adhered to by all members of that culture in what Hountondji calls the myth of unanimism (Hountondji, 1996: xviii). Moreover, from an ethnojustice perspective such a culture, even if in abeyance today, remains valid and should be revived. Against this ethnojustice discourse, I will try to meet Hountondji's demand that, instead of 'African traditional thought', we consider 'African *traditions* of thought' —

3. The following sections draw on Branch (2011).

or, in this case, traditions of justice — where those traditions are themselves plural, contrasting and contested (ibid.: xxiv, emphasis added). In so doing, I argue that peace and justice will not be found through the imposition of an inert, authoritarian order upon societies. It will emerge through the ongoing and contentious process of including more groups, interests and voices in the deliberations over the shape of those societies.

The outline of the ethnojustice approach can be found in the first major ethnojustice text on northern Uganda, Dennis Pain's *The Bending of the Spears* (1997), which purports to give an account of the 'traditional authority structure' of the Acholi. At the heart of Pain's account is his assertion that, among the Acholi, conflicts were traditionally regulated and resolved by the *rwodi-moo*, or traditional elders. He writes, 'The principle of conflict resolution in Acholi is to create reconciliation which brings the two sides together' and involves both paying compensation for harm done and ritually drinking a 'bitter root extract drink', known as *mato oput* (Pain, 1997: 56). In the current conflict, as in any conflict among the Acholi, according to Pain, the *rwodi-moo* should meet and decide on a route for its resolution. He then confidently proclaims, 'as with any idea in Acholi, if the proposal is good, all will accept and Acholi can then speak with one voice' (ibid.: 54). Reconciliation can proceed through the 'traditional approach to "cooling" the situation and healing the land and restoring relationships, far beyond the limited approaches of conservative western legal systems' (ibid.).

Today's crisis, according to Pain, is the result of 'social break-down', in particular a 'collapse of traditional networking and values' in which 'the elders have failed to take on the responsibility which they should have taken' (ibid.). The war is thus represented as an intra-Acholi conflict that has escaped the limits traditionally imposed by elders. Even though 'all clans (and subclans) are both victims and perpetrators' (ibid.: 51), the most important task is the reconciliation of LRA fighters: 'although the rebels are seen to have rejected society, if society now establishes the means of reconciliation, the rebels will accept that authority' (ibid.).

Pain thus internalizes the war as an intra-Acholi problem, while also counterproductively misrepresenting the politics of the internal crisis. He reduces the national politics of the war to a social crisis brought about by the breakdown of traditional authority, embodied in a patriarchal regime of elders and chiefs, and reduces the resolution of the war to the re-incorporation of the young, alienated LRA into that unreformed regime. Although it is true that there has been a significant loss of authority by male elders as a result of the war and displacement, to reduce the local and national political crises faced by the Acholi to that loss of authority is unwarranted. When a misconception like this informs transitional justice interventions, it can have counterproductive political consequences, entrenching the very forms of domination and inequality that gave rise to the crises. First, ethnojustice can be counterproductive as a result of its own internal logic, which empowers older men at the expense of youth and women. Second, ethnojustice is counterproductive as a result of its instrumentalization by the state, which uses ethnojustice to evade accountability for violence or repression and to entrench its power within Acholi society by manipulating a regime of unaccountable 'chiefs'. Ethnojustice also prevents the international dimensions of war from being rectified or even comprehended.

ACHOLI ETHNOJUSTICE

The ICC intervention sparked a flurry of research within the ethnojustice paradigm. One of the earliest and most important studies is *Roco Wat i Acholi: Restoring Relationships in Acholi-land: Traditional Approaches to Justice and Reconciliation* (Liu Institute for Global Issues and Gulu District NGO Forum, 2005), funded by the John D. and Catherine T. Macarthur Foundation and by the Royal Embassy of the Netherlands.[4] The purpose of *Roco Wat* was 'to provide an initial assessment of how traditional rituals and ceremonies could be further adapted to address the crimes committed during the 19-year old conflict in Uganda' (ibid.: 1). To this end, it seeks principally to 'identify and describe: a) Justice from the perspective of Acholi traditional culture; [and] b) the processes and mechanisms of traditional justice' (ibid.: 7). *Roco Wat* attributes the importance of ethnojustice to the fact that: 'After nearly two decades of conflict, social relationships and trust within a traditionally communal culture have been severely degraded. Consequently, so has Acholi culture, and the prominent role cultural leaders (Chiefs, Elders and Mego) once held in society. Due to mass displacement, youth have little opportunity to learn about their history or culture' (ibid.: 2).

The report presents the recently created body of Acholi chiefs and elders, Ker Kwaro Acholi (KKA), as key to this process of reviving traditional justice mechanisms in order to help restore relationships in Acholiland. *Roco Wat* intended to begin the project of the positivization and formalization of so-called Acholi traditional justice by collecting and writing down practices, rituals and ceremonies, which was to proceed in tandem with the empowerment of KKA as the privileged body that was to apply this formalized traditional justice system.

The ethnojustice of *Roco Wat* does not allow Acholi themselves to fully articulate their own traditional justice system. Instead, it is up to experts and outsiders, with the assistance of Acholi academics and elders, to compile and formalize the traditional justice system as a coherent whole, subsequent to which it will be up to outsiders to help revive those traditions among the Acholi. Although *Roco Wat* recognizes that some elders have considerable knowledge of the traditional justice system, it also implies that they still

---

4. Other, more nuanced accounts have been produced since this initial period; for example, see Komakech (2012) and Oola (2012).

need additional instruction, and it notes that outside organizations, funded by foreign donors, are conducting 'leadership training on traditional practices' (ibid.: 31). The situation of the youth is even more deplorable from the ethnojustice perspective; indeed, 'one Elder remarked that the younger generations do not know how to be Acholi' (ibid.: 22). The strangeness of foreign organizations teaching old men how to be proper elders is compounded by the fact that elders are then expected to teach recalcitrant youth and women how to be proper Acholi. This, as we will see, is a recipe for a potential disciplinary project, one based on the silence of actually existing Acholi people in favour of the 'true' traditional Acholi identity articulated and promoted by foreign actors with local partners.

The Unanimism of Acholi Tradition

So what are the characteristics of this Acholi traditional justice system, from an ethnojustice perspective? First, ethnojustice relies on the idea of a radical break with traditional culture as a result of British colonialism. Moreover, it assumes that before colonialism, a timeless, unchanging and clearly defined Acholi identity and set of cultural practices existed. In this spirit, *Roco Wat* repeatedly refers to 'how traditional justice was once practiced in Acholi prior to colonialism' (ibid.: 9). It thus displays the ethnojustice tendency to equate a pure, essential cultural identity and set of practices with the pre-colonial, and to contrast it with an impure colonial and post-colonial society that has been contaminated by Western ideas and practices. On the one side is the traditional, pre-colonial, non-state, communal, consensual and restorative. On the other is the Western, colonial/post-colonial, individualist and punitive which supposedly disrupted this earlier harmonious traditional justice system (ibid.: 16). However, the idea that a self-regulating, harmonious Acholi culture existed throughout the pre-colonial period in which a traditional Acholi justice system held sway, fails to take into account what many have described as the British invention of the Acholi as tribe. Furthermore, even if a pre-colonial Acholi identity did exist, it also fails to acknowledge the century of extensive violent conflict and upheaval that preceded the advent of British colonialism. This was a period not of primitive harmony and cultural purity, but of destructive foreign incursion, slave raiding and internecine warfare.

The report goes on to describe Acholi traditional justice as being rooted in the spiritual (ibid.: 3), whilst simultaneously being socially functional: 'in traditional Acholi culture, justice is done for *ber bedo*, to restore harmonious life' (ibid.: 14). In traditional Acholi culture, according to *Roco Wat*, belief in and consent to this justice system and the social order it supports is unanimous. All Acholi value the unity of the Acholi, or the clan, before they value themselves as individuals. The typical Acholi, then, believes absolutely in the spiritual world and in the punishment that the spiritual world sends down when rules are violated. Ethnojustice relegates the spiritual to the functional, in the service of reproducing a static social order. This is achieved by rendering the spiritual domain positive, that is, capable of being formalized in writing and codified in a series of specific normative rules and prescriptions.

Such positivization, however, is contrary to the very nature of the spiritual. As Allen (2010: 253) explains, through this process, rituals 'will lose their flexibility, and will no longer have all the many resonances and associations of lived ritual actions. They will have status that is at least partly based on their externally supported authority. They will become privileged rites and, most likely, the preserve of certain figures of male authority recognized by the government'. The spiritual is inherently a realm of surplus, a domain from which the potential for social or political rupture can always emerge. The idea that it can be contained in positive form without remainder, making it perfectly functional to an existing social order, is a fiction that those in power often want to maintain. Numerous examples can be found within Acholi society of the disruptive potential of the spiritual, a potential that ethnojustice denies.

Ethnojustice and Power

As Allen suggests, the ethnojustice discourse and its reification of the spiritual serve to legitimate the power of a specific social group: male elders, who are presented as the privileged repositories and guardians of tradition and the exclusive mediators with the spiritual world. They are in charge of 'a series of rituals within village settings and household compounds in order to appease the ancestors and ensure the moral order was upheld' (Liu Institute, 2005: 11). Thus, elders and *rwodi* are assigned the exclusive role of regulating Acholi society through their access to the spiritual domain.

Just as in the Pain report, ethnojustice here conceives of the empowerment of male elders as a project of reconstruction or rebuilding an authentic order that is in crisis, as ethnojustice is explicitly phrased in terms of 'reviving' traditional authority. There is truth to the crisis of older male authority. However, the attempt to resolve that crisis by forcefully re-imposing an imagined order of the past is bound to exacerbate the broader social crisis in which the breakdown of male authority is situated. The reason for this is because, at present, the lineage- and clan-based structure of patriarchal, generally gerontocratic, male leadership, which had held significant internal authority in Acholi society at various times over the last century, has been thrown into crisis by the war and displacement. Male Acholi elders and chiefs have largely lost their power of social regulation and political leadership, and while men have seen their authority and status within Acholi society wane, women, and to a lesser extent youth, have seen their economic, social and political authority and status rise. These latter groups have benefited from new business and educational opportunities, human rights interventions and associations made possible in the environment of displacement. Young people also found a form of sometimes ambiguous empowerment in the rebel groups and paramilitaries. Ethnojustice thus represents an opportunity for older men to assert their power under the guise of tradition and to dismiss challenges to that power as non-traditional and non-authentic.

The recently invented KKA is the main beneficiary of this. As *Roco Wat* favourably reports: 'Participants at the Consultative Workshop agreed that Acholi culture was in decline, and in need of revival, especially for youth. Ker Kwaro Acholi and its supporters should embark upon a cultural revival through the recommendations below, which should be supported by donors and the Government of Uganda' (Liu Institute, 2005: 74). The motivation is clear: to channel donor and state funding to the promotion of 'traditional authorities' who can lead a cultural revival and, through mechanisms of traditional justice, restore social order among the Acholi. It is a supposedly empowering, participatory project — where Acholi are empowered to participate as proper, 'responsible' Acholi under the authority of chiefs. The World Bank was among the donors who responded to the call. Their Northern Uganda Social Action Fund (NUSAF) envisioned two thousand 'interventions targeted at traditional institutions' to promote social order by reviving traditional authorities, in particular chiefs and elders. In the process, it was to stimulate inter-clan meetings and dialogue in order to help the process of reconciliation between the LRA and the Acholi. The Bank hired NGOs and individuals to identify the traditional leadership.[5]

A key assumption of the ethnojustice perspective is that these older men, as the proper guardians of tradition and the spiritual, will enjoy universal consent to their authority. A glance at social reality in Acholi, however, reveals this to be far from the case. Instead, following Hountondji's critique of ethnophilosophy, this putatively unanimous adherence to Acholi traditional justice and the social order it upholds is a mystification. It mystifies one particular version of traditional justice, which is in fact part of a dominant ideology and upholds the power of a specific group who claim exclusive access to the spiritual domain in order to ensure the reproduction of their preferred social order. The consequence is that ethnojustice can legitimize a disciplinary social project, one which imposes the same forms of domination and inequality that gave rise to conflict in the first place. As Erin Baines puts it, 'although local mechanisms emphasize reconciliation in a way that punitive approaches do not, it could potentially increase violence rather than restore relationships' (Baines, 2009: 184).

---

5. Interview with project coordinator, Office of the Prime Minister, Kampala, 5 March 2003.

The Violence of Ethnojustice

Although some revival of traditional authority seems to be widely supported among Acholi, there is controversy over just what that authority should comprise and what its domain should be. In interviews conducted among the Acholi soon after the end of the war, it was found that for women and youth, especially those in towns, a return to the idealizations of pre-war order advocated by many male elders would be neither practical nor just. For their part, however, elders and many men tended to demand a comparatively vast increase in their authority once back in the village in a bid to correct the corruption introduced into Acholi society during displacement. In the most extreme versions, elders saw themselves occupying a dominant and all-encompassing role in regulating society in the post-conflict period and dealing with everyone from ex-rebels to thieves, government informants, prostitutes, foreigners and all troublemakers. This revival of their traditional authority, men and elders explained, would take place by imposing discipline at the family and clan levels through warnings, fines, corporal punishment and, if all else fails, expulsion from the clan and curses.

Therefore, there is a possibility that post-war Acholi society may see a coercive project carried out by men, especially men with family or clan authority, designed to eliminate what they see as the corruption that had infected Acholi society during the war and displacement. This produces the potential for violence and upheaval within Acholi society around this kind of systematic exclusion of certain categories of people from clan membership and land possession. Indeed, many older men framed the re-establishment of traditional authority explicitly in terms of undoing the power gained by women and youth and imposing the power of men and elders over these formerly subjugated groups. This project could involve physical violence, as caning and other punishments can take place within the family or else at the clan level, administered by the husband or by clan enforcers. As a result, women's and youths' public space and the social and economic opportunities they enjoy with it may be erased as they are confined to the private world of the home, whereas the public space of older men re-opens through social interaction within the lineage and clan.

Ex-LRA returnees, often representing the most marginalized youth or those most unwilling to conform to the demands of older male authorities, could face particular difficulties under the imposition of an ethnojustice agenda. Indeed, tensions between male lineage-based authorities and armed young men have been one of the roots of the wars that have plagued northern Uganda for over two decades, so there is no historical precedent that would imply that ex-members of the LRA would necessarily submit to this older male authority now. Moreover, there is no guarantee that traditional authorities will not use their new authority *against* ex-members of the LRA whom they see as undesirable or who are without firm family or clan connections. In short, a number of factors — fear of revenge, refusal to submit to male authority and the possibility that male authorities may exclude them from clan membership and access to land — meant that ex-LRA members, especially those who had been in the bush the longest and were without strong family relations, could end up facing discipline and exclusion.

Indeed, as soon as movement out of the camps began in 2007, so former LRA began to report being dispossessed of their land by other members of the community, sometimes with the collusion of clan authorities. According to a study of the International Organization for Migration, 90 per cent of the male former LRA they surveyed in post-war Gulu towns 'reported experiencing acute isolation and/or fear of revenge upon return', and over 90 per cent of 'former Lord's Resistance Army combatants surveyed in Gulu municipality reported being unable to access land upon return' (McKibben and Bean, 2010: 8; see also Branch, 2013). Many took refuge in town, further adding to the poverty and social pressures there.

Therefore, the externally funded ethnojustice project could enable a wider project of imposing disciplinary male authority on an Acholi society where that male authority lost much of its legitimacy decades ago. This could amount to a transitional justice project carried out by men to redeem what they saw as a deeply corrupted Acholi society, an agenda that would ride on the coat-tails of the more public transitional justice agenda promoted by foreigners and the Ugandan government. However, because it would represent peace built on the backs of women and youth, there is the potential for further crisis within Acholi society around the exclusion of certain categories of people from clan membership and land possession, reinforcing the very forms of inequality and domination that helped drive on the conflict.

Just as ethnojustice effects a positivization of the spiritual, therefore, it also effects a reification of justice and social order, excising from each its inherent plurality and possibility for rupture. In fact, neither the spiritual, the moral, nor the social are the positive, singular and unanimous domains that ethnojustice insists they are, and they cannot exist in the closed, mutually supporting circuit that ethnojustice claims to identify. Each is a terrain where there is contradiction, conflict and struggle between dominant and non-dominant opinions, ideas and projects.

Importantly, it is not only male elders who benefit from the promotion of ethnojustice: its advantages can also redound to the Ugandan government. As discussed, the two-decade war stemmed from and exacerbated grievances both internal to the Acholi community, of youth and women against older men's power, and between the Acholi community and the Ugandan state. From this angle, the Ugandan government is instrumentalizing ethnojustice in ways that re-enforce the very forms of injustice that gave rise to the war and that will need to be rectified if the legacy of the war is to be overcome. For one thing, it seems likely that the Ugandan government is interested in promoting Acholi traditional justice precisely because traditional justice may guarantee state impunity. Indeed, rituals presided over by male lineage-based Acholi authorities are inadequate to deal with crimes committed by a modern state

(Baines, 2007). Ethnojustice also fails to take into account the international dimensions of the war, including the role of the donors in funding Uganda's militarization, and the role of the aid agencies in collaborating with forced displacement. The assertion of a uniquely Acholi traditional justice further tribalizes the conflict, making it an 'Acholi problem', and can make national political justice even more difficult (Allen, 2010: 257–60).

Second, the government has often made successful efforts to co-opt the newly established, and foreign-supported, set of chiefs whose unaccountable authority makes them good candidates for state manipulation. It remains to be seen whether this cadre of chiefs supported by foreign donors and the government will be able to establish legitimacy within Acholi society or if their dependence on external funds will make them tools of outsiders seeking political control or economic benefits. For these reasons, we might expect ethnojustice to appeal to other states that are involved in political violence and seeking to avoid demands for accountability. In these contexts, the promotion of ethnojustice can entrench the forms of state-driven inequality and injustice that give rise to political grievances and violent conflict.

The Plurality of the Spiritual and the Social

The lack of consensus among Acholi on the particular version of the spiritual and the social promoted by ethnojustice is very apparent even in recent Acholi history. Indeed, the spiritual domain has offered a wide scope for alternative and oppositional ideologies among the Acholi, most notably in the form of spirit possession and the work of the *ajwaka* (a medium or 'tamer' of spirits). The HSM and LRA can be seen as embodying counterhegemonic spiritual claims in part against the power of male elders. The spiritual is a terrain on which women and youth have asserted claims to power and authority beyond that of the male elders, and it is by no means the exclusive preserve of those elders, as ethnojustice would have it. Ethnojustice ignores the disruptive power of *ajwaka* and the fact that many *ajwaka* today come from outside Acholiland, and thus may draw on the spiritual to articulate national or even cosmopolitan identities and projects. Ethnojustice instead imposes the tribe, under the customary power of the chief, as the essential political and social unit, ignoring how the spiritual may rupture not only the power of the male chief but also the boundaries of the tribe as collective identity. Ethnojustice may retribalize political identity in the name of justice and social order, when it is a movement towards the national that may be needed to overcome the legacy of violence.

The domain of justice is a terrain of social struggle in northern Uganda at present and cannot be reduced to being functional to a certain patriarchal model of social order. This is seen with the contestation over what justice should mean in the wake of the war. Indeed, in one 2010 survey, only half of the respondents said that 'traditional justice ceremonies' were 'useful for transitional justice', and only 39 per cent said that they were useful for community reconciliation (Oola, 2012: 55–56). *Roco Wat*'s insistence on the 'consensual' nature of all 'traditional' Acholi justice should draw our attention to how that consent is enforced and at whose expense. The monopolization of justice and reconciliation by an externally supported male authority structure, as dictated by ethnojustice, fails to address the fact that different groups within Acholi society, in particular women and youth, might have their own particular demands for justice. Furthermore, these demands may be centred around alternative spiritual mechanisms or have nothing to do with the spiritual at all, oriented instead toward formal, state-based legal processes, non-spiritual community-based processes or other alternatives. As a result, ethnojustice has the potential to silence those who do not identify with this revived male authority and the version of the spiritual that it claims to uphold. It also has the potential to silence community demands for justice made against the state. Chiefs, empowered through state largesse, may be willing to serve as proponents of forgiveness, repressing claims for justice against the state.

Women, in particular, could be prevented from deciding for themselves what justice means in response to their own specific experiences during the war. It is unreasonable to assume that women would agree to male elders deciding what justice means for them, or to assume that women would be satisfied with men deciding that the perpetrators of violence against women should simply be forgiven, as male elders may very well do under the mantle of tradition. Men may be satisfied with a negotiated, ritualized solution among themselves that does not involve punishment or compensation, whereas women may not be willing to accept that as a just solution at all. The imposition of such justice could create a peace among men built on a reinforced regime of gendered violence.

The external promotion of this form of traditional authority does not enjoy unanimous support even among men. Some men see the project not as the redemption of a corrupt Acholi society, but as part of that corruption itself. Foreign and state sponsorship of traditional authority has provided supposed chiefs with the opportunity to grab land and enrich themselves under the mantle of KKA. Whites and their money are seen as promoting dependency among the Acholi, turning Acholi against Acholi within the NGO job market and creating a new breed of *Acholi matar*, or 'white Acholi'. Foreign agencies are accused of paying people sitting allowances to participate in workshops and sensitizations, a practice that has corrupted the traditional Acholi practice of sitting and meeting to resolve problems without concern for monetary compensation. So there are certainly those men who see ethnojustice not as a revival of traditional Acholi society with external assistance, but as corrupting Acholi society even further.

In short, community-based justice cannot be reduced to a male-dominated version of traditional justice because the community itself, especially now after two decades of war, is not reducible to those who would claim traditional authority (not that it was before the war either). Acholi society, like any society, is not a homogeneous, coherent whole. Acholi traditional justice as identified and celebrated by ethnojustice is only one ideology supporting a claim to power by one group, legitimated through an appeal to a singular tradition and Acholi identity. It is promoted at the expense of alternative traditions of justice and of the spiritual, social and political order *within* Acholi society.

CHALLENGING ETHNOJUSTICE

'The process of reviving traditional justice is not an easy task', *Roco Wat* admits (Liu Institute, 2005: 3), and at one point the report does indeed recognize that the imposition of a gerontocratic, patriarchal order on contemporary Acholi society might not be an unmitigated good. *Roco Wat* appears uncomfortable with the fact that physical punishment of women and youth through beating is a widely prevalent aspect of the traditional culture being promoted by older men — a traditional justice that supposedly rejects justice through punishment as Western. Indeed, this brings to light the double standards of the ethnojustice discourse and it belies the claim that traditional justice is restorative and non-punitive. Women and youth can be 'traditionally' subjected to punishment, physical violence, expulsion, even fatal curses by male elders, whereas men's transgressions — or really a certain category of men's transgressions of interest to male elders — are dealt with through the lofty language of reconciliation, forgiveness, and restorative justice.

Finding a way forward would require a refutation of the ethnojustice discourse and its assumptions. It must recognize that the changes produced by upheaval represent not a deviation from a genuine Acholi traditional order, but rather opportunities for new forms of local and national democratization and political inclusion — forms that go beyond the reduction of the local to the customary and Ugandan citizens to tribespersons. It requires the admission that internal plurality, conflict and contestation have always characterized Acholi society, and the recognition of the many traditions found *within* Acholi society pertaining to the spiritual world and to justice. Indeed, there are many African and many Acholi traditions of justice. Some may find their origins in the pre-colonial period, others find their origins in the colonial, and others in various times during the post-colonial period. Some are tied to the symbolic and embedded in the cultural, others are tied to local and national state-based institutions and others derive from international norms. These different traditions emerged at different times in response to different circumstances and reflect different configurations of power and authority. *All* these traditions can be drawn on now in order to deal with the legacy of the war. For this reason, it is better to speak not of traditional justice but of *traditions of justice* among the Acholi, where the Acholi are historicized, not essentialized, within pre-colonial, colonial and post-colonial political and social processes.

Just as traditional justice, as described by the ethnojustice discourse, is not really traditional, so is it not really justice. Justice by its nature must always be open, never closed, must always be plural and unfinished, and cannot be the preserve of a single group. Justice is 'yet to come', in Hountondji's phrase, in the sense that it is open to new voices, new opinions, new formulations and ideas into the indefinite future. There is no single true justice, for justice is a domain of ultimate uncertainty, a fact that ethnojustice rejects. Justice, spirituality, tradition and society are all realms of internal contradiction and struggle, and only if that is recognized can democracy have a chance to emerge. Then, justice will not be functional to the project of imposing an authoritarian social order, but rather will be the subject for deliberation, organization and action in an inclusive, open, contentious social order.

Times of violent upheaval represent opportunities for the emergence of new political and social orders. If the initiative in such situations falls into the hands of international donors, NGOs and the state, then transitional justice may end up equivalent to discipline and coercion and may set the stage for future conflict. If the community that has survived the conflict takes up the initiative, new forms of inclusive popular organization may emerge that reject the oppression of the past, demand that international intervention come into line with democracy, and lay the foundation for peace in the future.

REFERENCES

Allen, T. (2006) *Trial Justice: The International Criminal Court and the Lord's Resistance Army.* London: Zed Books.

Allen, T. (2010) 'Bitter Roots: The "Invention" of Acholi Traditional Justice', in T. Allen and K. Vlassenroot (eds) *The Lord's Resistance Army: Myth and Reality*, pp. 242–61. London: Zed Books.

Anders, G. and O. Zenker (2014) 'Transition and Justice: An Introduction', *Development and Change* 45(3): 395–414.

Arendt, H. (1990/1963) *On Revolution.* London: Penguin.

Baines, E. (2007) 'The Haunting of Alice: Local Approaches to Transitional Justice in Northern Uganda', *International Journal of Transitional Justice* 1(1): 91–114.

Baines, E. (2009) 'Complex Political Perpetrators: Reflections on Dominic Ongwen', *Journal of Modern African Studies* 47(2): 163–91.

Branch, A. (2007) 'Uganda's Civil War and the Politics of ICC Intervention', *Ethics and International Affairs* 21(2): 179–98.

Branch, A. (2011) *Displacing Human Rights: War and Intervention in Northern Uganda.* New York: Oxford University Press.

Branch, A. (2013) 'Gulu in War ... and Peace? The Town as Camp in Northern Uganda', *Urban Studies* 50(15): 3152–67.

Chandler, D. (2006) *Empire in Denial: The Politics of Statebuilding.* London: Pluto Press.

Chopra, J. and T. Hohe (2004) 'Participatory Intervention', *Global Governance* 10(3): 289–305.

Douzinas, C. (2007) *Human Rights and Empire: The Political Philosophy of Cosmopolitanism.* New York: Routledge-Cavendish.

Duffield, M. (2001) *Global Governance and the New Wars: The Merging of Development and Security*. London: Zed Books.

Gregory, D. (2008) '"The Rush to the Intimate": Counterinsurgency and the Cultural Turn', *Radical Philosophy* (150): 8–23.

Grovogui, S. (2011) 'Looking Beyond Spring: An African Perspective on the Arab Revolt in World Order'. CIHA Blog. http://sites.uci.edu/cihablog

Hountondji, P. (1996) *African Philosophy: Myth and Reality* (2nd edn). Bloomington, IN: Indiana University Press.

Huyse, L. (1995) 'Justice after Transition: On the Choices Successor Elites Make in Dealing with the Past', *Law & Social Inquiry* 20(1): 51–78.

Kagoro, B. (2012) 'The Paradox of Alien Knowledge, Narrative and Praxis: Transitional Justice and the Politics of Agenda Setting in Africa', in M. Okello et al. (eds) *Where Law Meets Reality: Forging African Transitional Justice*, pp. 4–52. Cape Town: Pambazuka Press.

Kirchheimer, O. (1961) *Political Justice: The Use of Legal Procedure for Political Ends*. Princeton, NJ: Princeton University Press.

Komakech, L. (2012) 'Traditional Justice as a Form of Adjudication in Uganda', in M. Okello et al. (eds) *Where Law Meets Reality: Forging African Transitional Justice*, pp. 64–79. Cape Town: Pambazuka Press.

Koskenniemi, M. (2002) 'Between Impunity and Show Trials', *Max Planck Yearbook of United Nations Law* 6: 1–35.

Lekha Sriram, C. and S. Pillay (eds) (2009) *Peace versus Justice? The Dilemma of Transitional Justice in Africa*. Scottsville: University of KwaZulu-Natal Press.

Lenin, V. (1964) *Collected Works: Volume 25*. Moscow: Progress Publishers.

Liu Institute for Global Issues and Gulu District NGO Forum (2005) *Roco Wat I Acholi: Restoring Relationships in Acholi-land: Traditional Approaches to Justice and Reintegration*. Vancouver: University of British Columbia Press.

MacGinty, R. (2008) 'Indigenous Peace-Making versus the Liberal Peace', *Cooperation and Conflict* 43(2): 139–63.

McKibben, G. and J. Bean (2010) *Land or Else: Land-based Conflict, Vulnerability, and Disintegration in Northern Uganda*. Kampala: International Organization for Migration.

Meister, R. (2011) *After Evil: A Politics of Human Rights*. New York: Columbia University Press.

Merleau-Ponty, M. (1980) *Humanism and Terror: An Essay on the Communist Problem*. Boston, MA: Beacon Press.

Murithi, T. (2012) 'Towards African Models of Transitional Justice', in M. Okello et al. (eds) *Where Law Meets Reality: Forging African Transitional Justice*, pp. 200–17. Cape Town: Pambazuka Press.

Oola, S. (2012) 'A Conflict-Sensitive Justice: Adjudicating Traditional Justice in Transitional Contexts', in M. Okello et al. (eds) *Where Law Meets Reality: Forging African Transitional Justice*, pp. 53–63. Cape Town: Pambazuka Press.

Pain, D. (1997) *'The Bending of the Spears'. Producing Consensus for Peace and Development in Northern Uganda*. London: International Alert/Kacoke Madit.

Paris, R. (2004) *At War's End: Building Peace after Civil Conflict*. Cambridge: Cambridge University Press.

Richmond, O. (2008) *Peace in International Relations*. London: Routledge.

Shklar, J. (1964) *Legalism*. Cambridge, MA: Harvard University Press.

Simpson, G. (2007) *Law, War and Crime: War Crimes, Trials and the Reinvention of International Law*. London: Polity Press.

Teitel, R. (2003) 'Transitional Justice Genealogy', *Harvard Human Rights Journal* 16: 69–94.

Zartman, I.W. (ed.) (2000) *Traditional Cures for Modern Conflicts: African Conflict 'Medicine'*. Boulder, CO: Lynne Rienner.

Zolo, D. (2009) *Victors' Justice: from Nuremberg to Baghdad*. London: Verso.

Index

Transition and Justice: Negotiating the Terms of New Beginnings in Africa, First Edition.
Edited by Gerhard Anders and Olaf Zenker.
Chapters © 2015 by The Institute of Social Studies. Book compilation © 2015 John Wiley & Sons, Ltd.